THREE HUNDRED YEARS
OF
AMERICAN DRAMA
AND THEATRE

Second Edition

THREE HUNDRED YEARS OF AMERICAN DRAMA AND THEATRE

*from YE BARE AND YE CUBB
to CHORUS LINE*

GARFF B. WILSON
University of California at Berkeley

Prentice-Hall, Inc., Englewood Cliffs, N.J. 07632

Library of Congress Cataloging in Publication Data

Wilson, Garff B.
    Three hundred years of American drama and threatre.

    Bibliography
    Includes index.
      1. Theater—United States—History.   2. American
drama—History and criticism.   I. Title.
PN2221.W5-1982   792'.0973   81-5838
ISBN   0-13-920330-3   AACR2

Printed in the United States of America

10   9   8   7   6   5   4   3   2   1

Editorial/production supervision
      and interior design by Joyce Turner
Cover design by Jerry Pfeifer
Manufacturing buyer: Edmund W. Leone

Prentice-Hall International, Inc., *London*
Prentice-Hall of Australia Pty. Limited, *Sydney*
Prentice-Hall of Canada, Ltd., *Toronto*
Prentice-Hall of India Private Limited, *New Delhi*
Prentice-Hall of Japan, Inc., *Tokyo*
Prentice-Hall of Southeast Asia Pte. Ltd., *Singapore*
Whitehall Books Limited, *Wellington, New Zealand*

For my namesake
GARFF THOMAS HATHCOCK
and for his parents
DICK AND DEEDEE
who honored me so highly

Contents

Preface

The first edition of this history was well received. Reviewers—and student readers in particular—endorsed my decision to combine a history of the theatre and the written drama; that is, to trace in one volume the development of plays and playwriting in America as activities complementary to the development of acting, stagecraft, management, and so on. Readers also expressed their approval of my imaginary visits to theatres of various periods beginning with the colonial theatre of 1770. They agreed that it is a useful way to summarize the details of playgoing and to recreate the impression of a total theatrical experience. I have therefore retained the imaginary visits in this revised edition and have also retained the overall pattern of recording the development of both the written drama and theatrical production.

The principal changes in this edition are the addition of material from the decade of the 1970s and the condensation of all the material in the first edition. The former was fairly easy to do; the latter was difficult because it involved the basic problems of deciding what material could be eliminated and then reorganizing and condensing the remaining material. Like the long-time owner of a beloved collection of paintings who suffers when he parts with any one painting, I have grieved over dropping from these pages the name of any actor or playwright or the description of any theatrical event. All of them are dear to me. But we live in a hurried, crowded age when young people do not have the time nor the desire to read long books or to linger over details that are interesting and revealing but, perhaps, of secondary importance. So I have had to be ruthless in my prunning. I apologize to the ghosts of the people and events of the past which have been banished from these pages, and I apologize to every reader who feels that I made the wrong choices. I hope each one will remember that the decisions have been harder on me than on anyone else. I hope that the readers will also feel that within the limitations of space a sense of overall completeness has been preserved.

As with the first edition, I must extend my sincere thanks for generous assistance to the following people and institutions: Bernard Perry and the Indiana University Press; Frederick J. Hunter and Jane Allen Combs of the Theatre Arts Library of the University of Texas at Austin; O.G. Brockett of Indiana University; Thomas A. Bailey of Stanford University; Helen D. Willard of the Theatre Collection of the Harvard College Library; and my colleagues at Berkeley, Travis Bogard and Robert Goldsby.

GARFF B. WILSON

THREE HUNDRED YEARS
OF
AMERICAN DRAMA
AND THEATRE

Prologue

Those who love the stage need no excuse for reading a history of the American theatre. They have experienced the excitement, pleasure, and illumination that can come from playgoing. Others, who know the theatre only through an occasional movie or television drama, may wonder about a book like this. Has a book about the theatre—indeed, has the theatre itself—any relevance for the average person?

The answer, of course, is an emphatic *yes*. If understanding oneself and other human beings is important, the theatre is relevant; if experiences that exalt the spirit and cleanse the passions are important, the theatre is relevant; if entertainment that relaxes us and adds a few moments of meaningful laughter to our existence is important, the theatre is relevant. A book that enhances these experiences and makes them more rewarding must also be relevant.

A history of the American theatre shares in the relevance, but it is useful in other ways, too. The events and characters that compose the history are intrinsically interesting. Their innate color and fascination can stir our feelings as we follow the pageant of triumphs and tribulations, courage and despair, glamour and drabness, wise men and fools.

The history of the theatre gives us a new perspective on the growth and development of the nation. We are accustomed to think of the history of the United States in terms of political events, economic crises, and social changes. As we follow the theatrical history of the country, we view the same developments from a sharply different angle—from a position inside the stage door. We begin to realize that political, economic, and social events all influence the theatre, while developments within the theatre, in turn, influence the complex social structure around it. Now and then theatre history and political history join in a moment of shattering crisis, as they did on the evening of April 14, 1865, when a demented actor assassinated Abraham Lincoln while Lincoln was sitting in a box at Ford's Theatre in Washington, D. C.

A study of American theatrical history also introduces us to a collection of dramas that are too often neglected. Many people know only the American plays of the twentieth century and either are ignorant of the dramas of past centuries or dismiss them as worthless. The first play written by a native-born American and produced by a professional company was staged as early as 1767, and hundreds of American plays were written and produced in the following century. True, few of these plays have high literary merit or enduring quality, but the same can be said of the plays of Western Europe during the same period. Yet even the inferior American plays of the late eighteenth and nineteenth centuries reveal attitudes, aspirations, ideals, and tastes that will fascinate anyone interested in the formation of the national character. Occasionally, one of these plays achieves genuine exellence, and together they constitute a body of literature that should not be lightly dismissed.

The theatre we now call American developed almost entirely from the theatre of England. It might have been otherwise. When Europeans first reached the New World, they observed beautiful Indian ceremonies and dance rituals that contained many of the elements of drama. But no further use was made of this material. Neither did the American theatre develop from the drama introduced into the New World by Spaniards and Frenchmen long before the English colonists arrived. As early as 1538 religious plays in Spanish were produced in Mexico; in 1567 two comedies were performed in a Spanish mission in Florida; in 1598 an original Spanish play was presented in the southwest portion of North America. Another record indicates that in 1606, thousands of miles to the northeast, a masque in French was presented at Port Royal in Acadia, now Nova Scotia. French and Spanish plays continued to be given in the New World for many decades, but their popularity was limited and their influence negligible. They made no major contribution to the development of the American theatre.

It was English actors, managers, and technicians who planted the drama in America. English tragedies and comedies comprised the repertory in colonial America, and English costumes, settings, customs, and speech were used in dramatic productions. Thus, the theatre in America was a living transplant from the English stage, and many decades passed before the transplant, responding to its new environment, developed a character of its own.

The English actors who came to the New World were the heirs of a rich theatrical tradition dating back several centuries. In England during the thirteenth, fourteenth, and fifteenth centuries, cycles of mystery and miracle plays dramatizing the biblical account of the human race from the creation to the last judgment flourished in many towns and villages. During the sixteenth century the revival of learning and the rediscovery of classical theatre began to be felt. In the second half of the century wholly secular plays began to be written. The influence of the Renaissance culminated in the glories of the Elizabethan theatre, whose supreme representative was William Shakespeare. For a few years a score of English playwrights poured out some of the greatest dramas of all time. When Shakespeare died in 1616, the tremendous creative impulses began to weaken. Plays were still written, but they lacked the greatness of an earlier age. Public playhouses were still popular, but opposition to them, fostered by the Puritans, was growing. In 1642 Puritanism, led by Oliver Cromwell, triumphed. Drama was prohibited and play-houses were closed, to remain closed for eighteen years. Then in 1660 Charles II was restored to the throne of England. He reopened the public theatres, and pro-duction of the great plays of the Elizabethan period and of later periods was resumed. The Restoration era was a gay, witty, carefree period that stimulated a new corps of dramatists to write superb comedies of manners. But in the opinion of good Christians, the period was tainted with immorality and corruption. Com-plaints from religious groups increased year by year and culminated in 1698 with the publication of a pamphlet entitled *A Short View of the Immorality and Pro-faneness of the English Stage,* written by Jeremy Collier. The pamphlet, and the widespread resentment that prompted it, were effective enough to start reforms in playwriting and to alter the behavior of actors and audiences.

This was the situation of the English theatre in the eighteenth century when dramatic activity was transplanted from England to her colonies in the New World. The curtain was ready to rise on the first act of the history of the American theatre.

1

The Curtain Rises— and Falls

The American theatre—like theatre everywhere—is a fabulous phoenix. For more than three hundred years it has been flourishing, then declining; sinking, then rising; dying, then springing to vigorous new life. Its birth in the wilderness of a new world among sober, puritanical settlers was slow and painful. For decades it struggled feebly. Just as it was gaining strength and stature, the Revolutionary War broke out and the theatre became an immediate casualty. But after the war it rose again, stronger than before, and it has continued its colorful, phoenixlike existence ever since.

The story of the theatre in America—that is, in the part of America which became the United States—is old as such things are reckoned in the New World. It began in 1665 when three young men of Accomac County, Virginia, were summoned to court for an offense that today seems incredible. They were accused of presenting a play entitled *Ye Bare and Ye Cubb,* written by William Darby, one of the accused men. The offense shocked certain local inhabitants, but the magistrate, doubtless an Englishman of some sophistication, found that the young men were "not guilty of fault."

This incident is the first recorded account of theatrical activity in the English language in North America. For the next eighty-five years the record is sketchy and unreliable. The historian feels like a spectator in a playhouse where the stage is obscured by a curtain of fog. He strains his eyes but only now and then does he glimpse the action on stage. These rare glimpses reveal a series of unrelated pieces of theatrical history, the main parts of which follow.

Sometime between 1699 and 1702, a Richard Hunter, of whom we know nothing, petitioned the governor of the province of New York for a license to present plays in New York City. The petition was granted but there is no record of performances.

In 1703 Anthony Aston, a strolling player, recorded that he "acted" in Charleston and New York, having arrived in the New World "full of Lice, Shame, Poverty, Nakedness and Hunger." After his arrival, he claimed, he turned "Player and Poet and wrote one Play on the subject of the Country."[1]

The next glimpse reveals a milestone in the history of the printed play. In 1714 the first play to be published in America appeared. It was called *Androboros; a Biographical Farce in Three Acts,* and is attributed to Robert Hunter, governor or the province of New York. The play was never produced.

Two years after the publication of *Androboros,* the first playhouse in America was built in Williamsburg, Virginia, by William Levingston, merchant, for the actors Charles and Mary Stagg, but almost nothing is known about these performers or their activities or associates. There is evidence that plays were acted in Williamsburg for a few years, but presently the playhouse fell into disuse—why, we do not know—until finally, in 1745, the building was converted into a town hall.

During this time, the colleges of America encouraged dramatic offerings in the form of dialogues and odes eulogizing the king and honoring notable events.

The next glimpse of theatrical activity carries us back to New York. In 1732 at the New Theatre, George Farquhar's popular comedy, *The Recruiting Officer,* was presented. It remained a favorite in colonial America for many years.

In January 1735, Thomas Otway's tragedy, *The Orphan,* another favorite drama of the time, was given in the courthouse in Charleston, South Carolina. The following month, the first opera known to be performed in America was presented in the same place. It was entitled *Flora, or Hob in the Well.* Our glimpse of these courthouse productions reveals little about the players and singers who performed them. They must have pleased their audiences, however, because in the following year, 1736, a playhouse was built to accommodate them. It was called the New Theatre in Dock Street and more performances were given there. But the playhouse was short-lived. It burned to the ground in 1740, in the first of a long series of fires that have plagued and impoverished American playhouses.

In 1736, the students of the College of William and Mary in Williamsburg, Virginia, performed Joseph Addison's *Cato.* Shortly thereafter, three comedies were acted by a group announced as "the company"—a group that may have been an organized troupe of players.

In 1750 the Puritan stronghold of Boston was contaminated by a production of Otway's *The Orphan,* presented in a local coffee house. The results were dire. Massachusetts authorities immediately passed a law forbidding any form of theatrical entertainment and establishing a schedule of fines to be levied against actors and owners of buildings where plays were performed.

From these tantalizing glimpses of theatrical history between 1665 and 1750, we can easily generalize that theatrical activity was meager, most of it generated by amateurs. A few professional players and productions seem to have material-

---

[1] Committee on Historical Research of the National Society of Colonial Dames of America, *Church Music and Musical Life in Pennsylvania in the Eighteenth Century* (Philadelphia: National Society of Colonial Dames of America, 1938), III: 1, 134.

ized out of the wilderness, but they could not have been well-organized or long-enduring. There were practically no playhouses anywhere, as acute hostility to all forms of playgiving discouraged the building of such structures. The colonial colleges were friendly to classic drama, but most of their activity was confined to the presentation of "colloquies" or "dialogues." Meager as this record is, one still senses that the impulse to produce plays was manifest very early in the development of the American colonies, that this impulse recurred stubbornly despite the hostility which greeted it, and that sooner or later it was going to establish itself firmly in the soil of the New World.

THE FIRST PROFESSIONAL COMPANIES

Now the mist begins to lift. The organized professional theatrical troupe makes its debut in the colonies and affords us a chance to watch dramatic activities in fairly clear outline.

The honor of being the first known professional company to perform in America (not counting the company—if there was a company—headed by Charles and Mary Stagg in Williamsburg, Virginia) belongs to a troupe headed by Walter Murray and Thomas Kean. The credit of being first, it seems, is the only real distinction which can be claimed for this group. Pioneers though they were, they left no record of their background or makeup, and their history is brief. The company made its debut in Philadelphia in the fall of 1749, moved to New York the following year, and presented a regular repertory of plays in a makeshift theatre on Nassau Street during the spring and fall of 1750 and the spring of 1751. The troupe then moved to Williamsburg for a short season and after that to other towns in Virginia and Maryland—towns that were less hostile to the sinful practice of playgiving than were the communities of New England. While the company was absent from New York, one member of the troupe, Robert Upton, who had been left behind, organized a company of his own that gave plays for a brief time, then vanished. The Murray-Kean company continued to perform for a few years more, with diminishing success; then it too faded from the scene completely. Apparently it could not meet the competition of a lively rival, the famous Hallam company, which arrived in the colonies in 1752 and dominated theatrical activity for many years thereafter.

The Hallam company was organized by a bankrupt but enterprising theatrical manager from London, William Hallam. Hallam's theatre had been closed in England because it had violated the Licensing Act. He therefore decided that the American colonies were the place to recoup his fortunes. He enlisted his brother and sister-in-law, Mr. and Mrs. Lewis Hallam, along with three of their children, to be the nucleus of his pioneer company; then he rounded up ten additional adult players to complete the troupe. The company could not have been better than third rate, composed of less successful players from the London stage. Still, they must have had spirit and zest because they accepted the challenge of bringing theatre to a distant wilderness—and they succeeded.

Under the guidance of William Hallam, the company was successfully organized into a congenial, cooperative group. A repertory of plays was selected, roles were assigned, costumes and scenery were acquired; and in May of 1752, the group set sail from England on a ship called *Charming Sally*. Lewis Hallam led the expedition while William remained in London to oversee the venture from afar.

After only forty-two days, "certainly a very quick passage," says Charles Durang, the *Charming Sally* reached the coast of Virginia. As the ship sailed into "the magnificent expanse of the Chesapeake bay," the pioneer actors on board "saw naught but a vast expanse of wood stretching all along the horizon and, while they admired the grandeur (and to them the novelty) of this oceanic sylvan scene, each one whispered to himself, what is to support a theatre here?"[2] It did not take them long to find out.

Before watching these pioneer players in their American debut and following their early years, let us take a brief look at conditions in the American colonies during the mid-eighteenth century. What kind of land, people, and situation did the Hallam company find? What were the factors favorable to the success of their venture—or conducive to failure?

The country which the Hallam troupe saw from their ship was vast, beautiful, wild, and empty. White inhabitants of the colonies totaled about a million and a half, and Negro slaves added another half million to the population. All these people were thinly scattered along a thousand miles of the Atlantic seaboard

The Atlantic Neptune view of New York, before 1773.

Courtesy of the New York Historical Society.

[2]Charles Durang, "The Philadelphia Stage from the Year 1749 to the Year 1855," *Philadelphia Sunday Dispatch*, 1854, 1856, 1860; reprinted in part in Bernard Hewitt, *Theatre U.S.A.* (New York: McGraw-Hill Book Company, 1959), pp. 4-14.

stretching from New Hampshire to Georgia.[3] All thirteen colonies had been settled and organized by 1752, beginning with Virginia in 1607 and ending with Georgia in 1733. In the entire loosely knit confederation, only four communities were big enough to be called cities. Philadelphia was the largest, with more than thirty thousand people, and was followed by Boston, New York, and Charleston in that order. Ninety percent of the population lived in rural areas and earned their living by farming the land.

From the start, colonial America was a melting pot of many races, creeds, and languages. The basic stock and language were English, but mixed with the English were sizable groups of Germans, French, Dutch, Swedes, Swiss, Scots, Irish, Africans, and others. This polyglot population was divided into classes with landed gentry and merchant princes at the top of the pyramid and Negro slaves at the bottom. An American citizen of today might be startled to learn that his colonial ancestors were often seated in church and school according to their social rank. Only a small number of the colonists were entitled to be addressed by the then exalted title of "mister." Social, political, or economic democracy as we know it did not exist.

For both free men and slaves—and certainly for the early theatrical companies—the problem of transportation was enormous. A few dirt roads connected the major communities, but there was not a single hard-surfaced highway. In summer the roads dissolved into clouds of dust; in winter they became quagmires. Travel at all times was slow, treacherous, and generally unpleasant. The trip to New York from Boston by carriage or horseback required four days. It took an additional three days to reach Philadelphia. A total of twenty-nine days was needed to carry the news of the Declaration of Independence from Philadelphia to Charleston. Because of the wretched roads, waterways were used whenever possible.

Education and cultural pursuits were scanty and confined to the aristocrats. Most of the colonists were too busy scratching out a living to have time or energy for anything but churchgoing. In the South, which was dominated by the plantation aristocracy, there were sports and dancing, and in the lonely pioneer settlements there was an occasional harvest or quilting bee. In general, life was hard and serious; the practical problems of making a living and saving one's soul occupied the colonists from dawn to midnight and left little time for entertainment such as playgoing.

Saving one's soul was especially important; the ministers of religion never let the colonists forget it. The Sabbath was observed rigidly and almost everyone went to church, where they listened attentively to sermons endless in length and dire in prediction. Every colony except Virginia and Maryland had laws forbidding the staging of plays. Such were the conditions which faced the players of the

---

[3] I am indebted for most of the facts about the colonies in the mid-eighteenth century to Thomas A. Bailey, *The American Pageant* (Lexington, Mass.: D. C. Heath & Company, 1961), with additional help from Homer C. Hockett and Arthur M. Schlesinger, *Land of the Free* (New York: The Macmillan Company, 1944), and John D. Hicks and George E. Mowry, *A Short History of American Democracy* (Boston: Houghton Mifflin Company, 1956).

Hallam company when it reached the New World in 1752. The same conditions, in diminishing degree, faced every other theatrical group for many years thereafter.

As soon as the *Charming Sally* landed in Virginia, the company of players disembarked and set out for Williamsburg, the capital of the colony. Reaching town, Lewis Hallam immediately applied to the governor of Virginia for permission to perform. The request was "freely granted," and the company set about refurbishing Williamsburg's playhouse (probably the one built for Murray and Kean the previous year) into "a regular theatre fit for the reception of Ladies and Gentlemen."[4] By September 15 everything was ready, and on the evening of that historic day support for the new company materialized. From the outlying areas, from the farms and plantations came a great stream of vehicles bearing a crowd of happy playgoers. They filled the house, enjoyed the prologue, which praised them as "an audience sensible, polite, and kind," and applauded the production of *The Merchant of Venice* so enthusiastically that Hallam and his company decided to remain in Williamsburg for an extended period. They did—for nine more months. Finally, in June 1753 they moved to New York and there, after some delay, repeated the success they had achieved in Virginia. The delay was caused by the difficulty they encountered in obtaining permission to perform, despite the complimentary letter of recommendation they carried from the governor of Virginia. It took three months to overcome the obstacles, so it was not until September that the first performance was given. Once started, the season continued until the end of March 1754, and then the company moved to Philadelphia. Here, after once more overcoming strong opposition from the churches, they performed for two months. At the end of this engagement the troupe moved to Charleston, then in 1755 sailed for Jamaica intending, it seems, to return to the colonies after only one season in the West Indies. Actually, they did not return until late in 1758, and when they did the company was altered in both management and personnel.

Lewis Hallam, manager and cosponsor of the enterprise, died after reaching Jamaica. This reversal might have destroyed the company, but providentially it was saved by amalgamation with another English troupe that had arrived in Jamaica in 1751 and was preparing to try its luck in the American colonies. This troupe was headed by an energetic young man named David Douglass, who cemented the two companies by marrying the widowed Mrs. Hallam. With her as leading lady, with eighteen-year-old Lewis Hallam, Jr. as leading man, and with himself as manager, promoter, diplomat, builder, and actor, David Douglass became theatrical king of North America for almost twenty years.

The activities of the Douglass company were many and varied between 1758, when the company returned to New York, and 1774, when it returned to Jamaica for the duration of the Revolutionary War. The most important activity, of course, was the presentation of a repertory of plays to growing audiences in an ever-increasing number of American towns. Year by year, in true pioneer fashion, the company extended its circuit and built up its audiences despite unfavorable circumstances.

[4] *Virginia Gazette,* 21 August 1752.

Another important activity was the building of new playhouses. Everywhere the company went—New York, Philadelphia, Annapolis, Newport, Charleston—Douglass constructed playhouses for his troupe. He had to. The only alternative was to perform in the public rooms of taverns or in vacant warehouses or similar places. The playhouses that Douglass built were, of course, small, flimsy structures, all of them modeled, so far as possible, after the playhouses of London. They were cramped and uncomfortable, but they served the company adequately and paved the way for the bigger, better playhouses that came later.

Two houses built during the period deserve special mention. The first, opened in 1766, was the Southwark Theatre in Philadelphia, famous in theatrical history as the first permanent playhouse erected in North America. The second was the John Street Theatre of New York. It opened in December 1767 with a performance of Farquhar's *The Beaux' Stratagem* and remained New York's leading playhouse until the Park Theatre was built in 1798.

Another development of the period is the name adopted by the Douglass company early in the 1760s. By this time hostility to British tyranny had grown, and anything with an English label was becoming unpopular and suspect. So David Douglass's troupe with semantical shrewdness decided to change its name from The London Company to The American Company. Under this title it continued its career until the Revolution.

Probably the most unusual and amusing achievement of the company during this period was the adroitness with which it circumvented Puritan opposition—in some cases. The New England colonies were aggressively hostile to all things theatrical; the middle colonies were a little less so because of cosmopolitan cities like New York and Philadelphia; only in the southern colonies where cavalier attitudes prevailed did theatrical companies find a warm welcome. But there were many more centers of population, and hence more potential customers, in the northern colonies than in the South. So David Douglass and his colleagues set about placating, cajoling, educating, and circumventing their enemies in the North. Their usual maneuver was to disguise a play as a "moral dialogue" or as a demonstration of the work of Douglass's "histrionic academy" and to deny that the activity presented under these labels had anything to do with drama. Shakespeare's *Othello* was presented in this way when the company invaded Newport, Rhode Island, in the summer of 1761. Douglass's cunning announcement of a "Series of Moral Dialogues" is famous in theatrical history:

King's Arms Tavern, Newport, Rhode Island
On Monday, June 10, at the Public Room
of the Above Inn, will be delivered a Series of
MORAL DIALOGUES
in five parts
Depicting the evil effects of Jealousy and
other Bad Passions and Proving that
Happiness can only Spring from
the Pursuit of Virtue.

MR. DOUGLASS will represent a noble and magnanimous Moor named Othello who loves a young lady named Desdemona, and after he has married her, harbors (as in too many cases) the dreadful passion of jealousy.

> Of jealously, our being's bane,
> Mark the small cause, and the most dreadful pain.

MR. ALLYN will depict the character of a specious villain, in the regiment of Othello, who is so base as to hate his commander on mere suspicion, and to impose on his best friend. Of such characters, it is to be feared, there are thousands in the world, and the one in question may present to us a salutary warning.

> The man that wrongs his master and his friend
> What can he come to but a shameful end?

MR. HALLAM will delineate a young and thoughtless officer who is traduced by Mr. Allyn, and getting drunk loses his situation and his general's estecm. All young men, whatsoever, take example from Cassio.

> The ill effects of drinking would you see?
> Be warned and keep from evil company.

The announcement continues in like manner to list all the principal characters in *Othello* and concludes with the following paragraph, the shrewd piety of which must have disarmed a few of the enemy:

> Various other dialogues, too numerous to mention here, will be delivered at night, all adapted to the improvement of the mind and manners. The whole will be repeated on Wednesday and Saturday. Tickets, six shillings each, to be had within. Commencement at 7, conclusion at half-past 10, in order that every spectator may go home at a sober hour and reflect upon what he has seen before he retires to rest.

> God save the king
> And long may he sway
> East, North, and South
> And fair America.

The first period of professional drama in America was ended not by Puritan opposition, but by the Revolutionary War. But before the war closed the theatres, much had been accomplished. The Hallams, Douglass, and their fellow pioneers had gained friends and followers in the colonies; they had built playhouses in many towns; they had presented a commendable number of plays in a commendable fashion; and they had established a promising theatrical circuit along the Eastern seaboard despite forbidding obstacles. They could, with good reason, look forward to increasing activity and prosperity. But in October 1774 the Continental Congress passed a declaration to discourage "every species of extravagence and dissipation, especially all horse-racing, and all kinds of gaming, cock-fighting, exhibition of shews, plays, and other expensive diversions and entertainments." This resolution, along with other evidence of growing hostility and rebellion, were too much even for the canny David Douglass to circumvent. He returned to Jamaica and the curtain, which had risen many years before, was rung down on the first act of professional theatrical activity in America.

ATTENDING THE THEATRE IN COLONIAL AMERICA

Attending the theatre in colonial America was a vastly different experience from what it is today. To grasp how conditions have changed in the past two hundred years, let us go back in imagination to the year 1770; suppose that we are members of the upper class in a colonial city and that we wish to attend a performance to be given by Douglass's American Company which, luckily, is playing a season in our town. In our imaginary visit, everything seen and described is based on historical record. All the details of ticket buying, playhouse architecture, stage scenery, and so on are facts of theatrical history.

A handbill distributed throughout the town informs us that there will be three performances in the coming week: on Monday, Wednesday, and Saturday evenings, each to commence at 6:00 P.M. The early hour of 6:00 P.M. is customary, and it is popular because it gives us the advantage of the daylight and gets us home at a respectable time. Plays are not performed in the afternoon—and never on Sunday.

We decide to attend the Wednesday night performance because *Othello* will be given then and we have heard that Mr. Douglass plays the leading part very well. To buy a ticket, we stroll down to the local tavern or to the shop where the tickets are printed. We decide to sit in a box, even though we note that the prices are higher this year than last: we paid six shillings last season for the best seats, and now they are seven shillings and sixpence. As we buy our tickets, we ask the tavern owner to notify us if, for some reason, the Wednesday night performance is canceled. Last season there were several last-minute cancellations when the manager of the theatre discovered that he had scheduled a performance on the day of a popular social or civic event.

When Wednesday comes, we send a servant to the playhouse early, so that he will arrive by 5:00 P.M. The doors to the boxes and pit are opened then and if we want choice seats, we must send a servant to occupy and hold them. Our ticket assures us a place in the box but not a particular seat. When we arrive at 6:00 P.M., our servant will return home or retire to the gallery where we have bought him a ticket.

The way to the playhouse is rather muddy because of a heavy afternoon shower, and because there are no sidewalks the going is rather sloppy. However, the air is balmy and we expect the interior of the playhouse to be comfortable. We rarely attend in the coldest weather because then it is a battle to stay warm despite heavy clothing and a charcoal foot warmer. The single stove in the pit is wholly inadequate to warm the patrons in the boxes. We rarely go in the early fall, either, when the heat, humidity, and insects are bad. This balmy spring weather is an excellent time for seeing a play, despite the mud underfoot.

As we approach the playhouse, we are accosted by vendors selling everything from peanuts and oranges to mince pies. We do not feel like buying anything now but may purchase something from a vendor inside the theatre during one of the entr'actes.

We have excellent seats in the front row of a box to the right of the stage. As we settle down, we notice that all the candles have been lighted: those in the central chandeliers, those in the brackets attached to the front of the boxes, and those in the holders set across the front of the stage. We prefer to sit in this particular box because it is out of the range of the dripping candles. Other things we notice with disapproval are the young men in the pit standing on the backless benches in their muddy boots; the noisy crowd in the gallery, all of whom seem to be munching peanuts, apples, or cakes; and the vain young ladies in the boxes, trying their best to attract attention. So far we have not noticed the hardness of our chairs—but we shall before the evening is over.

This playhouse, of course, follows the design and shape established by Restoration playhouses in London a hundred years ago. It holds about six hundred people. Other theatres in the colonies, we know, vary in size from a capacity of three hundred to one thousand. Generally they have a lower floor, or pit; a tier of boxes curving in a horseshoe from one side of the stage to the other and surrounding the pit; and above the boxes, a gallery. A forestage extends well beyond the curtain line. Opening onto this forestage are proscenium doors on each side. After the curtain rises, the actors will enter by these proscenium doors and will play most of their scenes on the forestage to be closer to the audience and to the source of light.

We do not wait long before we hear the stage manager's whistle—it has not yet been replaced by a bell—announcing that the performance is about to begin. The musicians take their places in the narrow space directly in front of the stage and start the overture. The audience begins to settle down after greeting the musicians with mingled applause, boos, hisses, and also a few apple cores flung from the gallery. When the overture is finished, the large green front curtain slowly rolls up and the play begins.

The action of *Othello* is laid in Venice and Cypress during a bygone period, but the actors' costumes are contemporary. They represent neither the time nor the places described by Shakespeare. Othello, for example, is dressed in the uniform of a contemporary British general; Desdemona wears a gown that is currently fashionable in London. These inconsistencies of dress do not bother us; we are used to them, and besides, we know that the company's wardrobe is small. The players have

Reconstruction of the Dock Street, or Queen Street, Theatre, Charleston.
Courtesy of The Footlight Players Inc., Charleston, S. C.

to supply most of their own costumes and rely on the company only for such attire as Roman dress, oriental turbans, and the like.

We are not bothered by the scenery on the stage, either. We have long been accustomed to it both in England and in the colonies. We are used to seeing the back of the stage masked by a large cloth or drop painted appropriately. Or, in place of a drop cloth, there may be a pair of shutters, large painted flats fitted into grooves. When the shutters are pushed into place, they join in the center of the stage to form a continuous back wall. Concealing the offstage area on each side is a series of wing pieces parallel to the backdrop and painted to continue the decoration of the backdrop. The wings, like the shutters, are made of canvas stretched on wooden frames that fit into grooves. Hiding the ceiling is a series of borders, short cloths hung high on battens that stretch from one side of the stage to the other. When we look at this scenery, we can imagine any kind of setting suggested by the painting on the canvas and by the lines of the play. The American Company has more than thirty plays in its repertory but only a limited supply of wings, drops, and shutters. Its resources are limited, and the vogue for realistic, historically accurate settings has not begun. Audiences of 1770 believe that universal truth, independent of time and place, is the aim of drama. Therefore, we feel

The first Mrs. Lewis Hallam, afterward Mrs. Douglass, as Daraxa.
Harvard Theatre Collection.

that scenery should be general and idealized to suggest the universal nature of the situations and problems presented in dramatic literature. The furniture and properties used with this scenery are scanty and the floor of the stage is uncarpeted, so that the actors sometimes make a clatter when they move about.

Shakespeare's *Othello,* like all his plays, has numerous scenes in each of the acts. The front curtain is not rolled up and down for each of the scenes—only for the acts, and we have the fun of watching many of the scene changes. One backdrop is rolled up and another is lowered; one set of wings is pushed off and another slid into place; at the same time, a couple of stage hands dressed as servants change the few pieces of furniture required for the action of the play. All the changes are made in a matter of seconds. The scenery may not be realistic, but it can be changed rapidly and easily; and the play moves along smoothly without long interruptions.

During the interval between the first and second acts of *Othello,* we are treated to a patriotic song presented by one of the young ladies of the company. It is greeted with great applause, but the comic dance performed by one of the gentlemen receives a mixed reaction. We expect, of course, to be continuously entertained between the acts because it is the custom of the times. It keeps the spectators in their seats—and under control. Another custom which we enjoy is the presentation of a farce or a comic opera after the main play is over. These afterpieces are always rollicking and send us home in a happy mood. Actually, we see a lot of entertainment for the price of a ticket: a long play, either comedy or tragedy; entertainment between the acts; and finally a comic afterpiece.

One especially interesting aspect of the performance we are watching is the acting itself. Close observation reveals that there is no single uniform style, but rather a blend of styles. We must remember that the players of the American Company were all born and trained in England and thus are inheritors of two acting styles that prevailed on the English stage in 1770: the neoclassical style of conventionalized tone and gesture and the realistic-romantic style made popular by the English tragedians Charles Macklin and David Garrick. The realistic-romantic style was inspired by the belief that "the closer the imitation of nature in art, the better the art." These two styles dominated acting on colonial stages during the quarter-century between the arrival of the first professional company in 1749 and the closing of the theatres in 1774.

The American Company has an extensive repertory of plays. When the troupe first landed in the colonies, the players were prepared to present twenty-four plays, including Shakespeare's *Merchant of Venice, Richard III, Hamlet,* and *Othello.* In addition, they played several modern tragedies, five comedies by George Farquhar, a comedy by Sir Richard Steele (*The Conscious Lovers*), and five farces or afterpieces. During their first year of touring they added six long plays to the repertory, including *King Lear* and *Romeo and Juliet,* and increased the number of afterpieces to twelve. Each year since then, the repertory has undergone some changes, as the latest comedies, tragedies, and farces from the London stage are added and some of the older ones dropped. The plays of Shakespeare remain the backbone of the repertory. We have the satisfaction of knowing that we are able to see many of the same plays that are popular in London. We are also conscious that the repertory contains no plays written by native-born Americans.

The company that has performed *Othello* is organized like an English provincial troupe. A player is hired for a season to act a "line of parts," or a "line of business"—that is, he specializes in one kind of role. If he is under contract to play eccentric comic characters, he is not cast as a romantic young lover; if portraying old men is his specialty, he is not given leading roles. The lines of business for both men and women are headed, of course, by the leading man and the leading lady.

They have first choice of roles whenever a play is cast; the other actors are assigned the role that best fits their specialty. In standard plays, the casting of parts according to lines is well established, but when a new play is introduced into the repertory, the manager often has a quarrel on his hands over which role fits which actor's line of parts. The manager of the troupe assigns roles and takes charge of rehearsals. However, the actor has great freedom in interpreting his role and in creating his own style of performance. The manager does little more than indicate entrances and exits and specify who gets stage center in a scene.

The members of the troupe do not receive fixed salaries; rather, they participate in a "sharing scheme," a system surviving from the English theatre of earlier days. Each major member of the troupe owns one or more shares in the company, depending on his importance. The income received by the shares varies with the prosperity of the company. When audiences are large, the actors make money; when attendance is scanty, they receive very little. We hear that this system of profit sharing has been abandoned by the London theatres. Actors there receive fixed salaries. The system will be abandoned by the American Company after the Revolutionary War, but it will continue in frontier companies well into the nineteenth century.

The performance of *Othello* moves steadily to its climax and conclusion. It is marred only by occasional boisterousness from the gallery, by the discomfort of dripping candles, and by the need for a stagehand to tiptoe onto the stage during a tense scene to snuff out a smoking candle. When the play is over, we applaud generously and decide to stretch out limbs instead of watching the incidental entertainment offered between *Othello* and the afterpiece.

When the afterpiece begins, we join in the fun with vigor and gusto. The evening finally ends at half past ten, and we walk home through the unlighted streets to reflect on what we have seen.

Such might be the experiences and thoughts of a playgoer in 1770. The conditions he or she knew and accepted were destined to prevail for many years to come. There was no sudden or dramatic change in any one period. Instead, small differences crept in gradually, and in the course of two hundred years produced the much-changed theatre of the late twentieth century. Our era, like all those preceding it, is witnessing the same slow but steady changes that will produce still another kind of theatre in the years to come.

2

The Curtain Rises Again

There was no professional theatre in America for almost ten years. The curtain, rung down in 1774, remained down for the duration of the Revolutionary War. It rose again soon after the end of the war. In October 1781 General Charles Cornwallis surrendered his British forces. A few months later John Henry, a popular actor of the American Company, was back in Philadelphia petitioning the authorities for permission to present, not a play, but a semidramatic offering that he billed as a "Lecture on Heads." The bulk of the American Company returned to Pennsylvania in 1784. The troupe—which was soon to be known as the "Old" American Company—reopened the Southwark Theatre in Philadelphia and presented a season of drama. Because the ban against plays was still in force, the company resorted to its old subterfuge of calling its productions "lectures," "moral dialogues," or "pantomimical finales." The opposition was angered by the subterfuge—but it succeeded. The company then moved to New York and gave a season of plays, now undisguised, at the John Street Theatre in the fall of 1785. The professional theatre was back in business.

During the war years, playgiving did not entirely disappear from the colonies. Professional performers had fled, but in their stead the soldiers of both the British and American forces presented plays. The British were especially active. They presented plays in Boston, New York, and Philadelphia. American troops were less active and stopped playmaking completely in 1778 when the Continental Congress passed another resolution to discourage playgoing and to forbid acting by anyone on the national payroll.

When the Revolution was won, conditions in the nation—and thus conditions for theatrical activity—began to change rapidly. The new nation experienced a period of growth and ferment, of progress and of setbacks. British restraints on American industry and commerce were removed, manufacturing in the new nation was stimulated, and both religious and social tolerance increased. The most miraculous advance was made politically. A constitutional convention met in Philadelphia in 1787 and after working four months submitted to the several states a plan for a remodeled federal government. In June 1788 New Hampshire became the ninth state to ratify the new plan of organization, and the United States of America was born. George Washington, hero of the Revolution, became the first president in 1789, and was succeeded eight years later by John Adams.

However, not everything went smoothly in national affairs during the postwar years. There was continuing friction with Great Britain, instability and worry under the old Articles of Confederation, bitter debate over the new plan of government, and a serious economic depression between 1783 and 1787. To add to the problems, an epidemic of yellow fever ravaged the country in 1792 and reappeared for several seasons thereafter.

The professional theatre, now reestablished on American soil, reacted to both the progress and the setbacks of the society surrounding it. It was badly hurt by the economic upheavals and the epidemics of yellow fever. It was greatly helped by steady growth, expanding prosperity, and increased social tolerance. Despite difficulties, the overall record of theatrical activity in the postrevolutionary years is a record of continuing expansion and increasing prosperity.

The growing health and vigor of the theatre during the period from 1782 to 1800 is evident in four major areas:

Acting: The number of professional companies and competent performers increased.

Attitudes: Many antitheatre laws were repealed.

Playhouses: More and better theatres were built.

Playwriting: Influential native playwrights appeared.

At the start of the Revolution there were about two and a half million colonists. By 1790 there were almost four million people in the thirteen states, and by 1800 the number exceeded 5.3 million. As potential customers increased, so did the need for additional theatrical companies. Most of the groups were offshoots of the Old American Company. Like a vigorous plant the original troupe kept dividing, albeit reluctantly, and producing new growth. The most successful of the new companies was organized by Thomas Wignell, the best comedian of the Old American Company and the favorite performer of George Washington. In 1791 he moved to Philadelphia where he combined his experience with that of a musician named Alexander Reinagle and together the two men founded a company that dominated the theatre of Philadelphia for many years. From the start, it was larger than the Old American Company—and more talented, too. Wignell recruited from the English theatre such talented performers as Mrs. Oldmixon, a popular comedienne and singer; Mrs. Eliza Kemble Whitlock, sister of the renowned Mrs. Siddons and a gifted tragedienne; and James Fennell, a handsome leading man. These were not all. Within two years three other outstanding performers emigrated from England. They were Mrs. Anne Brunton Merry (1768-1808), William Warren (1767-1832), and Thomas A. Cooper (1776-1849). All of them contributed to the distinction and the tradition of the American theatre. It was Thomas A. Cooper, for example, who introduced a new style of acting to the American stage—the stately school of grand declamation and idealized movement that had been established in England by John Philip Kemble and his sister Sarah Kemble Siddons.

Mrs. Merry, an early favorite of the Philadelphia stage, as Calista.

Hoblitzelle Theatre Arts Library, Humanities Research Center, University of Texas at Austin.

While Wignell was recruiting talented players and strengthening his Philadelphia troupe, the Old American Company was not idle. It had a famous name and an established following and exerted itself to preserve both. To meet the competition from Wignell, it too recruited new talent. In 1792 the glamorous and versatile John Hodgkinson joined the company, bringing with him from England a lady friend and fellow player, Miss Brett, who later became his wife. With them came several other able players, the most important of whom was Mrs. Pownall, formerly Mrs. Wrighten, who had earned a high reputation in England as an actress and a singer. The following year an even more celebrated tragedienne, Mrs. Melmoth, joined the American Company, and in 1794 the company was further strengthened by the lucky acquisition of Joseph Jefferson I, a remarkable comedian whose talent was transmitted, in part, to his son, Joseph II, and in full to his grandson, Joseph III. The latter gained theatrical immortality as Rip Van Winkle.

The new talent strengthened the acting ensemble of the Old American Company, but it also created rivalries and jealousies within the troupe, especially among the women. The record during this period is one of friction and strife, which sometimes resulted in open rebellion and in the secession of valuable players who formed troupes of their own. Also, the management of the companies changed several times during the last sixteen years of the century. These growing pains indicated that the American theatre was expanding to meet the needs of a burgeoning nation.

One of the happiest developments in the postrevolutionary years, besides additional companies and better performers, was repeal of the antitheatre laws. In all the years since the Hallam company had landed in 1752, actors and managers were forced to petition, struggle, and fight for a chance to perform, and even to evade the laws that had been passed to suppress the theatre. But in 1789 they finally enjoyed a significant victory. The antitheatre law of Philadelphia was repealed, thanks to a vigorous campaign waged by a Dramatic Association of influential citizens. Some years later the Puritan stronghold of Boston capitulated. Again, an association of leading citizens led the attack on the old law. With both the Quaker and the Puritan capitals surrendered, it was not long before other communities followed suit. By the end of the eighteenth century, dramatic companies enjoyed the novel luxury of freedom to perform openly and honestly in almost every city of the nation—the nation then being confined largely to the East Coast.

With public acceptance of the theatre rising and the number of companies increasing, more and better buildings were needed to house the plays and players. Usually these were bigger, handsomer, and more comfortable than any previous playhouses. New Orleans opened the Theatre St. Pierre in 1791, the first French-language theatre in the United States. Newport, Rhode Island, remodeled a market into a playhouse in 1793. Charleston, proud of its long theatrical tradition, opened two new playhouses at about the same time, one in 1792 and the other in 1794.

In 1794, Boston joined the ranks of playhouse builders. Although the Puritan stronghold had seen a few dramatic performances in a makeshift playhouse called the "New Exhibition Room," the first legal playhouse was the Federal Street Theatre, described as "a lofty and spacious edifice, substantially built of brick, with stone facias . . ."[1] Two years later a second playhouse was erected, "an immense wooden edifice . . . that overtopped every other building in Boston."[2] This was the Haymarket Theatre. Both houses boasted acting companies recruited from England, but neither company included first-rate performers, and both had a number of more or less unsuccessful managers until Snelling Powell, a member of the acting company, obtained control of the Federal Street Theatre in 1802. He gained the title of "first successful manager of a theatre in Boston" and was the leading impresario in the area until his death in 1821.

In 1794 Baltimore also saw the construction of a new playhouse, promoted by Wignell and Reinagle and served by their distinguished company from Philadelphia. The new building, described as a "huge wooden barn,"[3] stood until 1813, when it was replaced by a second house of the same name.

While theatres were being built for the standard drama, other structures for specialty entertainments were also appearing. Most spectacular among these were the circus amphitheatres constructed in New York and Philadelphia in the 1790s by a circus man named Ricketts. They originally featured clowning and horsemanship (Ricketts himself was an expert rider), but later bits and pieces from legitimate drama were added. For a time, Ricketts's circuses offered strenuous competition to the regular playhouses.

Of all the new structures built in the period before 1800, by far the most famous and enduring were the Chestnut Street Theatre in Philadelphia and the Park in New York. The Philadelphia house came first. It was built to serve the brilliant new company organized by Wignell and Reinagle and for a time was the finest playhouse in the nation. The Chestnut Street Theatre was begun in 1791 but did not open until February 1794 because of the fear of yellow fever. The new structure had a handsome interior, in contrast to an unimpressive exterior, and boasted a pit and three tiers of boxes with a seating capacity usually reported as two thousand. The pit was raked—that is, it had a gentle slope from the front row of seats to the back—something new in American theatrical architecture. The stage was gently raked, sloping upward from the footlights to the rear wall. There was a large forestage with proscenium doors opening onto it, and a commodious space for the orchestra immediately in front of the forestage. The color scheme of the interior was gray and gold, and the decor was considered to be restrained but elegant. The lighting and scenic arrangements were the same as in colonial theatres, but the painting of the scenery was superior and the main curtain was a tastefully embellished drop instead of the usual green baize.

The Chestnut Street Theatre, rebuilt after a fire in 1820, had a long, glamorous, and glorious career before it closed its doors in 1856 after a lifetime of sixty-two

---

[1] William W. Clapp, Jr., *A Record of the Boston Stage* (Boston and Cambridge: James Munroe and Company, 1853), p. 19.

[2] Arthur Hornblow, *A History of the Theatre in America* (Philadelphia: J. B. Lippincott Co., 1919), I:238.

[3] Ibid., p. 212.

Interior of the Park Theatre, New York, 1821.
Courtesy of The New York Historical Society.

years. It gained the affectionate title of "Old Drury of Philadelphia" and was beloved of actors as well as audiences. For several years it helped to make Philadelphia the theatrical capital of the United States—and it never acknowledged the loss of that position. But supremacy in theatrical affairs did gradually move to New York during the first twenty years of the nineteenth century, and one of the reasons was the opening in New York of the Park Theatre only four years after the debut of Old Drury in Philadelphia.

The Park Theatre was constructed in 1798 for the Old American Company. The new playhouse was built with funds contributed by 113 businessmen—which created serious financial difficulties for a time. The house enjoyed a life of fifty years, having been rebuilt after a disastrous fire in 1820, and during many of these years it was the leading playhouse of New York. After the theatres in Philadelphia fell upon evil days, it could claim to be the premier theatre of the United States. It was the place where foreign stars made their first appearance, it enjoyed the patronage of the most cultivated audience in New York, and at its best it boasted one of the finest acting companies in America.

By the end of the eighteenth century, four centers of theatrical activity were clearly visible in the youthful United States. The three most vigorous were Philadelphia, New York, and Charleston, while Boston—where theatrical development had lagged behind the other three—constituted a fourth center. The first three cities each boasted a strong acting company headed by a vigorous management. In Philadelphia it was the troupe directed by Wignell and Reinagle; in New York, the Old American Company was headed by William Dunlap; in Charleston the troupe was led by John J. Solee and Alexander Placide. In Boston the company of the Federal Street Theatre eventually emerged as the leader in the New England area.

During the closing years of the eighteenth century, each theatrical center developed a territory of its own and a circuit of towns that were visited regularly. Such traveling engagements were necessary to keep a company busy. Even though American cities were growing rapidly, none was big enough in the 1790s to support a company for an entire year. The result was that many smaller communities became regular "road show" towns with the happy consequence of being able to watch and enjoy the growth of theatrical traditions in America.

The activities of the 1790s—the building of new playhouses, the increased number of good performers and good companies, the lessening of prejudice, and the growing strength of native playwrights—were all happy auguries for the future of the theatre in America. Thus, as the eighteenth century ended, managers, performers, and patrons could face the new century with optimism, enthusiasm, and the expectation of a golden age to come. The new century proved to be everything they hoped for.

3

Enter the American Playwright

On April 23, 1767, an event of unusual significance occurred. On the stage of the Southwark Theatre in Philadelphia, the American Company of David Douglass presented a new play entitled *The Prince of Parthia,* written by Thomas Godfrey. The audience probably knew that the author was a native-born Philadelphian, that he had attended the College of Philadelphia, and that he had died four years before the production of his play. It is unlikely, however, that anyone in the audience sensed the significance of the occasion. The play was a poor one—turgid, static, and derivative—and it merited only one performance. Yet this performance was to be remembered in the history of the American theatre as the first professional performance of any play written by a native-born American. If that audience of two hundred years ago could have signed a guest book, their names would be forever preserved in a footnote to theatrical history because they witnessed the entrance on the world stage of the native American playwright.

The Prince of Parthia is unquestionably an inferior play. It is an improbable tragedy in blank verse presenting unmitigated villainy plotting against unsullied virtue, which leads to murder, seduction, insurrection, madness, and death. It has been ridiculed and lambasted for two hundred years. As recently as 1967, a critic called it "self-conscious bombast"[1] and lamented that American playwriting began so badly. Yet there is something to be said for this first professionally produced play.

To begin with, it was a first; not the earliest American play to be written, but the earliest to receive presentation by a professional company. Second, Thomas Godfrey was only twenty-three years old when he wrote the play, having just left the College of Philadelphia to serve in the Pennsylvania state militia. He had de-

[1] Joseph Golden, *The Death of Tinker Bell* (Syracuse, N. Y.: Syracuse University Press, 1967), pp. 65-67.

veloped a love for drama in college; had participated in the production of college dialogues, odes, and masques; and had witnessed the plays presented by the professional actors of the American Company. Inspired by them and stimulated by his college training, he wrote a play modeled after the great Elizabethans. The result was bad, but Thomas Godfrey's effort was part of a noble tradition.

American playwriting began not with Godfrey's tragedy, but long before 1759, when *The Prince of Parthia* was composed. It had already resulted in a modest body of writing, some of which is still extant. This native playwriting of the eighteenth century falls into four recognizable periods.

The earliest period is the era of odes and dialogues composed in the colonial colleges and recited publicly as a means of honoring notable events and of giving young men practice in the art of speaking effectively. These odes and dialogues were not really plays with setting, plot, and a cast of characters. They were generally commemorative or hortatory poems in ornate style recited by two or more speakers. The first of these dialogues may have been a "pastoral colloquy" presented at the College of William and Mary in 1702. Although this is not certain, it is certain that sixty years later Francis Hopkinson, America's first poet-composer and a friend of Thomas Godfrey, wrote "An Exercise: Containing a Dialogue (by Provost Smith) and Ode, Sacred to the Memory of his Late Gracious Majesty George II," which was recited at the commencement of the College of Philadelphia in 1762. The following year Hopkinson composed a similar tribute on the accession of George III, which was recited at the commencement of 1763. In the same year the College of New Jersey (later Princeton) saw the presentation of a dialogue on "The Military Glory of Great Britain." Eight years later, by 1771, sentiment had so altered that the subject of the dialogue presented at the College of New Jersey and coauthored by Francis Hopkinson was "The Rising Glory of America."

The emerging sense of national identity appears in the writing of the next and overlapping period of American national dramaturgy. This was the period just before the Revolution that saw the publication of several plays with a native flavor, a patriotic aura, or both. In 1764, three years before *The Prince of Parthia* was staged, a dramatic piece entitled *The Paxton Boys,* published anonymously, introduced American Indians as characters. In 1766 Major Robert Rogers published a play, *Ponteach, or the Savages of America,* in which an Indian chief is the leading character. The American Indian, thus introduced to American drama, was to have a permanent place in the American theatre and an undying vitality as a dramatic character.

The same year in which *The Prince of Parthia* was produced, Thomas Forrest composed the first comic opera written in America, a piece entitled *The Disappointed, or the Force of Credulity*. It was a satiric work containing the first stage Irishman in American drama, and its main thrust was to lampoon certain local types and individuals. It was never produced. Another piece presenting a different kind of native material was published the year the American Revolution began. It was *The Patriots* by Robert Munford, a plea to the revolutionary Whigs and Tories to use moderation and common sense.

Munford's play introduces us to the period of the American Revolution. During this time, as we have seen, the American Company left the colonies and the presentation of plays was suspended except for the productions given by both British and American troops. Yet the writing of dramatic pieces increased, stimulated by the passions of the war and the partisan feelings of Whigs and Tories. There was a lively exchange of insults in the form of satirical dialogues and dramas, usually in printed form, rarely acted. Two of the best of these propaganda pieces are the work of Mrs. Mercy Otis Warren, who effectively satirized her fellow citizens who were sympathetic to the British in *The Adulateur* (1773) and *The Group* (1775).

In response to such attacks General Burgoyne, the cultivated British military leader, lampooned American stupidity in *The Blockade of Boston* (1775) and was answered the following year by an anonymous piece entitled *The Blockheads, or the Affrighted Officers,* which ridiculed the complaints of British officers and Tory refugees over the inconveniences they suffered because of the American blockade of Boston.

Sometimes patriotic sentiment and satiric attack were combined in the dramatization of contemporary events, such as *The Battle of Bunker Hill* (1776) and *The Death of General Montgomery at the Siege of Quebec* (1777), both composed by Hugh Henry Brackenridge, a friend and supporter of the Revolution. These pieces, and several more like them, kept dramatic writing alive. When the war was over, Mrs. Warren turned to the writing of tragedies in verse, such as *The Sack of Rome* and *The Ladies of Castile,* both published in 1790. Other propagandists turned to other pursuits, and a few new dramatists appeared to nurture the fragile growth of American playwriting. The most notable of these were Royall Tyler and William Dunlap.

ROYALL TYLER

Royall Tyler was a versatile, dashing young man whose clever comedy, *The Contrast,* is still read with amusement—and sometimes even acted with success. Born with talent into a family of means and position, he accomplished the unusual feat of earning degrees from both Harvard College and Yale College in the same year, 1776. Four years later, after serving in the Revolution, he was admitted to the bar. He made law practice his major activity and was notably successful in it, achieving the positions of chief justice of the Supreme Court of Vermont and professor of jurisprudence at the University of Vermont. Before he settled down to such staid pursuits, he tried his hand at playwriting (among other things) and was an instant success. He wrote his memorable comedy, *The Contrast,* in three weeks in 1787. Later the same year he dashed off a comic opera entitled *May Day in Town, or New York in an Uproar.* He wrote other plays as well, all of which are now forgotten. *The Contrast,* however, is remembered and studied as the first native comedy to be produced in the United States and as the forefather of a long line of satiric comedies of manners which have enlivened the American theatre ever since. It was produced at the John Street Theatre in New York in April 1787. The response was so favorable that several additional performances were given. Later the play was presented in several other American cities. It has had numerous revivals in the twentieth century.

The Contrast deserves to be remembered. It is nimble and amusing; it can still be read with enjoyment; and it effectively reveals the state of mind of a young nation which has just achieved its independence. The plot is simple. Billy Dimple, an affected young man who apes British priggishness, is entangled with three young ladies: Maria, to whom he is engaged; Letitia, whom he wants for her money; and Charlotte, whom he wants for his own enjoyment. His schemes to achieve his way with these three ladies are thwarted by Colonel Manly, Charlotte's brother, who is a veteran of the Revolution and a model of rectitude. In the course of exposing Dimple's machinations, the contrast between deceitful British affectations and honest American virtue is emphatically preached and praised. The contrast is further emphasized by the differences between Jessemy, the snobbish servant of Billy Dimple, and Colonel Manly's sturdy Yankee servant Jonathan, the first stage Yankee to appear as a major dramatic character.

The contrast between British deceit and American virtue is the source of the title and theme of the play; it also provides many lines of patriotic praise for all

Royall Tyler, who wrote the first comedy by a native American
to be produced professionally in the United States.

Harvard Theatre Collection.

things American. George Washington, who was an active patron of the theatre in 1787, is singled out for special tribute. The play ends with Colonel Manly addressing the audience in these final patriotic words:

> And I have learned that probity, virtue, honor, though they shall not have received the polish of Europe, will secure to an honest American the good graces of his fair countrywomen, and I hope, the applause of THE PUBLIC.

The fervent patriotism which characterizes the play was not only an echo of the times but was to be echoed for many generations to come in literally hundreds of American plays. It was a prominent feature in the dramas of William Dunlap, the other notable American playwright to emerge at the end of the eighteenth century.

WILLIAM DUNLAP

Before the advent of William Dunlap, no American who had written plays could call himself a professional playwright—or even a professional man of the theatre. The principal activities of these authors were law, politics, teaching, or house-keeping. Then the versatile Dunlap stepped onto the stage, and occupied it, off and on, for thirty years. Before he bowed out, he had earned a reputation as painter, playwright, manager-producer, historian, patriot, and, in retrospect, the impressive title of "Father of the American Drama." He was our first professional man of the theatre because playwriting, together with his other theatrical activities, constituted his main occupation for much of his career—although even he could not keep it up to the end of his life.

Dunlap, born in New Jersey in 1766 and reared, for the most part, in New York, developed a love for the theatre—and for his native land—at an early age. Both loves were nurtured in 1783, when he painted a portrait of George Washington (Dunlap's first ambition was to become a painter), and in 1784, when he went to London to study painting under Benjamin West, America's first native painter. West was a product of the College of Philadelphia, where he had been a friend of Thomas Godfrey and had helped with the production of dialogues and odes. Whether in New York or London, Dunlap attended the theatre faithfully and watched the best productions of his time. Returning to New York in 1787, he was so stimulated by the possibilities he saw in Royall Tyler's *The Contrast* that he decided to write a play. His first attempt was a failure, but his second—a comedy of manners entitled *The Father, or American Shandyism*—was performed professionally in 1789. It launched Dunlap on a playwriting career that was to last until 1828 and to encompass the writing or adaptation of at least fifty-six dramas.

When Dunlap's career in the American theatre is surveyed, it is impossible not to admire and feel affection for the character of the man. He was versatile, talented, hard-working, eternally optimistic and generous, and unwaveringly patriotic and proud of his country. He continued to exhibit these characteristics in

William Dunlap, "Father of the American Drama."
Harvard Theatre Collection.

spite of recurrent failures and continuing adversity in his theatrical pursuits. As Richard Moody points out, "Dunlap seems never to have got far above a perpetually distressing economic state."[2]

Dunlap had extensive experience as a manager beginning in 1796 at the John Street Theatre in New York; it continued with interruptions and difficulties until 1811. After that date he was never again a manager, but his activity in other fields did not diminish. He painted portraits and huge religious canvases, taught painting and design, helped to found the National Academy of Design, and wrote many books, including the first *History of the American Theatre* in 1832. Most important for the development of American drama, he continued to write original plays and to translate and adapt the works of German and French playwrights.

In a way it is a wonder that Dunlap was not a more successful manager. He was sensitive to the tastes and preferences of his audience and earned the reputation of being the first producer to make the drama "acceptable to Puritan consciences."[3] His original plays appealed to American patriotism and morality; his adaptations from French and German playwrights introduced to the American stage a kind of sentimental, heroic, moralistic melodrama that became a reigning favorite. It was a kind of play that audiences everywhere found engrossing and

[2] Richard Moody, *Dramas from the American Theatre 1762-1909* (New York: World Publishing Company, 1966), p. 89.

[3] Margaret G. Mayorga, *A Short History of the American Drama* (New York: Dodd, Mead & Co., 1934), p. 56.

gratifying. In fact, melodramas, particularly those adapted from the prolific German dramatist Augustus Frederic Ferdinand Von Kotzebue, remained so popular on the American stage for so long that they blighted the growth of native American playwriting.

Only two of Dunlap's foreign adaptations are readily available to a modern reader. These are *False Shame* and *Thirty Years,* both published in Volume II of *America's Lost Plays.*[4] Far more popular than these two pieces were such plays as *The Stranger,* Dunlap's first borrowing from Kotzebue, which was presented in 1798 and held the stage for most of the nineteenth century, and *Pizarro in Peru, or the Death of Rolla,* another adaptation from Kotzebue, which was staged at least two hundred times, beginning in 1800. Because Dunlap's renderings of these plays are not available (although other translations made and used in England are), the two dramas reprinted in *America's Lost Plays* will be considered as typical of his foreign adaptations. They illustrate the kind of play which thrilled American audiences for many decades.

The first, *False Shame, or the American Orphan in Germany* (an adaptation from Kotzebue), was first presented by Dunlap in 1799, the year after his successful production of *The Stranger.* The plot of *False Shame* is made up of contrivances, mysteries, and discoveries, all rigged to illustrate the evil effects of false shame. In the household of the German Baron Flachsland is an attractive orphan named Emmy, who as a child was rescued from a burning building in Charleston, South Carolina, when the city was sacked by the Hessians during the American Revolution. The child's rescuer is Captain Erlach, close friend of the baron, who brought her to Germany because he was unable to find any trace of her parents. She has been his ward every since, living with the baron, but Captain Erlach has not seen her for eight years. Early in the play, the captain—who has just inherited a fortune from an old aunt—returns to the baron's household and the following events ensue: (1) the captain, a confirmed bachelor and woman hater, falls instantly in love with his ward; (2) the baron's sister, disgraced and lost for more than twenty years, returns to her brother's home and arms; (3) Emmy, the orphan, turns out to be the daughter of the lost sister; (4) the priggish French vicomte, a guest of the baron, turns out to be the son of the lost sister.

As a result of these disclosures, and after much contrived misunderstanding, virtue and true love achieve a resounding triumph: the baron and his young second wife repudiate false shame and reach a new level of understanding and marital bliss, the baron's daughter (by his first wife) finds her true love, Emmy and Captain Erlach are united as a couple, and the frivolous, priggish characters are all ridiculed and dismissed. The play ends with the following song:

> Joy, brightest spark from Heaven,
> Daughter of Elysium, come!
> Vice has fled our blissful garden,
> Virtue here has found her home.

[4] Originally published in 1940 by Princeton University Press. Reissued in 1963 by Indiana University Press.

The final song illustrates the kind of moralizing which ornaments the play. Every scene is full of maxims, preachments, and sermonizing. The play is also loaded with sentimentality. Every serious emotion is exploited and exaggerated. All the characters, men as well as women, weep frequently and copiously; there is continuous embracing, fainting, screaming, and other emotionalistic display.

The language, with some exceptions, sounds florid and artificial to modern ears. Ordinary conversation is carried on in such phrases as, "Maiden, is this thy real intention?" or "Oh, impart to me your conjectures," or "To thee, and thee alone, do I confess my weakness." In scenes of crisis or climax, the rhetoric is more inflated and is sprinkled with interjections such as "Confusion!" "Oh, cruelest one!" "Fie on thee. For shame!"

The second of Dunlap's dramas in *America's Lost Plays* is adapted from a French original and entitled *Thirty Years, or the Gambler's Fate*. It is heavy melodrama portraying the horrors of a gambler's life and the misery he brings upon his wife and children, who bear their suffering with unwavering piety and fortitude. Included in the play are scheming villainy, attempted seduction, murder and flight, storms, police raids, and an ending which sees the archvillain stabbed by his victim, who then commits suicide as a burning house collapses on them both—while watching the carnage is the long-lost son who clasps his mother to his heart with the news that they are rich once more.

Of the fifty-six plays attributed to Dunlap, a total of twenty-seven are adaptations from French or German authors, Kotzebue being the favorite. The outstanding characteristics of all these plays—contrived plot, unreal characters, artificial language, heavy moralizing, and exaggerated sentimentality—are all traits that modern playgoers ridicule and deplore. Yet they must remember that these plays were the standard fare of the nineteenth-century theatre, not only in America but also in Europe.

Dunlap's original plays are far more important to us than his foreign adaptations. His twenty-nine originals cover a considerable range of genre and subject matter. There are a few comedies of manners, represented by Dunlap's first two plays, *The Modest Soldier* and *The Father;* romantic tragedies like *The Fatal Deception* (published as *Leicester*); an occasional farce comedy like *Bonaparte in England;* many romantic melodramas like *Fontainville Abbey* and *The Mysterious Monk;* plays that follow the lead of Kotzebue's popular contrivances; and finally patriotic plays and pageants that glorify American history and rousingly express the patriot's pride in his native land. The most admired of the last group, and the one most often included in anthologies of American plays, is the historical drama *André*, later rewritten as *The Glory of Columbia: Her Yeomanry!* These two plays deserve attention because they represent significant achievements in the development of American playwriting.

André, first acted in 1798, is a serious historical drama that depicts a famous episode of the American Revolution. Major André is a British agent captured by the American forces and executed as a spy. The plot is unusually simple. When the play opens, André is condemned to death; when it closes, he is executed. There would seem to be little chance for suspense or dramatic action in such a situation, yet Dunlap skillfully managed to generate a fair amount of both. The substance of the action is the various attempts to save André—by the young American Captain Bland, a friend of André; by Bland's mother, brothers, and sister; by the British high command, which threatens reprisals if André is executed; and by André's sweetheart, Honora, who arrives unexpectedly from England to plead for him. The attempts to save the convicted spy generate a measure of suspense even though we know they will fail, and they provide the opportunity for dramatic confrontations between opposing characters. Through the pleas and counterpleas to save André, the noble character of George Washington is revealed and many moral, patriotic principles are propounded. It may surprise a reader in the late twentieth century to find that George Washington was admired extravagently in his own time and was, in fact, described as "first among men" while he was still alive.

The patriotic fervor which we have already noted in many American plays is nowhere better illustrated than in *André* and the other native dramas of William Dunlap. This fervor will be seen again and again in the course of American playwriting and will not disappear until the advent of the age of anxiety and disillusionment in the mid-twentieth century.

As a play *André* has many worthy qualities, and it has faults as well. Despite Dunlap's skill in creating a degree of tension and suspense from unpromising material, the plot remains fragile and inert. The confrontation between opposing characters is always tinged with melodrama and often appears contrived to allow the dramatist to make points.

André was originally presented in 1798 but was not very successful. In 1803 Dunlap rewrote the play and rechristened it *The Glory of Columbia: Her Yeomanry!* In this guise it became a popular Fourth of July spectacle for the next fifty years. The change in title suggests the changes in the play. American "yeomen" are introduced and extolled as shining examples of bravery, duty, and honor. They are the ones who capture the spy, André, and bring him to military headquarters despite threats and bribes. The central action remains the same as in *André*—that is, various attempts are made to prevent the execution of the condemned man. But these scenes are drastically reduced to introduce the glory of Columbia—her yeomanry. In *André* the patriotic content was verbal and dignified. In the rewritten play, flag waving, patriotic songs, and dazzling visual spectacle were added— which explains, of course, why *The Glory of Columbia* remained a popular Fourth of July vehicle for so long. What red-blooded American would not thrill to the finale of the play, which is worth quoting in its entirety:

SCENE 2

Draws and discovers York-town—at a distance is seen the town, with the British lines and the lines of the besiegers—nearer are the advance batteries, one more distant from the audience than the other—cannonading commences from the besiegers on the town—explosion of a powder magazine—the French troops advance towards the most distant of the advance batteries—the battery begins to cannonade—the troops advance and carry it at the bayonet's point—while this is yet doing, the nearest battery begins to cannonade, and the American infantry attack and carry it with fixed bayonets, striking the English colors—shouts of victory. Enter on one side, George Washington, Melville, Bland, officers, soldiers, drums and colors . . . .

General: Thanks, my brave countrymen! our toils are past. It now requires not the spirit of prophecy to see, we have gain'd our country's independence. May that spirit which has animated the sons of Columbia, in this glorious struggle, remain pure and unimpaired, for then long will she be free and happy.

Chorus: The fight is done!
The battle won!
Our praise is due to him alone,
Who from his bright eternal throne,
        The fates of battles and of men decides!
To him all praise be given,
    And under heaven,
To great Columbia's son.
    Blest Washington!
Who o'er the fight like fate presides.

A transparency descends, and an eagle is seen suspending a crown of laurel over the commander in chief, with this motto—"Immortality to Washington."

Chorus: All hail to Columbia's son!
    Immortal Washington!
By fame renown'd
By victory crown'd
    Hail Washington!

The end of The Glory of Columbia. [5]

William Dunlap and Royall Tyler were the most notable native playwrights to emerge in the period between the end of the Revolution and the turn of the century. Other American dramas written in this period possess only antiquarian interest. Besides the verse tragedies of Mrs. Warren and the minor dramas of Royall Tyler, which have already been mentioned, the following might be remembered as typical of the period: *Virginia* (1784) by John Parke, a play about George Washington with the explanatory subtitle of "a Pastoral Drama on the Birth-Day of an Illustrious Personage and the Return of Peace, February 11, 1784"; two plays by Barnabas Bidwell, *The Modern Mistake* (1784) and *The Mercenary Match* (1785), the latter being a domestic tragedy about a dissatisfied wife who murders her husband; Peter Markoe's *The Patriot Chief* (1784), a classical tragedy laid in ancient Lydia which illustrates the dangers of aristocratic government; and two plays by

[5] For the text of *The Glory of Columbia: Her Yeomanry!* see Moody, *Dramas from the American Theatre*, p. 94.

John Daly Burk, an Irishman turned American, entitled *Bunker-Hill, or the Death of General Warren* (1797), and *Female Patriotism, or the Death of Joan of Arc* (1798). The latter is considered "one of the bright spots that reward the reader of our early drama"[6] because it portrays Joan not as the saintly martyr of tradition but as an honest, appealing, and clear-headed human being.

OBSTACLES TO THE DEVELOPMENT OF AMERICAN PLAYWRITING

By the end of the eighteenth century native playwriting had made a start. American dramatists had achieved a modicum of success and had established attitudes and created characters that were to influence native dramaturgy for the next two hundred years. Yet the development of American playwriting was destined to be slow and faltering.

Probably the severest handicap that an aspiring playwright faced was the country's long cultural dependence on all things European, particularly British. The colonies were exactly that: colonies—dependencies of Great Britain. The professional players were all imports from the London stage; the repertory of plays was exclusively British. Even after political independence was won, British actors, playwrights, managers, and stagecraft continued to dominate the American stage and to claim a vast superiority over anything of native origin. Despite the aggressive patriotism of many citizens of the new nation, most Americans accepted the claim of British superiority and felt a deep sense of cultural inferiority.

A corollary to the acceptance of British-European superiority in matters theatrical was the ease of acquiring popular plays from abroad. There were no effective national or international copyright laws for many decades. Anyone could translate and adapt a European play and present it, without royalty, on the American stage. When tested European successes were easily obtainable, why encourage native playwriting? And why should a native writer labor to compose a play when his labor would earn him little or nothing? The contemporary European plays, so easily obtained, did not set a high standard of playwriting. They were obsessed with the techniques of melodrama, a genre which became increasingly and immensely popular, and American playwrights copied these techniques for years.

Another situation that was to retard the growth of native playwriting was the pioneer nature of the American scene. The presence of a frontier throughout most of American history has influenced every phase of the American character and activity. The continuing challenge of settling and developing a new continent directed American enterprise into practical channels. There was little time or energy for any of the arts—including the art of playwriting.

Despite all these handicaps, some energetic, gifted young men braved the obstacles and continued the development begun by the Thomas Godfreys, the Royall Tylers, and the William Dunlaps. Their story will be told in later chapters.

[6]Arthur Hobson Quinn, *A History of the American Drama from the Beginning to the Civil War,* 2nd ed. (New York: Appleton-Century-Crofts, 1943), p. 117.

4

The Setting and the Action, 1800-1850

Many events of the first half of the nineteenth century such as the election of Andrew Jackson to the presidency strengthened the American faith in the common man as well as America's pride in her own achievements. It was a period of territorial expansion: Louisiana was purchased from France in 1803; Florida was ceded by Spain in 1819; Texas was annexed in 1845; the Oregon territory was explored and then acquired by treaty with Great Britain in 1846; and after the war with Mexico, a vast territory which now comprises six western states was annexed in 1848. It was a period of conflict, too, which included a second war with England in 1812 and the Mexican war of 1846-48. The burgeoning national strength and confidence were great enough in 1823 to enable President Monroe to assert that the American continent was closed to further colonization, that the spread of European systems would be resisted, and that Americans were not concerned with Europe's quarrels.

The territorial expansion of the period was indicated by the increase in the number of states. Between 1791 and 1820, eleven additional states were admitted to the Union, alternately one free and one slave to preserve the North-South balance. In the next thirty years, seven additional states were added, so that when California was admitted in 1850 the Union boasted a total of thirty-one members.

Despite the increasing tensions, which were to end in the tragic war between the states, the nation was developing prodigiously. Throughout the new territories and in the old as well, population increased rapidly, cities grew in number and size, and industry mushroomed. Everywhere new shops and factories were built, new banks and insurance companies were opened. To serve the needs of the expanding economy, the means of transportation, via roads and waterways, were greatly improved. By 1825 it was possible to travel from Boston to New York in only two days; New York was only eleven hours from Philadelphia, and Philadelphia only fifteen hours from Washington. The increased prosperity of the period was shared by thousands of citizens who now, for the first time, had money and leisure for entertainment.

The growth and exuberance of the period encountered temporary setbacks. The financial panic that began in 1819 and lasted for several years resulted in deflation, depression, and an appalling number of bankruptcies. A similar panic struck the country in 1837 and caused severe and widespread distress. Such panics were to be a recurring peril to American economic development. Although they never stopped the steady forward surge, they slowed it—and exacted a toll from every kind of business including, of course, show business.

The trends and developments of the period and the attitudes and ideals that dominated it all had a marked effect on what happened in the theatre. The growth in population, the improvement in transportation, and the general increase in prosperity were great boons to show business. New playhouses continued to be built in many cities, and more and more playgoers appeared to fill them. In 1800, according to William Winter, there were only 150 professional actors in America, most of them concentrated in the towns on the Atlantic seaboard.[1] By 1850 more than fifty theatrical companies were performing in many sections of the country.

During the first half of the nineteenth century, important new developments accompanied the general growth in theatrical activity. Professional dramatic criticism appeared in the writing of William Coleman and Jonathan Oldstyle (the latter was the pen name of Washington Irving). Eventually professional observers gained great influence in molding public opinion. As the reading of newspapers and magazines increased, more and more playgoers came to depend on the judgment of the critics for their choice of plays and opinion of the performers.

The first gas lighting for the stage, supplanting candles and oil lamps, was installed in the Chestnut Street Theatre, Philadelphia, in 1816; the Camp Street Theatre in New Orleans used gas for illumination in 1824; two years later it reached New York. However, many years elapsed before it gained widespread use. The brighter and more flexible lighting provided by gas eventually influenced both acting and scenery in the direction of greater naturalness.

Foreign stars began visiting the United States. The first of these was George Frederick Cooke, in 1810, and he was followed by a glittering succession of players such as Edmund and Charles Kean, Charles Mathews, Junius Brutus Booth, William Charles Macready, and Charles and Fanny Kemble.

The visits of such stars, together with the rise of outstanding native actors, established the *star system,* which has remained a feature of the American theatre ever since. Before the system was developed, the resident companies used their own players almost exclusively. With the coming of the star system, the situation changed. The visiting star acted his favorite roles for a set number of performances, and the local company supported him. During the star's engagement, the leading man or

[1]William Winter, *The Wallet of Time* (New York: Moffat, Yard and Company, 1913), I:23.

lady of the local company stepped aside or accepted a supporting role. Often the local players were required to alter their usual manner of performance or their way of staging traditional business to conform to the wishes of the star. Since each company was given only a minimum number of rehearsals with the visitor, and since each star had his own repertory and standards, the local company often appeared awkward or inept in their support. Sometimes they were.

It was the ambition of every professional performer to achieve the status of star and to command the salary, prestige, and independence that usually accompanied the status. As the nineteenth century advanced, more and more American players reached stardom, and more and more foreign celebreties performed in the United States. Companies began to depend on visiting stars to attract customers. The theatregoer came to expect the excitement of new faces and talents; he grew dissatisfied with productions that featured only members of the local troupe. Soon the morale and strength of resident companies declined, and in the end many of them disappeared. Undoubtedly the star system provided American audiences with dazzling performances, and undoubtedly the visiting artists challenged and inspired native actors—which was the case, as we shall see, in the careers of Edwin Forrest, Charlotte Cushman, and many other performers. But it is also true that in the end the star system was a major factor in undermining resident companies.

Another major development of the first half of the nineteenth century was the rise of the *popular theatre*—vaudeville, minstrelsy, burlesque, circus, and so on—which featured specialty performers of various kinds. The popular theatre, in its many forms and genres, reached its greatest popularity during the second half of the nineteenth century. But certain forms that originated during the first half of the century constitute an important development of the period. The birth of Negro minstrelsy, for example, is dated from 1830, when Thomas D. Rice first performed his famous song-and-dance act, "Jim Crow," in blackface. Thirteen years later (1843) blackface entertainment had become so popular that the first complete minstrel show was created by Dan Emmett and his "Virginia Minstrels."

The production of *travesties,* or takeoffs on serious plays, also started in the first half of the nineteenth century. During the 1840s, successful actor-managers like William Mitchell, John Brougham, and William Burton entertained their audiences with a series of travesties, and such takeoffs of serious plays were eventually combined with leg art to become the form we know as *burlesque.*

Other forms of popular theatre, like vaudeville and the circus, originated before the early nineteenth century; in the United States they date back to colonial times. However, in the early years of the nineteenth century they began to expand, develop new character, and achieve an independent status they had not enjoyed before.

Of all the developments that occurred during the period from 1800 to 1850, however, by far the most important were the appearance of notable native actors and actresses and the further development of American playwriting. Each of these major developments requires a chapter of its own, but first let us survey briefly the course of events in the four principal centers of dramatic activity. These centers, just as in earlier times, were New York, Philadelphia, Boston, and Charleston. Baltimore, Richmond, Washington, Savannah, and Albany also provided good audiences. Spirited and adventurous troupes of players even began to invade the frontier, where in the face of hardships that bring shudders to a modern actor, they established theatre in the remote corners of the nation.

CHARLESTON

At the beginning of the nineteenth century, the city of Charleston was still vigorous and active in theatrical affairs. Alexander Placide was the principal manager and provided Charleston and the surrounding area with lively theatrical fare. He maintained an able resident company and succeeded in bringing many stars of the northern circuits to play guest engagements. His death in 1812 was a blow to activity in the area. In fact, for three years, from 1813 to 1815, the Charleston Theatre was closed and the city had no dramatic entertainment except concerts and circus acts. In 1815 the Charleston Theatre was reopened by Joseph Holman, who managed the house until 1817, when Charles Gilfert, a musician and actor and Holman's brother-in-law, succeeded him. Gilfert enjoyed considerable success. He revitalized the circuit around Charleston and continued Placide's policy of providing the area with an able resident company and a series of glamorous guest stars. He managed the Charleston Theatre until 1825. After this date, the city declined as a theatrical center until 1833, when the old playhouse was sold and became a medical college. Although a new Charleston Theatre was built and opened in 1837, and although it enjoyed several years of prosperity, the city never regained the theatrical vigor it had had at the turn of the century.

BOSTON

The northern capital of the nation, Boston, experienced a happier fate. Starting its growth as a theatrical center later than Charleston, New York, and Philadelphia, it developed steadily and sturdily. Snelling Powell managed the Boston Theatre on Federal Street (sometimes called the Boston Theatre and sometimes the Federal Street Theatre) with consistent success from 1802 until his death in 1821. A highlight of his management was securing the services, in 1810, of two young English players, Mary Ann Duff and her husband, John R. Duff. Mrs. Duff became a brilliant actress, and although she was English-born, she earned the title of "the American Siddons."

In February 1821, after engagements in New York and Philadelphia, the famous English tragedian, Edmund Kean, gave a sensationally successful series of performances in Boston. He was so encouraged by them that he returned for a repeat engagement in May. But the theatrical season was nearing its close and patronage was meager. Kean played to poor houses for two nights. On the third night, when he faced the prospect of performing in an almost empty theatre, he refused to act and walked out. The citizens of Boston were insulted—so outraged, in fact, that they never permitted Kean to appear again. The actor apologized in 1821 and again in 1825, when he made his second American tour. But the Puritan capital did not relent; the ban against Kean remained.

The playgoers of Boston may have been unrelenting in their hostility toward Kean, but they were increasingly friendly to the theatre in general. Patronage increased and soon the Boston Theatre in Federal Street faced competition from new playhouses. In 1823 the City Theatre was built; in 1827 the Tremont Theatre opened. The Tremont competed so fiercely with the Boston Theatre that both soon faced financial ruin. So, in 1829, the two managements amalgamated and ended their disastrous rivalry.

In 1832 another playhouse, the American Amphitheatre, opened its doors and, under various names, lasted for twenty years. But it was unimportant compared to the illustrious institution that opened in 1841, the Boston Museum and Gallery of Fine Arts. The institution was indeed a museum and a gallery of fine arts—and maintained these features throughout its long and prosperous history. (It did not finally close until 1903.) In addition to exhibitions of art, artifacts, and stuffed animals, the institution also housed a "Portrait Gallery" containing enough benches to seat nine hundred people. Here edifying programs of music, recitations, and variety acts were presented so successfully that after two years the Portrait Gallery became a place where standard plays were performed by a resident company. With this arrangement the Boston Museum prospered mightily. The good citizens of the town, many of whom still disapproved of playgoing, found it acceptable—even fashionable—to watch a "program" in the Portrait Gallery of a Museum. Thus, with the help of semantics and allied with religion and morals, the Boston Museum and the drama in general grew and flourished.

One of the first big hits of the Museum was the presentation in 1844 of W. H. Smith's temperance melodrama, *The Drunkard, or the Fallen Saved*. This highly moralistic play ran for one hundred performances at the Museum and helped greatly to establish the place as a center for edifying experiences.

Another notable date in the Museum's early history is 1847. In that year William Warren the younger joined the resident company and remained there, except for one season, until his retirement thirty-eight years later. Warren was unusually gifted and became one of the greatest comedians of the American stage. His presence in the Museum company added to its strength and contributed to its reputation as a first-rate troupe.

The last new playhouse built in Boston before 1850 was the Howard Athenaeum, which opened in 1845. Although it was destroyed by fire the following year, it was quickly rebuilt and became a worthy rival to the old Boston Theatre and the newer Boston Museum. Thus, by the middle of the nineteenth century Boston had become a flourishing center of theatrical activity, boasting fine resident companies and audiences large and discriminating enough to attract all the visiting stars.

PHILADELPHIA

Philadelphia had reason to claim that it was the strongest theatrical center in the nation at the turn of the century. Wignell and Reinagle, who dominated theatrical activity in Philadelphia and the surrounding area, boasted a troupe that was gifted, polished, and versatile. It was equal or superior to any other in the country. The Chestnut Street Theatre was as fine a playhouse as could be found; it was the first theatre in the United States to install a system of gas lighting. Foreign stars were as much at home in Philadelphia as in New York, and many native stars—like Edwin Forrest—made their debuts in Philadelphia. Also, a whole corps of native playwrights developed in the city. Audiences to support both performers and playwrights were large and enthusiastic.

Early in the new century, Philadelphia's happy situation began to change. The talented, energetic Thomas Wignell died in 1803. Thereafter, the Chestnut Street Theatre was managed through good times and bad by several different partnerships. The playhouse survived many disasters: ruinous fires, the disruptions caused by the War of 1812, several deaths and suicides within the company. Also, competition appeared. In 1809 a circus building was constructed, and within a few years, it was presenting standard plays. As the Olympic Theatre, and later as the Walnut Street Theatre, it actively competed for the patronage of Philadelphia playgoers.

In 1828 another competitor entered the field: a new playhouse on Arch Street, which seated two thousand spectators. The rivalry that ensued between the three houses was cutthroat and ruinous. At the end of 1828, all three went bankrupt. They soon reopened under new managers, the most astute and successful of which proved to be William E. Burton, a popular actor of the period. As manager of the Chestnut Street Theatre, he gained a dominant position in the theatrical affairs of the city during the 1840s. At the end of the decade, Burton was also astute enough to realize that Philadelphia had too many theatres for a city of its size and that better prospects for success lay in the rapidly growing metropolis of New York. In the fall of 1848 he left Philadelphia and opened a playhouse in New York. This was for Burton the start of a new and even more successful career in America's largest city.

NEW YORK CITY

Burton's move to New York was significant. It indicated that leadership in dramatic affairs had passed from Philadelphia to the larger city and that New York was now the theatrical capital of the nation. This change of leadership had been gradual and had resulted from several important developments. One vital factor was size. During the early years of the nineteenth century, New York became the largest city in the nation and thus was able to supply the largest theatre audiences. In the 1820s New York's population rose from one hundred twenty-five thousand to two hundred thousand; by 1840 it was three hundred thousand; by 1850 it was more than half

Walnut Street Theatre, Philadelphia.

Hoblitzelle Theatre Arts Library, Humanities Research Center, University of Texas at Austin.

a million. As the population increased, so did the activity of the port of New York. It became the busiest harbor in the country and the port where visiting stars landed first. Philadelphia, as we have seen, originally had more and stronger theatrical companies than New York but did not increase its population as rapidly as the rival city. At the turn of the century, Philadelphia was close to New York in size, by 1830, Philadelphia had one hundred sixty-one thousand people compared to New York's two hundred thousand; twenty years later, Philadelphia had grown to three hundred forty thousand but New York boasted an increase to five hundred fifteen thousand. Furthermore, Philadelphia contributed to its own theatrical decline by overextending itself. New York in the meantime was improving its position. The company at the Park Theatre steadily gained strength and new playhouses were opened; the Chatham Garden Theatre in 1822; the Lafayette Theatre in 1825; and a formidable rival to the Park, the Bowery Theatre, in 1826. All of them attracted patronage from the growing population.

By 1850 New York City was without question the most prolific producer of plays in the nation. The developments, innovations, debuts, and crises that had brought this about in the years between 1800 and 1850 were numerous and varied. A chronological summary will indicate the steadily increasing volume of activity that made New York City the theatrical capital of the United States by the middle of the nineteenth century.

DEVELOPMENTS IN NEW YORK: 1800-1850

1806	Lewis Hallam, Jr., retired. He died in 1808 after fifty-four years on the American stage.
1809	John Howard Payne, age seventeen, made his acting debut as Young Norval in *Douglas*. Ten years later (1819), his play *Brutus* was produced at the Park Theatre, after an earlier production in London. He became one of the most prolific dramatists of the period.
1810	George Frederick Cooke, first of the great visiting stars, appeared in New York. Other notable New York debuts: 1818, James Wallack; 1820, Edmund Kean; 1821, Junius Brutus Booth; 1822, Charles Mathews; 1824, William Conway; 1826, William Charles Macready; 1827, George Holland; 1832, Charles and Fanny Kemble.
1812-13	Financially poor season for the theatre because of fire, war, and competition.
1820	Park Theatre burned. It was rebuilt and reopened in 1821 to seat twenty-five hundred people. About this time six performances per week became standard.
1821	*Richard III* performed by Negroes in the African Grove, a tea garden. This is the first performance on record of a play with a Negro cast. Later a playhouse by and for Negroes opened nearby. Here in 1823 was presented *The Drama of King Shotaway*, written by Mr. Brown, owner of the playhouse. This is the first American play on record by a Negro dramatist.
1823	Henry Placide, one of the greatest American comedians, made his New York debut.

Park Theatre, 1822. Charles Mathews and Miss Johnson in *Monsieur Tonson.*
Hoblitzelle Theatre Arts Library, Humanities Research Center, University of Texas at Austin.

1825   Edmund Kean reappeared at the Park Theatre, New York.

1826   Edwin Forrest made his New York debut at the Park Theatre in *Othello*. The Bowery Theatre opened with a seating capacity of three thousand. It burned and was rebuilt four times.

1828　James H. Hackett began specializing in Yankee roles. He was followed by such famous Yankee actors as George H. Hill, Dan Marble, Joshua Silsbee, and John E. Owens.

1829　*Metamora* by J. A. Stone, the first of the Edwin Forrest Prize Plays, was produced at the Park Theatre. The Forrest prizes stimulated the work of American playwrights and provided Forrest with some of his most popular roles.

1832　Thomas D. Rice introduced his "Jim Crow" act at the Bowery Theatre.

1833　New York's first opera house opened but closed in two years. Also, *Mazeppa*, one of the first sensational spectacles, was produced at the Bowery Theatre and established the popularity of shows featuring lavish scenery, crowds of performers, and spectacular effects of all kinds.

1836　Charlotte Cushman, America's first major native-born actress, made her New York debut as Lady Macbeth.

1838　United States Premier of Bulwer-Lytton's *Lady of Lyons* with Edwin Forrest and Charlotte Cushman. It was to become one of the most popular plays of the nineteenth century.

1839　The Olympic Theatre under William Mitchell opened and for eleven years operated without stars, providing a lower-class audience with first-rate productions of comedies, farces, light musicals, and other popular entertainment.

1841　P. T. Barnum opened the American Museum and Garden and Gallery of Fine Arts with a "lecture room" where variety acts were given in 1842-43. Like the Boston Museum, it attracted many patrons who normally would not have gone to a theatre as such and helped to gain acceptance for theatre among more puritanical groups. In October Boucicault's *London Assurance* was produced at the Park Theatre with the first *box set* seen in New York, a box set being an arrangement of flats to form continuous walls representing the three walls of a room.

1842-43　Worst season in New York history. John Brougham, a popular English playwright and actor, made his United States debut. He remained a star for forty years. In February 1843, the Virginia Minstrels created the first Negro Minstrel Show at the Bowery Theatre.

1845　Anna Cora Mowatt's *Fashion* produced at the Park Theatre. Later Mrs. Mowatt, a member of New York's social set, made her debut as an actress and starred for nine years.

1846　Charles Kean introduced historically accurate scenery and costumes in *King John*.

1847　New Broadway Theatre opened. It succeeded the Park Theatre as chief home of stars in New York for the next few years. The Park burned in December 1848.

1848　William E. Burton opened his theatre (Burton's Theatre) in New York; it was popular for almost eight years. Francis F. Chanfrau starred as Mose, the Bowery Fireboy, in *A Glance at New York*, and thus started a series of plays about Mose, a native city type.

1849　In May the Astor Place Riots occurred, caused by Macready-Forrest quarrel. Twenty-two people were killed and thirty-six were wounded; it was the worst theatre riot in American history. In

September P. T. Barnum began giving standard plays in his lecture room, which he rebuilt to seat three thousand. Here in 1850 he produced *The Drunkard*, which broke all records. Later in 1850 he introduced Jenny Lind to the United States.

One entry in the chronology deserves special comment. In the fall of 1821 a playhouse by and for Negroes was opened in New York City. This was the African Theatre, located at the corner of Mercer and Bleeker Streets and operated by Mr. Brown, a steamship steward from Liverpool. His theatre was the further development of a nearby tea garden, called the African Grove, which provided a gathering place and a variety of entertainment, including an occasional play, for the Negroes of New York. In this garden on September 21, 1821, Shakespeare's *Richard III* had been acted by a Negro cast—the first American performance on record by a Negro company. The leading actor was James Hewlett, a native of the West Indies. When the performances were moved indoors from the Grove to the African Theatre, James Hewlett continued to be the star. From the beginning, unfortunately, the enterprise was ridiculed and harassed by white racists, many of whom attended the performances to make fun and cause trouble. The theatre managed to maintain a shaky, spotty existence until 1823, when persecution from the whites forced it to close permanently. Before this happened, however, the African Theatre made history by presenting a play written by Mr. Brown from his own experiences, entitled *The Drama of King Shotaway*, with James Hewlett in the leading role. Although no copy of the play survives, it is the first American play on record by a Negro dramatist. The African Theatre also helped to make history by providing inspiration for Ira Aldridge, America's first Negro star. Aldridge undoubtedly had his first experience in acting at the African Theatre before he emigrated to England to begin his impressive career as a tragedian.

THE FRONTIER THEATRE

The growth of theatrical activity along the Eastern seaboard in the years from 1800 to 1850 was exciting; equally exciting was the expansion of the theatre into the territories beyond the Alleghenies.

The years following the American Revolution saw the nation's frontier move steadily westward. By the turn of the century it crossed the Alleghenies. In the early decades of the new century it reached the Mississippi River, and by 1850 it made the great leap to the Pacific Coast. During all this time, as the covered wagons carried settlers and their families deeper into the wilderness, other wagons carrying actors followed close behind. The pioneering adventures of the original Hallam Company on the Atlantic Coast were repeated many times over by equally intrepid companies of players. Like the Hallams, these companies carried a scanty supply of scenery, costumes, and properties and performed in taverns, barns, warehouses, and any other place—including flatboats—which they could devise or improvise. Like the Hallams, these players were talented, ingenious, optimistic, and rugged of body

James Hewlett, first Negro star of the American stage, as Richard III
at the African Grove, September 21, 1821.

From George C. D. Odell's *Annals of the New York Stage*, Volume III, New
York: Columbia University Press, 1928, p. 34, by permission of the publisher.

and spirit. They were also versatile and considered themselves poorly trained if they
could not sing, dance, and play a musical instrument as well as act.

The story of the westward movement of the theatre is told in the lives of a
few famous pioneer showmen: Noble Luke Usher, Noah M. Ludlow, James H.
Caldwell, Sol Smith, the Chapman family, the Drake family, and a few others. All
of them were people of many talents. Management was only one of their jobs.
They were also actors, scene painters, theatre builders, script adapters, publicity

wizards, and diplomats. Two of them, Noah Ludlow and Sol Smith, wrote fascinating accounts of their careers in the frontier theatre.[2]

A vivid and typical illustration of the experiences and difficulties encountered by the frontier companies is recorded by Noah Ludlow. In December 1827, his company played a two-week engagement in Montgomery, Alabama. He proudly declares that *"those two weeks were the first performances by a regular dramatic company in Montgomery."*[3] He is less proud of the facilities that the town provided. He writes:

> The room that we performed in at Montgomery was, perhaps, the most inconvenient place that ever the descendants of Thespis had to encounter. It was in the upper story of a very large, roughly built frame house, that was called a "hotel." The garret, or topmost portion of which had been fitted up by some amateurs to perform plays in. The only way of reaching this attic temple of the muses, for either actors or audience, was by a flight of rough stairs on the *outside* of the building, and these seemed almost interminable; then, when you had reached the top of them, you had to make your entrance through a *window,* so low that a person of regular height had to stoop to get into the room. This room was fitted up with rough seats without any covering, and all on a dead level. There were no dressing-rooms contiguous to the stage; therefore the performers were compelled to dress in their own rooms of the stories below, and, wrapped in cloaks, thread their way through the audience to the stage. If a change of dress was required during the progress of the play, it had to be done behind a temporary screen across the corner of the room, and behind the back scene.[4]

Ludlow did not hold a grudge against the city of Montgomery for these primitive facilities. Writing many years later, he is careful to state, "I am told that the town has now a very well arranged theatre, a largely increased population, and in years not long past, supported the Drama very well."[5]

During these years a different and unique form of pioneering was begun by William Chapman, Sr., and his three sons and two daughters. They built a floating theatre that is now famous as the first showboat in America. It is probable that as early as 1817 Noah Ludlow had presented plays on a keelboat named *Noah's Ark,* which he had fitted out as a means of transporting his itinerant company down the Cumberland, Ohio, and Mississippi rivers to Natchez, Mississippi. However, William Chapman, Sr., wins credit for building the first vessel designed specifically to be a floating playhouse. This was in 1831 at Pittsburgh, Pennsylvania. The vessel, named simply the *Floating Theatre,* was a one hundred-foot-long barge with a barnlike superstructure containing a small stage lighted by tallow candles plus a pit and

[2] They are Noah M. Ludlow, *Dramatic Life as I Found It* (St. Louis: G. I. Jones and Company, 1880), and Sol Smith, *Theatrical Management in the West and South for Thirty Years* (New York: Harper & Row, Publishers, 1868).

[3] Ludlow, *Dramatic Life as I Found It,* p. 303.

[4] Ibid.

[5] Ibid.

gallery holding enough firmly anchored benches to seat two hundred spectators. This wonderful invention plied the waters of the Ohio and Mississippi rivers for ten years, and brought theatrical entertainment to dozens of communities that were outside the regular circuits. George D. Ford, a descendant of the original Chapman family, writes that the floating theatre "sometimes moored during the day at places that seemed like unexplored wildernesses, but . . . by nightfall, guided by candles in the windows of the craft, people found their way on foot, horseback, and by wagon."[6] The description is reminiscent of the scene, so long before, when the original Hallam Company gave its opening performance in Virginia and had the thrill of seeing an audience materialize out of what seemed to be a total wilderness.

The Chapmans' floating theatre satisfied the hunger for entertainment of the many river settlements for which the river was the principle or only link with the rest of the world. Soon other managers, noting the success of the Chapmans' enterprise, followed their lead and built similar floating playhouses. During the 1840s and 1850s, as Philip Graham records, "dozens of small showboats swarmed over the river systems of the Middle West bringing entertainment to hundreds of river landings."[7]

Showboating continued to prosper until the Civil War. It disappeared completely for the duration of the war, then was reintroduced to resume a development which established a tradition as glamorous as any in the American theatre.

In California, the last frontier, it was not showboats that brought the theatre to pioneer audiences; it was soldiers of the United States Army. The appearance of English-speaking drama in the Far West was the result of the 1847-48 war between the United States and Mexico. When the war began, the United States seized the various forts and presidios on the West Coast and garrisoned soldiers in them. Inevitably, as in every war, the troops became bored when there was little action. They amused themselves by presenting skits, plays, and minstrel shows. The first standard English play given in California was one of these soldier productions, a drama entitled *The Golden Farmer* by Benjamin Webster, presented in Sonoma on the stage of an improvised theatre in 1847. Other productions, less ambitious, were given in several other California towns. But Monterey, the Spanish capital of California, claims the first theatre in the Golden State. This, like many other improvised theatres of the frontier, was a lodging house built by Jack Swan, a retired sailor, and converted for use as a playhouse by the soldiers stationed in the town. In the spring of 1848 they gave a number of performances here and charged the astonishing sum of five dollars for admission. The season was short because the war ended and most of the soldiers left Monterey; except for occasional presentations by local thespians, the adobe structure was returned to its original use as a lodging house. But the building still stands, preserved as an historical monument and officially designated as the first theatre in California.

The first building erected expressly to serve as a playhouse took shape in Sacramento in the fall of 1849 during the feverish activity of the Gold Rush. It was

[6]George D. Ford, *These Were Actors* (New York: Literary Publishers, 1955), pp. 116-17.
[7]Philip Graham, *Showboats* (Austin, Tex.: University of Texas Press, 1951), p. 21.

Old Theatre, Monterey, California. The so-called first theatre in California.
Courtesy, The Bancroft Library, University of California, Berkeley.

named the Eagle Theatre; although it lasted only two and a half months, it is additional evidence of the irrepressible appeal of dramatic art—even in the wilderness.

The nineteenth century began with bright promise for the American theatre. The general developments during the first fifty years of the century fulfilled that promise—and so did developments in specific fields. In no activity of the theatre was the progress more gratifying than in the development of native actors and actresses. It is in order, therefore, to survey the appearance and the rise to fame of the first great American stars.

5

Enter the American Actor

American-born actors, most of them amateurs, appeared as early as colonial times. One of them, a Mr. Greville, deserted his studies at Princeton College in 1767 to join the Douglass company, thus earning the distinction of being the first American to become a professional actor. In the season of 1790-91, another young American, John Martin, made his debut in a leading role on the Philadelphia stage. Neither of these two, or even a young lady of American birth, Miss Tuke, made much impression on audiences of the time or is remembered as a great success. Apparently Mr. Greville never advanced beyond minor roles; and Mr. Martin, although he played major parts, is described by William Dunlap as "a useful, though not a brilliant actor," who "laboured hard, lived poor, and died young." Not until the appearance of such performers as Edwin Forrest, Mary Ann Duff, and Charlotte Cushman could America claim to have produced actors of genuine distinction.

The activity and achievements of distinguished American players, once they appear, are impressive—so much so that the age they inaugurate will come to be known as the golden age of the actor. In this golden age, the actor is the most important person in the theatre. He is often the manager of the company and the author or adapter of many plays in its repertory. Sometimes, like Edwin Forrest, he offers cash prizes to stimulate native dramaturgy. He is a pioneer who pushes the frontiers of the theatre further and further west; and he is, by all odds, the most important element in any production. During these years there is no régisseur, or master director, such as we have in the contemporary theatre. The leading actor decides how the play will be produced and performed. All elements of the production are subordinate to him; his virtuoso efforts will make or break the play. The history of the theatre of this period rightly yields center stage to the actor and his achievements.

During the greater part of the nineteenth century, almost all American actors performed as members of a resident company. They learned their art by serving an apprenticeship in one or more companies—beginning, usually, in minor roles and advancing if they had talent to major roles. Their constant association with seasoned professional players such as those in the troupes of the Park Theatre of New York, the Chestnut Street Theatre of Philadelphia, or the Federal Street Theatre of Boston, provided the novice players with a priceless education in dramatic art. When they achieved sufficient popularity and fame, they usually became independent stars. A few stars, like William Warren the younger, remained members of a resident company during their entire careers. But it was more common for star actors to become independent performers who were not attached to a resident company but traveled from company to company playing their popular roles with the support of the local troupe. Since much of American theatrical history was made by these independent stars, it is easy to forget the continuing importance of the resident company and to recall theatrical history in terms of individual performers only. But notable as the individual stars became, they were the products of the resident companies, they acted with the local troupes throughout their careers, and these local troupes remained the basic theatrical unit during all of the eighteenth and most of the nineteenth centuries.

EDWIN FORREST

When Edwin Forrest made his adult debut in 1820, the American stage was dominated by English actors, managers, and dramaturgy. Culturally, the United States was still dependent on Great Britain. With the advent of Edwin Forrest, this situation began to change. Born and reared in Philadelphia and passionately American in his loyalties, Forrest achieved a reputation at home and abroad as dazzling as the fame of the English stars. He played great roles for more than fifty years, during which his personality and style of acting were as typical of the vigorous young American democracy in which he grew up as were his rowdy young fans, the "Bowery B'hoys," who idolized him.

Forrest's formal education, both general and dramatic, was slight. His style of acting was largely the result of his study, observation, and experience on the stage. Fortunately, his early acting was done in the company of excellent players who had been trained in the English tradition of Drury Lane and Covent Gardens and who were mature and seasoned in their roles. Forrest learned much from his association with these players. His official debut was made in November 1820 at the flourishing Walnut Street Theatre of Philadelphia. He continued his apprenticeship by serving in other resident companies. In the summer of 1826, he made his New York debut at the Park Theatre as Othello and scored a triumph. In the fall of the same year, at the age of twenty, he was engaged as leading man for the new Bowery Theatre of New York, and the following year he became a star. He remained a star for the rest of his life, which meant that he was not permanently attached to any company. However, his allegiance to the Bowery Theatre was strong and he often played long engagements there.

Forrest learned much from his association with the companies in whose ranks he served his apprenticeship. He was also influenced by the visiting stars whom he watched or acted with. In the formation of his mature style two men exerted special influence on him: Thomas A. Cooper and Edmund Kean. From one he learned the dignified posture, the measured declamatory reading, and the ideal of poetic elevation that were characteristic of the Kemble school. From the other he learned the effectiveness of stormy, realistic acting—the style that had ended the vogue of the Kemble school.

The outstanding quality of Forrest's acting, as it finally developed, was strenuous realism. He sought to portray nature as it existed around him in actual life, aiming for complete, detailed character portrayals unchanged by idealization. His method of studying his roles illustrates his goals. In preparing for the part of King Lear, he visited many asylums and old men's homes, studied various manifestations of insanity, observed the walk, the gestures, and the movements of old men, and read the best scientific books on old age and insanity, discussing the ideas with eminent physicians. As a result, when he played Lear in London, the playwright Douglas Jerrold wrote: "We never saw madness so perfectly portrayed. It is true to nature—painfully so."[1] One is reminded of Forrest's remark when a young admirer praised his "acting" in *King Lear.* Forrest exclaimed, "By God, sir, I am King Lear."

Forrest was at his best in strenuous, heroic roles, but he had difficulty finding enough of them in the standard repertory of the time. Beginning in 1829 he began offering cash prizes for American plays that suited his needs. The first prizewinner was a play featuring a heroic Indian Chief, *Metamora,* written by John A. Stone and produced by Forrest in December 1829. During the next few years Forrest awarded twenty thousand dollars in prizes for American plays, thus helping the cause of native dramaturgy. Unfortunately, only a few of the plays were successful or remained very long in Forrest's repertory.

The heroic, muscular style in which Forrest acted these plays led some critics to assert that he was a melodramatic ranter who never used his mind but only his muscles. But despite his deficiencies, his style of acting was immensely appealing to the majority of playgoers. They idolized this man of handsome face and powerful physique who seemed to typify the power and strength of a growing young country. The heroic, strenuous style of acting he created was unique and exciting. Audiences never seemed to tire of it.

Forrest's acting was strenuous and tempestuous, and so was his private life. He is the leading figure in two scandals, both of which shook the nation when they occurred and even today are remembered with regret. The first of these is the fatal Astor Place Riot of May 1849, which grew out of a petty quarrel between the hot-tempered Forrest and the English tragedian, William Charles Macready, a vain, snobbish man. The tragic climax to the quarrel in 1849 occurred when Macready was completing a farewell tour of the United States, during which he had encoun-

---

[1] James Rees, *Life of Edwin Forrest* (Philadelphia: T. B. Peterson & Brothers, 1874), p. 226.

Edwin Forrest in all his roles.

Hoblitzelle Theatre Arts Library, Humanities Research Center, University of Texas at Austin.

tered hostility and insults from certain audiences. When he tried to act Macbeth at the Astor Place Opera House on May 8, he was howled down by the Bowery B'hoys who filled the house. The aristocrats of New York were outraged and unwisely persuaded Macready to appear again on May 10, when they filled the house and prevented abuse on the inside. But outside a huge mob of ten to fifteen thousand people gathered. As their anger and excitement grew, they started to stone the theatre. An infantry regiment was summoned to protect the structure. The soldiers marched into position facing the mob. Immediately they were attacked by a hail of stones and other missiles. The command to fire into the crowd was given. Several rioters fell to the ground. The infuriated mob attacked again. Another volley was fired. This time the mob was seized with panic, turned, and fled—leaving twenty-two dead and thirty wounded on the pavement in front of the opera house. It was the worst riot in the history of the American theatre.

Macready escaped from the theatre in disguise and was quietly conveyed out of New York and out of the United States. He never acted in this country again.

The second notorious scandal involving Edwin Forrest was his divorce from Catharine Sinclair, a talented Englishwoman whom he had married in 1837. About the time of the Astor Place Riot, Forrest became convinced that his wife was being unfaithful to him with another actor, George W. Jamieson. The evidence was flimsy but Forrest, sensitive and easily angered, could not bear the idea of infidelity. The couple separated quietly; then gossip began to circulate, and finally Forrest openly accused his wife of misconduct. He filed suit for divorce in Philadelphia; Mrs. Forrest filed a countersuit in New York. The case came to trial in December 1851

SCENE OF THE RIOT.

The Astor Place Riot, May 10, 1849.

Hoblitzelle Theatre Arts Library, Humanities Research Center, University of Texas at Austin.

and was the talk of the nation for six weeks. The judgment went against Forrest, who, enraged and embittered, appealed the case. He appealed five times, and each time he lost. The final verdict was handed down eighteen years after the original suit had begun. During this time, Forrest's multitude of followers remained loyal, and he continued to attract audiences wherever he appeared. However, the actor himself never overcame the heartbreak, bitterness, and sense of injustice that the divorce caused him. He became a brooding, melancholy man who nursed his grievances to the end of his life.

Edwin Forrest's style of acting was popular, and it was representative in many ways of the young, democratic society that helped to produce it. Other actors adopted a similar style of performance. Among the most successful of these were Augustus A. Addams, David Ingersoll, Charles H. Eaton, J. Hudson Kirby, John R. Scott, Joseph Proctor, and John McCullough. By far the most successful of the group, and the man who was generally considered Forrest's heir apparent, was John McCullough. He earned immense adulation and became the best-loved actor of his time.

JOHN MC CULLOUGH

The story of McCullough's life and career is heart-warming—and sad. Born in Ireland, he emigrated to America as a boy of fifteen years. When he arrived, he was penniless and illiterate. But he was endowed with a husky build, a handsome face, a lovable disposition, and a sincere ambition to make something of himself. He began his theatrical career with an amateur group, then earned a minor position in a Philadelphia company. Thereafter, he slowly and laboriously developed his talents. Following four years of apprenticeship, he was hired by Edwin Forrest to travel with him and play supporting roles. McCullough stayed with Forrest for five years performing such parts as Laertes, Macduff, Iago, Edgar, and Richmond. During these years his style of acting was described as being "virile without virtuosity," yet his looks and personality won him friends and admirers everywhere.

After leaving Forrest, McCullough settled in San Francisco, where he acted and managed the new California Theatre for several years. Occasionally he made tours of the United States as a star performer. He studied constantly and tried in every way to improve his acting. When he returned to the East, the critics felt that he had made a great leap in his art. "The native vigor, resonance, and fire were there," said A. C. Wheeler, but now "they were disciplined and controlled."[2] During the years from 1877 to 1883, McCullough's acting reached its highest level of achievement. In plays like *Virginius, Damon and Pythias,* and *The Gladiator,* he looked the parts, understood the parts, and embodied them convincingly and appealingly. His performance as Virginius was praised for having "dignity without bombast, and immense force without violence."[3]

[2] See Percy Mackaye, *Epoch: The Life of Steele Mackaye* (New York: Boni & Liveright, 1927), I:270-71.

[3] Henry A. Clapp in *The Boston Advertiser,* 26 February, 1878.

The popular John McCullough dressed as a Roman.
Ross Theatre Collection, University of California Library at Berkeley.

The solid success that McCullough achieved came to a tragic end in 1884. In that year he suffered a mental and physical breakdown and had to be helped from the stage of McVicker's Theatre in Chicago. His affliction was mortal. After a year of steady deterioration, he died—the victim of congenital syphilis—and was more deeply and universally mourned than any other actor of his time.

The style of acting practiced by Forrest and McCullough has never completely disappeared from the American stage. Throughout every era, performers have appeared whose primary appeal has been their muscular bodies, manly bearing, powerful voices, and realistic portrayals. In the twentieth century, the brawny heroes of Western movies and television serials are good examples of this style, established so many years ago by stars like Forrest and McCullough.

EARLY COMEDIANS

While Edwin Forrest and his fellow performers of the heroic school were establishing an American reputation for acting in serious drama, other native stars were gaining fame as comedians. Although the greatest achievements in comic acting were to come in the second half of the nineteenth century, recognition should be given to those earlier performers who pioneered in the development of American comic acting. Among the best of these were Henry J. Finn (c. 1790-1840), William B. Wood (1779-1861), Charles Burke (1822-1854), and James H. Hackett (1800-1871).

MARY ANN DUFF

Ten years before Edwin Forrest made his adult debut, a beautiful young woman named Mary Ann Duff appeared on the Boston stage and began a career that was to earn her the title of "the legitimate and undisputed Queen of the American stage."[4] In the history of the American theatre, Forrest takes precedence over Mrs. Duff because he was born in the United States. But Mrs. Duff must be included—and honored—because she adopted America as her homeland and contributed her artistry exclusively to the American stage.

Mary Ann Duff was born in London in 1794, the eldest child of an Englishman who served with the East India Company. Her maiden name was Dyke. In 1809, under her mother's tutelage and in the company of her two sisters, she made her stage debut as a dancer in Dublin, Ireland. The following year she married actor John R. Duff and accompanied him to the United States, where they settled. With the exception of one brief visit to England in 1827, she spent the remainder of her life in America and died in this country. It was in the United States that she learned the art of acting, built her career, and achieved her reputation as the foremost tragic actress of her time.

Beauty of face, grace of figure, and richness of voice were Mrs. Duff's initial—and very fortunate—endowments as an actress. For several years after her arrival in the United States, these were her principal assets. Her acting was considered to be

[4] Joseph N. Ireland, *Mrs. Duff* (Boston: James R. Osgood and Company, 1882), p. 146.

charming but weak. Presently her husband began to lose his popularity. The support of a growing family devolved more and more on Mrs. Duff. Apparently she decided that she had to exert herself to develop the latent talent that few people suspected she possessed. By 1817 her improvement was marked and caused favorable comment.

Mrs. Duff's growing ambition received a powerful stimulus when Edmund Kean visited Boston in 1821 and she was assigned to act Ophelia to his Hamlet, Cordelia to his Lear, and Hermione to his Orestes. By this time Mrs. Duff had achieved a reputation for passion and fire, and in her performances with Kean she outdid herself.

Mrs. Duff continued to demonstrate her newly developed powers, chiefly in Boston and Philadelphia, until 1835. She also appeared in New York and won a host of admirers. Horace Greeley, after visiting the Richmond Hill Theatre (New York) in 1832, recorded in his *Recollections of a Busy Life:* ". . . I saw Mrs. Duff personate Lady Macbeth better than it has since been done in this city . . . I doubt that any woman has since played in our city—and I am thinking of Fanny Kemble —who was the superior to Mrs. Duff in a wide range of tragic characters."[5]

In 1836 Mrs. Duff, who had been a widow for some years, married J. G. Seaver, an attorney. She accompanied him to New Orleans and became a resident of that city. In 1837 and 1838 she played brief engagements in New Orleans; and then, becoming deeply religious, she retired from the stage. She lived in self-imposed obscurity until her death, which occurred in New York in 1857 but was not re-vealed to her public until seventeen years later.

The acting of Mrs. Duff in her maturity was clasically fine. As she grew older, she retained great personal magnetism and in addition learned to project strong emotion and to stir her audiences by the controlled intensity of her feelings. The texture of her acting was even and rich, and she impressed her critics as being remarkably true to nature. The noted manager N. M. Ludlow praised her as "re-fined, quiet, yet powerful; not boisterous, yet forcible; graceful in all her motions, and dignified without stiffness."[6] Then he added, almost as an afterthought, that she was "undoubtedly the best tragic actress of the United States."

CHARLOTTE CUSHMAN

In the same year (1835) that Mary Ann Duff was playing her farewell engagement in New York City, nineteen-year-old Charlotte Cushman, descendant of one of the Pilgrim fathers, was making her debut in Boston. Miss Cushman's first appear-ance was not as an actress; it was as a singer in Mozart's *Marriage of Figaro*. She was successful enough to win favorable attention; and shortly after her Boston appear-ance she accepted an engagement in New Orleans, where she promptly ruined her voice by overstraining it in a large theatre. Since she was poor and burdened with

[5] Horace Greeley, *Recollections of a Busy Life* (New York: J. B. Ford & Co., 1868), p. 203.
[6] Noah M. Ludlow, *Dramatic Life as I Found It* (St. Louis: G. I. Jones and Company, 1880), pp. 463-64.

the support of her mother, brothers, and sister, she looked desperately for some other employment and was advised to try her luck as an actress. Without any professional dramatic training she launched a career that was eventually to win her great wealth and the topmost rank among American actresses of her time.

After Miss Cushman's dramatic debut in New Orleans, she returned to the North and played in stock for eight years. Slowly and earnestly, she learned the secrets of her profession. She had no formal instruction, but relied on experience and observation to teach her. By the fall of 1837, her success and popularity were great enough to win her the position of leading lady in the company of New York's famous Park Theatre. During the next seven years she divided her time between the Park Theatre in New York and the equally famous Walnut Street Theatre in Philadelphia.

In 1843 William Charles Macready played an engagement at the Park Theatre in New York, and Cushman supported him in several roles. Macready was impressed by her ambition and undisciplined power. He urged the young actress to visit London and gain the experience of playing with an English company. Borrowing the money for her passage, Miss Cushman made the trip in 1844, and it proved to be the turning point in her career. For almost five years in England she played such roles as Bianca, Rosalind, Queen Katherine, and Romeo—and they were hailed as masterpieces. She returned in triumph to the United States in 1849. She was judged the best American tragedienne and remained an independent star until her final retirement in 1875. She died a year later.

Just as Edwin Forrest's physique and temperament exerted a powerful influence on his manner of acting, so did Cushman's looks and personality affect her style. She was a tall woman with square shoulders and a sturdy frame. Though her movements were somewhat ungraceful and awkward, she gave the impression of strength and dignity. She was generally described as commanding, rather than handsome, and as masculine in appearance, rather than dainty or feminine.

There was a streak of masculinity in Miss Cushman's temperament, too. As a child she was a tomboy who smashed dolls, climbed trees, and tyrannized her brothers and sister. As a woman she was hard-headed and practical and enjoyed acting the masculine roles of Romeo, Cardinal Wolsey, Hamlet, and Claude Melnotte. Her style, as it finally evolved, had sweep and power and majesty. She painted with bold strokes and unmixed colors.

It is not surprising that with her particular physical and mental endowments Cushman should have avoided the tender feminine roles and excelled in those parts which, when not completely masculine, showed the strength and audacity of a Lady Macbeth, the majesty of a Queen Katherine, or the bizarre physical power of a Meg Merrilies.

The unique power of Cushman's personality was enhanced by an unusual voice. Overstraining on the opera stage had left her speaking voice with a husky, hollow quality. Pure, ringing, elastic tones had given way to what Murdoch terms "a quality of aspiration and a woody or veiled tone." This unique quality, plus wide range and unusual power, made Miss Cushman's voice capable of effects

Charlotte and Susan Cushman as Romeo and Juliet.
Hoblitzelle Theatre Arts Library, Humanities Research Center, Univeristy of Texas at Austin.

which few players could duplicate. She was able to express intense, sustained grief without loudness or sudden variations. She could also rise to great vocal heights in scenes of anger or denunciation. At times, it is said, she was over-expressive and extravagent, but despite occasional blemishes, her best moments in her finest roles have probably never been surpassed on the American stage.

IRA ALDRIDGE

A review of the beginnings of American acting must include another unusual career—that of Ira Aldridge, the first great Negro tragedian of the English-speaking stage. Aldridge was American-born and grew up in the United States. His love of the theatre was acquired in New York City, and his earliest experiences on the stage probably took place at the short-lived African Theatre in New York. Yet Aldridge left his homeland in 1824 or 1825, when he was only seventeen or eighteen years old, because there was no chance for a Negro actor to succeed in the American theatre. He never returned to the United States. His immensely success-ful career was achieved exclusively in England and on the Continent. Can he be called an American actor? Pride in his accomplishments tempts us to claim him, but recognition of the injustice and prejudice which forced him to leave the United States makes us acknowledge that we hardly have the right.

It has been clearly established that Aldridge was born in New York City on July 24, 1807, the son of a straw vendor and lay preacher. He attended the African Free School and somehow conceived a great love for the theatre—and the ambition to become an actor. His friends persuaded him that American prejudice against Negroes was too great for him to overcome and that his only chance for success on the stage lay in emigrating to England.[7] This he did in 1824 or 1825 because, by October 1825, he played an important engagement at the Coburg Theatre in London.

With this beginning—at the age of eighteen and with experience that must have been meager—Aldridge proceeded to perfect himself as a tragedian and to achieve a career that can only be called miraculous. Almost all of Aldridge's first roles cast him as a Negro struggling for freedom for himself or for his race. Billed originally as "Mr. Keene, Tragedian of Colour," he acted in such plays as *The Revolt of Surinam, or Slave's Revenge* (an adaptation of Thomas Southerne's *Oroonoko*), *The Slave, The Negro's Curse,* and *The Death of Christophe, King of Hayti.* Within six years Aldridge dropped the stage name of Keene and billed himself as "Mr. Ira Aldridge, the celebrated African Roscius." During this time he added the great role of Othello to his repertory and the part became his mainstay and his masterpiece. He acted it until his death in 1867. At the height of his career, he also played, in white makeup, the roles of Shylock, Macbeth, and King Lear, at the same time retaining *Oroonoko* and one or two other antislavery plays in his repertory.

---

[7]Herbert Marshall and Mildred Stock, *Ira Aldridge, the Negro Tragedian* (London and Amsterdam: Feffer and Simons, Inc., 1958). Reprinted by Southern Illinois University Press, Arcuturus Books, April 1968.

In 1852, after twenty-five years of successful acting in England, he launched his first tour of the Continent. The response he created in Belgium, Germany, Austria, and Switzerland was so enthusiastic that for the rest of his life he divided his time between appearances in England and tours of the Continent, which eventually included Sweden, Poland, and Russia. While on a tour of the theatres of Eastern Europe in 1867, Aldridge died. In failing health for several years, the tragedian did not decrease his activities but, in fact, increased them. His strength finally failed him in the city of Lodz, Poland, where he had gone to fill an engagement. He died there of a serious lung condition, and is buried in Lodz in a grave that is still cared for by the Society of Polish Artists of Film and Theatre.

Ira Aldridge as Othello.

Hoblitzelle Theatre Arts Library, Humanities Research Center, University of Texas at Austin.

The style of acting that brought fame and fortune to Aldridge during his forty-two-year career was a unique blend of the dignity and nobility practiced by the Kembles of England and of the fiery, realistic emotion displayed by Edmund Kean. Evidently Aldridge studied and observed performers of both schools and adapted elements of both to his own endowments of body and mind. He was always described as having a noble bearing and a striking countenance. His body, well shaped and muscular, was flexible and responsive, and his deep, rich voice had wide range and carrying power. His capacity for projecting strong emotion, suppressed or overt, was great enough to make his Othello a memorable portrait.

In view of the triumphs won by Ira Aldridge in a hostile world, it is fitting that his biographers should declare: ". . . Ira Aldridge was the first to show that a black man could scale any heights in theatrical art reached by a white man—and create with equal artistry the greatest characters in world drama. And he did this alone . . . without any subsidies or scholarships, on his own two feet, with his own skill, versatility, and talent."[8]

In the decades that followed the death of Ira Aldridge, many American Negro comedians, singers, and entertainers gained fame, but no Negro tragedian of Aldridge's stature was destined to develop in the United States until the advent of Charles Gilpin and Paul Robeson in the twentieth century.

Even though Negro actors were not destined to flourish in the United States during the nineteenth century, acting in general enjoyed a period of superb development. With such native giants as Forrest and Cushman leading the way and providing inspiration and example, American performers in great numbers began to demonstrate their talent and versatility. Before the nineteenth century ended, they gave the American stage a golden age and proved that in the art of acting native players could be as great as any in the world.

[8]Ibid., p. 335.

6

Melodrama Takes Center Stage

American Playwriting, 1800-1850

If the first half of the nineteenth century witnessed the appearance of the first distinguished native actors and actresses, it also saw a great increase in the quantity and variety of American playwriting. As theatres multiplied, as audiences grew, equipment improved, and the Golden Age of the actor dawned, native playwrights, too, appeared in greater numbers and with greater confidence and skill. But unfortunately, the same blight that was afflicting playwriting in England, Germany, and France spread to American dramatists. It distorted and stunted their work to such an extent that, with few exceptions, no enduring dramatic literature was written for a hundred years. The nineteenth century was immensely fruitful in many ways; in playwriting it was a disappointment.

The blight that perverted American dramaturgy was the love of melodrama. Every type of play from high comedy to heroic tragedy was afflicted. The addiction to melodrama did not weaken until the end of the century, when native playwrights, along with their European colleagues, felt the cleansing, therapeutic effects of such giants as Ibsen, Strindberg, and Chekhov.

In the nineteenth century, melodrama was a relatively new genre. It is true that dramatists ever since Euripides have used devices that can be called melodramatic, yet the kind of play we now label as melodrama developed in the late years of the eighteenth century. Originally the term described lines spoken to a musical accompaniment. Georg Benda's *Ariadne auf Naxos* and *Medea,* both performed in Germany in 1775, are examples. Melodrama as a type of stage play developed in France as a result of J. J. Rousseau's romantic drama *Pygmalion* and, more importantly, as a result of the work of Guilbert de Pixérécourt, who is generally regarded as the father of the genre. His drama, *Coelina, or l'Enfant du Mystère,* produced in 1800, was translated into English two years later by Thomas Holcroft and stimulated tendencies toward the lurid and the sensational that were already present in English dramaturgy. Meanwhile, in Germany, August Friedrich Ferdinand von Kotzebue, who became the most popular playwright in the western world, developed new kinds of dramatic thrills and excitement and greatly increased the popularity of melodrama. The genre, once established, flourished luxuriantly.

The basic premise from which melodrama derives its characteristics is an overly simplified view of life, particularly of morality. In the world of melodrama the moral code is a simple set of principles of right and wrong. The code is fixed and unchallengeable; it applies to all people everywhere. Men and women who observe it are rewarded with good fortune and prosperity, but those who violate it must suffer. People are either completely good or completely bad; there is little shading or complexity in their characters and little possibility for development or change. In their world, evil is initiated by villains who try constantly to manipulate events for their own purposes at the expense of good characters. For their part good characters struggle to escape the evils forced upon them by the villains. In the end, the moral code demands that the good characters be rescued and rewarded and that the villains be exposed and punished.

Plays based on such a simplified view of human beings and their problems will inevitably exhibit artificiality and contrivance. The playwright must manufacture a plot that will illustrate the workings of the simplified, inflexible moral code. Instead of character development in complex moral situations, the dramatist substitutes contrived thrills and heightened emotionalism. Instead of the suspense that comes from internal conflict, the dramatist presents struggles between good and evil whose outcome is foreordained, and embellishes them with every device and surprise he can invent. Thus, the world of melodrama, although offered as a serious interpretation of life, is inevitably contrived and falsified.

The era preceding the nineteenth century had been dominated by monarchy in politics, aristocratic privilege in social life, and neoclassicism in literature. All of these forces confined and limited the energy and creativeness of the citizen. At the end of the eighteenth century came the American and French revolutions, and their liberating spirit inspired people everywhere; "everywhere in the west," that is. The heady exuberance of such an age conditioned people, including playgoers, to admire what was daring, novel, adventurous, and unorthodox. The exotic and sensational elements of melodrama seemed a kind of liberation and a refreshing change from the confines of aristocratic neoclassicism.

The tastes of the average person also encouraged the development of melodrama. Although these tastes were influenced by the political climate, there is a natural love of melodrama in the average person. The great dramatists of Greece recognized this; Shakespeare was keenly aware of it. Motion pictures, from their very inception, built a large measure of their appeal on melodrama, and today it is the opiate of the television-watching masses. The western, cops-and-robbers, and science fiction serials are all as melodramatic as any play of the nineteenth century. For better or worse, most people enjoy escaping into the never-never land of surprises and sensations; they enjoy stock characters, the unbeatable hero and the dauntless heroine whom they can understand easily; they enjoy uncomplicated emotions; and they especially enjoy the comfort of a simple morality that always rewards the good and punishes the bad.

The nineteenth century saw a great increase in the number of people who responded to such simple and exciting appeals. The industrial revolution brought thousands of unsophisticated workers into the cities. These people, sooner or later, had money to spend on amusements, and if they attended the theatre, they were likely to get more pleasure more quickly from a colorful spectacle, a sensational melodrama, or a knockabout farce than from a subtle play. In the United States the numbers of such people were immensely increased by the waves of immigration from foreign countries. Every year thousands of people who spoke no English were added to the population of the burgeoning cities. The immigrants provided large audiences for the popular forms of theatre like vaudeville, burlesque, minstrelsy, and the circus. They also swelled the ranks of those who enjoyed melodrama.

The size of playhouses encouraged spectacle and broad, strong emotion. During the nineteenth century theatres grew steadily larger and larger. For example, the Chestnut Street Theatre of Philadelphia, built in 1791, seated two thousand. The Park Theatre of New York, when it was rebuilt in 1821, seated twenty-five hundred. The Bowery Theatre of New York, which opened five years later, seated three thousand, and when it was rebuilt in 1845 after its fourth disastrous fire it was enlarged to hold four thousand. Such a cavernous auditorium as this, besides coarsening the style of acting, inevitably encouraged the production of plays that were loud and spectacular. Melodramas were admirably suited to fill the bill—and the house.

The improvement of stage machinery in the nineteenth century may also have encouraged the production of melodramas. Fires, floods, storms, earthquakes, and other cataclysms that appear so frequently in melodrama require special effects and machinery. The more such devices were invented, the more they were used and, as the century advanced, the more realistic they became. In one now-famous instance, the availability of spectacular scenery inspired the rewriting of a play to use that scenery. This was the case of *The Black Crook* in 1866, involving not only trick scenery, but also a ballet troupe imported from Europe. The playhouse where the ballet was scheduled to open burned down; the scenery and the ballet girls were acquired by the manager of Niblo's Garden. To use both the girls and the scenery, he reworked a melodrama entitled *The Black Crook* and the result was a production that ran a record-breaking 475 performances.

Conditions favorable to the growth of melodrama were general throughout the western world. In the United States, several additional influences strengthened the trend. The religious establishment favored the simple morality of melodrama. The democratic temper of the people was gratified by the humble heroes and heroines of the genre. Besides, with the nation so busy pioneering, building, and expanding there was little time for serious analysis of contemporary problems which, an optimistic nation felt, would certainly be solved in due course. And, were not the best dramatists in Europe writing melodramas? Why not follow their lead?

The beginning of melodrama in American playwriting can be seen as early as *The Prince of Parthia*. The characters in this first professionally produced American play are stock, the action is manipulated, and the ending is unconvincingly contrived. But we recognize that these are the faults of a young, inexperienced playwright and not the result of a trend or an ideal. Thomas Godfrey had the great plays of Shakespeare in mind; he tried to emulate them—and failed.

The same cannot be said for William Dunlap. His best original plays—like *André*—have only a trace of melodrama. But his adaptations from French and German writers, particularly from Kotzebue, are aggressively and undisguisedly melodramatic.

The principal American playwrights who followed Dunlap during the first half of the nineteenth century were all addicted to the devices of the genre. These dramatists can be grouped in several ways: according to the subject matter of their plays (Indian plays, Yankee plays, and so on), according to the type of drama they wrote (heroic, tragedy, satiric comedy, and so on), according to the amount of foreign influence contrasted to native influence and ideas. However, the grouping we shall use is simpler. All the plays (with a few exceptions) are influenced by the attitudes and techniques of melodrama. To a greater or lesser degree, these attitudes and techniques are the common factors which unite the dramatic output of the century. A survey of the most popular and successful plays of the period, whether comedy, tragedy, or romance, reveals this passion for the melodramatic.

MORDECAI M. NOAH, 1785-1851, AND JOHN HOWARD PAYNE, 1791-1852

Two playwrights who wrote successful melodramas early in the century were Mordecai M. Noah and John Howard Payne. The former is chiefly remembered for a drama first produced in 1819 and popular throughout the century for fifty years. It was entitled *She Would Be a Soldier, or the Plains of Chippewa*. Payne is remembered as a playwright for his heroic tragedy of 1818 entitled *Brutus, or the Fall of Tarquin*, which held the stage even longer than Noah's drama. Both plays contain praiseworthy elements, but each clearly reveals the devices and weaknesses of melodrama. Their authors had only a minor influence on American playwriting.

JAMES NELSON BARKER, 1784-1858

Of far greater significance for the development of American drama is the work of James Nelson Barker. He was a zealous patriot, like Dunlap and Noah, and deplored America's inferiority complex and dependence on European culture. In an effort to bolster native drama, he wrote ten plays using largely American material and themes. Of the ten, only five have survived in print. His output was small because he had little time to spend on playwriting. Most of his life was devoted to public affairs.

Barker's devotion to his country is clearly shown in his plays. The first of these, entitled *Tears and Smiles* (1807), is a comedy like *The Contrast* in which American manners and customs are lauded while everything European is ridiculed. Barker's second play, produced in 1808, is *The Indian Princess, or la Belle Sauvage,* which enjoys the honor of being the first surviving Indian play to be performed. Major Rogers's *Ponteach* was published in 1766 but never produced.

More important than either of these or than Barker's dramatization of Sir Walter Scott's *Marmion* (1812) is the play *Superstition,* produced in 1824, a full twelve years after *Marmion. Superstition* is a graphic illustration of how a promising dramatic theme can be spoiled by melodramatic treatment. Barker apparently intended to write a play on the destructive effect of bigotry and superstition. He laid the action in New England in 1675 when the fear of witchcraft was widespread. His central character is Ravensworth, a hard-hearted, bigoted father who hates the mysterious stranger, Isabella, a cultured Englishwoman living quietly in town. Ravensworth is convinced that she is a witch and should be burned at the stake. The play portrays the evil, suffering, and death that can be caused by such superstition. The theme is provocative and promising, and antedates Arthur Miller's treatment of a similar theme in *The Crucible* by more than 125 years. However, Barker's good intentions are ruined by his employment of all the devices of melodrama. The characters are either completely noble or the opposite. The action is enormously contrived and unnatural. For example, in the course of the play, Charles—the supposed son of the mysterious Isabella—becomes lost in the woods and encounters a sort of superman in skins, "The Unknown." Later, the Unknown suddenly appears to save the village from destruction by the Indians, and still later he reveals that he is Isabella's refugee father and that young Charles is actually the son of the king of England. During this time we also meet a dissolute Englishman, George Egerton, who attacks the lovely Mary, daughter of the bigot Ravensworth. Mary is saved from dishonor by the fortuitous appearance of Charles—with whom, of course, she is already in love—and Charles, for the sake of honor, challenges Egerton to a duel. The duel takes place. Egerton is wounded in a fair fight but the duel is used as an indictment against Charles. At the climax of the play, Isabella and Charles are both dragged before a tribunal on charges trumped up by Ravensworth. Amid a raging storm everything goes wrong for the accused. Charles refuses to defend himself, and Mary, whose testimony might have cleared him, faints and cannot testify. So Charles is led away to an immediate execution. The Unknown appears too late to save him. When the young man is carried in on his bier, Mary goes mad and Isabella drops dead.

In traditional melodrama, the good characters do not perish, as they do in *Superstition.* Barker breaks the general rule and contrives a tragic end to his play to establish his thesis—namely, that superstition and bigotry can take a severe toll in any social group. But the provocative theme of the play is buried under an avalanche of contrived complications and sensational coincidences. Spectators are so absorbed, or repelled, by the manufactured surprises and shocks that they completely forget the ideas that the play is supposed to communicate, or they reject them because their development is so farfetched.

Barker is honored as a playwright more for his sound intentions than for his actual accomplishments. He sensed the direction that American playwriting ought to take, but along the way he was trapped in the quicksand of melodrama—like most of his colleagues.

SAMUEL WOODWORTH, 1785-1842

Far more successful than *Superstition* is Samuel Woodworth's play, *The Forest Rose, or American Farmers.* Produced in 1825, it escapes the blight of melodrama almost entirely, yet it was an immensely popular success on the stage. Richard Moody calls it "the first 'Hit' show of the American theatre" and "the first successful musical play."[1] After its opening run, it continued to be staged all over the country for the next forty years.

The Forest Rose is a lively comedy of rustic intrigue replete with sentimental music. The pastoral atmosphere is idyllic and idealized. The girls are all charming, artful, and coy. The Yankee farmer, Jonathan Ploughboy, is shrewd and witty. One of the Englishmen, Bellamy, is stupid and ridiculous. Praise of the honest American farmer is consistent throughout and so is the mood of sprightly good humor. When the play is over, we have enjoyed a series of minor misunderstandings and complications ending in the happy union of three pairs of lovers.

In addition to *The Forest Rose,* Woodworth wrote seven other plays in the course of his varied career as journalist, printer, editor, and writer. Such titles as *The Widow's Son, or Which Is the Traitor, The Cannibals, or the Massacre Islands,* and *The Foundling of the Sea* are enough to convince us that *The Forest Rose* is an exception to Woodworth's overall commitment to the techniques of melodrama.

THE FIRST NEGRO PLAYWRIGHT

The first play by a Negro dramatist belongs to this period of American playwriting. In June 1823 at the short-lived African Theatre on Mercer Street in New York, a Negro company headed by James Hewlett performed a play called the *Drama of King Shotaway.* Unfortunately, little is known of its contents or treatment. Its author was Mr. Brown, the onetime ship's steward who had organized the African Theatre, and the play, according to a rare printed program, was "founded on facts taken from the Insurrection of the Caravs in the Island of St. Vincent." Further-

---

[1]Richard Moody, *Dramas from the American Theatre 1762-1909* (New York: World Publishing Company, 1966), p. 147.

more, it was "written from experience by Mr. Brown." As George C. D. Odell writes, "First Negro drama, Hail!"[2]

JOHN AUGUSTUS STONE, 1800-1834

If *The Forest Rose* is the first American hit play, the second must be John A. Stone's Indian drama, *Metamora*. The play was a sensational success when Edwin Forrest first produced it in 1829, and it remained in Forrest's repertory for the next forty years. Moody reports that "whenever Forrest played *Metamora,* the audiences crowded the theatres to capacity."[3] After Forrest's death, other actors of the heroic school continued to present the play for at least two decades.

Metamora was the first and most successful of Forrest's prize plays. Audiences could not resist the appeal of the noble red man who fights and dies heroically for his people, his family, and his ideals of freedom—especially when the part was played by the young, handsome, muscular actor who typified American democracy. Forrest could win cheers and tears from his audiences with his stirring appeals for freedom and fair play. Without Forrest, however, the play was less successful. And without the nineteenth-century infatuation with melodrama, the play is less than overwhelming. It presents most of the familiar devices of the genre. Besides Metamora's central struggle for freedom and justice there is the lovely white maiden whose scheming father wishes her to marry a dissolute nobleman—English, of course. There is the virtuous young man, an orphan, in love with the maiden. He turns out to be the long-lost son of the fine old man who has reared him. There is intrigue, villainy, courage, and sacrifice, and in the final scene, a heartbreaking climax when the great Indian chief stabs his beloved wife to save her from the white man. As she dies in his arms, before he himself falls dead, he cries, "She felt no white man's bondage—free as the air she lived—pure as the snow she died! In smiles she died! Let me taste it, ere her lips are cold as ice."

Although the author wrote several other plays, none of them very successful, his principal contribution to American drama remains the Indian play that provided Forrest with an ideal starring role.

GEORGE WASHINGTON PARKE CUSTIS, 1781-1857

Metamora increased the interest in Indian plays that had been developing since *Ponteach* was published in 1766 and since *The Indian Princess* was performed in 1808. But the real vogue for this kind of drama began the year after the debut of

[2]George C. D. Odell, *Annals of the New York Stage, 1821-1834* (New York: Columbia University Press, 1928), III:70-71.

[3]Moody, *Dramas from the American Theatre,* p. 201.

Edwin Forrest as Metamora. This Indian play was the first
and most successful of Forrest's prize plays.

Hoblitzelle Theatre Arts Library, Humanities Research Center, University of Texas at Austin.

Metamora, when a play called *Pocahontas, or the Settlers of Virginia,* was produced. The author of the play, a descendant of Martha Washington, bore the
imposing name of George Washington Parke Custis. He had written an earlier
Indian play in 1827 called *The Indian Prophecy.* He is also the author of several

dramas based on American history, such as *North Point, or Baltimore Defended* (1833), and *The Eighth of January* (1834), both of which portray events from the War of 1812. Custis's most successful play by far was *Pocahontas.* First produced at Philadelphia's Walnut Street Theatre in January 1830, it achieved an initial run of twelve performances—an unusual success for the era. It was later given in New York and then revived in Philadelphia. Audiences loved the excitement and thrills provided by the drama and elaborately staged by the Walnut Street Theatre. In fact, the theatre was closed for several days preceding the premier of the play to allow the management time to devise the scenic efforts necessary for the storms, battles, and other exciting episodes that embellish the drama.

For thirty years after the production of *Pocahontas,* Indian plays enjoyed a widespread popularity. At least fifty of them were written and performed. There were so many, in fact, and they became so extravagent in action and characterization, that by 1847 John Brougham was able to present a successful burlesque of the genre called *Metamora, or the Last of the Pollywogs.* Eight years later he wrote a similar satire on the Pocahontas-John Smith story called *Pocahontas, or the Gentle Savage,* which was even more successful. These burlesques were evidence of the diminishing appeal of such plays. The vogue declined steadily, but the Indian play and the Indian character never disappeared entirely. Years later when the motion picture was developed and started to mine the seemingly inexhaustible lode of dramatic gold in the stories of the old West, Indians appeared in greater numbers than before, but now they had changed from heroes to villains. They continue, still in stereotyped guise, to provide melodramatic material for films and television.

ROBERT MONTGOMERY BIRD, 1806-1854

If *Metamora* was the most successful of the prize plays written for Edwin Forrest, a close second in popularity proved to be *The Gladiator.* It was the work of a gifted and versatile man of letters, Robert Montgomery Bird, and proved so stirring to nineteenth-century audiences that Forrest performed it at least a thousand times between 1831 and 1854. It remained in Forrest's repertory all his life and subsequently was acted many times by John McCullough, Forrest's heir apparent. Bird, who was trained as a physician but quit the profession after a single year. had written an earlier classical tragedy entitled *Pelopidas.* Forrest had accepted this for production but shelved it in favor of *The Gladiator,* which offered greater scope for his heroic style of acting. The leading character of *The Gladiator,* Spartacus, was perfectly tailored to Forrest's talents and temperament. Spartacus, a handsome, powerful man, is a captive from Thrace brought to Rome as a slave. He reluctantly accepts the challenge to become a gladiator when he discovers that his wife and child, also captives, will be given their freedom if he performs well in the arena. He does so, kills his first opponent, and is prepared to fight his second. But the second opponent turns out to be his brother. After a few agonized moments the two men turn on their masters and shout a ringing call to freedom. The gladiators and slaves revolt, form an army with Spartacus and his brother as leaders, and begin a campaign for universal liberation. In the end, after much intrigue and treachery, the revolt is crushed and the brothers are killed.

Bird's next play, *Oralloossa, Son of the Incas,* produced in 1832, is another melodrama cast in heroic mold. It was played by Forrest with moderate success, then dropped from his repertory.

A far better play, probably Bird's best, is a tragedy entitled *The Broker of Bogota,* first performed in 1834. The play uses many of the devices and trappings of melodrama. It has an exotic setting; it is full of conflict, intrigue, and villainy; the action is often rigged for effect; the emotions are strong and grandiloquently expressed. Yet the play carries appeal and conviction because the leading character, Febro, is a plausible human being, and in the conflict with his erring but likable son he enlists our understanding and compassion. But nineteenth-century audiences were not impressed by the play and continued to prefer the contrived passions and excitement of *The Gladiator.* Bird himself was aware of the difference in the appeal of the two plays. He deplored the bombast that the public enjoyed in such a play as *The Gladiator,* and declared that he preferred *The Broker of Bogota*—for the same qualities that redeem it in our eyes.

RICHARD PENN SMITH, 1799-1854, ROBERT T. CONRAD, 1810-1858, AND NATHANIEL PARKER WILLIS, 1806-1867

The Gladiator and *The Broker of Bogota* were both romantic tragedies with melodramatic aspects. So were two other plays that received prizes from Forrest and that enjoyed success because of Forrest's vigorous acting. One of these, written in 1831, the same year as *The Gladiator,* is entitled *Caius Marius.* It is the work of a moderately prolific and fairly versatile dramatist, Richard Penn Smith, who tried his hand at writing historical plays, tragedies, melodramas, and an Indian play. *Caius Marius* and a French-inspired melodrama, *The Actress of Padua,* are Smith's best-remembered dramas.

The other tragedy that Forrest raised to success was Robert T. Conrad's *Jack Cade* (1835), which portrays the insurrections and struggles for freedom of the serfs of England in 1431 and 1450. For a time the play ranked in popularity next to *Metamora* and *The Gladiator.* It exhibits the same virtues and weaknesses as other tragedies of its kind.

One other play of an entirely different kind must be mentioned: the romantic comedy *Tortesa the Usurer,* written by Nathaniel Parker Willis and first produced in 1839. The play is different because it is comedy. There are contrivance and intrigue, farfetched developments, and other melodramatic devices. But the play is redeemed by its tone and treatment, which are consistently fanciful and amusing. Whenever the situation threatens to become serious, Tomaso, a low comic character, takes the stage and restores the comic atmosphere.

W. H. SMITH, 1808-1872 AND *THE DRUNKARD*

In the final decade of the first half of the nineteenth century, two additional plays enlist attention. They were not only enormously successful, but they strikingly illustrate the techniques of melodrama and the popularity of the genre.

The first of these, originally produced in 1844, is the famous temperance drama, *The Drunkard, or the Fallen Saved.* Written by W. H. Smith, stage manager of the Boston Museum, this play has come to epitomize for the modern playgoer the height of absurdity reached by melodrama in the nineteenth century. Dozens of modern acting groups, both professional and amateur, have presented the play as burlesque, and thousands of contemporary playgoers have roared with laughter at lines, scenes, and effects that once were accepted with dead seriousness. The story of a weak young husband brought low by Demon Rum and the connivance of an archvillain, then saved and restored by the ministrations of a pious temperance worker, is too well-known to need retelling. Every character in the play is a carica- ture, every line banal, every sentiment false, every scene manipulated to squeeze out the maximum horror or sentimentality. For example, here are the climactic lines from the famous delirium scene, which was sometimes reenacted as a separate moral lesson. The drunkard, Edward, writhes on the ground and moans:

> Here, here, friend, take it off, will you—these snakes, how they coil around me. Oh! how strong they are—there, don't kill it, no, no, don't kill it, give it brandy, poison it with rum, that will be a judicious punishment, that would be justice, ha, ha! justice! ha, ha!

Edward decides to end his agony by swallowing poison. As he raises the vial to his lips, the temperance crusader, Rencelaw, steps in, seizes the poison, flings it away, and says, "Nay, friend, take not your life, but mend it." Edward answers, "Friend, you know me not. I am a fiend, the ruin of those who loved me; leave me," and Rencelaw replies, "I come not to upbraid you, or to insult you. I am aware of all your danger, and come to save you. You have been drinking." In this way, the fallen is saved.

A modern spectator finds it hard to believe that such a play was ever taken seriously. Yet it was indeed! During the first year of its performance in Boston it was staged a hundred times; at Barnum's Museum in New York it was the first play ever to achieve an uninterrupted run of one hundred performances; at one time in New York four different theatres were presenting it at the same time. It spread from the East Coast to every corner of the nation; for many years touring compa- nies, playing *The Drunkard* exclusively, traveled from coast to coast. It is safe to conclude that "no play before *The Drunkard* . . . so completely captured the public's fancy."[4]

[4] Ibid., p. 278.

How can such popularity be explained? Was the taste of playgoers in the mid-nineteenth century so execrable that they could not see the absurdity of the play? Certainly the nineteenth century was an age of melodrama; some of the reasons for this have been discussed. The devices and techniques of *The Drunkard* were merely exaggerations of effects seen and accepted in other plays. The public was used to this sort of thing—and liked it. Yet the play could not have succeeded as it did if the temperance movement had not been sweeping the country at the time. The campaign against Demon Rum was in full swing and had aroused the Puritan consciences of average Americans. They were ready to feel guilty, to repent, and to be uplifted. Smith's play gave them a chance to do all these vicariously. They welcomed the experience, and *The Drunkard,* despite its absurdity, became the hit play of its era.

ANNA CORA MOWATT 1819-1870

Today we view *The Drunkard* as blatant nonsense, a museum piece that creates laughter and incredulity. Not so with the other significant play of the decade. That is Anna Cora Mowatt's comedy, *Fashion,* which is still admired as one of America's best satirical comedies and a worthy successor to *The Contrast.* Yet *Fashion,* with all its merits, is an example of the weakening effect of the nineteenth-century passion for melodrama. This is clearly seen if it is compared to *The Contrast.*

In their main plots, *Fashion* and *The Contrast* are very similar. Both concern a double-dealing suitor who is involved with three young ladies. Both plays have comic servants, and both have the bluff shrewd American gentleman (a relative of Jonathan) who cannot be easily fooled. In both plays, hypocrisy and affectation are exposed and punished while sincerity and virtue are rewarded.

This basic design was sufficient for Royall Tyler in 1787. It was not enough for Mrs. Mowatt in 1845 when she wrote her play. She added, undoubtedly because she felt her audience demanded them, several of the familiar devices of melodrama. Mr. Tiffany, the father of Seraphina and husband of the foolish, pretentious social climber, Mrs. Tiffany, is involved in embezzlement with the connivance of his clerk, Snobson. Snobson blackmails Tiffany, demanding social recognition and the hand of Seraphina. Snobson is thwarted and Tiffany is saved from ruin by the shrewdness and wealth of the bluff American farmer, Adam Trueman. Added to this melodramatic subplot is the mystery of Gertrude. This beautiful, virtuous maiden is an orphan of unknown parentage. In the end it is revealed that she is the granddaughter of rich old Mr. Trueman, who has had her reared in modest obscurity so she will not be corrupted by wealth. Before the restoration is accomplished, Gertrude is involved in intrigue and disgrace, but it is all a mistake and she is completely exonerated in the end.

The Contrast is simple in design and pleasantly satirical in atmosphere. *Fashion* is complicated in structure and has an atmosphere that varies from vigorous comic ridicule to sinister villainy. In addition, *Fashion* has farcical elements lacking

Anna Cora Mowatt Ritchie.

Hoblitzelle Theatre Arts Library, Humanities Research Center, University of Texas at Austin.

in *The Contrast.* Mrs. Tiffany and the phony nobleman, Jolimaitre, are the principal objects of satire. Also, there are such characters as the "modern poet," T. Tennyson Twinkle, the "drawing-room appendage," Augustus Fogg, and Zeke, the comic Negro servant who fulfills the stereotype of the shuffling, eye-rolling, dialect-speaking, good-natured darky.

Mrs. Mowatt, whose contributions as an actress will be discussed in a later chapter, wrote one other play, not counting two youthful pieces that were never produced professionally. Her second mature play, entitled *Armand, the Child of the People,* written in 1847, was successful in both the United States and England. However, Mrs. Mowatt's claim to fame as a dramatist and her major contribution to the development of American playwriting is her play *Fashion.* It was widely popular in its own time and even today retains a good deal of vitality.

THE REPERTORY IN THE FIRST HALF
OF THE NINETEENTH CENTURY

Our survey of the American plays popular during the first half of the nineteenth century has stressed the blight of melodrama as the reason these plays are now considered old-fashioned and inferior. A natural inference is that playgoers a hundred years ago must have had terrible taste if they enjoyed this kind of drama. The inference is only partially correct. In justice to the nineteenth-century playgoer, it should be pointed out that few contemporary plays of any period survive as masterpieces; however popular they are at the moment, most of them quickly become dated and disappear from the stage. It should also be pointed out that during the nineteenth century, contemporary plays, whether American or European, were only one part of the repertory, although a substantial part, and that the American plays we have surveyed were only a very small part of the total offerings. A recent study of the types of plays produced in representative American cities from 1800 to 1850 shows that in Philadelphia the repertory in 1811 contained only 2 percent of American plays; it rose to 7 percent in 1820, 8 percent in 1830 and 14 percent in 1850. In New Orleans American plays made up 9 percent of the total dramas produced in 1820 and rose to 15 percent in 1840.[5]

Far more popular than American plays were the works of the great English dramatists from Shakespeare to Sheridan. There were more of these plays available, to be sure, and their vogue tapered off as the century advanced. Still, their popularity indicates that playgoers of the time enjoyed and supported other types of plays besides contemporary melodrama. The great plays of the era from Shakespeare to Sheridan constituted 58 percent of the programs given in Philadelphia in 1811, fell to 20 percent in 1820, rose again to 45 percent in 1830, and then declined to 12 percent in the repertory of 1850. In New Orleans the pattern was much the same: a drop from 40 percent in the early years of the century to 10 percent in 1840.

The number of "classic" plays declined during the first half of the nineteenth century, and the percentage of American plays rose only slightly. What plays filled in the remainder of the repertory? Here the facts and figures do not compliment the taste of the playgoer of the time. The figures reveal that at least half the repertory consisted of importations from contemporary European dramatists: Kotzebue, Bulwer-Lytton, Sheridan Knowles, and so on—all of them purveyors of melodrama. In Philadelphia and Charleston from 1800 to 1816, the most often produced play was Kotzebue's *Pizarro in Peru*. From 1816 to 1831, *Pizarro* was second in popularity only to Shakespeare's *Richard III*. During the next twenty years, Bulwer-Lytton's tearjerker, *The Lady of Lyons*, rose to top spot. During those years, the ten most frequently performed plays in Philadelphia, Charleston, New Orleans, and St. Louis included four by Shakespeare and six by various European exponents of melodrama.

[5] See David Grimsted, *Melodrama Unveiled: American Theatre and Culture*, 1800-1850. (Chicago: University of Chicago Press, 1968), pp. 250-61.

During all these years of fervid melodrama, did American writers contribute anything original to the art of playwriting? Was there anything in mid-century American drama to distinguish it from its European counterpart? In many cases— Payne's *Brutus* or Bird's *Gladiator,* for example—the plays had no distinctly American elements. In material, treatment, and point of view, they followed the European pattern exactly. However, other American plays contained elements that were clearly native and that set them apart from European drama. One of the most important of these elements was the new character types developed in American plays. These original characters include the American Negro, the Yankee, the Red Indian, the Irish immigrant, the fire laddie, and many more.

Other elements helped to distinguish the drama of the United States from that of Europe. Now and then the material of a play was distinctly American, as in the dramas and pageants based on historical episodes. Sometimes the problem presented in the play was uniquely American, as in *Metamora,* which dramatized the plight of the Indian. Frequently the native playwright identified himself by praising everything American and ridiculing all things foreign. On the whole, however, nineteenth-century American dramatists achieved no innovations in playwriting technique. They cannot be credited with marked originality or creative distinction—only with occasional impulses toward these qualities. The flowering of distinctive American playwriting had to wait until the twentieth century.

7

The Setting at Mid-Century

The United States
and its Theatre in 1850

The United States in 1850 was a dynamic, exciting nation. It provided a colorful setting and a continuing stimulus for its developing theatre and created American attitudes and characters that brightened some American plays and gave them a measure of distinction. It inspired actors like Edwin Forrest to develop a style of performance that reflected the nation's tastes and ideals. A look at conditions in the country at mid-century reveals the close relationship between the general setting and developments in the theatre.

One of the most fascinating phenomena of the nineteenth century was the emergence of distinctly American citizens. As early as Jonathan and Van Rough in *The Contrast* of 1787, they began to emerge. By 1850 they were clearly recognizable—a product of their long struggle with the continent that they had chosen to subdue. As Gertrude Stein wrote, "In the United States there is more space where nobody is than where anybody is. That is what makes America what it is."[1]

Americans of mid-century were restless, thanks to the invigorating climate and the continual challenge of tremendous tasks. They were always "a-doin'" and always on the go. Even when they tried to relax they were whittling, chewing, jiggling, or rocking. A characteristic American device was the rocking chair, "the chair that travels but stays at home."

Typical Americans were often crude, ruthless, and even brutal. They were so accustomed to chewing tobacco and spitting in public that a visiting Englishman suggested that the spittoon, not the eagle, should be the national emblem. They were accustomed to a type of wrestling where no holds were barred and where noses were bitten off or eyes were gouged out. When the Indians stood in the way

[1] For much of the material that follows, I am indebted to Thomas A. Bailey, *The American Pageant* (Boston: D. C. Heath & Company, 1966). Professor Bailey has graciously given me permission to borrow and adapt the material as I see fit.

of their expansion, the Indians were brushed aside—or killed off like the buffalo of the great plains.

Americans were ingenious, inventive, resourceful, and self-sufficient. They had to be a jack of all trades if they wanted to survive on the frontier. They were strenuous, courageous, and endowed with the belief that they could "lick all creation." In their mighty struggle with the wilderness, they learned to laugh at adversity and to fight everybody and everything, man or beast, that stood in their way.

Isolated by the geography of their continent, Americans became self-centered and provincial, loving what was native and distrusting what was foreign. They relied on themselves and on their skill with an ax and rifle. The rifle, they said, made everyone "equally tall." Besides being provincially self-reliant, Americans were confident and optimistic. Anyone who crossed the Atlantic and braved the challenge of an unknown continent had to be optimistic. "The cowards never started; the weak died on the way."

Americans were boastful. As a defense against the ridicule of supercilious foreigners, they bragged of their accomplishments and of the future of their land. They worshipped bigness and had unlimited faith in progress and in the American Way of Life.

Americans were basically democratic, too. They rejected the class distinctions of colonial times and never asked, "Who is he?" but only "What can he do?" Economic and political democracy extended to almost everyone, and so did religious freedom. In general, citizens were able to worship as they chose, and if none of the established religions attracted them, they could found one of their own. They loved their freedoms and they cheered whenever a struggle for freedom was waged anywhere in the world.

Finally, the Americans of mid-century were intensely patriotic and nationalistic. They loved the land they had fought to make their own and they resented any criticism from the outside. In thousands of speeches and in hundreds of theatrical performances, they "made the eagle scream" by shouting praises of their country and by affirming their faith in the American Dream.

How many of these unique Americans were there? An astonishing number— and they continued to increase with amazing rapidity, doubling their number every twenty-three years just as they had done in colonial days. On the eve of the Revolutionary War, the population of the colonies was about 2,500,000. By 1800 it had increased to 5,308,483, and by mid-century it was 23,191,876! The United States was the fourth most populous white nation in the world.

The growth of cities, of special importance to the development of the theatre, kept pace with the general increase in population. At the close of the Revolution, only 5 cities in the country had more than 8,000 inhabitants. In 1850, there were 141 such cities representing every section of the nation. New York, with a population of 515,000, was the largest metropolis in the country. Trailing New York were Philadelphia with 340,000 (including suburbs) and Boston with 137,000. New Orleans was "Queen of the South" with 116,000 people, and Cincinnati dominated the Midwest with 115,000. Chicago at this time had only 30,000 people but was developing rapidly. On the Pacific Coast, San Francisco boasted a population of 50,000 compared to the 11,000 of Los Angeles.

The continuing fertility of the typical American accounted for most of the increase in population. However, by mid-century immigration was adding significant numbers. Before 1840, immigrants had been arriving at the rate of about 60,000 per year; in 1840, the influx tripled, and in the 1850s it quadrupled to 240,000 per year. By 1850, 12 percent of the population was foreign-born—which was to have significance for the development of motion pictures at the end of the century.

Economically the country was enjoying a lush period of expansion and prosperity, despite the setbacks caused by recurrent "panics" or depressions. The ingenuity of the native American was showing itself in the invention of hundreds of new machines that stimulated the economy to prodigious growth. Paralleling industrial expansion, and partly responsible for it, was improvement in all means of transportation. Such improvements were a boon to industry—and to the expansion of theatres as well.

During the years of invention and industrial expansion an irresistible movement toward social reform developed. Most Americans believed that a perfect society could be achieved; and with characteristic zeal, inspired leaders set about arousing the conscience of the country and correcting the evils in American life.

Since Americans at mid-century were devoting most of their time and talent to territorial expansion, political controversy, business activity, and social and economic reform, it is not surprising that they had little energy left for achievement in the arts, or that artistic contributions were relatively slight. The most significant accomplishments were probably in literature and in acting. In literature, the Knickerbocker Group, led by Washington Irving, and later the Transcendentalists, represented by Ralph Waldo Emerson, produced a body of writing that is still meaningful and admired. Playwriting did not share in the inspiration of these movements because it was still imitating European melodrama. In acting, the achievements of native performers like Edwin Forrest and Charlotte Cushman were notable and led to the development of a corps of versatile tragedians and masterful comedians whose art has never been surpassed in the American theatre. In painting, sculpture, and music, important beginnings were made, but the most distinguished achievements were still to come.

ATTENDING THE THEATRE IN NEW YORK IN 1850

The theatre in 1850 faithfully represented the nation of which it was a part. It was lusty, confident, colorful, noisy, and versatile. To savor what it was like, let us for the second time imagine an evening at one of the playhouses of New York City, remembering that everything seen and described is based on historical record.

New York City is now the theatrical capital of the nation, with ten playhouses offering everything from Shakespeare and grand opera to vaudeville and animal acts. In addition, several halls present minstrel shows and other specialties to enthusiastic audiences. The six playhouses that generally offer regular plays in the spring of 1850 are the Broadway, the Bowery, Burton's, the National, the Olympic, and Barnum's Museum. The latter was started as a museum to exhibit freaks and curiosities of all kinds and boasted, in addition, a "lecture room" where edifying entertainment was offered. Now the lecture room has become a playhouse with a resident company and a repertory of plays.

We note with regret that the famous old Park Theatre has disappeared. After a long and brilliant career dating from 1798, it slowly declined and finally closed forever after a destructive fire on December 16, 1848. Its closing severed the link that had bound the nineteenth century with the original Hallam company that established professional theatre in America one hundred years before. The Park can never be replaced, but before 1850 is over, a new popular playhouse, Brougham's Lyceum, will open and add another center of entertainment to the growing list.

A study of the attractions available on Friday, March 29, the date of our visit, reveals an impressive variety of offerings and a large number of performances. Eighty years before, plays were given on only two or three evenings of the week. Now all the regular theatres are open six nights a week. There are usually no performances on Sunday, but in a few cities like New Orleans, even Sunday programs are given.

Scanning the advertisements in the *New York Herald*—there are now several newspapers to keep us informed of theatrical events—we notice that the attractive Jean M. Davenport is appearing at the Broadway in such popular pieces as *The Stranger, The Lady of Lyons,* and *The Hunchback,* as well as in a couple of Shakespearean roles. The Broadway Theatre is known as the house of stars now that the Park is gone. We notice, also, that *Dombey and Son,* a dramatization of Dickens's novel, is again at Burton's Theatre with a fine cast of performers. However, after considering the offerings at all the playhouses, we decide that the bill at the Bowery looks like the best bargain available. It is a benefit night for Mrs. James W. Wallack, Jr., and two full-length plays will be presented. Mrs. Wallack and Miss Katherine Wemyss will star in Shakespeare's *Romeo and Juliet.* Afterward, Mr. and Mrs. Charles F. Addams will perform the perennial favorite, *Pizarro in Peru.* These two plays are representative of the taste of the time. Shakespearean drama is still popular, but romantic melodrama like *Pizarro* is even more popular. During the current season the Bowery has been offering about 20 percent Shakespearean drama, 65 percent romantic melodrama, and the remaining 15 percent has been equestrian spectacles, frontier plays, and "old" comedy.

The production of *Romeo and Juliet* scheduled for Friday night offers a novel situation because two women will play the title roles: Mrs. Wallack will act Romeo and Miss Wemyss will be Juliet. This was made acceptable by the great Charlotte Cushman, and now several accomplished actresses are doing it.

The program scheduled for Friday evening represents a frequent variation of the typical evening at the theatre. The usual bill is one full-length play supplemented by entr'acte entertainment and by a comic afterpiece, a curtain raiser, or both.

However, it is not uncommon to see two full-length plays without the supplemental features. This will be the situation on Friday night.

Because the March 29 performance will be a benefit, we purchase our tickets from a friend of the Wallack family rather than from the box office of the playhouse. Actors and actresses are not well paid. Their salaries (now that the sharing scheme has disappeared) range from about six dollars per week for utility men and women—generally apprentice performers who carry messages, haul trunks, and shout in the mob scenes—to seventy-five or eighty dollars per week for leading performers. A benefit performance allows the actor being benefitted to pocket a percentage of the evening's receipts, which varies according to the importance of the actor and the bargain he can strike with the manager. In return, the actor is expected to assist in selling the tickets. So we visit a friend of Mrs. Wallack and buy our tickets from him. Certainly the prices are reasonable. Most theatres charge fifty or seventy-five cents for seats in the pit or boxes, twenty-five cents for the family circle or upper boxes, and twelve and a half cents for the gallery.

When Friday, March 29, arrives, we walk the few blocks to the theatre, starting early enough to arrive in good time for the 7:30 P.M. curtain. It is a pleasant walk. The weather is fair, much of the walkway is hard-surfaced, and there are still many gardens and open spaces in the neighborhood. When the Bowery was built in 1826 on the location of the old Bull's Head Tavern, the neighborhood was woodsy, or "bosky," as the early critics called it, and the theatre took its name from the pastoral setting, which was like a bower. Now the green areas are disappearing but the name of the theatre is permanently fixed.

The playhouse itself has a dignified classical exterior. Although it has been destroyed by fire four times and rebuilt each time, it still retains the tall Corinthian columns of its facade. The four rebuildings have altered various features of the house. The lobby area is still roomy and well upholstered—a vast improvement over the cramped little entrance of colonial playhouses. The auditorium itself is almost overwhelming in size. It now seats 4,000 spectators, and the stage is 126 feet in depth. It is no wonder that regular plays often give way to equestrian drama and spectacular productions of all kinds.

The system of stage lighting is vastly improved. The drippy candles and smoky oil lamps of earlier theatres have given way to jets of gas housed in ground glass. These lamps can be brightened or dimmed by regulating the flow of gas, and thus wonderful stage effects can be obtained. Gas is also used to light the auditorium, and the annoying candles have been removed—with the result that the audience is much better behaved. There is still a good deal of shouting, hissing, stamping, and applause; and a prodigious amount of food is still consumed, especially in the gallery.

Even though the Bowery Theatre of 1850 is many times the size of the average colonial playhouse, the general arrangement of the auditorium has not changed. The auditorium is still divided into pit, boxes, and gallery. Also, there are still proscenium boxes, although the proscenium doors have disappeared.

When the curtain rises on the play, another thing is evident: the scenic traditions have not changed much since colonial times. Painted wings, drops, and borders

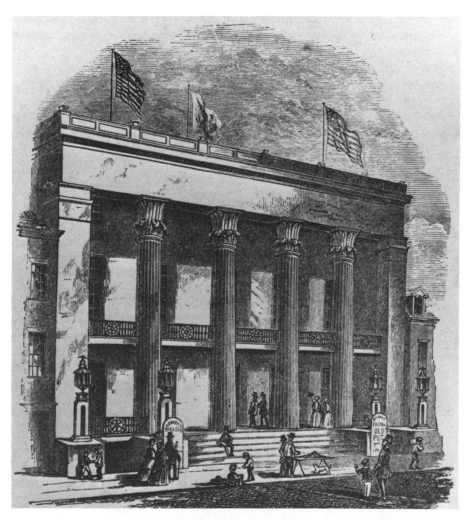

Old Bowery Theatre, 1865.
Hoblitzelle Theatre Arts Library, Humanities Research Center, University of Texas at Austin.

are still in general use. They are far larger and grander than in earlier days, but they operate on the same principles. The improved gas lighting has enabled the scene painter to use subtler colors and effects, but he still creates the illusion of trees, mountains, rivers, stairways, and buildings of all kinds on his canvases. During the past nine years a few producers have experimented with the use of *box settings*—that is, with settings made of side walls joined to a back wall which give the effect of an actual room. Such a setting was used in a production of Dion Boucicault's play, *London Assurance,* in London in 1840. It stirred interest both in England and in America and led to additional experiments in both countries. Six years later in 1846, the English tragedian Charles Kean brought Shakespeare's *King John* to New York and thrilled American audiences with the first full-scale production whose scenery and costumes were as accurate historically as the scholarship of the time permitted. These historically accurate settings were painted on canvas, yet they were a departure from the conventional painted scenery. The Bowery Theatre continues to use conventional painted scenery on wings and drops, a system that allows a speedy change of setting from scene to scene.

Mrs. Wallack and Miss Wemyss perform admirably as Romeo and Juliet. Mrs. Wallack modulates her voice and strengthens her movements so that she conveys the impression of a young man. Her costume is masculine and dashing and her wig very convincing. Miss Wemyss, surely a favorite here at the Bowery, is perfectly cast as Juliet. She is winsome, graceful, lovely in appearance, and her voice has sweetness in the love scenes and force in the climaxes. Of course both the actresses are projecting their voices strongly and enlarging their gestures and movements. The large playhouse demands it.

The second play is the ever popular *Pizarro in Peru*, which has held the stage, on and off, for fifty years. There is an air of happy expectancy in the upper tiers where the Bowery B'hoys congregate. They are the exuberant young fans—some people prefer to call them rowdies—who take delight in expressing their likes and dislikes by shouting, applauding, stamping, hissing, and throwing fruit. and vegetables. They prefer the gaudy melodrama of Kotzebue to the poetry of Shakespeare. *Pizarro* has an exotic setting and plenty of action. The leading characters are Rolla and Cora, portrayed this evening by Charles F. Addams and Mrs. Addams. In the play, Rolla is the heroic leader of the Peruvians in their struggle against Pizarro and the Spanish. After a series of battles and intrigues, Rolla has a chance to kill his enemy, Pizarro, but chivalrously refrains from doing so. He loses his own life when he rescues Cora's baby and, against great odds, restores it to its mother. The performance of the play is lusty and colorful. The patriotic speeches that Rolla utters are delivered resoundingly and often draw applause or cheers from the audience. Mr. and Mrs. Addams are competent performers but do not compare in power or artistry with Mrs. Wallack. The rest of the cast is skillful and experienced and shows that the Bowery has a strong company this season. The practice of hiring a full company for the whole season, according to lines of parts, is still standard, as it was in colonial times. Now, however, there are numerous guest stars, like Mr. and Mrs. Wallack and Mr. and Mrs. Addams.

When the roaring drama of *Pizarro* is over, the audience departs. It has been a long evening, typical of the taste of the time and of the theatrical bargains available almost everywhere in the United States. Tomorrow it will be possible to read criticisms of the performance in several newspapers, which now make a practice of reviewing plays. Three favorite publications for such criticism are *The Spirit of the Times,* the *New York Herald,* and a weekly journal, *The Albion.* All of them carry lengthy and perceptive reviews and are reminders of the great growth and improvement in theatregoing on the East Coast since 1770. Even "palmier" days are to come during the next twenty-five years.

ATTENDING A FRONTIER THEATRE IN 1849

As yet, the palmy days have not reached the theatre of the frontier. Let us examine the situation by an imaginary visit to the colorful but short-lived Eagle Theatre in Sacramento, California, in the fall of 1849.

This playhouse, the first edifice in California built to be used as a theatre, has been open only since October 18, when it was inaugurated with a performance of *The Bandit Chief, or the Forest Spectre.* We decide to see the same play during the following week. We stroll to the theatre in the early evening, happy that the fall weather is pleasant, and happy, also, that the rainy season has not started. The playhouse faces the levee of the Sacramento River and has no ventilation and practically no heat. It is identified by a painted sign announcing "Eagle Theatre"; otherwise it would be mistaken for a saloon. It appears, in fact, to be an appendage of the adjacent saloon. Playgoers enter through the barroom and buy tickets at the bar. They are high in price: three dollars for a box seat and two dollars for the pit. One can pay in coin of the realm or in gold dust. Several miners purchase their tickets with gold dust, worth twelve dollars an ounce,[2] which they pour onto the treasurer's scale.

The inside of the theatre is amazing. The flimsy structure cost the incredible sum of seventy-five to eighty thousand dollars because of the rampant inflation of the Gold Rush era. And what did so much money produce? The "building" is about sixty-five feet long and thirty feet wide; it has a dirt floor and a timber framework. Lumber is almost worth its weight in gold. This is why the roof of the theatre is sheet-iron and tin and the sides are canvas—not an entirely happy arrangement. When it rains, the metal roof makes a terrible din; and the canvas sides, sealed by the water, shut off any breath of ventilation. Before the fall season is finished, the river will flood over the nearby levee and inundate the theatre. Spectators will be forced to stand on their seats and then, finally, flee to higher ground. But tonight there is no danger of a flood, so we settle as comfortably as we can on the hard seats and survey the audience and the stage. The stage is sixteen feet deep, built of packing boxes, and it boasts a front curtain and three backdrops representing a wood, a street, and an interior. The audience is even more colorful than the garishly painted front curtain. It contains an array of humanity varying from grimy miners dressed in knee-length boots and felt hats to a number of "fine looking, well-costumed ladies."[3] The house holds about four hundred persons, three hundred of them in the pit and the rest in a tier of boxes.

The evening's play, entitled *The Bandit Chief,* is a typical melodrama of the time, filled with ghosts, violence, sensation, and "the usual amount of fighting and

---

[2]The material on the Eagle Theatre is taken from Walter M. Leman, *Memories of an Old Actor* (San Francisco: A. Roman Co., 1886), and Bayard Taylor, *Eldorado, or Adventures in the Path of Empire* (New York: G. P. Putnam's Sons, 1850), II.

[3]Leman, *Memories of an Old Actor,* p. 232.

View of Sacramento City as it appeared during the great inundation of January 1850.

terrible speeches."[4] The acting is declamatory, extravagent, and unconvincing. A journalist named Bayard Taylor, who sees this performance, describes one of the climactic scenes involving the leading lady, Mrs. Ray, in these words:

> At this juncture Mrs. Ray rushes in and throws herself into an attitude in the middle of the stage; why she does it, no one can tell. This movement, which she repeats several times in the course of the first three acts, has no connection with the tragedy; it is evidently introduced for the purpose of showing the audience that there is, actually, a female performer. The miners, to whom the sight of a woman is not a frequent occurrence, are delighted with these passages and applaud vehemently.[5]

Between the acts of the play, there are the usual singing, dancing, and comic turns. But the quality of the entr'acte entertainment is not high. In fact, several men in the pit provide better entertainment for themselves by playing a game of monte "using the seats to make their 'layout' upon."[6] The tragedy finally reaches its heartrending conclusion, the curtain falls, and a good many people leave the theatre. Others remain to sample the additional entertainment that follows the tragedy.

As the evening ends and the audience departs, we experience a variety of feelings. On the one hand, the primitive building and bad performance are appalling. Yet on the other hand, in the ramshackle Eagle Theatre and its inept company can be sensed the same irrepressible love of drama and the same willingness to meet and overcome any obstacle that planted the theatre on the East Coast, that carried it to the Midwest and the South, and that is now establishing it on the last frontier. Within two years Thomas Maguire will build the Jenny Lind Theatre in San Francisco, seating two thousand people and "rivalling the best theatres in the Atlantic States,"[7] and very soon all over the last frontier new playhouses will appear that will quickly bridge the gap between the primitive programs of the Eagle Theatre and the elegant productions of the East Coast.

[4] Taylor, *Eldorado,* pp. 30-31.
[5] Ibid., p. 31.
[6] Leman, *Memories of an Old Actor,* p. 231.
[7] Ibid., p. 233.

8

The Golden Age
of American Acting

In the third quarter of the nineteenth century, the American theatre was blessed with a galaxy of performers who have never been excelled. Mary Ann Duff was dead, but Edwin Forrest and Charlotte Cushman were still at the peak of their powers and were not to retire until the 1870s. John McCullough and other members of Forrest's heroic school of acting were enjoying wide popularity. Anna Cora Mowatt was ending nine years of fame and fortune as an actress, and Matilda Heron's star reached its zenith. Laura Keene was enjoying her best years; Fanny Davenport and Clara Morris were starting their careers. A dazzling corps of comic geniuses led by William Warren, Henry Placide, John Gilbert, and William E. Burton were setting new standards of versatility in the acting of comedy, and Joseph Jefferson III was embarking on his career as the immortal Rip Van Winkle. Most impressive of all, perhaps, were a group of superb tragedians, headed by Edwin Booth, who were performing the great roles of Shakespeare in a classic manner that has become legendary. In addition to this wealth of talent, the popular theatre of minstrelsy, burlesque, vaudeville, and the circus was creating a group of specialized performers who were unexcelled in their fields and whose art greatly enriched the life of the theatre. It was, indeed, a golden age of acting.

At one period during this era of great acting, the life of the nation was endangered by the bloody conflict of the Civil War. The years preceding 1861 were dominated by mounting tension over the issues of slavery and states' rights. The four years between 1861 and 1865 were the terrible years of open warfare. The ten years following 1865 were marked by tremendous growth but also, in the South, by the chaos and bitterness of Reconstruction.

During this quarter century, the theatre continued to prosper and expand despite the war and despite recurrent economic crises like the panic of 1857-58. Even during the years of open conflict, activity in the theatre was not seriously curtailed—at least in the northern states, which were now the theatrical center of the nation. The moral conflicts of the day revived old Puritan prejudices against the theatre, and some citizens, feeling guilty, renounced their patronage of the stage. Showboats on the Mississippi River system disappeared. Otherwise, the effects of the war were slight. At the start of the conflict, many theatres gave patriotic plays, and some companies shortened their seasons. Some actors joined the army; others, like James Murdoch, gave up regular professional appearances and devoted their time to entertaining the troops. In army camps here and there, soldiers produced plays for relaxation and amusement. In metropolitan centers, attendance at the theatre fell off for a time, then revived as spectators returned in large numbers to escape the tensions and terrors of the conflict. At the end of the war, the world of drama suffered a shock when President Lincoln was assassinated by an actor in Ford's Theatre while watching Laura Keene perform in *Our American Cousin.* Miss Keene's company, and all theatre folk, were under suspicion for a time. When the shock and suspicion had passed, show business resumed its growth and expansion.

From 1850 to 1875, certain general developments in the theatre deserve mention. The first copyright law to protect the interests of the playwright was enacted in 1856 through the influence of Dion Boucicault. Although it was a step in the right direction and gave the playwright a firmer legal status, it did not provide the protection the dramatist needed.

In 1860 Boucicault, motivated partly by the failure of the copyright law he had sponsored, began to promote the idea of road, or "combination," companies. The idea was not original with Boucicault. Ever since colonial days, professional companies had, in a sense, been road companies because they traveled from town to town, usually taking their scenery along. However, they presented a repertory of plays, not a single drama—as advocated by Boucicault. Even the touring of a single play had been done earlier—by companies playing *Uncle Tom's Cabin,* for example. Still, Boucicault added originality to the plan by insisting that any play, after a successful initial run, could be sent on the road with a single cast performing only the single play. The new system was given impetus by the rapid growth of railroads, which provided safe and dependable transportation for both performers and scenery. But it steadily undermined the old system of resident stock companies, eventually destroying them. In 1860 there were probably more than fifty resident companies operating in the United States and providing a wonderful training ground for versatility in acting. Twenty years later only seven or eight of these remained.

Several other developments altered the nature of theatregoing during these years. The presentation of farcical afterpieces went out of fashion. The vogue for box settings and realistic stage furnishings increased greatly, another trend attributed to the energetic Boucicault. The practice of hiring actors to play a particular line of parts began to change. When Augustin Daly organized his company in 1869, he engaged the performers without specifying the traditional lines of business such as leading man, eccentric comedian, walking gentleman. He started a trend that eventually ended the old practice. Even more significant were the increasingly long runs given to popular new plays and the consequent decrease in the total number of productions per season. In the early years of the century, a popular new play might hold the stage for seven to fifteen performances; later on, twenty to fifty became the average, and sensational hits like *The Black Crook* and *Uncle Tom's Cabin* might hold the stage for many months. The result of such long runs was inevitable: each year, fewer and fewer plays constituted the season. In 1851-52 the Boston Museum produced a total of one hundred forty different plays; New York theatres offered almost as many. Twenty-five years later, only forty to sixty full-length dramas were given at the Museum, and the typical New York theatre produced only fifteen to twenty-five.

New York's continuing leadership in theatrical affairs was illustrated by several important events. In 1855, for example, the first guest star performing in a foreign language appeared in America—at the Metropolitan Theatre in New York. This was Mlle. Rachel, reigning queen of the French theatre, who presented plays like Corneille's *Horace* and Racine's *Phèdre* in their original language. Developments such as this remind us that foreign-language theatres have, throughout the entire history of the American theatre, provided an exotic thread in the general tapestry. Companies speaking every language from Spanish to Chinese have been heard in American playhouses and have contributed significantly to the richness of theatre history.

An important new playhouse, Wallack's Theatre, opened in New York in 1852 and, with the help of new structures in 1861 and 1882, augmented the city's theatrical glory for more than thirty years. Under the management of James William Wallack, and featuring the acting of both himself and his son, Lester, Wallack's Theatre was a model of good taste, well-balanced repertory, and excellent acting.

The success of Wallack's Theatre marked the opening years of the third quarter of the nineteenth century in New York. The final years were distinguished by the opening, in 1869, of two other famous playhouses that added to the twenty-one theatres already operating in New York in 1868. One of the new playhouses was Daly's Fifth Avenue Theatre, which, under the autocratic direction of Augustin Daly, began to reshape the American stock company. The other new theatre was Edwin Booth's, which the great actor hoped to make into a national theatre presenting only the best in classic and poetic drama. Booth's dream, unfortunately, was never realized. Financial difficulties forced him to relinquish the management of the house after only four years, and the whole impressive structure was torn down in 1883 after only fourteen years of existence.

Although New York was clearly the theatrical capital of the nation in the third quarter of the nineteenth century, there was ample activity in other cities and towns. In Philadelphia, Mr. and Mrs. John Drew dominated the scene both as performers and as managers. They founded the famous Drew-Barrymore dynasty, which contributed colorfully to American theatre for a hundred years. Mrs. Drew was not only a consummately skillful comedienne; she was also the most brilliant and successful female manager the country has ever seen. For many years after her husband died in 1862, she made the Arch Street Theatre a showplace of talent and excellence, and here a number of famous players received their early training.

In Boston five theatres—sometimes six—were in operation, of which the Museum and the Boston were the most prominent. When the old Boston Theatre in Federal Street burned in 1852, it was replaced, in another location, by a lavish new structure that was the pride of the city for several decades.

Providence, Charleston, St. Louis, and New Orleans all supported varying amounts of theatrical activity; but other cities, many of them further west, enjoyed the greatest new growth. This was made possible by the continuing expansion of the railroad, climaxed in 1869 by the completion of the first transcontinental line connecting the East Coast with the West Coast. Henceforth, theatrical companies could travel with ease and comfort to almost any town in the nation.

In Chicago in 1857, John McVicker built the first playhouse to bear his name, and in the years that followed he became the leading impresario of the city. Much further west, in Salt Lake City, the Mormon church—which had always sponsored artistic and recreational programs—built a splendid theatre and opened it in 1862. It was the first playhouse erected in America by a religious organization; and its subsequent success, due in part to the vigorous support of Brigham Young, head of the Mormon church, would have gladdened the hearts of the original

The California Theatre, Bush Street between Grant Avenue
and Kearney Street, San Francisco, in the 1870s.

Courtesy, The Bancroft Library, University of California, Berkeley.

Hallam company and all those other pioneer actors who struggled against religious prejudice all their lives.

On the Pacific Coast, theatrical activity made rapid progress. Although the original Eagle Theatre in Sacramento lasted only two and a half months, shortly thereafter, in 1850, Thomas Maguire built a playhouse over his gambling saloon in San Francisco and called it the Jenny Lind Theatre.

The Jenny Lind Theatre soon had a rival. In 1853 San Francisco's second legitimate playhouse, the Metropolitan, was opened. The manager was none other than Catherine Sinclair, the ex-wife of Edwin Forrest. Other playhouses, as well as many variety halls, soon followed, but all were eclipsed in 1869 when the new California Theatre opened. San Franciscans claimed that this playhouse surpassed in elegance, scenery, and lighting facilities any other playhouse in America—and they maintained the boast even when Booth's Theatre was opened in New York a few weeks later. The California Theatre immediately set high standards. An excellent company was assembled, headed by Lawrence Barrett and John McCullough, which proceeded to present plays that often equaled the best theatrical productions of New York. From such companies flowed traveling troupes that carried the drama to cities, towns, and mining camps up and down the state and into adjacent states as well.

Against the background of these developments, American acting enjoyed the last years of its golden age. Individual stars emerged from the resident companies and made dazzling careers for themselves as independent performers who traveled from city to city presenting their favorite roles with the support of the local troupes. The contributions of these independent stars were so varied, exciting, and splendid that they made the third quarter of the nineteenth century a memorable period in theatrical history. American playwriting may not have reached maturity; American acting certainly had.

THE CLASSIC SCHOOL OF ACTING

The most memorable achievement of the age, perhaps, was the acting of Edwin Booth and a group that can be termed the "classic" school—classic in the sense that their manner of performance was "of the first rank; perfect in its way; a model of its kind." These players, as Lewis Strang has written, were "destined in the end to outlive and outact the school of heroic histrionism of which Forrest was the founder."[1]

Two actresses who belong in this group, Mary Ann Duff and Charlotte Cushman, have already been discussed. Their methods, practices, and attitudes were characteristic of the classic school. Typical players of the school were close to the best traditions of the European theatre. They had rich and varied apprenticeships, served in the resident stock companies of the day, and prided themselves on the

[1] Lewis C. Strang, *Plays and Players of the Last Quarter Century* (Boston: L. C. Page & Company, 1903), I:129.

range and versatility they developed as members of such companies. In their mature years they became independent traveling stars who specialized in the great roles of Shakespeare and other standard dramatists. They were masters of the techniques of speech and movement; and although they aimed to give the impression of being perfectly natural, their naturalness was the suggestive, idealized behavior that suited the characters of poetic tragedy. Players of the classic school studied their roles penetratingly, fitted them into the overall design of the play, and rehearsed their effects carefully so that in performance, their acting appeared spontaneous and effortless. In every part they played they tried to transform their personalities so as to project the illusion of separate dramatic characters, and they sought to feel the emotions of their roles without losing control of their bodies or voices and without wallowing in their emotions.

Edwin Booth, 1833-1893

Edwin Booth, the greatest actor of the classic school, may well be the greatest actor America has produced. He was born in Belair, Maryland, on November 13, 1833, the fourth son of a famous father, Junius Brutus Booth, who was considered a worthy rival of Edmund Kean. As a boy, Edwin had little formal education but much informal education in the hard school of experience. For several years he traveled throughout the country with his gifted but half-mad father, serving him as a friend, guardian, and valet. Naturally, Edwin's first conceptions of acting were gathered from his illustrious parent. The elder Booth was a fiery, impulsive actor who dazzled his audiences with mighty outbursts of emotion and thrilling vocal displays. Inevitably Edwin was influenced by this style, but the influence did not persist for long. The elder Booth died when Edwin was nineteen, and thereafter the young man began cultivating an individual style that was to win him worldwide acclaim.

Edwin's debut on the stage was almost accidental. In 1849, while his father was performing in Boston as a traveling star, Edwin assumed the bit part of Tressel in *Richard III* to relieve the burden of an overworked prompter. Thereafter, Edwin occasionally played minor roles in the productions that starred his father. His serious apprenticeship began in San Francisco, where he had gone with his father in 1852. The elder Booth died later the same year, but Edwin remained in the West until 1856, playing a great variety of roles, both tragic and comic, in various resident and traveling companies. After this apprenticeship, he returned to the East and immediately scored an enduring triumph. Although his art was not yet fully developed, he was successful enough to be hailed as "the hope of the living drama."

From the time of Booth's Eastern debut in 1856 until his death in 1893, he remained an independent star of the first magnitude. Except for the years from 1869 to 1873 when he managed his own company in his own theatre, he was not attached to any single resident company but made star appearances with practically all of them—east and west, north and south. At the peak of his career, after Forrest had passed his prime, he was acknowledged to be America's greatest tragic actor. He performed before admiring audiences in both England and Germany, and in the United States he was the first actor to play the role of Hamlet one hundred consecutive times.

The major premise in Booth's artistic creed was his belief that art should interpret, exalt, ennoble. To achieve his high ideals he used all his physical and mental endowments, which were many. His admirers claimed that he possessed the ideal combination of mind, voice, and body. His power to illuminate his characters through imaginative poetic insight was his chief glory. One critic called him "the foremost poet of his profession,"[2] and another declared, "The distinctive quality that illuminated his acting was the personal one of poetic individuality."[3]

Edwin Booth as Richelieu.

Ross Theatre Collection, University of California Library at Berkeley.

[2] Quoted in Strang, *Plays and Players of the Last Quarter Century*, I:156.
[3] Winter, *The Life and Art of Edwin Booth*, p. 223.

Booth's style of acting in his mature years excelled in consistency and lack of mannerism. His art was smooth, even of texture, and marvelously relaxed. It never depended for its effect on tricks or explosions, and it was never static. He studied his parts as long as he played them, tirelessly probing for deeper meaning and more effective expression.

The three Booth brothers on November 25, 1864 in *Julius Caesar.*
Junius Brutus, Jr., as Cassius, Edwin as Brutus, John Wilkes as Mark Antony.
Mother Booth watched from a private box.
Hoblitzelle Theatre Arts Library, Humanities Research Center, University of Texas at Austin.

Among the great players of the nineteenth century Booth was the finest artist. He was also one of the more versatile. His greatest creation, Hamlet, tended to obscure the numerous other characters that he created with equal skill. Yet the discriminating critics were well aware of his ability to act lovers and villains, rogues and heroes. He achieved so greatly during his career and impressed the playgoers of America so profoundly that after his death one of the best dramatic critics wrote, "When he made his final bow, the curtain—so far as the American stage was concerned—fell also upon the legitimate drama."[4]

James E. Murdoch, 1811-1893; Edward L. Davenport, 1815-1877; and Lawrence Barrett, 1838-1891

Three other versatile tragediens whose talent and success place them close to Booth are James E. Murdoch, Edward L. Davenport, and Lawrence Barrett. Their careers and accomplishments are impressive, but space in this volume permits only a brief mention of each.[5]

James E. Murdoch is remembered not only for his versatility—he was successful in the great tragic roles, in romantic parts, and in high comedy—but he also became an eminent teacher of elocution. His three published books influenced the course of dramatic instruction in America for many years.

Edward L. Davenport was so versatile that this very gift tended to obscure his brilliance. The range of parts he played covered everything from Bill Sykes to Hamlet and from Sir Lucius O'Trigger to Othello. Each role had symmetry and balance from first to last, and each presentation was remarkable for grace and repose.

Lawrence Barrett was the least gifted but certainly the most persevering of the group. His endowments were limited compared to those of Booth, Murdoch, and Davenport, but by arduous self-training he raised himself slowly but surely to success in many difficult roles. The climax to his career came in the 1880s when he arranged the famous partnership with Edwin Booth during which, as manager and costar of the combination, he achieved the prestige of equal billing with America's greatest tragedian.

VERSATILE TRAGEDIANS OF LESSER RANK

Associated with the versatile tragedians of top rank were several other capable actors whose ideals and methods belong to the same school. These performers, more limited in talent and less eminent in position than Booth, Murdoch, Daven-

---

[4] John R. Towse, *Sixty Years of the Theatre* (New York: Funk & Wagnalls, Inc., 1916), p. 171.

[5] For a more detailed discussion of the careers of these men, see the present author's *A History of American Acting* (Bloomington and London; Indiana University Press, 1966).

port, or Barrett, played the same roles and demonstrated to a lesser degree the same range of versatility. Among the actors who belong in this group are the following:

George C. Vandenhoff, 1803-1885
Edwin Adams, 1834-1877
Charles W. Couldock, 1815-1898
Joseph Haworth, 1855-1903
Peter Richings, 1797-1871
William Wheatley, 1816-1876
Charles Barron, 1843-1918
Steele Mackaye, 1842-1894

THE GREAT COMEDIANS

The performance of serious plays was superb during the golden age of American acting. The performance of comedy was equally brilliant. During this period there flourished a host of players prodigal both in number and in comic genius. Their enormous versatility, unending variety, and astonishing achievements dazzle an admirer who studies their careers a full hundred years after their great performances. To understand the unique kind of acting they achieved during their time, we must glance at the type of comic acting that is seen today.

Most of the comedians of the present time fall, roughly, into two classes. There are the clowns and gagsters, like Bob Hope, Jack Benny, and Red Skelton, and the sophisticates, like Jack Lemmon and Cary Grant. The first group includes men who have created a unique stage personality for themselves and who exploit it largely through verbal gags and absurd situations that lead to gags. They are amazingly successful because the public enjoys the characters they have created and because the players behind the characters are expert in manipulating themselves through an endless succession of situations. The sophisticated comedians are a different breed. They are charming, polished, urbane drawing-room heroes with a dash of romantic appeal. They appear on stage, screen, and television in sprightly comedies that feature witty dialogue, ingenious action, and romantic glamour. Generally, the comedians who star in these comedies do not vary their roles but play their attractive and clever selves over and over again.

The great decades of the nineteenth century had clowns and sophisticates, but they had, in addition, a group of expert actors who can be called *character comedians*. These gifted players could change their personalities with their roles, they could produce uproarious laughter through careful portrayal of character, and they could and did create rich galleries of unique comic portraits.

To understand the kind of character acting they developed and the versatility they achieved, we must recall the extensive comic repertory of the period. The comedies of Shakespeare were part of the standard repertory; they offered such challenging roles as Bottom, Dogberry, Falstaff, Malvolio, Sir Andrew Aguecheek, and so on. The so-called old comedy, best represented by the plays of Goldsmith, Sheridan, and Farquhar, offered such popular parts as Sir Peter Teazle, Sir Anthony Absolute, Bob Acres, Sir Lucius O'Trigger, Tony Lumpkin, and a galaxy of other characters that no comedian could resist. A third group of plays, which furnished some of the most popular vehicles of the century, were the dramas and adaptations of recent or contemporary playwrights. A few of the best-known examples are Boucicault's adaptation of *Rip Van Winkle,* which provided Joseph Jefferson with his greatest role; Morris Barnett's *The Serious Family,* which included the character of Aminidab Sleek; Tom Taylor's *Our American Cousin,* which included the roles of Asa Trenchard and Lord Dundreary; and George Coleman's *The Heir-at-Law,* which featured the popular characters Dr. Pangloss and Zekiel Homespun. A final group of plays, providing further tests for the skill of comedians, were the farces that generally appeared as afterpieces to the main drama of the evening. Representative examples are the lively inventions of J. Madison Morton such as *Slasher and Crasher, Betsey Baker,* and *Poor Pillicoddy.* A character comedian in the mid-decades of the nineteenth century customarily played a major role in the main drama of the evening; then, very likely, he performed comic songs or turns in the entertainment that separated the main drama from the farce; and finally, he cavorted an additional hour in the afterpiece or farce.

A surprising number of superlative character comedians flourished at this time. Heading the company are four great names: Henry Placide, William E. Burton, John Gilbert, and William Warren.

Henry Placide, 1799-1870

Henry Placide, the first of the great comedians to make his debut, was called "almost a faultless actor,"[6] and "the best comedian the United States has yet produced."[7] He had every personal requisite for success—a handsome, expressive face; a supple figure of medium height; a clear, melodious voice; a spirited, vivacious personality; and an alert, inquiring mind that savored all the peculiarities and eccentricities of human nature. Born into a family of actors and acrobats, he became one of the troupe at an early age and subsequently underwent a long and intensive apprenticeship. The results were rare and wonderful: he emerged as an actor whose range of roles was extraordinary. He could play every variety of comic part from broad farce to exquisite high comedy, and was unequaled in three kinds of roles: middle-aged gentlemen, drunken servants, and simple country lads. In addition, his French ancestry and knowledge of the French language gave him an

---

[6]*New York Mirror,* 20 June 1829; quoted in Brander Matthews and Laurence Hutton, *Actors and Actresses of Great Britain and the United States—Kean and Booth, and Their Contemporaries* (New York: Cassell & Company, Ltd., 1886), p. 153.

[7]G. C. D. Odell, "Some Theatrical Stock Companies of New York," p. 8 (an essay issued by the Brander Matthews Dramatic Museum, Columbia University, to accompany its exhibition, "Two Centuries of the New York Theatre," March-October 1951).

immense advantage in parts requiring Gallic background. During his twenty years at the Park Theatre in New York, he acted more than five hundred roles and was the first portrayer of over two hundred of these.

William E. Burton, 1804-1860

In the minds of thousands of theatregoers, Placide was great, but William E. Burton was "the funniest man who ever lived." The very sound of his voice off-stage could send an audience into an uproar, and in the famous drunk scene from *The Toodles* he could hold his spectators convulsed for a full fifty minutes without speaking a line. He could also make them weep, mingling laughter and tears in miraculous combination. No comedian, perhaps, has ever exercised such complete command over the responses of his audience.

Burton had a rather heavy figure, a broad, genial face, and a voice of extraordinary flexibility. Some of his funniest effects came from his voice and face. Both were protean: he could vary his tones from the boyish squeak of the terrified adolescent to the roar of the enraged sea captain, while his face was a huge map on which was outlined every degree and kind of comic emotion.

Like the other great comedians of his time, Burton was marvelously versatile and creative. He could embody with exquisite humor a sharply conceived character like Shakespeare's Bottom, or he could take a sketchily written part in a modern farce and could so build, shape, and embellish it that it became a full-length master-piece.

Burton had been a leading manager in Philadelphia from 1838 to 1848 and had won success and admiration in the Quaker City. He was even more successful in New York. From 1848 to 1856, his Chambers Street Theatre became nationally famous. It delighted its audiences with a wealth of wonderful comedies and it dazzled playgoers with occasional Shakespearean productions both colorful and historically accurate.

John Gilbert, 1810-1889

John Gilbert, who made his debut five years after the advent of Placide and Burton, was noted for the polish, grace, dignity, and exquisite finish of his style. He was a master technician who modeled his acting after the style of the English comedian William Farren and who became so expert that no matter how painstaking his preparation of a role, the final effect appeared spontaneous and unrehearsed. He portrayed a great number of old men, but each was individual and distinct; for he was another actor gifted with the supreme power to submerge his own personality and transform himself into the character conceived by the dramatist. His range was prodigious, and the perfection of his portraiture was the subject of boundless praise. John R. Towse said that his acting of Sir Anthony Absolute "has never been equalled anywhere in the last half century! . . ."[8] William Winter believed that he gave "the best performance of Caliban that ever was seen in America,"[9] while Brander Matthews declares, ". . . I have never seen, nor has anyone else in the past half-century, any rendering of Sir Peter Teazle comparable with John Gilbert's."[10] These are only 3 of the 1,150 parts he performed during his lifetime—and in all these parts, as William Winter wrote, he was "sometimes a great actor . . . always a correct one."[11]

William Warren, 1812-1888

William Warren, son of the famous actor-manager of the same name, is the final member of the top quartet of comic geniuses and is considered by many critics to have been the greatest of them all. In view of the achievements of Placide, Burton, and Gilbert, it is difficult to contend that another actor could be greater than they. But Warren's claims are strong, and certainly he is a peer of the greatest if, indeed, he does not surpass them.

Warren's career on the stage covered more than fifty years, for he made his debut in 1832 and retired in 1883. The final thirty-six of these years were spent at one theatre, the Boston Museum. Except for a single starring tour in 1864-65, the world had to travel to Boston to see Mr. Warren. Warren was a meticulous student, a penetrating observer, and a genuine lover of his fellow men. Each of his comic creations was "complete, uniform, and fulfilled to its absolute possibilities."[12] and each was suffused with a delicious, genial humor that lacked any trace of sarcasm or satire. Whenever he stepped on the stage—or even before, when his voice was heard off-stage—a thrill of joy went through the audience and lasted through his entire performance.

Warren's versatility as a portrayer of comic types was practically limitless. He seemed able to create complete and unique portraits from every part assigned to him. During his professional life, he performed thirteen thousand five hundred times in almost six hundred different roles. Joseph Jefferson said, ". . . it is safe to conclude that this versatile comedian studied and created more parts than any other actor of his day,"[13] and Lewis Strang declares, ". . . he was, beyond a reasonable doubt, the greatest comedian that the American Theatre has produced."[14]

Placide, Burton, Gilbert, and Warren form a quartet whose comic genius was without peer. But so vital was the American theatre in their day, and so rich was

[8] Towse, *Sixty Years of the Theatre*, pp. 99-100.
[9] William Winter, *The Wallet of Time* (New York: Moffat, Yard and Company, 1913), I:158.
[10] Brander Mathews, *These Many Years* (New York: Charles Scribner's Sons, 1917), p. 349.
[11] Winter, *The Wallet of Time*, I:157.
[12] Catherine M. Reignolds-Winslow, *Yesterday with Actors* (Boston: Cupples and Hurd, 1887), pp. 127-28.
[13] Joseph Jefferson, *Autobiography* (New York: The Century Co., 1889), p. 403.
[14] Strang, *Plays and Players of the Last Quarter Century*, I:267.

the array of talent, that this quartet of actors was challenged by six other comedians whose talent was close to theirs. Of these six, William Rufus Blake (1805-1866) and William J. Florence (1831-1891) belong at the top, in a position close to the greatest. Ranking slightly below them were Charles Fisher (1816-1891), John Sleeper Clarke (1833-1899), John E. Owens (1823-1886), and William P. Davidge (1814-1888). All of them were famous for certain specialties as well as for a worthy versatility.

With this group of versatile male performers should be mentioned several women: Mrs. John Drew (1820-1887), Mrs. A. H. Gilbert (1821-1904), and Mrs. Sarah Ross Wheatley (1790-1872?). All these ladies were known for their brilliant portrayal of such famous comic characters as Mrs. Malaprop, Lady Teazle, Lucretia McTab, and Lady Creamly, and in many ways their art paralleled that of the great male performers.

Dion Boucicault, 1820-1890

In a somewhat different category, yet still deserving mention in the ranks of the character comedians, was that tireless and multitalented Irishman, Dion Boucicault. Although he was thirty-three when he arrived in the United States in 1853, the "Ubiquitous Boucicault" immediately became a dominating influence on the American stage, and during the remaining thirty-seven years of his life he left his stamp on every department of the American theatre. He died in the United States in 1890.

Born in Dublin about 1820, he became stage-struck at an early age and eventually found his way to London where, said William Winter, he "haunted theatres and wrote plays."[15] In 1841, after serving as an actor in the English provincial theatres, he established a name for himself by writing the highly popular success, *London Assurance*. From then until the year of his death he never ceased his many activities in the theatre.

One of his principal activities was acting. As a performer he exhibited the same cleverness and skill that he showed in constructing his plays. He did not attempt the varied comic roles of the great comedians like Warren, Burton, or Gilbert. It was as a lovable Irish character in his plays based on Irish life that he achieved his greatest success. Three such roles are especially notable: Myles-na-Coppaleen in *The Colleen Bawn,* Daddy O'Dowd in the play of the same name, and Conn in *The Shaughraun.*

Boucicault's influence on the American theatre came not only from his acting, but also from his wide range of other activities. He introduced fireproof scenery, sponsored the first successful copyright law for the protection of American playwrights, helped found the system of road or combination companies, directed innumerable productions and coached hundreds of players, promoted the use of box settings and realistic furnishings, and, during fifty years, supplied the theatres

---

[15]William Winter, *Other Days* (New York: Moffat, Yard and Company, 1908), p. 125.

Dion Boucicault as Conn in *The Shaughraun.*

Hoblitzelle Theatre Arts Library, Humanities Research Center, University of Texas at Austin.

of both America and Great Britain with more than 130 of the most popular plays of the century. It is not surprising that he earned the title of the "Ubiquitous Boucicault."

Single-Role Comedians

Allied with these versatile character comedians was another group of superlative comic actors who based their fame on the creation of a single part or line of parts. They were similar to the Hopes, Bennys, and Skeltons in that they generally played a single role into which they infused the richness of their own personalities. They were unlike their modern counterparts in that the single roles they played occurred within the framework of a drama and were not presented as independent, vaudeville-type entertainment. Prominent among the single-role comedians were such talented players as the following.

John T. Raymond (1836-1887) so injected his own buoyant personality into the role of Colonel Mulberry Sellers in *The Gilded Age* that he made it internationally famous. E. A. Sothern (1825-1881) immortalized the eccentric Lord Dundreary in *Our American Cousin.* Francis S. Chanfrau (1824-1884) started a national craze with his dashing portrayal of Mose the Fireboy and played the frontiersman and the Arkansas traveler, Kit, equally well. James Lewis (1838-1896) made priceless portraits of the fussy old men who were his specialty. Barney Williams (1823-1876) won the hearts of both British and American audiences with his portrayal of the Irish peasant boy. George Holland (1791-1870) was the greatest jokester of his time and converted every part he played into a vehicle for his own gags and slapstick. Stuart Robson (1836-1903) had a drolly innocent appearance, a squeaky, unpredictable voice, and eccentric movements that dominated every role he undertook and titillated audiences for over fifty years. John Brougham (1810-1879) had a fair measure of versatility; but his breezy, genial Irish personality infused all his roles, and his fame at making impromptu curtain speeches was as great as his popularity as an actor. George "Yankee" Hill (1809-1899), Denman Thompson (1833-1911), and a host of other skillful interpreters of the stage Yankee carried the fame of Jonathan Ploughboy and other Yankee types to every corner of the country and to England as well, where James H. Hackett's pioneering in similar roles had paved the way for later American comedians.

Many other skillful actors specialized in light romantic comedy, like the Cary Grants and Noel Cowards of the twentieth century stage. Two of the best of these were Lester Wallack (1820-1885) and John Drew (1853-1927). Their charm, dash, and sophistication could easily challenge the matinee idols of today. All these single-role performers were popular and successful, but by far the greatest of them, whose fame surpassed and outlasted the others, was Joseph Jefferson III, the immortal Rip Van Winkle.

What a wonderful creation Rip Van Winkle turned out to be! As finally perfected by Jefferson, his portrait was a masterpiece that warmed the hearts and tickled the funny bones of several generations of playgoers throughout the entire United States. The artistry that Jefferson lavished on this part was considered by the public to be ample recompense for the actor's lack of versatility; the public did not want him to play a different role—just as the public today would rebel if Bob Hope changed his personality. They considered Jefferson's single role reason enough for classing the comedian as one of the truly great actors of the American stage.

It is not surprising that Joseph Jefferson succeeded so brilliantly in the theatre. He sprang from a long line of successful actors. He made his debut at the age of four, and seventy-one years later, only a year before his death, he gave his final performance as Rip. Jefferson established himself as a popular comedian early in his career, but he was not satisfied with the roles he played. He began searching for a character in whom, as he says in his *Autobiography,* "humor would be so closely allied with pathos that smiles and tears should mingle with each other,"[16] He found such a character in Washington Irving's Rip Van Winkle, and he decided to make Rip his own even before the character was embodied in a play. Not until 1865 when Jefferson was thirty-six years old did Dion Boucicault dramatize Irving's story. Jefferson produced it at the Adelphi Theatre in London. The play was shoddy and the character of Rip sketchily drawn, but Jefferson's interpretation won hearty approval. For the rest of his life Jefferson continued to shape and develop the role of Rip. As he finally played the part, the character was more his own creation than the dramatist's. Into it Jefferson poured all the warmth of his personality and all the artistry of his many years of acting. His portrayal of Rip was notable for its ease and naturalness and absence of tricks, bombast, or the striving for effect. The character had a kindliness, spirituality, and humor that were projected so deftly and effortlessly that they seemed inseperable from the actor—which they were. As Lewis Strang wrote, "Jefferson's Rip Van Winkle is a wonderful thing, a unique achievement, an astonishing exhibition of virtuousity, a creation impossible to anyone but Joseph Jefferson."[17]

THE SCHOOL OF EMOTIONALISM

During the golden era of the great tragedians and comedians, another school of acting gained wide popular appeal and added to the rich variety of performances that the period offered. This was the school of emotionalism, developed by a group of actresses as a fitting style for performing melodramas. Emotionalistic acting was confined almost exclusively to female performers for the simple reason that emotionalistic roles were not often written for men. The most notable exponents of the emotionalistic school include Anna Cora Mowatt, Laura Keene, and Matilda Heron.

---

[16] Jefferson, *Autobiography,* p. 223.

[17] Strang, *Plays and Players of the Last Quarter Century,* I:268. For the story of Jefferson's career and a discussion of his artistic principles and practices, see his famous *Autobiography* (New York: The Century Co., 1889).

Joseph Jefferson in *Heir-at-Law.*

Hoblitzelle Theatre Arts Library, Humanities Research Center, University of Texas at Austin.

As a manner of performing, emotionalistic acting can be recognized by three dominant characteristics. First, the actress of this school actually experiences the feelings and passions of her role and surrenders herself to these emotions. Second, she cultivates a lush, overt display of the passions she is feeling. Her performance is marked by sobs, tears, screams, shudders, heaving, writhing, panting, growling, trembling, and all manner of other physical manifestations. The third major characteristic of the emotionalistic school is neglect of technique. In surrendering to emotion and cultivating lavish, overt expression, the emotionalistic actress disregards discipline and control.

Emotionalistic acting also needs a certain kind of play for its fullest development—a drama of abundant sentiment, melodramatic action, and contrived emotional crises. Playwriting of the nineteenth century, as we have seen, provided hundreds of such vehicles, and by exploiting them the emotionalistic actresses were highly successful.

Anna Cora Mowatt, 1819-1870

During the years when Charlotte Cushman's star was rising, there flashed across the theatrical sky a meteor of uncommon brilliance. In May 1845 Mrs. Anna Cora Mowatt, whose play *Fashion* had succeeded brilliantly just two months earlier, suddenly decided to become an actress. Three weeks later her debut became the sensation of the New York season. For nine years she illuminated the dramatic heavens as an actress and then withdrew as suddenly and unexpectedly as she had appeared. Her career in acting is significant because it marks the beginning in the American theatre of the school of emotionalism. Mrs. Mowatt is the first of a long line of actresses who achieved success primarily through personal charm and emotional exhibitionism.

Anna Cora Mowatt was without question an unusual and remarkable woman. She had unusual intelligence, keen aesthetic perception, thorough education, wide cultural experience, an excellent speaking voice, and beauty of face and figure, all of which are invaluable endowments for any actress. In addition, she had an emotional sensitivity that enabled her to "abandon herself to a role," to "live the part." This ability, added to her other endowments, won her success on the stage for nine prosperous years. Mrs. Mowatt herself recognized the source of her appeal. In her autobiography she wrote, "I never succeeded in stirring the hearts of others unless I was deeply affected myself. The putting off of self-consciousness was, with me, the first imperative element of success."[18]

Laura Keene, 1826?-1873

Another woman of strong will and varied abilities, who made her American debut just two years before Mrs. Mowatt quit the stage, was the imperious beauty, Laura Keene. Like Mrs. Mowatt, Laura Keene had boundless energy, abiding self-confidence, and enough ability to demonstrate competence in several fields. She was a charming and graceful actress, a successful manager, a respected business

[18] Anna Cora Mowatt, *Autobiography of an Actress* (Boston: Ticknor, Reed and Fields, 1854), p. 224.

woman, and an able enough student of aesthetics to lecture occasionally on the fine arts and to edit, for a brief time, a magazine devoted to the fine arts. Though she made no lasting impression on the American theatre and though her popularity and success declined long before she quit the stage, her name is associated with the careers of many great stars of the American theatre, and her acting was a worthy example of feminine charm and emotionalism. Her name is forever linked with American history because she was the star of the play being presented in Ford's Theatre the night Abraham Lincoln was assassinated, and she was the one who recognized John Wilkes Booth as he made his escape and who held the dying president's head in her lap until he was carried from the theatre.

Matilda Heron, 1831-1877

As early exponents of the emotionalistic school, Mrs. Mowatt and Laura Keene emphasized feminine charm and sentiment in their acting and gave secondary place to displays of strong feeling. They occasionally indulged in lavish exhibitions of tears, rage, and hysteria, but such exhibitions were not their stock in trade. Moreover, the roles they played and the tastes of the time caused them to subdue and to idealize, in some degree, their emotional pyrotechnics. With the rise of performers like Matilda Heron, primary emphasis was placed on extravagent displays of the more violent feelings. Moreover, the representation of feelings became realistic and naturalistic. Instead of refining or sentimentalizing their emotional exhibitions, the later actresses reproduced the overt manifestations of passion in detail and with clinical accuracy. By these means they shocked and fascinated their audiences and won notoriety for themselves.

The first influential actress of this branch of the emotionalistic school was Matilda Heron. Her contribution to American acting is her single outstanding role, Camille. This role brought her fame and fortune, and in it she most effectively displayed her naturalistic, emotional style of acting, influencing many other actresses to join the school of emotionalism. And this role was also remembered at the time of her death: on her coffin was engraved the single word, *Camille.*

The naturalism of Miss Heron's style was not the photographic realism developed by David Belasco in the twentieth century, but her acting had several characteristics new enough in the mid-nineteenth century to cause excited comment. Miss Heron did not make her entrance with her face to the galleries, waiting for a "reception"; she walked in naturally and ignored the audience. She did not raise her voice or project her words perceptibly, but spoke in what seemed to be a commonplace, conversational tone. On occasion, she even dared to turn her back to the audience. Another aspect of her naturalism was her inclusion of a multitude of realistic details. She made no attempt to idealize or refine her characters; she did not even select and arrange her effects, but included commonplace business of every sort, no matter how awkward or distracting it appeared. Finally, she portrayed physical and clinical reactions that were rarely if ever exhibited on the stage at that time. Many of her scenes were called repulsive and revolting. Her

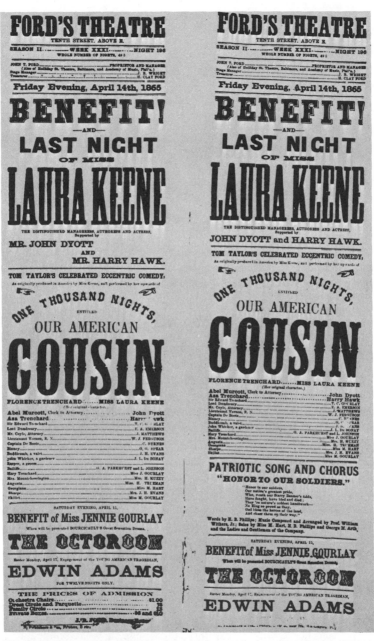

The "assassination" playbills are the most famous in American theatrical history. The one on the left was being printed when word came that President Lincoln intended to visit the theatre that night. The printing was suspended, the patriotic song added, and then the playbill on the right was printed. Both were distributed on the fatal evening. Many forgeries were subsequently printed and sold.

Hoblitzelle Theatre Arts Library, Humanities Research Center, University of Texas at Austin.

Ford's Theatre, Washington, D. C.
Hoblitzelle Theatre Arts Library, Humanities Research Center, University of Texas at Austin.

deathbed scene was considered especially painful. But all of the "disgusting minutiae" added to the fascination of the play and attracted thousands of spectators.

The golden age will long be remembered in the history of the American theatre. It produced an impressive number of great actors and actresses who performed in a variety of fascinating styles. The individuals described in this chapter are the most noteworthy examples of these performers; there were many others. The achievements of all of them are amply recorded in the reviews, memoirs, and biographies that are a rich source of information—and of pride—to those who love the history of their country.

9

The Popular Theatre
Grows Up—
and Captivates the Crowd

Phineas T. Barnum once said that "show business has all phases and grades of dignity from the exhibition of a monkey to the exposition of that highest art in music and the drama . . ."[1] As usual, Barnum was right. The "highest art" in show business was represented when Edwin Booth, Charlotte Cushman, or William Warren performed in one of the plays of Shakespeare. But as Barnum shrewdly realized, show business included the exhibition of a monkey—and ten thousand other little variety acts, burlesque skits, minstrel shows, animal exhibitions, and circus performances. These forms of "popular theatre" were the common theatrical activity which, like Whitman's leaves of grass, "bathed the globe" in the nineteenth century. From them developed a unique type of performance, and to them the American theatre owes much of its individuality and excitement.

Do not be misled by the term *popular theatre*. It does not imply that a Booth or a Cushman performing Shakespeare was *un*popular. Rather, the term is meant to suggest a theatre "of the people," or, more strictly, a form of theatre that is different from the "legitimate" stage and that has a powerful appeal to great numbers of people who seldom or never attend a regular play.

Like television, radio, and the motion pictures of today, the popular theatre of the nineteenth century provided much of the entertainment for the masses. For example, Barnum's American Museum, which featured many kinds of popular entertainment before it started to present regular plays, drew the tremendous total of 37,560,000 admissions from 1841 to 1865. New York City alone in 1869 boasted a total of six hundred "concert saloons." In 1846 Christy's Minstrels established themselves at Mechanics Hall in New York and began a series of shows that ran continuously for ten years, reaching a total of at least 2,792 performances.

[1] Phineas T. Barnum, *Life of P. T. Barnum* (Buffalo, N. Y.: The Courier Company Printer, 1888), p. 37.

The lusty growth and great drawing power of the popular theatre were due mainly to the rapid growth of cities and to the polyglot population that poured into these cities. Recall that by 1850 there were 141 cities in the United States with a population of eight thousand or more, and by the end of the century there were over 500. Recall also that into these cities flowed a constantly increasing flood of immigrants. Before 1840 immigrants arrived at the rate of about sixty thousand per year. In 1840 the influx tripled, and in the late 1850s it quadrupled. In every decade thereafter, from 1850 through the 1870s, more than two million aliens arrived. In the 1880s more than five million poured in. By 1890 Chicago's foreign-born numbered as many as had the entire population of the city ten years earlier. In New York City there were as many Italians as in Naples, as many Germans as in Hamburg, twice as many Irish as in Dublin, and two and a half times as many Jews as in Warsaw.

Such a city, composed of so many nationalities speaking so many languages, could not be expected to support the standard repertory of the English-speaking theatre exclusively. The polyglot crowds failed to understand its language and intentions. These patrons flocked to the popular theatre, where spectacle, vaudeville, burlesque, and minstrelsy offered something to please everyone—and to be understood and enjoyed by everyone.

In the early years of the nineteenth century, vaudeville, burlesque, and minstrelsy were appendages of legitimate drama. A standard play was usually embellished with entr'acte specialties and a farcical afterpiece. As the century advanced, the specialties drew away from legitimate drama and emerged as a distinctive type of entertainment housed in theatres of their own.

VAUDEVILLE

The variety show, or vaudeville, was perhaps the first type to achieve independence. A kind of variety show, revealing most of the elements of vaudeville, is as old as public entertainment itself. Since the beginning of recorded history there have been gatherings where the singer, the reciter, the dancer, and the mimic have performed their bits. For many centuries professional entertainers performed their tricks in inns, beer halls, and public squares. So the entr'acte specialties in the American theatre of the nineteenth century were nothing new. But during the century they broke away from legitimate drama and set up shop in public museums like Barnum's and in saloons, beer halls, and concert halls. By the middle of the century, they had grown so popular that every city of any size had regular theatres devoted to variety programs. In New York City, one house was renamed the "New Theatre of Mirth and Variety" and presented on a single bill such numbers as "Elboleros, Cachuchas, Scotch Flings and Strathspeys," a selection of "the most astonishing feats of gymnastics and contortions ever presented in this country," and an act described as the "Flying Cord by the unequalled Mr. Ruggles."[2] Clearly this was the type of

[2] Foster R. Dulles, *America Learns to Play* (New York: Appleton-Century-Crofts, 1940), p. 119.

popular entertainment that was to culminate in the great vaudeville circuits of the early twentieth century.

The first successful chain of vaudeville theatres whose entertainment was supplied for a whole season by a central booking agency was the work of two men: B. F. Keith and E. F. Albee. Both men had experience in circuses and in the Barnum type of museum. In 1885 they formed a partnership and opened the Bijou Theatre in Boston. For the admission price of a single dime, a spectator could watch a vaudeville show that was continuous from ten in the morning until eleven o'clock at night. The venture was a huge success, and the partners quickly capitalized on it. Within two years they opened similar theatres in Philadelphia and Providence, and later in New York. From these beginnings grew Keith and Albee's huge vaudeville circuit, which blanketed the East. From such success grew other circuits, like the Orpheum and the Pantages, which covered the rest of the country.

MINSTRELSY

Vaudeville itself had a powerful competitor in Negro minstrelsy, a type of entertainment that rose suddenly and took the country by storm. Before 1830 American audiences had seen the forerunners of Negro minstrelsy. Many actors had "blacked up" for specific occasions and appeared between the acts of legitimate plays. Very often Negro songs had been sung by circus clowns riding on the backs of horses. However, it was Thomas D. Rice, in 1830, who began the real vogue for minstrel entertainment when he invented his famous song and jig in imitation of an old darky named "Jim Crow." It was an appealing reproduction of Negro character, and Rice instantly became a star. He traveled all over the United States and Europe, playing to packed houses wherever he went. Carl Wittke says, "He was the first blackface performer, who was not only the main actor, but the entire act."[3]

Not until 1843 was the first complete minstrel show invented—that is, a show composed entirely of the singing, dancing, and "gagging" of a blackface company. The first performance was the inspiration of Dan Emmett and three other actors who styled themselves "The Virginia Minstrels." In costumes that later became traditional, they serenaded the audience with music from a violin, a banjo, a tambourine, and bones.

About the same time there was organized the "Christy Minstrels," the most famous troupe in the history of blackface entertainment. This organization gave to the show the traditional form for which it became noted. There was a "first part" with the performers in a semicircle, the interlocutor in the center, and the endmen holding bones and tambourine at the extreme ends. During the first part the performers sang their sentimental ballads, played their banjos and one-string fiddles, and danced their soft-shoe routines, giving way frequently to interruptions from the endmen and interlocutor, who exchanged jokes and insults with each other. The "second part" of the show featured an "olio," or miscellaneous collection, of

---

[3]Carl Wittke, *Tambo and Bones* (Durham, N. C.: Duke University Press, 1930), p. 20.

variety acts, a farcical "stump speech," and a lively "hoe-down" dance for the whole company at the end.

Christy's Minstrels, who perfected this form, played continuously in one hall for ten years. They were so popular and their appeal was so profitable that by 1854 E. P. Christy, the founder, was able to retire with a large fortune. Other troupes were almost as successful. Every city had its resident companies, and traveling groups toured the country from Maine to the gold fields of California. In the urban centers the craze was so great that three performances a day—morning, afternoon, and evening—had to be given.

Many famous performers were developed by nineteenth-century minstrelsy. Two of the most memorable teams were McIntyre and Heath, and Primrose and West. The latter pair headed their own company for thirty years. Probably the most famous single performer was Lew Dockstader, who began his career in blackface in 1873 and continued it well into the twentieth century. He helped to develop other popular minstrels, the most successful of whom was Al Jolson.

The history of the minstrel show reveals two curious developments. First, it was a male profession exclusively. Women never successfully broke into the business. The second curiosity is even stranger. Minstrelsy became a white man's show even though it derived its color, music, humor, and mannerisms from the black man. A few Negro companies competed for attention in the nineteenth century, the most famous, perhaps, being the Georgia Minstrels, organized in 1865 by a Negro named Charles Hicks. This group endured and prospered through several changes of management and finally emerged in 1882 as "Callender's Consolidated Spectacular Colored Minstrels."

During the 1880s the popularity of minstrelsy began to decline. The entertainment lost its characteristic Negro flavor and became a collection of vaudeville acts in blackface. Today the genre survives in the specialty acts of a few blackface teams and as a form of amateur entertainment. An abundance of standard scripts and recorded performances can be found in almost any music store.

BURLESQUE

Burlesque has always been one of the poor but saucy relatives of legitimate drama. Originally, it was what its name implies: a takeoff, or travesty, on a serious play or on serious personalities and events. An Englishman named John Poole is said to have started the modern vogue for takeoffs on classic plays when in 1811 he produced a burlesque of Shakespeare's *Hamlet*. During the 1840s and 1850s in New York, three successful managers—Brougham, Burton, and Mitchell—produced a series of travesties. Presently a new element was introduced into the genre. This was *leg art*—and eventually the new element caused a complete change in the nature of burlesque. Leg art had already been used to embellish melodrama and spectacle. For example, a great sensation was created in 1861 when Ada Isaacs Mencken appeared in a revival of the spectacle *Mazeppa*. Miss Mencken titillated her audience by wearing only tights in a big scene when she was borne off the stage "strapped to the back of a living horse." Five years later a spectacular extravaganza called *The Black Crook* exhibited a veritable forest of ladies' limbs. The gorgeous scenes and female legs were alluring enough to draw audiences to the spectacle for sixteen months and to pour a million dollars into the box office of Niblo's Garden.

The first American presentation that combined leg art with the parody of a serious subject came in 1868, and it was an English import! In that year Lydia Thompson and her "British Blondes" offered New York a production entitled *Ixion, or the Man at the Wheel*. It was a hodge-podge of songs, dances, gags, and impersonations set in the framework of a story from Greek mythology. Most of the dramatic critics were scathing in their ridicule of this "bewilderment of limbs, bella donna, and grease paint," but the public loved it. Miss Thompson and her blondes became the fashion, and from New York they embarked on a series of nationwide tours that continued for ten years and reached as far west as Virginia City, Nevada.

Lydia Thompson, "Mother of Burlesque," as Robinson Crusoe.

Ross Theatre Collection, University of California Library at Berkeley.

The early burlesque shows were considered racy, risqué, and revealing in their time. They would seem dull and decorous to later audiences that attended burlesque to see bumps, grinds, and striptease acts. They would appear without interest or significance to a late-twentieth-century audience that has grown accustomed to completely nude players performing "symbolic and socially significant" sex acts, as in the Living Theatre of Julian and Judith Beck that flourished in the late 1960s.

MUSICAL ENTERTAINMENT

Musical entertainment was a favored feature of the American theatre long before burlesque emerged. During the whole of the eighteenth century, almost every form of dramatic amusement included musical embellishment. Before the curtain rose on a regular play, an orchestra performed; during the intervals between the acts, vocal and instrumental numbers were presented; the afterpiece was often interspersed with songs or was itself an "opera." Even the main drama of the evening was often embellished with incidental songs. Similarly, musical numbers of all kinds strengthened the appeal of circuses, vaudeville, and minstrelsy, and were the principal attraction at the summer pleasure gardens. As early as 1735, in Charleston, the first *ballad opera* to be advertised for performance in America was presented under the title of *Flora, or Hob in the Well.* It was a new form of theatre: a popular play with spoken dialogue and a large number of songs fitted to existing tunes. This new form, ballad opera, had been introduced in England in 1728 by John Gay's *The Beggar's Opera.* Now *Flora* adopted the same format, but *Flora* did not achieve a long life. As soon as *The Beggar's Opera* crossed the Atlantic, John Gay's work became the rage.

America had to wait until 1796 to enjoy a musical show written and composed by Americans. This was *The Archers, or Mountaineers of Switzerland,* a version of the William Tell story written by none other than the father of American drama, William Dunlap, with music composed by Benjamin Carr. The production included solos, duets, trios, choral music, love songs, comic songs, dances, and marches as well as plot and dialogue, and thus may qualify as America's first musical comedy.

In the last quarter of the nineteenth century, a more sophisticated form of musical show, the comic opera, achieved popularity in America. French *opéra-bouffe* and Italian grand opera had already established a following in this country. Then in 1879, *H. M. S. Pinafore,* by the English team of William Gilbert and Arthur Sullivan, appeared on Broadway and introduced a captivating kind of comic opera that increased the popularity of musical drama. This popularity was further enhanced at the end of the century and during the early years of the twentieth century, when such romantic light or comic operas as Franz Lehar's *The Merry Widow* (1907) and Oscar Straus's *The Chocolate Solider* (1910) were produced. These forms of musical drama exerted an influence on the American musical show by presenting more sophisticated scores, better integration of plot and music, and greater attention to character development.

The further developments of the American musical play that occurred during the twentieth century and the landmark productions that illustrated these developments—such as *Show Boat* of 1927 and *Oklahoma!* of 1943—will be outlined in later chapters.

CIRCUS

Still another form of theatre that became dear to the heart of the common man was the circus. It appeared very early in American history. During colonial days, little menageries and bands of itinerant acrobats flourished on the East Coast. They traveled from town to town, delighting the country folks who never saw any other kind of theatre. In the eighteenth century, many of these troupes ceased traveling. Amphitheatres were built for them, and here they took up permanent residence and played for a complete season, just like the resident companies of legitimate drama. To embellish their offerings, they added variety numbers from the regular stage and riding acts from equestrian drama. In the early years of the nineteenth century, they surrendered their permanent homes and took to the road again. The traveling troupes were small at first, comprising a few performers and a few wagons. However, as the population of the country increased and as the roads improved, so did the circus. Before 1830, the first circus tent appeared; by the 1840s the first bands were added as well as bareback riding and other dangerous feats. The development of the railroad provided an additional boost and gave rise to the convenient system of housing the entire circus in specially built cars owned by the troupe and capable of rolling from town to town during the performance season.

Almost as important as the railroad to circus development was the personality and ingenuity of P. T. Barnum. He joined the ranks of circus managers in the 1850s and became the greatest showman of them all. His inventiveness and originality built the circus into a dazzling combination of riders, acrobats, clowns, musicians, alluring ladies, freaks, and ferocious wild animals like the "blood-sweating" hippopotamus—all of them performing, not in a single ring, but simultaneously in two or three rings.

Barnum was not the only big name in circus business. Other successful managers who contributed to the development of this unique form of entertainment were William C. Coup, James H. Bailey, the Ringling brothers, the Sells brothers, and the Forepaughs. However, Barnum had the knack of outdistancing them—or of joining them. In 1880, for example, when his circus was wiped out by a devastating fire, he quickly rallied and joined forces with James A. Bailey. Thus was born the famous partnership of Barnum and Bailey and with it, "the greatest show on earth."

The golden age of the circus came at the end of the nineteenth and the beginning of the twentieth centuries. During those years, the Greatest Show on Earth and many other competing troupes criss-crossed the nation, bringing thrills and glamour to towns of all sizes. Circus day was unforgettably exciting to the

P. T. Barnum, the greatest single name in circus history.
Courtesy, The Bancroft Library, University of California, Berkeley.

smaller towns, which as yet had no movies, radio, or television. It provided spectacle and entertainment, romance and color, and a wealth of memories that older fans still cherish. With the rise of the movies, of automobile transportation, and of the many forms of sports and of mechanical entertainment, the great days of the circus dwindled. Today there is little left of the tradition. The remaining troupes have abandoned tents and now appear, if at all, only in the great sports arenas of the big cities.

EDWARD HARRIGAN

Another achievement in the history of the popular theatre is the dramatic work of Edward Harrigan. For a time during the last quarter of the nineteenth century, Harrigan produced a unique and wonderful form of farce that was truly theatre and truly popular.

Harrigan and his partner Tony Hart began their stage careers as variety artists. They specialized in sketches of city life, presenting humorously and faithfully a wide variety of familiar American characters. In these skits Harrigan acted the male role and Hart impersonated the female, but the authorship of the skits was almost entirely the work of Harrigan.

From these vaudeville acts the full-length plays of Harrigan emerged. The process was a gradual one. In their first form the sketches were popular songs ridiculing some well-known personage or type. The song led to the duet and the duet to the dialogue. Under the inspiration of audience response, the dialogue was elaborated and lengthened. New incidents were improvised from performance to performance, and eventually enough material was created for a full-length play. Just when the first of these was born is not known, although one of the earliest and most enduring is the comedy *Old Lavender,* first produced in 1877 and expanded in 1878.

Out of the skits on Irish and German immigrant types grew the most famous Harrigan plays, the "Mulligan Guard" series. The first of these, *The Mulligan Guard Ball,* was produced in 1879 and ran for one hundred nights. It was followed with great success by seven or eight other plays all recounting the adventures of a group of Irish and German immigrants, the Mulligans and the Lochmullers, and their Negro and Italian friends. These plays, remarkably free from coarseness and lewdness, were glorious mixtures of wild burlesque, lilting songs, dancing and military drills, outrageous puns, breathtaking spectacle, and—above all—knockdown, dragout, slambang farce. They were so popular in their time that together with other comedies from the facile pen of their author, at least twenty-three of them achieved runs of more than one hundred performances each on Broadway—"phenomenal displays of longevity in those days."[4]

Another colorful figure who contributed to the tradition of the popular theatre in America was Charles Hoyt. His plays were related to the comedies of Edward Harrigan because, like the Harrigan plays, they were close to the vaudeville tradition. Songs were interspersed throughout, low comedy "gagging" was plentiful, and the actors were given ample opportunity for comic improvisation. In the first scene of Hoyt's *A Texas Steer,* for example, the action stops while four cowboys sing a quartet. At the end of each act of the play there are gags and tableaux suggested for use in the curtain calls, a feature included in many other plays of the period. Our modern musical comedy is directly influenced by the vaudeville-Harrigan-Hoyt tradition.

OTHER FORMS OF POPULAR THEATRE

Three other entertainment phenomena of the nineteenth century might be included as forms of popular theatre. One of them is the "Tom Show"—the colloquial name given to a traveling circuslike production of *Uncle Tom's Cabin.* The other two, Chautauqua and Lyceum, were started as lecture series or educational institutes to satisfy the American passion for self-improvement. They eventually presented entertainment of all kinds, including regular plays. However, they should be considered not as a separate dramatic genre like minstrelsy, but rather as a mechanism for presenting various established forms of theatre both popular and legitimate.

[4] E. J. Kahn, Jr., *The Merry Partner: The Age and Stage of Harrigan and Hart* (New York: Random House, Inc., 1955), p. 14.

From a survey of the motley and sprightly offerings of the popular theatre —burlesque, vaudeville, minstrelsy, circus, and the Harrigan-Hoyt comics—two interesting conclusions emerge: (1) these types are intimately related, and (2) in all of them the technique of presentation is similar.

Successful actors in the popular theatre needed diverse abilities. They had to possess attractive personalities and the ability to project them quickly and directly. They had to establish a feeling of fellowship with their audiences and be instantly intelligible, but never labored or highbrow. They had to perform with easy speed and possess skill at improvisation. The total effect, as Walter Prichard Eaton wrote, had to be one of "unforced, jovial intimacy between audience and stage, of spontaneous fooling, of impromptu jest. . . ."[5]

The American stage was enriched by the training and the opportunities offered by the popular theatre. Thousands of performers of every level of competence served their apprenticeship there. One of the most famous, and who epitomized all the skills and endowments of the variety artist, was the sensationally successful Charlotte Crabtree, affectionately known and better remembered as "Lotta." Her career and style of acting will serve as a representative example of the countless performers who were produced by the popular theatre and who exhibited the essential characteristics of the variety artist: personal magnetism, congeniality, deftness, naturalness, articulateness, and skill at improvisation.

Lotta began her dramatic training in California at the age of six as a pupil of the notorious Lola Montez, who taught her to dance, sing ballads, and ride horseback. Presently the child also learned to play the banjo, and with these skills, plus her captivating looks and personality, she launched a career that was to make her a national favorite. She first became the darling of the California mining camps, which she trouped for ten years under the shrewd and tireless supervision of her mother. In 1864 she left the Golden State and began her rapid and complete conquest of the rest of the nation.

In 1867, at age twenty, she appeared in New York as the star of a play written especially for her by the talented John Brougham. This was a dramatization of Dickens's *Old Curiosity Shop* called *Little Nell and the Marchioness.* It was a great success and ran for six weeks. Later it proved a smash hit whenever it was presented in the United States. Thereafter and for the rest of her life, Lotta appeared either in burlesque or extravaganza or in light, flimsy vehicles that had been written especially for her and that enabled her to exploit her sprightly charms and captivating skills.

The influence of the technique of the popular theatre was felt early in the legitimate theatre. Audiences became accustomed to entertainment that was varied, moved swiftly, and appealed to the eye. In the legitimate theatre they became restless during long speeches and wordy dialogue. Theatrical managers began to speed up the action and dialogue in their productions and embellish them with eye-filling costumes and scenery. For several decades American plays, in contrast

[5]Walter Prichard Eaton, *The Actor's Heritage* (Boston: The Atlantic Monthly Press, 1924), p. 214.

Lotta Crabtree as a drummer boy.

Ross Theatre Collection, University of California Library at Berkeley.

to British, were notable for the swiftness of their pace. Today even British productions have succumbed to the speeding-up process begun many years ago by American performers.

The American popular theatre of the nineteenth century was a rich and lusty creation. With its roots deep in the fun-loving, polyglot character of America, it achieved a glorious popularity and revealed the magic of theatre to countless thousands of citizens, old and new. It also shaped the development of several forms of native drama and created a recognizable technique of acting, the influence of which is still discernible.

10

Melodrama Continues to Star-- with a Rival in the Wings

American Playwriting, 1850-1890

The mass audiences of the nineteenth century loved the offerings of the popular theatre. They also supported an astonishing variety of plays of every kind. The range of dramatic offerings during the second half of the century was more extensive, perhaps, than it has ever been in the history of the American theatre. Besides vaudeville, minstrelsy, burlesque, and the circus, there was the standard repertory of Shakespeare and other established dramatists. Besides the unique comedies of Harrigan and Hoyt, there were the romantic tragedies of George Henry Boker and his followers. Besides the comedies featuring Yankees, fireboys, or other American types, there were importations from England, France, and Germany. Besides plays dramatizing American history, past or present, there were dramas that touched on contemporary problems. The means of producing such varied offerings were as extensive as the offerings themselves. The nation was amply supplied with playhouses, companies, and versatile performers capable of meeting any challenge created by the dramatist.

Most of the plays of the period, whatever their intention or subject matter, continued to exhibit the attitudes and devices of melodrama. The conditions that had originally created the love of this genre persisted well into the second half of the nineteenth century. In fact, the second half of the century begins with the success of the most popular melodrama ever written: *Uncle Tom's Cabin.*

UNCLE TOM'S CABIN

Consider some of the records set by *Uncle Tom's Cabin* after it was dramatized by George L. Aiken in 1852:

Following its premiere in Troy, New York, it ran one hundred nights in that city, which had a population of only thirty thousand.

After its premiere in New York City at the National Theatre, it ran almost three hundred performances and during some weeks was played three times a day.

At one time, five playhouses in New York and an equal number in London were presenting it simultaneously.

By 1854, traveling companies performing the play in tents were blanketing the country.

By 1879, after hibernating for the duration of the Civil War, the play was being toured by forty-nine traveling companies. By 1899, five hundred traveling companies were presenting it.

The countries of Western Europe, from Denmark to Spain, joined in the craze for the play.

In 1901, a spectacular New York production used two hundred singers and dancers and eighteen gigantic sets.

After the turn of the century at least twelve movie versions were filmed.

As late as 1927, a dozen traveling companies continued to produce the play.

It is safe to conclude that no other play in the history of drama has been produced so many times. *Uncle Tom's Cabin* is an all-time world champion.

Harriet Beecher Stowe's novel, from which the play was made, appeared in 1852. Early that year two different dramatizations were tried unsuccessfully. Not until Aiken's version was produced in Troy, New York, late in the year did the rage for *Uncle Tom* begin. George L. Aiken, only twenty-two years old, was commissioned to construct the play by his uncle G. C. Howard, manager of the theatre in Troy and father of a talented little daughter named Cordelia. Howard felt that Cordelia would make an ideal Little Eva, and he was right. She became the most famous Little Eva in the history of the play, a phenomenon within a phenomenon. Supported by her father, her mother, and three other relatives, she was the star of a company that performed the play for thirty-five years, until her father died in 1887.

George Aiken's dramatization, one of the many that appeared, is a loose sequence of scenes that closely follow the course of the novel and faithfully reproduce Mrs. Stowe's dialogue. The opening scenes are laid in the Shelby household in Kentucky. We meet kindly Mr. and Mrs. Shelby and three of their slaves: the saintly Uncle Tom, the handsome Eliza, and her child. We also meet Eliza's husband, George Harris, a gifted, proud Negro who is being abused by his master (not Mr. Shelby). George decides to run away to Canada; and Eliza, after she learns that Shelby is so deeply in debt that he must sell her and her child to raise money, decides to follow her husband. Then come the scenes of Eliza's flight, her pursuit by lawyer Marks and his men, and her escape by crossing the Ohio River on cakes of ice. In later scenes we see Eliza reunited with her husband. Both of them escape their pursuers and reach freedom through the help of Quaker friends.

In the famous scene of Eliza crossing the ice, there are no bloodhounds either in Mrs. Stowe's novel or in Aiken's play. The ferocious dogs were added later by ingenious stage managers and became an indispensable addition to the thrills of the play.

In the second act, the setting shifts to the St. Clare mansion in New Orleans. We meet the dashing husband, St. Clare; his spoiled and selfish wife, Marie; his

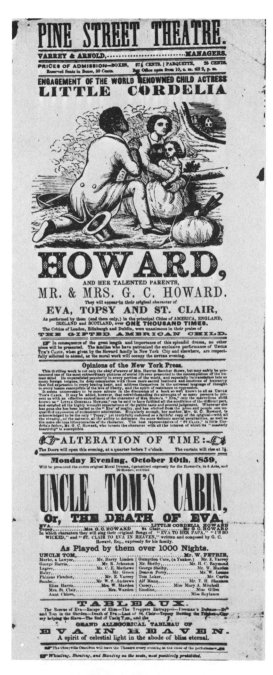

Playbill for *Uncle Tom's Cabin.*

Mrs. George C. Howard in her original character of Topsy.

Hoblitzelle Theatre Arts Library, Humanities Research Center, University of Texas at Austin.

eccentric aunt, Ophelia; and his angelic daughter, Eva. We also meet the impish young pickaninny, Topsy, and again the saintly Uncle Tom. Uncle Tom has been sold by Shelby and purchased by St. Clare after Uncle Tom rescued Little Eva from drowning. A beautiful spiritual relationship has developed between Eva and Tom, but it is too beautiful to last. Eva fades and dies, her father is killed before he can free Uncle Tom as he had promised, and Uncle Tom is once again sold, this time to the wicked Simon Legree. The final scenes of the play show Uncle Tom's persecution and torture, his saintly endurance and forgiveness, and his death—just as he is about to be rescued by young George Shelby, son of his former owner.

The play, without question, is melodrama. It exhibits all the devices and appeals so popular in earlier melodramas. Yet the material is often good, and its tremendous impact on nineteenth-century audiences is understandable. The characters and situations were accepted as real. Certainly the slavery issue was agonizingly real, the unhumanity of human beings to each other was real, and a belief like Uncle Tom's in a benevolent heaven was real to most playgoers. If they could sympathize with the misfortune of a Spartacus or a Metamora, it is no wonder that they were aroused by the tribulations of Uncle Tom—as long as these tribulations were effectively dramatized.

A host of special traditions became associated with this extraordinary play. Choruses singing sentimental and religious music were commonly added; so were the bloodhounds that pursue Eliza, in addition to many other spectacular effects. The touring companies adopted many of the practices of the circus. They carried their own tents and equipment; they staged street parades with bands, horses, floats, singers, and dancers; they ballyhooed their productions with gaudy posters and stentorian barkers; they sometimes presented sideshow attractions; and in a few instances they even tried to equal the appeal of the three-ring circus by presenting the play with a double cast: two Uncle Toms, two Evas, two Topsys, and so on were on the stage at the same time. This incredible absurdity was managed in a number of ways. Sometimes the two performers of the single character took turns delivering the lines; sometimes one actor did all the speaking while the other pantomimed the action.

The entire history of *Uncle Tom's Cabin,* as a novel and as a play, is unique and extraordinary. There may never be another phenomenon like it. Although dramatic literature was not enriched, and although the devices of melodrama were glorified by the success of the play, still the history of the American theatre would be poorer if the prodigy of *Uncle Tom's Cabin* had never occurred.

THE OCTOROON

Uncle Tom's Cabin dominated the stage in the years preceding the Civil War. A few—very few—other plays revealed the evils of slavery. One of these, entitled *The Escape, or a Leap for Freedom,* was never produced but holds the distinction of being the earliest extant play written by an American Negro. The author was William Wells Brown, who lived from about 1816 to 1884 and is not to be confused with the Mr. Brown who was impresario of the short-lived African Theatre of 1821-23. William Wells Brown wrote his play in 1858 and read it to audiences for several years thereafter, always with favorable effect. The play, however, is a typical melodrama that presents a harrowing account of a slave's experience in the leap for freedom.

Probably the best of the antislavery plays is Dion Boucicault's drama, *The Octoroon,* presented somewhat daringly in 1859, just two years before the attack on Fort Sumter. This play is astonishingly complex and action-filled, a classic example of melodrama in full flower. In fact, it contains almost every melodramatic device and thrill invented by the human mind. For example, there is the heavily mortgaged plantation with the upright young man, George, and his kindly aunt trying to save it. There is the honest, shrewd Yankee attempting to help them and the dastardly villain who steals the letter from Liverpool that will save the plantation. There is the beautiful octoroon slave girl, Zoe, noble, self-sacrificing, and silently in love with George. There is the theft of the papers that would free Zoe and the murder of the boy, Paul—both by the villain, with the murder being

Scene from Dion Boucicault's *The Octoroon:* The slave market,
sale of the octoroon (November 30, 1861).

Hoblitzelle Theatre Arts Library, Humanities Research Center, University of Texas at Austin.

recorded on the film of an unnoticed camera. There is the heiress who wants to marry George and is willing to buy the plantation to get him; the foreclosing of the mortgage; the revelation that Zoe is a slave; and her sale to the villain. There is the trial of an innocent Indian boy for the murder of Paul, the sudden appearance of the photo that shows the murderer, and the recovery of the stolen letter from Liverpool. Then occurs the trial of the real villain; his escape; the burning of a ship; the villain's pursuit, capture, and death at the hands of friends of the murdered boy. Finally, there is Zoe's midnight visit to obtain a dose of poison, her suicide just before the arrival of the good news that the plantation is saved, and her death in the arms of George, the man she cannot marry because she is an octoroon.

If there exists a classic example of the contrivances of melodrama, this is it. If any evidence is needed to prove that melodrama continued to flourish in the second half of the nineteenth century, this is it. Finally, if any proof is needed that the writing of good melodrama requires inventiveness, skill, and professional talent, this also is it.

OTHER PRE-CIVIL WAR PLAYS

Although few plays in the pre-Civil War years dealt with the agonizing conflicts between the North and the South, there were dozens of plays of every other type. Some of these plays dramatized episodes in American history, continuing a tradition established by many of our earlier dramatists. In 1857, for example, a play by Oliver Bell Bunce entitled *Love in '76* was produced. Its setting is the Revolutionary

War, its heroine a sprightly American beauty, Rose Elsworth, who outwits the British commandant and saves her lover through a series of audacious intrigues and maneuvers. In the following year, 1858, an example of contemporary American history in satiric form appeared on the stage. It was a play by Thomas D. English entitled *The Mormons, or Life in Salt Lake City*, portraying in comic fashion how Brigham Young outwits a New York alderman who has traveled west to teach Mr. Young about politics.

Another type of play that continued to be written after mid-century was the comedy of manners. These plays, in the tradition of *The Contrast* and *Fashion*, sometimes portrayed the virtues of the American citizen in contrast to the stupidity and affectation of Europeans; sometimes they exposed the foolishness of American parvenus and social climbers. Mrs. Sidney F. Bateman's comedy *Self* (1856) does the latter, satirizing the social and business morality of New York City in a manner reminiscent of *Fashion* but much less skillfully than Mrs. Mowatt's play. A funnier, better-written comedy of the same type appeared in 1858. Called *Americans in Paris*, and written by William H. Hurlbert, it amusingly presents the misunderstandings and complications that develop between two American couples who are living in Paris and trying to be a part of the society of that city.

Contemporary with the many social comedies of that period were a variety of other types of entertaining plays. For example, a whole series of comedies featuring Mose the Fireboy began in 1848 and continued for twenty years. Each of these plays was a loosely knit sequence of scenes presenting the exploits and adventures of the dauntless hero, Mose. The first, entitled *A Glance at New York*, by B. A. Baker, shows Mose protecting an out-of-town visitor from the big-city crooks and then introducing the visitor to the colorful low life of New York City. This first play was so successful that, like Tarzan of the Apes in the twentieth century, it sired a whole series of plays revolving around Mose. The popular audiences loved him and followed his melodramatic adventures for many years.

Another exciting adventure play that thrilled New York in 1857 was Dion Boucicault's *The Poor of New York*, which was borrowed from a French play, *Les Pauvres de Paris*. Boucicault, with customary ingenuity, capitalized on the popularity of the play by producing it many times in the United States and England, each time changing the title to give it local impact. As the play made the rounds of theatrical cities it became *The Poor of London, The Poor of Liverpool*, or *The Poor of San Francisco*. But whatever the title, it remained the same plot and action, including a spectacular fire scene, and it remained a typical nineteenth-century melodrama exhibiting every contrivance that could be invented by the master contriver, Boucicault. Today, it lends itself to burlesque as easily as does its famous relative, *The Drunkard*.

FRANCESCA DA RIMINI

In 1855, when the stages of America were largely monopolized by such plays as *Uncle Tom's Cabin*, the Mose series, and the dramas of Boucicault, there appeared an unusually fine specimen of romantic tragedy. It was George Henry Boker's

Francesca da Rimini, destined to be admired and played long after melodramas of the time had lost their appeal.

George Henry Boker (1823-1890) was a cultivated man of letters who had chosen writing as a career. Fortunately he was financially well off and did not have to depend on his writing to earn a living. In 1855, after authoring six dramas—five of which were produced—he composed his masterpiece. *Francesca da Rimini.* The play was produced at the Broadway Theatre in New York with Edward L. Davenport cast as Lanciotto, the leading man, and Madame Elizabeth Ponisi, a popular English tragedienne, as Francesca. The initial production was not as successful as it should have been, considering the merits of the play, but it was applauded by many discerning playgoers and admired by actors as well. Twenty-seven years later, in 1882, Lawrence Barrett revived *Francesca* at Haverly's Theatre in Philadelphia and continued to produce it with success for several seasons. In 1901 Otis Skinner again revived it, this time at the Grand Opera House in Chicago, and once more it drew admiring audiences throughout the country. It is still produced occasionally by community or college theatres.

The tragic tale of Paolo and Francesca is one of the great love stories of the Western world. It has fascinated and inspired artists of all kinds—poets, musicians, sculptors, and playwrights. Boker's drama is considered the best rendering of the

Otis Skinner's *Francesca da Rimini,* Act III.

Hoblitzelle Theatre Arts Library, Humanities Research Center, University of Texas at Austin.

story in English and possibly in any language. It is based on historical characters. In the latter part of the thirteenth century, there was a Francesca, daughter of the lord of Ravenna, who married Giovanni, son of the ruler of Rimini. Giovanni was a man of great valor but was deformed of body and vengeful of mind. When he discovered that his wife and his brother Paolo were in love, he killed them both.

Boker set his drama in the correct historical period, which provided rich opportunity for color and pageantry, but he transformed Giovanni, now called Lanciotto, into an admirable leader who, although misshapen of body, has "the noblest heart in Rimini." He and Boker's other characters are human and believable; their actions develop from their character and from the situation in which they are placed. The tragic sequence of events is not contrived but develops step by step from small mistakes and errors of judgment. The play has no real villain. Pepe, the spiteful jester who informs Lanciotto that his brother and his wife are in love, does not motivate the action; he only expedites it. The three principal characters all enlist our sympathy and understanding. If there is guilt, they all share the guilt and the tragic consequences.

Francesca da Rimini is generally considered to be the culmination and conclusion of the vogue for romantic tragedy in American playwriting. It may well be the culmination, but it is not the conclusion. The demand for such plays dwindled but did not disappear. Romantic tragedies and romantic historical plays continued to be written and produced in every succeeding decade after 1855. They are still being written, and sometimes even produced.

RIP VAN WINKLE

Francesca da Rimini was a refreshing change from the contrived melodramas so beloved of the public in 1855, but it altered no tastes and redirected no trends. This is forcefully illustrated when we consider the history of *Rip Van Winkle,* a play produced in 1865, ten years after *Francesca,* which held the stage for forty years. It held the stage, in fact, as long as Joseph Jefferson III played the leading role. When he died in 1905, the play died too, which suggests that it was not the drama but the performance that earned the play its vast popularity.

The legend of Rip Van Winkle, as created by Washington Irving, is simple and charming. Rip is a happy-go-lucky idler, beloved of children and dogs, who leaves the care of his scraggly farm to a hard-working, sharp-tongued wife. One afternoon he goes hunting, climbs higher into the Catskill mountains than usual, and stays longer than usual. When he starts to descend he is led to a mysterious amphitheatre in the hills, where he finds Henrick Hudson and his ghostly crew playing at tenpins. Rip, pressed into service as the bartender, begins to tipple on the side and soon falls into a deep sleep. When he awakes, the amphitheatre is gone. He returns to his village to find that his wife is dead, his son is grown up, and his daughter is married. He realizes that he has been asleep for twenty years. After he establishes his identity, his daughter gives him a home and he becomes a happy old relic who spends his time spinning tales.

This simple and intriguing sketch was written by Washington Irving in 1819. Within a few years, at least three dramatic versions were tried but without much success. However, Jefferson was captivated by the possibilities of the story and in 1865 commissioned the ubiquitous Boucicault to rewrite one of the early dramatic versions. Boucicault, as usual, obliged. His dramatization was a flimsy thing; but Jefferson produced it both in London and New York, and his portrayal of Rip won great acclaim. For the rest of his life, Jefferson continued to play Rip. He also altered, reshaped, reworked, and improved the play year by year so that as the drama finally evolved, it was as much the work of Jefferson as of Boucicault.

But what a change from the sketch of Washington Irving! The simple tale of a ghostly crew and a twenty-year sleep was not enough to satisfy the taste of the times. What was added? Intrigue, villainy, and the eventual triumph of virtue, of course. The villainy is furnished by a scheming pair of villagers named Derrick and Cockles who wish to beat Rip out of his property. They also want to ensnare his wife and daughter into marrying them. Rip is unaware of the marriage scheme, but he does suspect villainy when Derrick presses him to sign a deed involving Rip's farm. Rip refuses to sign and tucks the deed away into his game bag, where it remains for twenty years. Later the same day, when Rip returns to his home in a tipsy state, the patience of his wife is exhausted and she drives him out of the house—into a raging storm, of course. Then follow Rip's climb into the mountains, his adventure with the ghostly crew, and his twenty-year sleep. When he finally awakens and returns to his village, which is now much changed, he discovers that Derrick has married his wife and has reduced her to the status of a household drudge. Cockles is about to force himself on Rip's daughter, who has held him off, hoping for the return of her childhood sweetheart who apparently has been lost at sea. When everything seems hopeless, Rip reveals himself, claims his wife, and produces the twenty-year-old deed, which proves that the farm is still his. The daughter's long-lost love miraculously reappears and saves her from Cockles. The villains are utterly routed, the Van Winkle family is happily reunited, and the play ends with Rip summoning the neighbors, their children, and their dogs for an old-time celebration.

Just as Mrs. Mowatt in 1845 added a melodramatic subplot to her social satire, *Fashion,* so Boucicault in 1865 embellished the sketch about Rip Van Winkle with the same kind of villainy and intrigue. Jefferson retained the embellishments as long as he performed the play, which was until 1904. The appeal of melodrama, obviously, is tenacious.

AUGUSTIN DALY

As the years went by, the continuing popularity of melodrama placed greater and greater demands on the ingenuity of the dramatist. So long as the characters of a play were stereotyped and the emphasis was on plot, playwrights were continually called upon to manufacture new twists and surprises, mysteries and sensations, thrills and excitement of all kinds. They responded with remarkable inventiveness.

For example, in James J. McCloskey's thriller, *Across the Continent, or Scenes from New York Life and the Pacific Railroad,* written in the 1860s, the climactic moment comes when the hero, a railroad station master, taps out a message on that new invention, the telegraph, to summon help that will save him and his friends from massacre by Indians. The use of the telegraph for suspense and for rescues was repeated many times thereafter, one famous example being in William Gillette's play about espionage during the Civil War entitled *Secret Service* (1896). But it was Augustin Daly, producer, director, and playwright, who introduced some of the most sensational thrills to be found in the plays of the period. His first original drama, *Under the Gaslight* (1867) presents the spectacle of the hero tied to a railroad track with a train rushing down upon him. *The Red Scarf,* produced in 1868, introduces the horror of the hero tied to a log which is about to be sawed in half. *The Dark City* (1877) shows the hero in a perilous situation, descending from a roof by a rope which the villain cuts from its anchorage. Other plays by Daly feature burning ships or buildings, attacks by wild Indians, raging storms, and numerous other sensations that were the stock thrills of melodrama. Undoubtedly Daly had learned to use such effects from studying the plays of Boucicault and other popular writers of melodrama.

Augustin Daly wrote original plays and also made or helped to make numerous adaptations from British and American novels and from the works of continental dramatists. His list of accomplishments is long. With substantial help from his brother, Joseph, he had a hand in creating at least ninety plays that reached public production—most of them by his resident company. These plays—both his adaptations and his original works—cover an amazing range of settings and subject

Scene from *A Working Girl's Wrongs.*
Hoblitzelle Theatre Arts Library, Humanities Research Center, University of Texas at Austin.

matter. His first original play, *Under the Gaslight* (1867), has a realistic setting in contemporary New York and purports to give an authentic account of life in the big city. Four years later, he tried his hand at a frontier drama, calling the play *Horizon,* and he earned the praise of several critics by portraying the West in a more realistic manner than other frontier plays had done. After this, Daly turned to social comedy or melodrama in such plays as *Divorce* (1871) and *Pique* (1875), whose settings are the fashionable homes of the wealthy.

Daly's plays were usually great popular successes. Like William Dunlap before him, Daly possessed a keen sense of what the public enjoyed and a flair for creating episodes, characters, and staging that were novel, appealing, and exciting. His talents were exercised not only in the plays he wrote or adapted but also in his productions of such standard dramatists as Shakespeare and Sheridan. He made important contributions as one of the first master directors, or règisseurs, in the American theatre. He was a prolific dramatist who achieved outstanding popular success with many of his plays, but whose contributions, following the tastes of the times, did not revitalize contemporary dramaturgy in any significant way.

BRONSON HOWARD

A more important figure in the development of American playwriting is Bronson Howard (1842-1908), often called the dean of American drama and our first truly professional playwright. In 1888 he produced the most successful drama to use material and ideas from the Civil War. This is *Shenandoah,* an immensely popular melodrama that made a place for itself in the history of the American stage. It achieved its fame during a time when the older traditions of playwriting were on the wane and the movement toward realism in literature was gaining strength. Yet *Shenandoah,* as contrived a drama as can be found, entranced its audiences for several years. It still entrances its readers because of the craftsmanship of its construction.

Many Civil War plays had been produced before *Shenandoah,* some of which deserve mention. While the war was being fought, playwrights often presented dramatizations of climactic battles within a few weeks, or even days, after the actual event. For example, four weeks after the battle of Bull Run, a play by the same name was presented at the New Bowery Theatre in New York. Far more astonishing is a play entitled *The Capture of Fort Donelson,* which was seen just six days after the event. These plays, of course, were not documentary in the modern sense of the word. They used standard melodramatic plots modified to fit the current situation. They added spectacular battle scenes that purportedly reproduced the actual battle being celebrated. Contemporary titles, names, and allusions lent topical interest. Instant drama of this kind, or the illusion of instant drama, had been a tradition of the American theatre since the Revolutionary War.

After the Civil War was over, many plays about the conflict appeared. Most of them are of negligible merit or interest. An exception is Dion Boucicault's *Belle Lamar,* produced in 1874, which portrays the complications that arise when a girl from the South must choose between loyalty to her region and loyalty to her sweetheart, who is an officer of the Union army. Although the play is full of suspense, surprises, and exciting action, like all of Boucicault's dramas, it failed to stir much interest in its time. But when *Shenandoah* came along, the public was captivated.

The action of *Shenandoah* is far too involved to be summarized briefly. It is sufficient to say that few plays of any genre have a more intricate plot than *Shenandoah* and few manipulate so many characters and complications so adroitly. Certainly it is a triumph of craftsmanship to introduce four pairs of lovers and to maintain interest in them through misunderstandings of all kinds, to introduce several varieties of comic relief, and at the same time to fight a war complete with bombardments, espionage, villainy, heroism, retreats, rescues, and final victory. Yet Howard's play accomplishes all of this with dexterity and ease. Moreover, the contrivances are unobtrusive because the characters involved are more lifelike and their conversation is more natural than in many other plays of the period. The eye is diverted by colorful spectacle and the senses are dazzled by numerous realistic effects. General Sheridan, for example, actually gallops across the stage on his heroic horse. A final triumph is the balance of sympathies between North and South. The points of view of both areas are presented fairly and sympathetically and the spectator is never asked to take sides.

Eighteen years before *Shenandoah,* Howard wrote his first successful play. This was a clever farce comedy entitled *Saratoga* that was produced with success at Augustin Daly's Fifth Avenue Theatre in 1870. Howard continued to write plays for the next thirty-six years, ending with an unproduced drama called *Kate* written in 1906, two years before his death. Of the eighteen or nineteen plays that he wrote or helped to write, two or three besides *Shenandoah* achieved outstanding success. One of these was *Young Mrs. Winthrop* (1882), a satire on the growing social restrictions of Howard's world. Another was *One of Our Girls* (1885), which contrasts the differing standards of American and French girls; it enjoyed a run of two hundred nights. An even greater success was achieved by *The Henrietta* (1887), which satirizes the conflict between a domineering capitalist father and his two sons.

In all his plays Howard demonstrated with increasing impressiveness his skill at inventing original situations, his gift for writing clever dialogue, and his mastery of theatrical effects. His settings are always refined, his characters are always ladies and gentlemen, and his aim is always to entertain and amuse. When he introduced social problems, they were used as a framework for the dramatic situations he was so good at inventing and for the clever dialogue he was so good at writing. *Shenandoah* is an excellent example of his talent as a playwright and of his conviction that a dramatist should not consider himself a literary man but a craftsman of the theatre.

Howard will be remembered for *Shenandoah* and also for the leadership he gave to American playwrights. He organized them into a successful guild—originally called the American Dramatists Club, later the Society of American Dramatists and Composers—and he led the campaign to strengthen the copyright laws. Through his leadership the royalty system was established, whereby every playwright was guaranteed the right to collect royalties on his own writing. In earlier years a few dramatists, like Boucicault, had been strong enough to demand and collect royalties. Now, through Howard's efforts, every playwright was legally empowered to do so. For the first time in the history of the American theatre, playwrights could support themselves successfully by the single activity of writing plays. Howard was the first to do so through playwriting alone.

FRONTIER DRAMA

While Bronson Howard was excelling in the presentation of life among the upper classes, other dramatists were depicting life on the American frontier. Such plays have an enduring appeal for American audiences. They were popular in the nine-teenth century; they are the delight of millions of moviegoers and television watchers in the twentieth century. During all this time, the genre has followed the same basic formula of melodrama. The hero is the rough but valiant and resourceful frontiers-man; the heroine is a pure, modest maiden with hidden strength in her character; the villain is either an ugly gunslinger or a suave, polished hypocrite; the conflict that develops runs a predictable course, but after the perils, fights, narrow escapes, and misunderstandings have occurred, the villain and his bad guys are defeated; the hero and his good guys are victorious.

The locale of the early frontier plays is a good index of the progress of the westward movement. *Nick of the Woods,* produced in 1838, is set in Kentucky, then a part of the frontier. *The Arkansas Traveller* (1870) and *Davy Crockett* (1872) indicate that the frontier had moved to Arkansas and Tennessee. It had actually moved farther than that because Augustin Daly, in 1871, used California as his principal setting in *Horizon.* So did a host of other frontier plays like Bret Harte's *Two Men of Sandy Bar* (1876), and his *Ah Sin,* written with Mark Twain in 1877. In the same group are Joaquin Miller's *The Danites in the Sierra* (1887) and Bartley Campbell's *My Partner* (1879).

My Partner, considered to be the best of Campbell's plays, was first produced at the Union Square Theatre, New York. It achieved wide popularity and held the stage for several years. Although its characters and plot have few original touches, *My Partner* is representative of the general run of frontier plays and can serve as an example of the type. The setting of the play is a small mining town high in the mountains of northern California. Joe and Ned are long-time partners, and both love the same girl, Mary. Ned has won her heart—and has seduced her. When this is discovered by the blunt, honorable Joe, whose love for Mary has never been re-vealed, he forces Ned to swear to marry the girl. Before it can be arranged, Ned is killed by the villain Scraggs, who steals Ned's gold and arranges the evidence to cast suspicion on Joe. Joe is arrested for murder. Mary runs away and has her baby, which dies. On the last day of Joe's trial, Mary returns to claim forgiveness. To protect her and conceal her guilt, Joe declares that they are secretly married; to prove it he goes through a ceremony, supposedly for the second time, which actually makes Mary his wife. The hastily arranged wedding is just concluded when word comes that the jury, which has been deliberating Joe's fate, has found him guilty of murder. He is being led away to justice when the Chinese servant, who has provided most of the comic relief of the play, appears with evidence—including the stolen gold—which shifts the guilt from Joe to Scraggs, and the play ends as follows:

Joe *(looking at gold):* Boys, he speaks the truth; that is my partner's gold. And here stands the man who killed him. *(Rushes at Scraggs. . . .)*

Scraggs: It's a lie! He struck me first; he would have killed me; 'twas in self-defense.

Omnes *(rushing at Scraggs):* Hang him! Hang him! Lynch him!

Joe: No! Let him live long enough to realize the doom that's waiting for him. Sudden death would be too much mercy to show to such a wretch as him. . . .

Sam: All right, Joe! But he swings in one hour. . . .

Bran *(advancing to Scraggs):* Josiah, I'm sorry—very sorry.

Scraggs: I don't want your sorrow! I despise your pity! Besides you have none to waste! Go to Lady Mary and hear her story, or will I tell it to you here, before all your friends?

Joe: No! No! You must not hear this. Take him away. *(Exit* Scraggs *followed by* Miners, *shouting.)* Lynch him! Lynch him!

.   .   .

Mary: Is it true? Has the light come at last?

Joe: Yes, dear! The night has been long and dark. But on the heights of happiness, where we are standing now, our love will illuminate our lives forever.

(Music. Curtain.)

A frontier drama like *My Partner* and other plays of the same kind are evidence that fondness for the comforting morality of melodrama and for the exciting devices that characterize the genre continued to dominate American drama in the second half of the nineteenth century. Melodrama continued to star—but waiting in the wings was the new and powerful influence of realism, which was soon to claim the center of the stage.

11

Realism Begins
to Upstage Melodrama

American Playwriting at the Turn
of the Nineteenth Century

The movement toward realism in literature that began in the waning years of the nineteenth century was destined to work great changes in American playwriting. It slowly lessened the dominant influence of melodrama, eventually relegating the genre to a minor role, and prepared the playgoer for the new kinds of dramas written by Ibsen, Chekhov, O'Neill, and their followers. It also turned the attention of American playwrights to American scenes, characters, localities, and problems, and thus helped to free American writers from their long bondage to European models and materials.

The romantic movement in literature, beginning in the late eighteenth century, provided a climate favorable to the development of melodrama. A century later, the movement had run its course. The world had changed and the need for a literature relevant to the times was urgent. Everywhere people were becoming aware of the deeply disturbing problems created by the industrial revolution, the urbanization of the population, and the impact of science, especially the conflict between science and religion. The conventions and attitudes of romantic literature were criticized for being outmoded and artificial. A desire for relevance and truth developed. Instead of exotic settings, there was a demand for the settings of everyday life. Instead of battles for political liberty, there was a demand for social and economic freedom. Instead of princes, noblemen, and Byronic heroes, there was a demand for characters who represented the average person. Instead of the romantic problems of love and honor, there was a demand for a discussion of the disturbing economic, social, and personal problems of the day. Instead of the language of poetry or elaborate rhetoric, there was a demand for the diction and rhythms of ordinary speech. A radically altered concept of the mission and method of literature was needed. The new leaders of the art of novel writing and playwriting said that realism could fill the need. They began a campaign to persuade creative writers to abandon conventions, clichés, and artificialities of romantic writing and to devote themselves to portraying the unglamorized truth. They also urged the choice of American subject matter. The movement, like all such movements, began slowly and with few adherents. It gradually gained strength and support. Little by little, it altered the literature of the time, including playwriting, until finally it became the dominating literary creed.

American playwriting saw no sharp break with the past. The influence of realism—which had already been seen in the stage effects and dialogue of many melodramas—was exerted in small ways before it altered the basic conventions of dramaturgy. Consider the case of Steele Mackaye's play *Hazel Kirke* (1880), often cited as an early example of realism. It was enormously popular in its time and held the stage for many years. Yet a modern reader finds the characters unreal and the action hopelessly contrived. Only a few elements indicate the beginning of a shift to realism. The setting is not exotic; it is a mill. The characters, except for the hero and his mother, are not aristocrats; they are people of the working class. There is no conventional villain; the man who holds the mortgage on the mill is a sympathetic, understanding neighbor. The language is not blank verse or inflated rhetoric; it is a fair approximation of colloquial speech. So *Hazel Kirke* takes a step toward realism without really achieving it.

WILLIAM DEAN HOWELLS

The writers of fiction and drama who lagged in the pursuit of realism, or who had never begun the pursuit, found themselves prodded, exhorted, and encouraged by a group of literary figures whose leader was William Dean Howells, America's most influential man of letters in the late years of the nineteenth century. Howells was a spokesman and also a doer. He not only preached realism in the critical essays he wrote for *The Atlantic Monthly* and for *Harper's Magazine* between 1866 and 1920, but he also practiced it in both his novels and his plays. His influence was enormous: he had a profound effect on American writers of fiction and directly affected the work of such playwrights as Edward Harrigan, James A. Herne, Augustus Thomas, and Clyde Fitch.

Howells, recognized in his own time as a master novelist, was also a skillful dramatist—yet his plays are not well known. They never achieved the professional success that many critics think they deserve. However, his one-act plays, many of them published in the *Atlantic Monthly, Harper's Weekly,* or *Harper's Magazine,* had a tremendous following and were the favorites of amateur actors everywhere. Among the best known of these are *The Sleeping Car* (1883), which uses the realistic setting of a Pullman car; *The Elevator* (1885), which shows the characters of the play trapped in an elevator between floors; and several other playlets of diverse setting such as *The Garroters* (1886), *The Mouse Trap* (1889), *A Letter of Introduction* (1892), and *Unexpected Guests* (1893). In this series of one-act plays, Howells recorded, with skill and charm, the adventures of two young American couples, Mr. and Mrs. Edward Roberts and Mr. and Mrs. Willis Campbell. He made them so distinctive, yet so American and so lifelike, that for millions of readers and spectators they seemed like actual friends or neighbors.

Howells also wrote full-length plays, some of which were produced on the professional stage. The most successful of these is entitled *A Counterfeit Present-ment.* It was produced by Lawrence Barrett in 1877 and remained in his repertory for some time.

More influential than Howells's playwriting, however, was his critical championship of the realistic movement. Through his essays, letters, and personal encouragement, he persuaded many aspiring dramatists to believe that real life should be the subject matter of their plays, and that it should be recorded faithfully without resort to contrivances and artificialities.

JAMES A. HERNE

James A. Herne is a fascinating representative of the transition from melodrama to realism. He began his career by writing one kind of play, then came under the influence of two of the leaders of the realistic movement in literature, Howells and Hamlin Garland, and ended his career as a champion of the realistic movement in drama.

Herne began his life in the theatre as an actor. His first appearance was in Troy, New York, in a part in *Uncle Tom's Cabin.* After several seasons on the East Coast, he appeared in California; presently he settled in San Francisco and remained there for some years. In 1874 he became stage manager for Maguire's New San Francisco Theatre and two years later assumed the same post at the new Baldwin Theatre, where he was also the leading character actor. At the Baldwin Theatre, Herne met David Belasco, who was also employed there. Herne's first serious attempts at playwriting were in collaboration with Belasco. Previously, Herne had tried his hand at dramatizing novels, a regular activity of many playwrights. He had acted in several successful adaptations of Dickens's novels and these had impressed him. He noted how warmly audiences responded to the original, realistic characters of Dickens's world. No doubt he remembered this response when he created the homespun, realistic rural characters of his own later plays. However, the three early dramas he manufactured with David Belasco cannot be called realistic or original. These three—*Within an Inch of His Life* (1879), *Marriage by Moonlight* (1879), and *Hearts of Oak* (1879, originally entitled *Chums*)—all followed the old conventions of melodrama. The characters and action are contrived to be theatrically effective and to provide the maximum of sentiment and sensation.

Herne next turned to American history and wrote an original play called *The Minute Men of 1774-75* (1886), which was not successful. By this time the actor-playwright was back on the East Coast and close to the leaders of the realistic movement in literature. Here, after the failure of *The Minute Men of 1774-75,* he wrote a play originally called *Mary, the Fisherman's Daughter,* then renamed *Drifting Apart.* The piece featured American rural types delineated with so much naturalness that the play attracted the notice of Hamlin Garland, a staunch disciple of William Dean Howells. Garland praised the play warmly, introduced Herne to Howells, and encouraged Herne to continue writing in the realistic mode. About the same time Herne was introduced to the plays of Henrik Ibsen, the Norwegian giant, and was deeply affected by them. Herne became not only a convert to realism but also a dedicated crusader for truth-to-life in literature, so much so, in fact, that he was willing to sacrifice commercial success, which he had already won with his earlier, contrived plays, for a kind of artistic success that brought him approval from literary leaders but little support from theatregoers. Mass audiences were not enthusiastic about realism.

Herne took a giant step toward realism when he produced his next play, *Margaret Fleming,* in 1890. It was an artistic triumph but a commercial failure, even though it had several tryouts and the public backing of literary leaders. Playgoers praised the acting of Herne and his wife in the leading roles (the part of Margaret Fleming had been written for Katharine Corcoran), but they rejected the play. Yet *Margaret Fleming* is one of the first American dramas that breaks with the old conventions and clearly presages a new kind of playwriting.

The setting, the home of Philip and Margaret Fleming, is a middle-class household in contemporary America. The action of the play concerns an urgent social problem: the double standard and the consequences of marital infidelity. Philip, an attractive, likable man, has sired an illegitimate child by a working girl named Lena, who is the sister of Maria, a domestic servant in the Fleming household. Margaret, Philip's wife, knows nothing of this affair but is happily absorbed in her own new baby and her household activities. Lena, mother of the illegitimate child, dies soon after her baby is born. In a letter written on her deathbed, she reveals that Philip is the father of her child. Margaret, nobly and compassionately, adopts the baby to rear as her own. But the shock of discovering her husband's infidelity complicates an ailment of her eyes and causes her to go blind. Philip, overcome with contrition, disappears for a time. On his return he expects Margaret to reject him. She tells him that although their old relationship as husband and wife cannot be resumed, his duty is to accept his responsibility as a father, to support the two babies, and to rebuild his life as best he can.

During the course of the play, several episodes remind us that the influence of melodrama is still strong. Yet the theme of *Margaret Fleming* was important and relevant to the lives of most Americans. Herne posed the old question of a man's infidelity to his wife and asked, who suffers? who is to blame? what can be done? A play like *Shenandoah* posed no such questions and illustrated no theme except the old cliché that "love conquers all." In *Margaret Fleming,* Herne created characters with enough plausibility to carry conviction; the course of events developed from the natures of these characters. In *Shenandoah* Howard introduced a gallery of stock characters—skillfully constructed, but stock nevertheless—who were created and manipulated to suit the action. The emphasis in *Margaret Fleming* was on theme as revealed through the events that ensue from the actions of the characters. In *Shenandoah* the emphasis was on the action itself. The unsensational ending that Herne chose might not be pleasing, but it is certainly closer to what happens in actual life. Nineteenth-century audiences disliked the ending, and they disliked what they considered to be the seamy reality of the play as a whole. In contrast, the advocates of honesty and realism were enthusiastic about the play. William Dean Howells wrote a letter to Herne praising *Margaret Fleming* in these words: "Your fidelity to the ideal of truth, the only ideal worth having, is witnessed in every part of it, and it will be recognized by everyone who can feel and think, as a piece of nature and a great work of art." [1]

Herne's next play is entitled *Shore Acres* (1892) and introduces other elements typical of the early romantic movement. Written while Herne was living in a small town on the coast of Maine, the play was inspired by the town. Although the plot and subplot are strictly melodramatic, the characters and their manner of speaking were copied from the local residents. The settings introduced actual horses, poultry, and farm tools in the barnyard scenes and steaming hot food in the kitchen scenes. The play is as strongly American in setting, speech, and character portrayal as Herne could make it.

It may be significant that *Shore Acres,* after a shaky start, achieved substantial commercial success and ran a whole season at Daly's Theatre, while *Margaret Fleming* never attracted a following until it was revived early in the twentieth century. The different receptions accorded the two plays is explained by a modern critic as follows: "With *Margaret Fleming,* Herne was ahead of his time. The American theatre public was fascinated with American folk realism, the realism of authentic local color, the theatrical realism of exciting lifelike spectacles, but it was not yet prepared to tolerate the free thinker's psychological realism, inner realism, the new outspoken, imported, Ibsen-like realism." [2] Thus, *Shore Acres* was a popular success and *Margaret Fleming* a failure.

The casting and production of both *Margaret Fleming* and *Shore Acres* reveal a significant change in American theatre practice. The plays were not given to a resident company to present; special companies were organized to produce them. The performers were not members of an established troupe; they were individually engaged for a specific role in a specific play, and generally continued to play a single, specific role during the entire run of the play. This change in the way a play was cast and produced had been used with increasing frequency ever since Dion Boucicault promoted combination, or road, companies in the 1860s. It became the dominant practice in the twentieth century.

Following the success of *Shore Acres,* Herne wrote three additional plays, only one of which stirred any enthusiasm. The two failures were a romantic Irish play called *My Colleen* (1892) and a historical play entitled *The Reverend Griffith Davenport* (1899). The successful play was a reworking of *Hearts of Oak,* which Herne called *Sag Harbor* (1899) and which uses the rural characters, natural speech, and homey American settings that Herne had found to be so attractive in *Shore Acres.*

[1] Richard Moody, *Dramas from the American Theatre 1762-1909* (New York: World Publishing Company, 1966), p. 659.
[2] Ibid., p. 660.

Sag Harbor was Herne's last play. He died in 1901 and will be remembered both as an accomplished actor and as an influential playwright. He introduced Ibsen-like realism in *Margaret Fleming,* strengthened the trend toward folk realism in *Shore Acres* and *Sag Harbor,* and in several plays showed that American characters in native setting could be as appealing as foreign exoticism.

WILLIAM GILLETTE

Another playwright who often turned to native material was William Gillette (1855-1937). Like Herne, he was both actor and dramatist, and successful in both activities. However, the plays of Gillette did not make a major contribution to the development of realism as did the best of Herne's dramas. Gillette's three most famous plays are *Held by the Enemy* (1886), *Secret Service* (1895), and *Sherlock*

William Gillette as Sherlock Holmes.
Hoblitzelle Theatre Arts Library, Humanities Research Center, University of Texas at Austin.

Holmes (1899). The first two are spy thrillers using the American Civil War as the setting and source of subject matter. The third is based on the adventures of the famous detective created by Conan Doyle and is considered the grandfather of all American detective plays and one of the best ever written. All three plays are deftly constructed melodramas whose thrills and suspense seem to develop naturally from the nature of the material. A. H. Quinn credits Gillette with fathering the "realism of action," and certainly there is some truth in this. The characters in Gillette's thrillers behave and speak far more naturally than do the characters in earlier melodramas like *Uncle Tom's Cabin* or *The Octoroon.* To make sure that they do so, Gillette carefully worked out specific movements, gestures, facial expressions, and stage business for each character and inserted them in the texts of his plays.

In his own acting Gillette was as carefully true to life as his written stage directions indicate. He impressed his audiences as being remarkably realistic. He was the ideal hero—firm-jawed, resourceful, and imperturbable—in *Held by the Enemy* and in *Secret Service.* His acting of Sherlock Holmes was such a perfect embodiment of the character that for several generations of playgoers Gillette *was* Sherlock Holmes. Some historians claim that his performance of these roles establishes him as the founder of modern naturalistic acting. He was certainly one of the performers of his time who adapted his style to the more realistic material he was acting, but he was only one of many—and he practiced his naturalistic style long after Mrs. Fiske had established it in her own performances, performances that are discussed at the end of Chapter 15. Gillette was not an innovator, yet he strengthened the trend toward realism in playwriting and acting by the greater logic and reasonableness that he introduced into the plots of his melodramas and by his true-to-life acting in these plays.

WILLIAM CLYDE FITCH

Contemporary with Herne and Gillette is another playwright who at the start of the twentieth century was considered the best dramatist of his day. Certainly he was the most prolific and, for a time, the most successful. He is William Clyde Fitch. His dramatic writing illustrates the greatly improved craftsmanship of American playwriting and also illustrates, in some respects, the growing commitment to the new creed of realism.

Fitch's brief life, from 1865 to 1909, was one of feverish activity and prodigal output. Born in Elmira, New York, and educated at Amherst, he showed very early in life an interest in the theatre and a gift for writing. To further his dramatic ambitions, he moved to New York City. His first chance to write for the theatre came when he was commissioned by Richard Mansfield to dramatize the story of *Beau Brummell.* His successful completion of the commission gave Mansfield a play that the actor used for years and that established Fitch as a professional dramatist.

Fitch proceeded to write plays of many kinds: one-acts, social comedies, historical romances, and adaptations from the French. These plays met with varying

Clyde Fitch, considered the best American playwright of his day.

Hoblitzelle Theatre Arts Library, Humanities Research Center, University of Texas at Austin.

success, but all of them sharpened Fitch's skill as a dramatist. In 1898 and 1899, he turned to American history and produced *Nathan Hale* and *Barbara Frietchie*, both of which were well received. In 1900 Fitch wrote a satirical comedy of manners entitled *The Climbers*, and the following year he turned out two plays, *Captain Jinks of the Horse Marines* (which gave Ethel Barrymore her first starring role) and *Lover's Lane.* In 1901 Fitch had the thrill of seeing four of his plays running on Broadway at the same time, all doing good business. He continued writing for eight more years. In 1902 he produced *The Girl with the Green Eyes;* in 1905 came *Her Great Match;* in 1907, *The Truth;* and in 1909, *The City.* Altogether in the nineteen years following the production of *Beau Brummell,* Fitch wrote a total of sixty plays of which thirty-six were original. He also insisted on assuming complete responsibility for every detail of the casting, directing, and staging of his plays. No wonder that he was too exhausted to survive an operation for appendicitis and died in 1909 at the age of forty-four.

To the audiences of his own day, such plays as *The City, The Truth,* and *The Girl with the Green Eyes* were marvels of truthful portraiture and realistic action. To a modern reader or playgoer with an additional sixty years of perspective, these dramas are dated by their contrived situations and half-believable characters. Consider Fitch's last play, *The City,* which was produced in 1909 after his death by the Shubert brothers at the Lyric Theatre, New York, with Walter Hampden, Lucille Watson, and Tully Marshall in leading roles. The play was hailed as Fitch's masterpiece. It ran for 190 performances in New York and afterward enjoyed a successful tour of the United States.

Fitch planned his play as a drama of ideas. It was to be a searching analysis of the corrupting influences exerted by a big city on a family that has been reared in the strict but humdrum morality of a small American town. Such a theme is consistent with the realist's desire for plays that discuss the pertinent problems of contemporary society. How does Fitch present the problems and convey his convictions?

The play concerns the Rand family, which includes the father, George Sr., the mother, and three grown children—a son, George Jr., and two daughters, Teresa and Cicely. The Rands are the leading family of Middleburg, a small town in upstate New York, but all of them except George Sr. despise the dull life of Middleburg and hanker to live in New York City. Although George Sr. is the leading banker and most respected citizen of Middleburg, it is revealed in the first act that he is guilty of many dishonest business deals. Moreover, he has sired an illegitimate son and kept his affairs from public knowledge by sending the mother out of town and supporting her in secret. When the play opens the mother is dead but the illegitimate son, Fred Hannock, now grown, is blackmailing George Sr. without knowing that the banker is his father. All this background is adroitly brought out in a long scene between the banker and Hannock. The scene reaches its climax when Hannock threatens to reveal the banker's affair with his mother; George Sr. succumbs and pays the money Hannock demands. Then, worn out, George Sr. confesses his past misdeeds to his son, George Jr., and exacts a promise from him that he will take care of the illegitimate son. George Sr. leaves the room only to fall dead of a heart attack. The Rand family is now free to move to the city.

The second act of the play takes place five years later. The Rands are now ensconced in a fashionable home in New York. Mrs. Rand is a social climber; Teresa, who has married a dissolute society playboy, is unhappy and wants a divorce; George Jr. has become a powerful and successful big-city banker. He is about to be nominated for governor of the state. Also, he is engaged to marry the lovely Eleanor Vorhees. He has established a reputation not only for ability but also for absolute honesty and integrity. Hannock is his confidential secretary. Just when George is congratulating himself on the wisdom of moving to the city, a series of crises develops. The committee that is backing George's nomination for governor demands that he fire the unsavory Hannock, who, besides being shifty and unreliable, is also a drug addict. Hannock, when told of the committee's demand, threatens to expose George's crooked business deals. George, it seems, has been more unscrupulous than his father without fully realizing his own dishonesty. At this point Hannock and the younger sister, Cicely, announce that they are in love and plan to be married. George is aghast and absolutely forbids it. Then the couple reveals that they are already married. In desperation, George sends Cicely from the room and reveals the frightful truth to Hannock—namely, that he, Hannock, is Cicely's half-brother. Hannock refuses to believe it. When George declares that he must reveal the ugly truth to Cicely so that the marriage can be annulled and calls

Cicely into the room, Hannock shoots her dead to spare her the nightmarish revelation. George snatches the gun from Hannock, who is about to kill himself. Hannock begs to be allowed to die and almost persuades George to return the gun by describing the scandal and disgrace that George will face if Hannock is brought to trial for murder. George weakens when he realizes that all his hopes and ambitions will be destroyed unless Hannock commits suicide. Then his better nature asserts itself, and facing Hannock, he declares, "You must take your punishment as it comes, and I *must take mine!* This is my *only chance to show I can be on the level!. . .* God help me *do it!*" Thus ends the second act.

In the third act we witness the redeeming effect of the death of the innocent Cicely. Mrs. Rand confesses that she is a social failure in New York and should have stayed in Middleburg. Teresa's husband renounces his mistress and makes a reconciliation with his wife. George confesses all his shady business deals, withdraws as a candidate for governor, vows to make full restitution to everyone he has cheated, and declares that he will rebuild his life on absolute honesty. He also bids a sad farewell to his fiancée, Eleanor Vorhees, believing that she can never marry a blackguard like himself. But Eleanor tells him that in owning up to the wrongs he has committed, his real self has triumphed and he is now the man she loves. The play ends with George declaring, "Now I know what those people mean who say a man gets all the *Hell* that's coming to him *in this world*—and *all the heaven, too!*"

The preceding synopsis of the action clearly reveals the weakness of the play. The realistic theme that Fitch wishes to document—the corrupting effect of big-city life—is all but forgotten in the sensational developments of the plot. Furthermore, the experiences of the Rand family are so exceptional that they seem to have little relationship to the general problem. How many families who migrate to the city are so wealthy? How many have such hidden scandals in their backgrounds? How many are so corrupt *before* they move to the city? How many include a potential governor? These situations are so untypical that they afford little or no insight into the usual problems of a family adjusting to urban life. The play fails, also, to convince us that the characters are real people, plausible, motivated, and true to their natures.

If the play fails as a realistic presentation of representative human beings under stress, it succeeds as first-class melodrama. Fitch constructs the action smoothly and skillfully. The pieces fit together well. The tension mounts steadily in each act. The surprises are timed for maximum effectiveness, and although contrived, they do not come without preparation. Other virtues of the play are the sharpness and naturalness of the dialogue, the realistic details of speech and action that make the characters acceptable, and the effective, if occasional, self-revelation of the characters.

The virtues and weaknesses of *The City* are typical of Fitch's playwriting. In two other very successful plays, *The Truth* and *The Girl with the Green Eyes,* he devoted more attention to a single character, building the play around one person who is dominated by a single trait. However, despite the atmosphere of modernity found in these plays, they are not convincing to a modern reader. The central characters are too extreme in their dominating trait, too pathological to be representative. Also, the regeneration at the end of each play is hard to accept, just as the reform of the Rand family is difficult to believe.

Of the thirty-six original plays written by Fitch, all but one use American subject matter. All of them exhibit a superior mastery of the dramatist's craft, and all exhibit a growing sense of the need for realism in drama. In these ways, Fitch contributed to the advancement of American playwriting.

In summary, playwriting in America at the end of the nineteenth century was more vigorous, varied, and competent than ever before. Plays of every type continued to be written and produced. Many of them appealed strongly to public taste, provided attractive opportunities for actors, and were enormously popular. Yet most of them followed the traditional formulas and thus were contrived, melodramatic, and second-rate. But gaining strength and favor amid the old traditions were several new trends. One of these was the growing emphasis on American subject matter and characters. Another was the commitment to portray human existence honestly and realistically. Still another was the increased concern for the social, economic, and personal problems that beset the average person. Dramatists like Harrigan and Hoyt, Howells, Herne, Gillette, and Fitch all contributed to these trends, which in time were destined to alter radically the kinds of plays written by Americans.

Many other dramatists of importance contributed to the development and transformation of American playwriting. Before discussing them, we must examine some of the other activities in the American theatre in the last years of the century.

12

The Lively Scene at the Close of the Nineteenth Century

A look at the American stage in the last years of the nineteenth century reveals a theatre that had color, vigor, variety, and dimension. The theatre was prosperous, enjoying the patronage of large numbers of playgoers everywhere. It was expanding, with playhouses being built from New York to California. In some ways it was also sterile. Many of the traditions and practices that had served the nineteenth century so well were now outmoded, like those in playwriting, but they persisted and inhibited experimentation and change. Yet challenging them were new ideals, theories, and techniques in every branch of dramatic art. Within the first two decades of the twentieth century, these new movements were destined to transform and revitalize not only playwriting, but also every other activity of the theatre. Within the same period the living theatre was to face a formidable challenge from that mechanical miracle, the motion picture.

In the last years of the nineteenth century the popular theatre was especially prosperous. Variety shows had become chain-store vaudeville, with circuits and weekly programs covering the nation from coast to coast. Negro minstrelsy was a national institution. Burlesque was standardized and largely respectable. Mammoth, mobile circuses like Barnum and Bailey's "Greatest Show on Earth" were touring the country. Lyceum and Chautauqua were welcomed in hundreds of villages, hamlets, and towns. Showboats, which had reappeared on the Mississippi after the Civil War, were enjoying some of their palmiest days. Palatial vessels such as the *New Sensation*, the *Floating Palace*, and the *Water Queen* floated majestically from town to town attracting customers along the waterfront with the powerful music of their steam calliopes and thrilling audiences with all kinds of entertainment from grand opera and Shakespeare to melodrama and minstrelsy.

The regular theatre offered a vast range of plays and entertainments. With increasing skill, native playwrights turned out melodramatic thrillers and farce

The showboat *Cotton Palace.*

Hoblitzelle Theatre Arts Library, Humanities Research Center, Univeristy of Texas at Austin.

comedies, spectacles and extravaganzas, plays of local color and local types, sentimental romances and historical tragedies, adaptations of novels, and almost every other genre in the repertory. Along with the flood of commercial plays, audiences could still see a reduced number of Shakespearean productions, revivals of Old Comedies—that is, the plays of Goldsmith, Sheridan, Farquhar, and the like—and importations from every European country. Musical plays were popular, and grand opera was established in a few of the larger, wealthier cities.

With productions of every kind and from numerous periods and nations, it is logical that a variety of acting styles would be needed. The golden age of acting had ended, but there was a considerable afterglow. The older styles of performance continued to be represented, and several new styles appeared. American acting at the end of the nineteenth century had color, variety, and considerable vigor. Indeed, it was often first rate.

Perhaps the two most important new developments to occur during the last decades of the nineteenth century were the emergence of the master director, or *régisseur,* and the adoption of a new kind of realistic stagecraft that encouraged and complemented the growing realism in playwriting and acting. The two developments are closely related, because the men who emerged as régisseurs were also leaders in the movement for realism in staging and in acting as well.

ENTER THE RÉGISSEUR

Ever since the establishment of the American theatre, the actor had been the focus and the deciding voice in a production. The stage manager held the book during rehearsals and indicated entrances, exits, and the positions of minor characters. He was the director insofar as there was one, but he did not coach actors in their roles nor did he guide their interpretation of a part. He worked with the company manager—sometimes he *was* the company manager—and conferred with musicians and scene painters. He was a coordinator of activities but not the artistic czar of the production.

In the final three decades of the nineteenth century, a need arose for strong, resourceful managers. Audiences became more sophisticated, productions more complicated, and demand more insistent for realistic, authentic scenery and stage effects. The thrills, surprises, and tricky scenic effects of many plays needed to be carefully staged if they were to succeed. The old, more or less laissez-faire method of preparing a production was ineffective. A strong, controlling authority was needed to coordinate and unify all the elements that contributed to the final presentation. Thus, the régisseur, or master director, emerged. Earlier in the century, strong company managers had approached the status of régisseur. The emotionalistic actress Laura Keene was one of these during the years she ran her own theatre. So were William E. Burton and Dion Boucicault. Lester Wallack was another, after he assumed control of Wallack's Theatre in 1864 upon the death of his father. He managed the company, acted important comic roles, discouraged the use of guest stars, and maintained a distinguished troupe of players that included at times such notable performers as John Gilbert, E. L. Davenport, and John Brougham. Because his personality, tastes, and authority dominated all the activities in his theatre, Wallack came close to being a régisseur. When such men as Augustin Daly, Steele Mackaye, A. M. Palmer, and David Belasco appeared, it was certain that the régisseur had arrived.

REALISTIC SCENERY

During the time the régisseur developed, a new, realistic stagecraft steadily gained acceptance. The old, generalized, and easily manipulated settings of wings and drops, which had served so well when the emphasis in playwriting was on universal principles rather than on specific problems, were giving way to box settings with authentic furniture and properties. At the same time there was a growing demand for scenery and costumes that faithfully reproduced the historical or modern setting of a play. The new régisseurs contributed significantly to the development of new ways of mounting and staging a play. They were not, of course, the first or the only advocates of realistic scenery and lifelike stage effects. Many other producers and productions had already established the trend. For example, the spectacular scenes of melodrama—fires, floods, and special effects—had been reproduced with increasing realism for many years.

In 1846 the English tragedian Charles Kean thrilled New York audiences with his production of *King John,* which presented acres of canvas painted to reproduce Shakespeare's settings with scrupulous historical accuracy. The production also exhibited costumes that were historically correct and even more realistic than the scenery. Edwin Booth followed the example set by Kean. When he managed his own theatre from 1869 to 1873, he was praised not only for the impressive mountings of his Shakespearean productions but also for their realism and historical correctness. Booth's productions were also noted for combining authentically painted canvas with heavy, three-dimensional pieces of scenery.

At the same time, the new drama of ordinary life was creating interest in another kind of realism: one that was intimate, photographic, and naturalistic. This interest exerted considerable effect in altering the design of playhouses and particularly the machinery of the stage. A notable illustration of these alterations is the Madison Square Theatre, which Steele Mackaye remodeled in 1880. He reduced the seating capacity to seven hundred, creating an intimate playhouse where the audience could see or hear every movement, gesture, and word of the performers. To bring the audience as close to the actors as possible, he eliminated the forestage and the proscenium doors; he also eliminated the orchestra pit and installed a recessed musician's gallery above the proscenium arch. Thus, only a narrow, unencumbered space separated the audience from the stage. Most revolutionary of all was the elevator stage that Mackaye invented and installed for the quick shift of scenery. The elevator had two levels, or stages, each one twenty-two feet wide, thirty-one feet deep, and over twenty-five feet high. The mechanism used a system of cables, pulleys, and winches and could be operated by four men. When a scene was being performed on one stage of the elevator, the other level—out of sight of the audience—could be prepared for the following scene. Only forty seconds were needed to raise or lower the elevator and reveal the new scene. Here was a system that permitted use of the realistic three-dimensional settings and yet had the advantage of the old system of wings and drops—namely, speed and ease in the changing of scenery. Despite these advantages, the new machinery was not adopted by other theatres. Evidently the cost of installation and the allegiance to traditional methods of scene shifting were too great.

AUGUSTIN DALY, 1839-1899

Augustin Daly was the first producer who can clearly claim the title of régisseur. He began his career as a manager in 1856 when he was only eighteen. His first venture failed but he never lost his interest in the theatre and his urge to produce plays. He tried his hand at dramatic criticism. In 1862 he began adapting and writing plays. In 1869 he opened his first playhouse, the Fifth Avenue Theatre, and from then on he was a major producer and a powerful influence in the theatrical affairs of the nation. At the height of his career, in the early 1890s, he directed his own Daly's Theatre in New York and another Daly's Theatre in London, operating them with an authority and sureness of grasp that earned him the title, "autocrat of the stage." He permitted no voice but his own to be heard in the preparation of a play. He trained and molded every intonation, gesture, and movement of his performers, always in the direction of greater simplicity, suggestiveness, and naturalness. He carefully supervised every detail of the stagecraft, which included scenery, lighting, properties, and costumes. He was in the theatre from early morning until midnight or later looking after every detail, large or small. One member of his company said that he seemed "to know instinctively just how everything should go to get the best effect."[1]

Daly had an outstanding ability to discern and develop talent, and he demonstrated it by making stars of such players as Clara Morris, Fanny Davenport, Ada Rehan, and several more. Daly's company, including his stars, became famous for polish, sprightliness, and teamwork. Daly was the first manager to discard the practice of hiring actors for lines of business; he engaged them without designating specialties and cast them in whatever roles he felt they could play. Under his sure and autocratic guidance, the company at its best became a well-balanced team that boasted a quartet of players who earned the title of the "Big Four." These were the romantic matinee idol, John Drew; two comedians of inimitable skill, Mrs. John Gilbert and James Lewis; and the captivating, wholesome Ada Rehan. With this quartet Daly was able to present some outstanding revivals of Shakespeare's plays and of old comedies like *She Stoops to Conquer, The Rivals,* and *The School for Scandal.*

During Daly's early years as a producer, before 1880, his productions were likely to feature ensemble playing and scenic effects that were charming but not lavish. After 1880 Daly came to rely more and more on the attraction of his stars, principally Ada Rehan. The need to make money in the highly competitive and risky theatrical market led him to tailor plays to fit and exploit the personalities of his most popular players.

Daly's later productions also became increasingly elaborate in scenic and lighting effects. He used grand, painted backdrops and wing pieces supplemented by solid three-dimensional balconies, staircases, ramps, and platforms. All of these, and the costumes as well, were as authentic and realistic as he could make them. Often these lavish, realistic mountings proved highly popular; sometimes they were considered obtrusive and distracting.

Daly's productions of Shakespearean plays and old comedies were a minor part of his overall repertory. Most of the plays he adapted or wrote for his company and his stars were romantic comedies and contrived thrillers that, in retrospect, are worthless as dramatic literature. But for a long time they were immensely popular

[1]Marvin Felheim, *The Theater of Augustin Daly* (Cambridge, Mass.: Harvard University Press, 1956), p. 18.

Steele Mackaye's "double stage" in use.

Photograph is reproduced from EPOCH, the Life of Steele Mackaye, by Percy Mackaye, with the permission of Liveright Publishing Corporation. Copyright 1919 by Percy Mackaye and Harry Barnhart. Copyright renewed 1947 by Percy Mackaye.

and made Daly financially secure. When the public taste for this kind of play began to diminish, Daly experienced real difficulty, and the last years of his life were troubled ones. But before he died in 1899, he had, among other contributions, securely established his status as a régisseur and demonstrated the usefulness of such a position.

The Daly Company in *Twelfth Night.*
Theatre Collection, University of California Library at Berkeley.

Three other manager-régisseurs who were active in New York during the same years as Daly were Steele Mackaye (1842-1894), A. M. Palmer (1838-1905), and David Belasco (1859-1931).

STEELE MACKAYE

Steele Mackaye was one of the most gifted and idealistic men ever to grace the American theatre. He was an actor who had studied in Paris and could perform Hamlet creditably in either English or French. He was a teacher who introduced the United States to a method of acting developed by the Frenchman François Delsarte. The theatre school that Mackaye established in connection with the Lyceum Theatre in New York later became one of the leading American centers for the teaching of dramatic art, the American Academy of Dramatic Art, whose director for many years was Franklin Sargent, a pupil of Mackaye. But acting and teaching were only a small part of Mackaye's activities. As a dramatist he wrote several plays, the most popular of which, *Hazel Kirke,* has already been discussed. He was also an architect-inventor who is credited with devising such conveniences for the playgoer as folding seats with hat rack and umbrella holder; such architectural reforms as better sightlines, wider aisles, and more intimate relationship between player and spectator; and such technical equipment for the stage as improved systems of lighting and scene shifting, illustrated by the innovations already described, which he introduced into the remodeled Madison Square Theatre. The mammoth theatre that Mackaye proposed for the Chicago World's Fair of 1893, to be called a "spectatorium," was designed to include all of his inventions and innovations. Although the Spectatorium was never built (the plan was abandoned because of the financial panic of 1893), a smaller version of it called the "Scenitorium" was completed and used for public presentations.

The last of Mackaye's many accomplishments was managing and directing in the kind of way that qualifies him to be called a régisseur. His career in this field, like all of his other activities, was brilliant but erratic. He managed the St. James Theatre in New York during the season of 1872-73. Seven years later he produced his own *Hazel Kirke* at the Madison Square Theatre. But he resigned after one season, realizing what a disastrous contract he had signed with the backers of the theatre. It was a contract that gave them all the profits from *Hazel Kirke,* which amounted to two hundred thousand dollars in two years, but left Mackaye with a salary of only five thousand dollars per year. Mackaye turned to management again in 1885 when he joined Daniel Frohman in remodeling and opening the Lyceum Theatre in New York. This partnership, too, was brief and once more Mackaye began free-lancing. In 1887 he produced his play, *Paul Kauvar,* which is remembered because of the convincing way Mackaye directed the crowd scenes and developed the ensemble playing. Mackaye's directing in *Paul Kauvar* was authoritarian and creative and qualifies him to be called one of the first American régisseurs. His skill in many other areas of theatrical activity qualifies him to be remembered as a gifted artist who never wholly fulfilled the promise of his abundant talents.

A. M. PALMER

Mackaye's brilliant failures in many theatrical activities are in sharp contrast to A. M. Palmer's solid success as a manager-régisseur. Palmer did not have Mackaye's varied talents, but he became a shrewd and able man of the theatre. Trained in law, with no real experience in theatrical affairs, he was suddenly in 1872 handed the management of the Union Square Theatre in New York by the owner of the house. Palmer met the challenge. He quickly developed a flair for choosing popular plays and attracting popular players. The plays were sentimental melodramas like *The Two Orphans* and *Rose Michel,* both adapted from the French; the players were accomplished and attractive actresses like Agnes Ethel and Kate Claxon. Palmer also developed a skill for coordinating all the artists of his theatre into a harmonious organization and for directing the team with shrewdness and good taste. He managed the Union Square Theatre for eleven successful years, during which it was one of the most popular playhouses in New York. He retired for a year, then returned as manager-régisseur of the Madison Square Theatre, where he produced Clyde Fitch's first play, *Beau Brummell,* in 1890 and Augustus Thomas's *Alabama* in 1891. From 1891 to 1896 Palmer directed his last theatre, Wallack's old playhouse, refurbished and renamed Palmer's. The enterprise, however, was not very successful. Palmer retired in 1896 with his reputation as a régisseur still high and his contributions to the end-of-the-century theatre still admired.

DAVID BELASCO

Outlasting all of his fellow régisseurs and outdistancing them in several areas was David Belasco. He must be accounted the most successful régisseur and credited with engineering the final triumph of realism in stage effects. Belasco was born in San Francisco in 1859 and served his apprenticeship there. He worked laboriously and eagerly at every theatrical job that came his way. He was copyist, callboy, errand boy, and boy-of-all-trades at several theatres. When he was old enough, he traveled up and down the coast as a vagabond player. Between 1871 and 1880, he acted over 170 roles. Unfortunately we know very little about his style of performing during this period.

In 1876 he became assistant stage manager, and later stage manager, at San Francisco's newest theatre, Baldwin's Academy of Music. He continued to hold this position, with a few interruptions, until 1882. It was a job that gave wide scope to his talents. He not only directed the plays that were produced in the theatre, he also wrote some of them and adapted many more. Whenever there was an opportunity, he acted in them, too. During this period he also served briefly as a secretary to the active and prolific Dion Boucicault.

Early in his apprenticeship Belasco began to question the effectiveness of the old type of scenery where objects were simulated by being painted on canvas. He noted how eagerly an audience responded to real touches and how much these seemed to add to the illusion of a play. In one of his first productions in San Francisco, he experimented with using a flock of real sheep; and in the play he wrote with Herne, *Hearts of Oak,* he introduced a real cat, a real baby, and real food on the table. The public was delighted with all these effects, and Belasco continued to supply more and more of them.

Belasco left San Francisco in 1882 to assume his first New York position, that of stage manager of the Madison Square Theatre. This was the playhouse that Steele Mackaye had remodeled just two years earlier and equipped with the latest stage machinery. It was an ideal setting for Belasco. Here he found the means to fulfill his long-standing desire for authentic settings. He remained at the Madison Square Theatre for two years and then became stage manager of the new Lyceum Theatre, another playhouse that had been designed and equipped by Steele Mackaye. In 1895 Belasco withdrew from stage management to assume responsibility as an independent producer. He remained one for the rest of his life. In 1902 he remodeled the Republic Theatre into the first Belasco Theatre, and four years later he built a new playhouse that became the second theatre to bear his name.

In all these theatres he proceeded to practice the ideal of realistic staging he had developed during his apprenticeship. At the zenith of his career, he came as close to his goal, perhaps, as was possible. His settings were marvels of solid walls, illusionistic lighting, and authentic properties. "I will allow nothing to be built out of canvas stretched on frames," he said. "Everything must be real."[2] His production of *Du Barry* displayed furniture and ornaments actually owned and used by Mme. Du Barry. *The Darling of the Gods* used brocades, swords, and trappings imported from Japan.

The lighting of a Belasco production was designed to heighten the reality of the scenery. Belasco began his career as a director and producer just at the time electric lighting was being introduced into the theatre. Which American theatre was actually the first to install the new source of light and to use it regularly is a matter of dispute. However, it is a fact that during the 1880s in the United States and elsewhere, all the principal playhouses installed electricity. It was safer, and as it was developed and improved, it became brighter, more easily controlled, and thus more capable of meeting the demand for realistic effects.

Belasco was an innovator in the use of electric lighting on the stage. As early as 1877 he anticipated modern gelatin slides by using colored silks to add hue and variation to the lights. Later, in New York, he did away with footlights because they were unnatural; and he evolved a system of diffused lighting from above that realistically simulated sunlight. In his own theatres, after 1902, he maintained a laboratory for developing and testing new lighting effects.

Some attention must be given to another aspect of Belasco's varied career, that is, his playwriting. He adapted, wrote, or helped in the writing of thirty-four plays after he arrived in New York, and his output of lesser-known plays in San Francisco was even greater. He can be called, therefore, a prolific dramatist. It is also possible to call him a twentieth-century dramatist because the most important of his plays appeared in the early years of this century, and his writing continued until 1928. Yet in structure, spirit, and style, these plays belong to the nineteenth century. They do not participate in or anticipate the spirit of the new era. They appealed to popular tastes and were perfectly tailored vehicles for Belasco's stars. They were so expertly, lavishly, and often spectacularly mounted that they appeared to be thoroughly modern. But they were not.

At the start of his career Belasco was hailed as a pioneer and an innovator. At its end, his productions were considered old-fashioned in most respects. Yet during his long and successful life in the theatre, he represented better than any other single person the powerful new concept of the régisseur and the triumph of realism in staging. His total career illustrates the transition that the theatre was making from the traditions of the nineteenth century to the changed ideals of the twentieth.

---

[2]David Belasco, *The Theatre through its Stage Door* (New York: Harper & Row, Publishers, 1919), p. 61.

David Belasco in his workshop.
Ross Theatre Collection, University of California Library at Berkeley.

ENTER THE BUSINESSMAN

Régisseurs like Belasco and Daly were managers and businessmen. They were also creative artists dedicated to the noble traditions of the theatre. Developing side by side with them in the later years of the nineteenth century was another kind of manager who was not a creative artist but a businessman and a money-maker exclusively. It was inevitable that a manager of this sort should arise.

In 1900 more than five hundred theatrical companies were on the road. Obviously big money could be made by producing popular plays and selling them to the nation. Enterprising businessmen, many of them with little or no experience in the theatre, recognized the opportunity and entered the field as producers and entrepreneurs. Two of the most representative and successful of this new breed were the Frohman brothers, Daniel (1851-1940) and Charles (1854-1915). Daniel started his career as Steele Mackaye's business manager at the Lyceum Theatre in 1880. Charles began as a company manager, booking agent, and organizer of road companies. He emerged as a big-time producer in 1889 when he presented a revised version of Bronson Howard's *Shenandoah* and made it a smash hit. Both the Frohmans eventually managed or owned theatres in New York and controlled many others throughout the country. Both commissioned the writing of plays, developed stars, promoted the building of playhouses, and spent huge sums on advertising. When Charles was drowned in the sinking of the *Lusitania*, Daniel took over and carried on many of his brother's enterprises.

There was another consequence of the emergence of such theatrical entrepreneurs as the Frohmans: the organization of a business monopoly designed to control a chain of playhouses throughout the nation, and thus to control the productions that visited them. This was the famous—or infamous—Theatrical Syndicate, organized in 1896 and destined to be the object of controversy and reaper of fat profits for many years to come. Charles Frohman was one of the founders of the Syndicate, together with a group of fellow entrepreneurs named Sam Nixon, J. Fred Zimmerman, Al Hayman, Marc Klaw, and Abraham L. Erlanger. They successfully enrolled the best playhouses in every city under their aegis and then demanded that producers and managers book their plays exclusively in Syndicate houses, with a high fee paid to the Syndicate for "booking charges." Such a monopoly had advantages because it organized a central office where bookings could be planned, coordinated, and administered in an orderly fashion. But the Syndicate created more evils than it corrected. It stifled competition. Producers like Belasco and stars like Minnie Maddern Fiske, who were unwilling to be controlled by the Syndicate, had great difficulty finding housing for their productions. They were forced to use second-rate or improvised theatres; sometimes they were shut out completely.

As serious as the stifling of competition was the cheapening of the dramatic product. Since the Syndicate was a business organization whose aim was financial profit, plays that appealed to the masses, however shoddy, were given priority in dates and playhouses. The aim of elevating public taste and character through the presentation of masterpieces, which had motivated an actor-manager like Edwin Booth, was entirely ignored by the Syndicate.

Some of the most famous and successful performers and managers of the era were bitterly opposed to the Syndicate and battled it unrelentingly. Among its notable opponents were David Belasco, Joseph Jefferson, James A. Herne, Minnie Maddern Fiske, and James O'Neill. They used their prestige to get bookings from reluctant theatre owners; they produced their plays in makeshift theatres if regular ones were not available.

Such opposition, continuing for ten years, maintained a certain amount of competition and free enterprise and helped to break the monopoly of the Syndicate. Far more successful in loosening the grip of the Syndicate was the organization of a rival monopoly about 1905, by the Shubert brothers, Sam, Lee, and Jacob. During the lush, money-making years of the early twentieth century, the two monopolies controlled most of the playhouses and theatrical companies in America. The struggle between them continued into the era of World War I with the Shuberts, once established, becoming almost as ruthless as the Syndicate had been originally. Eventually, however, the battle between the Syndicate and the Shuberts and between them and the independent producers dwindled into inconsequence. The reason? Road show business, on which the monopolies subsisted, decreased disastrously when the motion picture started its wildfire advance from coast to coast. The Great Depression of the 1930s completed the decline of the road show.

END-OF-THE-CENTURY CRITICS

William Winter, who raged against the Theatrical Syndicate, was a venerable representative of another significant activity of the end-of-the-century theatre. He was the dean of theatrical critics and represented a corps of reviewers who had dominated dramatic criticism for several decades. These men, scholarly and thoughtful, were reared in the traditions of the nineteenth century and steeped in the aesthetics and morality of the Victorian age. Winter (1836-1917) was the most prolific of them. During his forty-four years as drama critic for the *New York Tribune* he composed hundreds of detailed reviews and also wrote an impressive array of theatrical biographies plus several volumes of stage reminiscences and general criticism. Three of his most distinguished contemporaries were John Ranken Towse (1854-1927), drama critic of the *New York Evening Post* for fifty-three years and author of a wise and mellow volume of memories called *Sixty Years of the Theater;* Henry Austin Clapp (1841-1904), who served as drama and music critic of the *Boston Advertiser* in the 1880s and of the *Boston Herald* in the 1890s, and whose book *Reminiscences of a Dramatic Critic* is still stimulating and insightful; and Lewis Strang (1869-1935), drama editor and critic of the *Boston Journal* in the 1890s, then critic for the *Washington Times* and author of several useful volumes of theatrical biography.

These critics, and others like them, were expert in their knowledge of dramatic literature and intimately acquainted with the performances of the superb actors and actresses of the golden age. They wrote detailed analytical reviews of the plays they witnessed, and the newspapers they served provided ample space to print them. In creating a rich, varied, and extensive portrait of the nineteenth-century theatre, they served their age nobly and well. But by 1900 their era was passing. Many of them were unable to adjust to the changes. The new kinds of plays and concepts of production that were gaining acceptance seemed alien and unappealing. William Winter, for example, thought the dramas of Ibsen were filthy and morbid. His voice, and those of his colleagues, still dominated theatrical criticism as the century closed, but they were soon to be replaced. A new corps of young critics with a different philosophy and background was preparing to come forward and to analyze and interpret the altered theatre of the twentieth century. But before surveying the theatrical renaissance of the twentieth century, let us look at the galaxy of performers who still graced the stage in 1899-1900.

13

The Lively Scene in Acting

American acting in the closing years of the nineteenth century was as varied, vigorous, and colorful as the other activities of the theatre. During this time, actors surrendered their controlling voice in production to directors or régisseurs. But they were still a focus of attention.

The greatest stars of the classic school were gone. Mary Ann Duff, Charlotte Cushman, and E. L. Davenport were dead. James Murdoch retired in 1883; Edwin Booth and Lawrence Barrett followed in 1891. However, the ideals and practices of the classic school were carried on by three gifted actresses, one of them American by birth and two American by adoption. Their careers and achievements are unusual.

HELENA MODJESKA, 1840-1909, AND FANNY JANAUSCHEK, 1830-1904

The two foreign-born actresses who adopted America as their native land were Fanny Janauschek (Franziska Magdalena Romance Janauschek) and Helena Modjeska (Helena Modjeska Chlapowski, Countess Bozenta). Both were already stars when they came to America. Janauschek, born in Prague in 1830, had been educated for the stage in Germany, where at the age of eighteen, she became the leading actress in Frankfurt-am-Main. She remained in Germany for twenty years, winning adulation and renown as one of the greatest tragediennes of Europe. Her American debut occurred in 1867. Modjeska, although an actress of equal fame in Europe, came to the United States as an immigrant rather than as a star. She had been born in Cracow, Poland, in 1840 and had received her first theatrical training in a small provincial stock company organized and directed by her husband. At age twenty-five she returned to Cracow and made a successful debut. Three years later she was invited to appear at the Imperial Theatre in Warsaw where, it is said, her triumph was the greatest ever known in the annals of that theatre. She was engaged for life as the leading lady of the Imperial Theatre and for seven years was the reigning actress of the nation. In 1876, nine years after Janauschek made her debut, Modjeska traveled to California with a group of other Poles to establish an ideal colony where she could regain her health and escape the oppressive Russian regime in Poland. Only when the colony failed did Modjeska return to the stage, making an unheralded debut at the California Theatre in San Francisco in 1877. Her genius was recognized instantly; she appeared in New York before the year was over and was soon accepted as the great actress she was known to be in Europe.

Modjeska made her American debut in English, which she had learned in a six months' period after her resolve to become an American actress. Janauschek, on the other hand, made her first American appearances in German, sometimes performing with German-speaking actors and sometimes with an English-speaking company. Persuaded by Augustin Daly to learn English, she retired from the stage for a year and reappeared in 1870 as an English-speaking actress.

Madame Janauschek as Marie Antoinette, June 18, 1894.
Ross Theatre Collection, University of California Library at Berkeley.

In the first years after her debut in English, Janauschek achieved such popularity and success on the American stage that, following a return to Germany, she decided to make her home in the United States. For some time her career prospered, but presently the public taste for her style of acting began to decline and she slowly sank in popularity and fortune. When she died in Brooklyn in 1904, she was both impoverished and forgotten. Modjeska, on the other hand, maintained her hold on the public to the end of her career. She played almost continuously from the time of her American debut in 1877 until her last tour in 1907, which she was forced to cut short because of ill health. She died in California two years later, on April 8, 1909.

Although there are many similarities in the careers of Fanny Janauschek and Helena Modjeska, and although they both acted in the classic tradition, their styles of performance were markedly different. Janauschek's acting was intense, powerful, and heroic. She was ideal in the roles of Medea, Brunnhilde, and Lady Macbeth. Modjeska's acting, in contrast, was graceful, symmetrical, and poetic. She excelled in such roles as Viola, Rosalind, and Adrienne Lecouvreur. The contrasting styles of the two actresses might be compared to the differences between Charlotte Cushman and Mary Ann Duff.

MARY ANDERSON, 1859-1940

Modjeska and Janauschek, Duff and Cushman all clearly belong to the classic school of acting. Mary Anderson belongs to the classic tradition, also, but with her the old order weakens. Her training was different and her repertory was limited. She chose her roles from the standard drama, but they were roles that required womanly emotion rather than tragic power. Her appeal was based more on personal charm than on dramatic genius. She was not of the school of feminine emotionalism illustrated by Matilda Heron, but neither did she achieve the same high plane as Duff and Cushman or Modjeska and Janauschek.

Mary Anderson became stage-struck very early in her life. At age twelve she was given a volume of Shakespeare's dramas and was immediately entranced. Some time later, Edwin Booth played in Louisville, Kentucky, Miss Anderson's hometown, and the excited young lady decided to become an actress. After ten lessons in elocution and stage deportment—plus a few months of self-training—she made her debut as Juliet on the stage of Macauley's Theatre in her hometown of Louisville in November 1875. Three months later she again acted at Macauley's, playing the leading roles of Bianca, Julia, Pauline, and Juliet. Then followed short engagements in St. Louis, New Orleans, Owensboro, and San Francisco. In 1877 she made her debut in Philadelphia, Boston, and New York, and these cities gave her tremendous popular acclaim. For the next twelve years, until her retirement in 1889, she acted throughout the United States and England, winning a public adoration such as few players ever enjoyed.

The qualities that won public affection for Mary Anderson were the same qualities that made her acting acceptable. They were an attractive personality, a

Mary Anderson, a postcard portrait.

beautiful face and figure, a rich, melodious voice, a fair measure of dramatic instinct, and an admirable intellectual earnestness. On these endowments her acting was built, and it developed only so far as the limitation of these resources permitted.

Miss Anderson's repertory, compared to that of the other actresses of the classic school, was very small. Her most successful characters were Galatea in Gilbert's *Pygmalion and Galatea,* Parthenia in Holm's *Ingomar,* and Perdita in Shakespeare's *Winter's Tale.* She acted no more than eighteen roles during her entire career. But neither this limitation nor any other seemed to matter to her adoring public. They ignored the carping of the critics and flocked to see her. When she retired, before the age of thirty and at the height of her popularity, her departure from the stage was loudly lamented by audiences in both the United States and Great Britain.

CLARA MORRIS, FANNY DAVENPORT,
AND MRS. LESLIE CARTER

Equally as fascinating as the later classic actresses, and even more colorful, were three representatives of the emotionalistic school. These ladies, heirs of the tradition established by Mrs. Mowatt, Laura Keene, and Matilda Heron, set new records for dazzling displays of emotional pyrotechnics during the last ten years of the nineteenth century. The most fascinating of the three was Clara Morris (1848-1925).

In the first volume of her reminiscences, Miss Morris asked the question, "What could *you* do to make yourself cry seven times a week for nine or ten months a year?" And then she wonders, ". . . did I ever do anything else?"[1] It was precisely this ability—to weep all kinds of tears at every single performance, season after season—that distinguished the acting of Clara Morris.

Miss Morris's career in emotionalistic acting was longer and more varied than the careers of her predecessors. Her apprenticeship began in 1862 in Cleveland, Ohio, and ended seven years later when she became leading lady at Woods Theatre in Cincinnati. But she remained in Cincinnati for only one season. The encouragement she received from critics and friends led her to apply for a position in Augustin Daly's New York company. Daly engaged her, at a nominal salary, with the idea of making a comedienne of her. But Clara Morris never acted comedy for Daly. When Agnes Ethel, one of Daly's stars, refused the feminine lead in a play called *Man and Wife,* Miss Morris was given the part. It was an emotional role in a domestic drama, and the young actress from the West played it with triumphant success. Henceforth, she became a specialist in domestic emotionalism. Parts in comedy or high tragedy were abandoned for the tearful heroines of contemporary French melodrama.

Miss Morris's power to manufacture stage tears was phenomenal. She could weep any time the dramatic situation demanded it. The tears were real, too, not simulated by trickery or illusion. They flowed whenever the actress turned her thoughts to sad or pitiable things.

The actress not only wept herself; she could make an audience weep and suffer with her. Spectators experienced an immediate, strong empathic response to her acting; they identified themselves personally with her struggles. Few actresses have ever possessed so much personal magnetism. Almost everyone felt it, but no one could explain it. Most of the critics agreed that her appeal defied analysis.

During the early years of her career Clara Morris maintained her popularity. As she grew older and stouter and failed to develop in versatility or artistry, and as the public taste shifted away from domestic melodrama, the critics began to ridicule her methods. Ill health and waning popularity forced her to retire from regular stage appearances in the 1890s. For several years thereafter she was seen occasionally in vaudeville and revivals and kept very much in the public eye by her lecture tours and writing. She died in 1925.

Clara Morris launched her career as an emotionalistic actress when Daly gave her the leading role in *Man and Wife.* Another actress in the company might have

---

[1] Clara Morris, *Life on the Stage* (New York: McClure, Phillips & Co., 1901), pp. 317, 141.

Fanny Davenport as Cleopatra

been given the part and she might have proved equally successful in it. This was Fanny Davenport (1850-1898), daughter of the eminent tragedian E. L. Davenport. She had been engaged by Daly in 1869, a year before Miss Morris joined the company, and had already established herself as a charming, vivacious comedienne. However, Daly feared that she did not possess the emotional power for the lead in *Man and Wife,* yet before Miss Davenport ended her career she had metamorphosed from a sparkling comedienne to an emotional star in four melodramas by Victorien Sardou.

The metamorphosis began in 1873 when Miss Davenport played the role of Madge, the tramp, in W. S. Gilbert's play *Charity*, and demonstrated considerable emotional power. Daly, always ready to capitalize on the talents of his players, recognized Miss Davenport's new potentialities and in 1876 wrote a play for her called *Pique*. It required Miss Davenport to exhibit emotional power and range. She succeeded brilliantly, and *Pique* ran for 238 consecutive performances. Shortly thereafter, Miss Davenport formed her own company and toured the United States as a star, building a repertoire that included more and more emotional roles. In 1883 she secured the American rights to Sardou's *Fedora*, and from then until her death in 1898 she was strictly a devotee of "Sardoodledom." *Fedora* lasted for five seasons and was followed by *La Tosca, Cleopatra,* and *Gismonda,* all of which were enormously successful. Miss Davenport will be remembered as a good though not a great actress, who succeeded both as an exponent of the personality school and as a leader in the field of feminine emotionalism.

The school of feminine emotionalism found another prominent exponent in Mrs. Leslie Carter (1862-1937). She was born Caroline Louise Dudley in Lexington, Kentucky, and at the age of eighteen married the prominent and wealthy Leslie Carter. The marriage lasted nine years, ending in a divorce suit that was the sensation of the period. Left without a means of support, Mrs. Carter determined to try the stage. Since she had no experience or training, her only assets were the publicity received from her divorce suit, her determination, and the beauty of her face and voice.

After her appearances in two Broadway productions—*The Ugly Duckling* in 1890 and *Miss Helyett* in 1891—in which she did not achieve any particular distinction, Mrs. Carter retired for two years and placed herself under the tutelage of David Belasco. Her training during this period was unique. Belasco recruited a company whose sole purpose was to rehearse with Mrs. Carter. With only Belasco as critic and audience, the would-be actress prepared and acted forty roles ranging from Shakespeare to French melodrama, from old comedy to modern farce.

Mrs. Carter emerged from training in 1895 to act the leading role in Belasco's production of *The Heart of Maryland.* She was sensationally successful and played the role for three years. Then followed her triumphs in Belasco's *Zaza, Du Barry,* and *Adrea.* The first two plays received as much notoriety for their "lurid" and "immoral" subject matter as for the emotional pyrotechnics of Mrs. Carter's performances.

In 1906 Mrs. Carter defied the wishes of her tutor and manager, Mr. Belasco, and married an obscure actor named William L. Payne. She never again acted for Belasco. Her career, however, continued for twenty-five years under other directors or under her own management. Although she flourished to a degree, her subsequent success was never so brilliant as it had been under Belasco. Her last stage appearances were in 1929, and she died eight years later at the age of seventy-five.

The bases for Mrs. Carter's success as an actress are clear. She had striking beauty: a mass of red hair "one shade hotter than Titian," an exquisitely pale complexion, soft blue eyes, and a slender, shapely figure. She had a mellifluous, musical voice, capable of great range and variety and trained for clarity and cadence; she had a fiery temperament to match her red hair; and finally, she had the ability to lose herself in the emotions of her role and to involve the audience in the hysteria of her own feelings. In her later years on the stage, after her break with Belasco, and after her youth and emotional powers had declined, she changed her style to fit her roles in such plays as Pinero's *The Gay Lord Quex* and Maugham's *The Circle*. However, it is as a successful emotional actress in plays such as *Zaza* and *Du Barry* that Mrs. Carter earned her place as a successor to the vanishing tradition of Mowatt, Keene, Heron, Morris, and Davenport.

THE PERSONALITY SCHOOL

During the late years of the nineteenth century, the ladies of the emotionalistic school enjoyed a wide popularity—but they were not without rivals. Competing for public esteem was a group of beautiful young players, mostly women, whose style of performance was different and who appeared in plays that were a sharp contrast to the fervid emotional dramas favored by Clara Morris and Mrs. Leslie Carter. This group of performers, whose most prominent representatives at the end of the nineteenth century were Maude Adams, Julia Marlowe, Viola Allen, and Ada Rehan, constituted a group that can be termed the *personality school*. Its outstanding characteristic is the appeal of the personality of the individual player—that is, the substitution of the performer's personality for the dramatic character, or the portrayal of dramatic characters that fit the performer's personality so exactly that performer and character are practically identical. In addition, the typical actress of this school offered the appeal of womanly loveliness and feminine virtue unsullied by coarseness or passion. She confined herself to roles that were sweet, wholesome, and refined—like herself. She was a deft and artful performer with unusual personal magnetism who used the stage as a means of projecting her feminine charms to inspire her audience with a feeling of purity and optimism.

Although the personality school flourished most prominently at the turn of the nineteenth century, it was ably represented much earlier in the history of American acting. Two notable early exponents of the style were Clara Fisher (1811-1898) and Maggie Mitchell (1837-1918). They both achieved great popularity and large public followings, and they rank as worthy predecessors of the Adams-Marlowe-Allen-Rehan group.

Maude Adams, 1872-1953; Julia Marlowe, 1866-1950; Viola Allen, 1869-1948; Ada Rehan, 1860-1916

Julia Marlowe, who was born in England and came to America at age four, began her theatrical career at the age of eleven, playing children's roles in musical shows. She made her adult debut as Parthenia in the old-fashioned tragedy of *Ingomar*. For the ensuing nine years she acted nothing but classical roles. Then, bowing to popular taste, she appeared in modern romantic comedies and played in them for six years. Returning to the classics, she began starring in Shakespearean drama with E. H. Sothern, and from 1904 until her retirement in 1924 she and Sothern became famous as the leading exponents of Shakespearean drama in the United States. Although she performed such parts as Cleopatra and Lady Macbeth, her success in these roles was negligible, whereas her achievements as Rosalind, Viola, and Juliet were admired and praised in both England and America. The latter roles suited Miss Marlowe exactly, for she was the epitome of womanly virtue and feminine loveliness and earned the reputation of being the foremost romantic actress of her time.

Allen, like Julia Marlowe, received her initial training in the classics. Her second adult role was Desdemona, which she played to the Othello of John Mc-Cullough. She also supported McCullough in *Virginius, The Gladiator,* and *Richard III.* She continued her theatrical education by playing engagements with Lawrence

Julia Marlowe

Theatre Collection, University of California Library at Berkeley.

Barrett and Tommaso Salvini, after which she acted for two seasons in old comedy with Joseph Jefferson, V. J. Florence, and Mrs. John Drew. Such thorough early experience in the standard drama of the mid-nineteenth century gave Miss Allen's style an elevated poetic quality that she never lost. It enabled her in later life to succeed admirably in romantic drama but handicapped her performance of modern comedy. Her best parts—which suited her refined, ladylike personality—were Shakespeare's Viola and Rosalind and the role of Gloria Quayle in a wholesome modern drama entitled *The Christian.*

In the training they received, Marlowe and Allen represent the survival of the classic repertory in the American theatre, but Maude Adams, who exceeded both of them in popularity, was identified almost exclusively with contemporary drama. She began her career acting modern roles and scored her greatest triumphs in the plays of James M. Barrie. Whereas we remember Marlowe for her Rosalind and Allen for her Viola, we remember Maude Adams for her captivating and enduring appeal in Barrie's *Peter Pan* and *The Little Minister.*

During her most active years, Maude Adams was the top money-making star in the entire United States. The public paid over a million and a half dollars to see

Maude Adams as Peter Pan in the souvenir program of
J. M. Barrie's *Peter Pan, the Boy Who Wouldn't Grow Up* (1907).

Theatre Collection, University of California Library at
Berkeley.

her in Chicago and Boston, and almost twice as much in New York City. At the peak of her career, she was "the most conspicuous figure upon the English-speaking stage, the most notable woman in a nation of a hundred million people. . ."[2]

The attraction of Miss Adams was the irresistible appeal of joyfulness, goodness, optimism, and eternal youth. She symbolized all that was fine, pure, and hopeful. Her acting filled the spectator with a clean, sweet sense of happiness and well-being. She avoided roles that portrayed the seamy side of life, and she rarely attempted parts that included the fierce, elemental passions of hate, jealousy, anger, or sex. In the realm of sentiment, of wholesome ideals, and heart-warming charm—all of which suited her personality—she excelled.

Adams, Marlowe, and Allen constitute a group that might be called the sisterhood of sweetness and light. They were not only admirable performers, they were also a strong moral influence on the life of the nation. For the first time in the his-

Viola Allen as Viola, James Young as Sebastian,
in Viola Allen's production of *Twelfth Night*.

Hoblitzelle Theatre Arts Library, Humanities Research Center, University of Texas at Austin.

[2]David Gray, "Maude Adams, a Public Influence," *Hampton's Magazine,* XXVI (June 1911), 725.

tory of the American theatre, uplifting influence became a major element in the appeal of popular stage performers. Audiences were attracted by the individual virtues of these ladies and by their reputations as moral leaders. With their appearance, the venerable Puritan prejudice against plays and players was reversed.

The talented and popular Ada Rehan should be listed as a fourth member of the sisterhood of sweetness and light. She was born in Limerick, Ireland, on April 22, 1860. When she was five years old, her family moved to Brooklyn, where she grew up and went to school. Except for professional trips abroad, she lived her whole life in the United States and died in New York City on January 8, 1916.

Ada Rehan, after a sound, practical apprenticeship, attracted the attention of Augustin Daly. In 1879 he engaged her as a permanent member of his company. She became his leading lady and remained in this position until Daly's death in 1899. During this time she played over two hundred parts, all with a skill, charm, and magnetism that placed her in the front rank of American comediennes. Daly selected her roles with the greatest care. All of them were designed to exhibit her radiant personality. Some of them were Shakespearean roles: Katherine in *The Taming of the Shrew,* Julia in *Two Gentlemen of Verona,* plus Viola and Rosalind —parts in which Julia Marlowe and Viola Allen excelled. More often, however, Miss Rehan was cast in farces and melodramas borrowed from German dramatists and reworked by Daly. In such plays as *Red Letter Nights, The Transit of Leo,* and *The Countess Gucki,* Rehan always portrayed the gay, mischievous, charming girl who filled the stage with wholesome merriment.

Continued repetition of the same kind of role in the same style of acting eventually arrested Miss Rehan's growth as an actress and limited her range of accomplishment. In 1905, at age forty-five, she made her final appearance on the stage. She died eleven years later, leaving the memory of an actress who had provided wholesome pleasure for thousands of playgoers by bringing to life a whole gallery of sprightly, charming, attractive women, all endowed with her radiant personality.

COMEDIANS OF THE LATE NINETEENTH CENTURY

The great tradition of comic acting, so brilliantly established early in the nineteenth century by players like Henry Placide, William Wood, and Henry J. Finn and so marvelously enriched later in the century by geniuses like William Warren, William J. Florence, and Joseph Jefferson, was carried on for a number of years at the end of the century by a corps of younger comedians reared in the shadow of their towering predecessors. For a time the younger group acted the same roles and fulfilled the same ideals. But as the repertory decreased in quality and as theatre practice pandered more and more to a debased public taste, the style and quality of comic acting underwent a change. Yet the players who met the demands of the new repertory and the changed conditions were often of the highest caliber and in many cases might have equaled their illustrious predecessors had they been faced with as stern a challenge. Outstanding in this group were E. M. Holland (1848-1913), who carried on the tradition of his father, George Holland, by acting the roles of classic comedy and then starring in such parts as Colonel Moberly in *Alabama* and Captain Redwood in *Jim the Penman;* and May Irwin (1862-1938), who after her apprenticeship acted comic roles for seven years at Tony Pastor's variety theatre, then joined Augustin Daly's company for four years, and finally returned to vaudeville to spend the remainder of her career sharing her infectious high spirits and her ability to create laughter with audiences all over the nation. Other accomplished performers who deserve mention were Nat C. Goodwin (1857-1919), a skillful light comedian; Francis Wilson (1854-1935), a successful star of comic opera and comic drama; Fritz Williams (1865-1930), an adept creator of fun in farce and sentimental comedy; Sol Smith Russell (1848-1902), a specialist in awkward, eccentric roles; Roland Reed (1856-1901), famous as Dr. Ollapod in *The Poor Gentleman* and as Dr. Pangloss in *The Heir-at-Law;* and William H. Crane (1845-1928), the perfect embodiment of such characters as David Harum and Colonel M. T. Elevator in *Our Boarding House.*

ACTORS OF THE TRANSITION

Another group of native performers who were prominent at the end of the nineteenth century might be called actors of the transition. The three most representative and illustrious of these were Richard Mansfield, E. H. Sothern, and Otis Skinner. In some respects all three were heirs of the classic school of Edwin Booth and carried on the classic tradition; in others, they illustrate the new influences that were reshaping the theatre, and they assisted in the reshaping. Instead of outlining the several aspects of their careers, which were many and notable, it might be more illuminating to note in what ways each one represented the transition from the ideals and practices of the nineteenth century to those of the twentieth.

Richard Mansfield

Richard Mansfield (1854-1907) began his career as an entertainer and singer. He scored his first triumph in acting at the age of twenty-eight when he created a vivid and startling portrait of a doddering old lecher in a play called *A Parisian Romance.* Within five years he was able to become his own manager and to star in his own productions. His roles covered a fascinating range of characters from Richard III to Beau Brummell, from Henry V to Cyrano de Bergerac, and from Shylock to Peer Gynt. The parts he played and the pattern of his seasons clearly indicate that he performed in an era of change. Like a star of the nineteenth century, he was close to the repertory tradition; he produced and acted fine plays (including Shakespeare) in the grand manner; and he, the star performer, was the dominating force and the center of attraction in all his productions. At the same time, Mansfield anticipated the changed theatre of the twentieth century: he acted far fewer

Richard Mansfield as Ivan the Terrible.

Hoblitzelle Theatre Arts Library, Humanities Research
Center, University of Texas at Austin.

roles than his great predecessors and his seasons of repertory were secondary to the
long runs of his hit plays; he produced two plays of George Bernard Shaw and
performed them in a manner that suited their satiric, modern content; and he was
the first to produce Ibsen's *Peer Gynt* in the United States and contributed to the
growing recognition of the great Norwegian.

E. H. Sothern

Edward Hugh Sothern (1859-1933), a second representative of the transi-
tional period, did not move toward the theatre of Shaw and Ibsen during the early
years of the twentieth century as did Richard Mansfield. Instead, he returned to the
traditions of an earlier period. During the first seven years of his career, he excelled
as a light comedian of charm and adroitness. He then started to appear in the dashing, romantic roles of cloak-and-sword drama such as *The Prisoner of Zenda*. Finally,
in 1899, he astonished and delighted his public with his performance as the hero of

E. H. Sothern in *The Prisoner of Zenda.*

Hoblitzelle Theatre Arts Library, Humanities Research Center, University of Texas at Austin.

Hauptmann's poetic tragedy *The Sunken Bell.* During the rest of his career, he devoted himself with dogged perserverence and earnest studiousness to developing himself as a tragedian and as a specialist in Shakespearean drama. After his marriage to Julia Marlowe in 1904, he and his wife became the leading Shakespearean performers in America.

Otis Skinner

Otis Skinner (1858-1942), a third outstanding actor of the transition, served a rich and vigorous apprenticeship. During the early years of his career, he played the varied and ever-changing roles characteristic of the versatile actors of the nineteenth century. But the influences of an era of transition overtook him. At the height of his career he succumbed to the long run. He played Colonel Bridau in *The Honor of the Family* for two and a half years; he played Hajj in *Kismet* for three years. He succumbed also to the changed public taste in drama. Instead of roles in Shakespeare, old comedy, or Restoration tragedy—the roles in which he had

Otis Skinner as Hajj in *Kismet.*
From the collection of Cornelia Otis Skinner.

learned his art—he played mostly in quaint, sentimental comedies or in romantic costume dramas. The list of these is long but among the most popular, in addition to *Kismet* and *The Honor of the Family,* were such favorites as *His Grace de Grammont, Prince Otto, Mister Antonio,* and *Blood and Sand.*

ROMANTIC HEROES

The romantic costume plays that formed too large a part of the later repertory of Otis Skinner were attractive to many other players. Actors who might have developed varied skills under different circumstances became specialists in romance and confined themselves largely to one kind of role. There have always been romantic heroes on the American stage and love for the kind of play in which they appear. The late nineteenth and early twentieth centuries are notable for the unusual popularity of this kind of drama, and the players who developed a style of acting appropriate to the romantic costume plays are first cousins—albeit more suave and sophisticated—of Edwin Forrest and the members of the heroic muscular school.

An outstanding example of an actor who specialized in romantic roles was James O'Neill (1847-1920), father of Eugene O'Neill. He began his career as a versatile player who acted many parts and showed promise of becoming a worthy successor to Booth, Davenport, and Barrett. But after he was cast as the Count of Monte Cristo in the famous play of the same name by Alexandre Dumas *père,* his fate was sealed. His success in the part was so great and the monetary returns were so enormous that he continued to play the role year after year. As an actor he is remembered solely as the dashing, romantic hero of *Monte Cristo.*

Other actors who starred as heroes of romance include the following:

William Faversham (1868-1940). Faversham was called in his prime "a matinee girl's ideal" and the "hero of a thousand matinees." He won great popularity as the vigorous, masculine hero of such plays as *Under the Red Robe, The Squaw Man,* and *The Prince and the Pauper.*

James K. Hackett (1869-1926). Hackett, son of the fine comedian James H. Hackett, caused heart palpitations in thousands of ladies who watched him as *The Prisoner of Zenda* or *Rupert of Hentzlau.*

John B. Mason (1857-1919). Mason excelled in romantic roles but was also successful in comedy, especially old comedies such as *The School for Scandal.* Later he made the transition to roles in the comedies of Arthur Wing Pinero and Henry Arthur Jones and won the accolade from Lewis Strang of being "the finest modern comedy actor in the country."

Many other popular players earned reputations as romantic heroes. Among them was William Gillette, already introduced as a playwright and an actor. He can be grouped with the later players of the heroic school. However, instead of performing his heroics with cape and sword, as O'Neill, Faversham, and Hackett usually did, Gillette used a pistol, a magnifying glass, and native cunning in such famous parts as the detective Sherlock Holmes and the spy Captain Thorne. With his strong, manly personality he created vivid portraits of a special kind of romantic hero.

FOREIGN STARS IN THE LIVELY SCENE

Adding to the busy theatrical scene in the last years of the nineteenth century and enriching the kinds of acting that made the period so varied and colorful were a host of foreign stars. Following in the footsteps of the first visiting celebrity, George Frederick Cooke, they trouped the nation from coast to coast, lending distinction and international color to the American scene.

Three of them came from Italy. They were Adelaide Ristori (1821-1906), a powerful actress of such roles as Lady Macbeth and Medea, who made her first American tour in 1866 and her last in the season of 1884-85; Tommaso Salvini (1829-1916), an actor with muscular physique, magnificent voice, and tremendous emotional intensity, who visited America five times between 1873 and 1889 and was a sensation, especially in his greatest role of Othello; and Eleonora Duse (1859-1924), often considered by her contemporaries to be the greatest actress in the world, who made her first American tour in 1893 and her last in 1924 performing the plays of both the nineteenth century, like *Camille,* and the twentieth century, like Ibsen's *Ghosts* and Gabriele d'Annunzio's *La Gioconda.*

France contributed two of its brightest stars to the American circuit. One was Sarah Bernhardt (1844-1923), "the Divine Sarah," who toured the United States many times between 1880 and 1917 performing an astonishing number of parts that ranged from neoclassical tragedy like *Phèdre* to nineteenth-century domestic melodrama like *Camille.* She attracted unlimited publicity wherever she went by her temperament and her eccentricities. Her colleague from the French theatre was Benoit Constant Coquelin (1841-1909), the great star of the Comédie Francaise, who was as brilliant in tragedy as he was in comedy and who toured the United States three times, in 1888, 1894, and 1900. On his final visit he teamed with Sarah Bernhardt to present two popular dramas by Rostand: *L'Aiglon* and *Cyrano de Bergerac.*

Scotland contributed one actor to the American scene, Robert Mantell (1854-1928), who, after 1890, organized a company and toured the United States many times in a repertory of Shakespearean tragedies, thus keeping alive one of the great traditions of the nineteenth century.

England provided the greatest number of visiting stars, just as she had been doing since the beginning of the American theatre. There were many of these, but especially notable were Adelaide Neilson (1846-1880), Sir Henry Irving (1838-1905), Ellen Terry (1847-1928), and Sir Johnston Forbes-Robertson (1853-1937).

It is clear that the galaxy of players, both native and foreign, who livened the American theatre at the close of the nineteenth century offered excellent performances in every style of acting. One important new school of acting that gained influence at this time has not been mentioned. It is the school of psychological naturalism developed by Minnie Maddern Fiske and destined to become the dominant style of acting in the twentieth century. Because it was an important influence in the theatrical renaissance of the twentieth century, it will be described later when those influences are discussed. It is sufficient to note that the new style was another contributor to the lively scene at the close of the nineteenth century.

14

Attending the Theatre in 1902

Before leaving the lively theatrical scene that prevailed at the turn of the century, let us pay another imaginary visit to a playhouse and savor the changes that have occurred since 1850. We shall find a mixture of old traditions and modern improvements. In some ways, it is a new world; in other ways it is still the world of the nineteenth century.

There are many performances to choose from during the period from 1899 to 1902. We decide, however, to relive the night of September 29, 1902, because that is the night when David Belasco, the most famous independent producer of the era, will open the first playhouse to bear his name. The production will be a revival of his own play, *Du Barry,* starring his special protégé, Mrs. Leslie Carter. The playhouse, the play, and the performance will all offer revealing illustrations of the state of the theatre at the beginning of the twentieth century.

As the year 1901 closed, Belasco was worried about his fortune as an independent producer. The Theatrical Syndicate was tightening its grip on playhouses in New York and elsewhere. Belasco's hit of 1901, *Du Barry,* was playing at the Criterion Theatre in New York, a Syndicate house. If Belasco were denied the use of this house and of other first-class houses throughout the nation, his future would be bleak—unless, of course, he accepted the profit-squeezing terms offered him by the Syndicate. Belasco had vowed never to surrender to the Syndicate; fortunately, he never had to. In January 1902, he was unexpectedly offered a five-year lease on the Republic Theatre by Oscar Hammerstein, its owner, who was also fighting the Syndicate. Belasco accepted instantly, and thus was born the first Belasco Theatre.

When Belasco inspected his newly acquired playhouse, located on Forty-second Street off Broadway, he found it needed extensive remodeling. "The stage," he told his friends, "was wrong, the house was wrong, and the colors set my teeth on edge."[1] He began his alterations in April 1902, intending to spend no more than twenty thousand dollars at the most. Before he finished, he had rebuilt the entire theatre except the four main walls and part of the roof. In the process he blasted out basement space for retiring rooms and machinery rooms (striking a subterranean spring that had to be sealed up) and spent one hundred fifty thousand dollars.

Theatregoers have been fascinated by the news of Belasco's rebuilding and redecorating, which has been reported from time to time in the daily newspapers. The first announcement of the opening of the new house appears on September 15, 1902. The advertisement, carried by all the metropolitan dailies, reports that the first performance will be Monday, September 29, and that seats for the opening night will be "allotted entirely by subscription." This means that a playgoer has to sit down immediately, write out a check, and mail an application for tickets. All seats in the orchestra and first balcony cost three dollars, but after the opening night prices will be two dollars, a dollar fifty, one dollar, and fifty cents. All the playhouses in New York have box offices now, and mail orders are usually filled promptly. Prices vary from twenty-five cents to two dollars; many good shows can be seen for fifty cents. However, the ticket speculator has now appeared; he buys up blocks of seats for the biggest attractions and then resells them at inflated prices.

The opening play at the Belasco will be a revival of, or rather a continuation of, *Du Barry*, starring Mrs. Leslie Carter. The play was a hit last season and ran from December 25, 1901, to May 31, 1902, when it closed for the summer.

On Sunday, September 28, a search of the newspapers yields only scanty information about the new Belasco Theatre. The opening performance, scheduled for the next day, is mentioned in the theatre columns and there are fair-sized advertisements in all the papers, but no detailed stories. The *New York World* does reprint a statement from Belasco on the purpose of his new theatre. In the first paragraph Belasco says, "The house is primarily intended as the dramatic abode of Mrs. Leslie Carter and the plays in which she will appear." In the second paragraph, he declares, ". . . in all ways I am anxious to make this new dramatic home of mine a standard of refinement, good taste, good entertainment, and good art." Those patrons who are not admirers of Mrs. Carter will find the last statement inconsisent with the first.

Although the Sunday papers on September 28 carry little news about the Belasco opening, there is plenty of other theatrical news, both colorful and amusing. On the front page of the *New York Times,* for example, we read that Wilton Lackaye, a popular actor, has been jailed in St. Louis for his involvement in a brawl; and on page eight is the story that the stage manager of the Garrick Theatre in New York has shot and killed his wife to avenge his "outraged domestic honor."

The pleasanter theatrical news, however, is the long list of amusements available to New Yorkers during the coming week. The Sunday *Times* lists forty different offerings typical of the varied attractions of our era. Included are nineteen regular

[1]William Winter, *The Life of David Belasco* (New York: Moffat, Yard and Company, 1918), II:53.

plays, eight musical shows, one grand opera, seven programs of vaudeville, three concerts, and finally, two circuses. Remember that the theatrical season is just starting. In a month or two there will be many more than forty attractions.

In the long list of playhouses we note only two venerable names. One is Wallack's, which has just celebrated the fiftieth anniversary of its opening. The other is the Murray Hill Theatre, the only house on the list to advertise a play by Shakespeare. During the current week, the Murray Hill is presenting Hoyt's farce, *A Rag Baby*, but beginning October 6, Elita Proctor Otis will appear as Lady Macbeth. During the coming season there will be additional performances of Shakespeare's dramas and other classics, but the number of such productions has shrunk steadily during the past half-century. Now the repertory is mainly farce, romance, melodrama, and musical comedy.

On Monday, the twenty-ninth, we start for the theatre in a horse-drawn cab at the early hour of 6:45 P.M. in order to have ample time to inspect the new playhouse before curtain time. When we reach the playhouse at Broadway and Forty-second Street, two or three hundred people are already waiting to enter. It is a cultivated, well-dressed crowd. Promptly at seven o'clock, the new wrought-iron doors are swung open by attendants in livery, and we enter the new lobby. It is an elegant reception area that resembles a lounge in an exclusive private club. The walls and ceiling are paneled in oak; the carpets and draperies are a combination of reds blending into browns and greens. The whole area is artfully lighted by electric fixtures.

We are about to enter the auditorium but remember all the talk about the elegant retiring rooms for ladies and gentlemen, made possible by blasting out a basement area under the lobby. A visit to these reveals much about Mr. Belasco's good taste. The smoking room for gentlemen is furnished with carpets, drapes, a writing desk with a supply of fine stationery, and lounge chairs close to a table on which are placed copies of the best magazines. The total effect is subdued and gracious. The ladies who inspect the "boudoir," or powder room, report that it is even more elegant than the lobbies. It is furnished in the style of Marie Antoinette and is claimed to be exactly true to the period.

As we enter the auditorium of the playhouse, the ladies are given a souvenir booklet entitled *The Story of Du Barry*. Handsomely printed on heavy paper, it contains—in addition to the story—several elegant photographs of the production and the autographs of both Mr. Belasco and Mrs. Carter.

The interior of the auditorium continues the color scheme of the lobby: subdued tones of green, red, and golden-brown. The side and back walls are hung with tapestries depicting an autumnal forest. The seats, with arms, are richly upholstered, a great improvement over the seating found in mid-century playhouses. The upholstery is done in shades of silver-green, and on the back of each seat is embroidered the Napoleonic bee, signifying Mr. Belasco's belief that "work is the greatest good." The ceiling dome of the house is decorated in shades of gold, gray, and rose, while the principal-act curtain is of plain green baize, to continue the original tradition of the colonial theatre. The subdued richness of Mr. Belasco's new playhouse is a reminder of his public statement that he has tried to make the surroundings "more those of a cozy, comfortable drawing room than a theatre."

One important feature of the house that has helped Mr. Belasco to accomplish his aim is the moderate size. The new theatre seats only 950 people: 450 on the lower floor, 200 in the balcony, and 300 in the gallery. Compared to the 4,000 seats that the old Bowery Theatre once boasted, the new Belasco house is small. Its size indicates that a new kind of play, a new kind of acting, and a new concept of production are beginning to supplant those that dominated the theatre for so many years just past.

From seats in the front row of the balcony, the elegance of the audience is readily apparent. We are especially interested in watching the stage boxes, which are now located outside the proscenium frame and no longer overhang any of the acting area as they did in the early years of the nineteenth century. One of these boxes is occupied by Mrs. Carter's mother and her son, Dudley Carter, a young man who has inherited many of his mother's features. Mrs. Carter seems to play directly to him, and her own emotionalistic style of acting is heightened by his presence. After the big scene in which she beats her lover into insensibility and hides him in order to save his life, she is pelted with flowers from all sides—but she acknowledges only her son's spray of lilies of the valley by a profusion of kisses and tears. It is as emotional as any moment of the play.

Mrs. Leslie Carter in a scene from *Du Barry*.
Theatre Collection, University of California Library at Berkeley.

The audience adds to the excitement of the evening, but the real spectacle is on the stage. The lavish scenery, the new machinery for quick scenic changes, and the Belasco wizardry with lights provide fascination all evening. The play requires a cast of fifty speaking parts plus many supernumeraries. Mr. Belasco uses his people so artfully that we feel that there are hundreds in the crowd scenes. The action of the drama is divided into five acts and eight scenes that move from a French milliner's shop to the palace of Versailles, and finally to the street in front of the milliner's shop. The most spectacular scenes are the fete, given in the gardens of Versailles, and the final scene where Du Barry is dragged in a cart through the streets of Paris to her death on the guillotine. Belasco, true to his reputation, has made every scene as authentic and realistic as human ingenuity can contrive.

Eight scenes, if they are to be changed in a reasonably short time, require elaborate machinery. Not too long ago, when wings and drops sufficed, there was no need for complicated devices for shifting the scenery. As soon as the desire for authentic, three-dimensional, often heavy settings developed, the need for machinery developed too. The audience knows that Mr. Belasco is a leader in equipping his stages with the machinery required by these settings. The devices in his new playhouse are the talk of the town. The entire acting area of the stage is trapped. The center trap, which reminds us of a similar device in Booth's Theatre of 1869, measures fifteen by thirty feet and is an elevator that can be lowered to the basement area. In the basement an entire scene on a wagon stage can be rolled onto the elevator, then raised to the stage level. Thus, to shift the central segment of a scene requires only the time it takes to lower the elevator, replace one wagon stage with another, and raise the elevator again. To supplement this central device, there is a complete set of lines for raising scenery and drapery into the overhead area, then lowering it again when needed.

Belasco's new theatre is also equipped with the latest electrical devices, as one would expect from a man who is always experimenting with lights. The sources of the light are all concealed, each light is individually controlled by a dimmer so that variations in intensity and direction can be easily achieved. No wonder that Mr. Belasco is regarded as the master craftsman of the American theatre.

The play itself is from the industrious pen of Mr. Belasco. It uses historical characters and settings, but the events depicted are entirely fictional. Mr. Belasco's fertile imagination has invented a romantic story about the life and loves of Jeanette Vaubernier, the young lady who becomes Madame Du Barry. The play is typical of his dramaturgy. It is colorful, contrived, sentimental, and emotional. It offers grand opportunities for scenic displays, dramatic confrontations, and emotional pyrotechnics from the leading lady. Mrs. Carter, however, is not at her best on opening night. She is suffering from a severe cold and also from the tensions of an opening night with her only child watching her. In the early scenes, trying to be charming and coquettish, she seems forced and awkward. In the big scenes her famous emotionalism exerts its usual fascination and stirs the audience to enthusiasm. When Mrs. Carter is aroused, she has an animal attraction that is magnetic; when she lacks inspiration, her acting is ordinary and empty.

The dramatic critics are divided in their evaluation of Mrs. Carter's performance in *Du Barry*. The reviewer of the *New York Times* calls it a "strenuous and unmodulated impersonation";[2] *Leslie's Weekly Magazine* declares it a "wonderfully strong performance."[3] William Winter, one of the most influential critics, recognizes what he calls the "executive force and skill in Mrs. Carter's performance" and also her "abundant physical fascination." However, he says that her method in the big scenes of *Du Barry* is "to work herself into a state of violent excitement, to weep, vociferate, shriek, rant, become hoarse with passion, and finally to flop and beat the floor." He adds that he does not consider this to be acting but "it is merely the facile expedient of transparent artifice. . . ."[4]

The fascination of the opening night is enhanced by the excited responses of the audience and by admiration for Belasco's versatility and accomplishments. After each act his name is called, but he delays his appearance until after Act IV, when the calls become vociferous and insistent. He then steps modestly before the curtain, amid great applause, and makes a graceful little speech. He ends it with a very human confession by saying, "You cannot know what it means to me to speak to you at last, after thirty years of labor in the dramatic calling, from the stage of my own theatre. Ladies and gentlemen, I thank you—I thank you—I can say no more."[5]

After this effective speech the final curtain calls following the last act seem almost anticlimactic. As the playgoers leave the elegant new playhouse, they are aglow with pleasure and with high hopes for the future of the theatre in New York. The old Bowery Theatre of the 1850s had much to recommend it. Despite its vast size, the repertory and the acting were superb and the appeal was immense. However, Belasco's theatre at the start of the new century also has much to recommend it. The repertory is deficient in the classics and the acting is emotionalistic, but the playhouse is more comfortable than any in past history, and the stagecraft is the most advanced of its kind. Playgoers feel that they can look forward with pleasure to what the next few years will bring.

[2] "Plays that Run On," *New York Times,* 5 October 1902.
[3] *Leslie's Weekly Magazine,* 2 October 1902, p. 317.
[4] Winter, *The Life of David Belasco,* p. 38.
[5] Ibid., pp. 61, 62.

15

The Theatrical Renaissance of the Twentieth Century

By the beginning of the twentieth century, the United States of America had achieved world power. The Spanish-American War of 1898 shocked the nations of Europe into realizing that fact. As a result, American prestige throughout the world rose sharply, as did American national pride. Also, United States involvement in imperialism began. The Spanish-American War gave the United States possession of Puerto Rico, Guam, and the Philippine Islands, and made it protector of Cuba. Subsequent events increased its involvements in international affairs. In 1900 America helped form an international force to suppress the Boxer Rebellion in China. During the following decade the country aided and abetted the Panamanian revolution, arbitrated the dispute between Germany and Venezuela, arranged the Portsmouth Conference, which ended the Russo-Japanese War, mediated the Moroccan dispute between France and Great Britain, and sent the United States Navy around the world to impress the nations with its military prowess. The American nation, which a hundred years before had been viewed with contempt, was now a colossus playing a dominant role in world affairs.

The role of leadership was justified by the internal growth of the United States, which had been swift and tremendous. In 1850 the population was 23,191,000; by 1900 it had swelled to 76,094,000. In 1850 there were thirty-one states in the union; by 1900 there were forty-five states extending from coast to coast and from Canada to Mexico. The burgeoning population of these states was tending more and more to concentrate in towns and cities. In 1790 at least 90 percent of the population lived in rural areas. By 1900 40 percent lived in towns with more than 2,500 inhabitants. Twelve of the largest cities of the nation were now located in the Middle West; San Francisco and Los Angeles, on the Pacific Coast, were both metropolises; New York and Philadelphia, in the East, boasted more than 1,000,000 inhabitants each.

The population continued to be polyglot. The stream of immigrants that had increased so rapidly in the mid-nineteenth century was now an annual inundation. In the three decades since 1870, almost eleven million immigrants had arrived in America. By 1900 one-third of the people of the country were foreign-born or the children of immigrants. However, the population was less diverse than these figures might suggest, because more than three-quarters of the newcomers were from Canada or Northwestern Europe; they either spoke English or learned it quickly and were soon assimilated. Less than one-quarter were from Southern or Eastern Europe and tended to huddle in ethnic groups in the big cities.

As a whole, American society was remarkably homogeneous. One could travel three thousand miles east and west and fifteen hundred miles north and south and see the same flag, hear the same language, and observe the same culture. Because of the nationwide distribution of manufactured goods, Americans everywhere wore the same styles in clothing, used the same household gadgets, and ate the same brands of food. In all sections of the country, people tended "to talk alike, think alike, act alike." Their towns were alike.

The homogeneity of American life was strengthened by the improved means of transportation between the various sections of the country and by the ease of communication. Many states were linked by waterways; all of them were connected by roadways and by two hundred thousand miles of railways. The telegraph and the telephone were everywhere, while the same books and magazines were circulated from Maine to California. As a warning of things to come, eight thousand automobiles were registered by 1900.

In the first years of the twentieth century, the country enjoyed boom times. Natural resources seemed unlimited, while the energy and inventiveness of American citizens seemed inexhaustible. The energy had raised the country, since the Civil War, to first place among the industrial nations of the world; the ingenuity had resulted in the registration of more than two hundred thirty-four thousand inventions in the decade of the 1890s and more than three hundred fourteen thousand in the years from 1900 to 1909. Prosperity and optimism were in the air.

The American zeal for reform was undiminished in 1900. In 1850 it had focused on such institutions as the penal system, insane asylums, and the little red schoolhouse. Now the crusading, reforming spirit, inflamed by new problems, was directed toward a huge variety of evils and deficiencies. For example, conservation and reclamation received major and much-needed attention. A new Department of Commerce and Labor was established to mediate the conflicts between capital and labor. The dormant antitrust laws were invoked against the giant monopolies, which sought to limit free enterprise. There was an outcry against "bloated plutocrats," "dirty-handed millionaires," and "predatory wealth." The cry was raised by the leaders of the movement known as "muckraking." It began in 1902 when Lincoln Steffens exposed the corrupt alliances between big business and municipal governments. Other gifted journalists soon began exposing such evils as the railway barons, the Beef Trust, the "white slave" traffic, the abuse of child labor, the plight of slum dwellers, the exploitation of Negroes, the conditions in the food and drug industries, and graft and corruption in many agencies of government. These exposés strengthened the movement for more democratic processes in government. This, in turn, led to such reforms as the popular election of senators, the city manager plan of municipal government, nomination of candidates by direct primary, and lawmaking by initiative and referendum.

The exposés of the muckrakers and the growing consciousness of social problems were reflected in the playwriting of the period—not to a great extent and not with great effectiveness, it must be admitted, but to some degree nevertheless. Consider three plays that we have already discussed. Clyde Fitch planned his last play, *The City*, to be an exposé of the corrupting influence of urban life on a small-town family. Although the play failed to do this, Fitch at least recognized a pressing contemporary problem. James A. Herne, in *Shore Acres*, introduced another such problem, the spoilation of a beautiful stretch of seacoast for commercial gain. The problem is only lightly touched in the play, but it is there. Herne did a far better job of discussing a social problem in *Margaret Fleming*. The whole play concerns the consequences of infidelity in marriage and the double standard in morality. Other plays of the period present a wide range of problems and thus represent the awakened social conscience of the American public in the early years of the twentieth century.

However, the zeal for reform that characterized these years was most vividly felt in the theatre in another way. The theatre made its greatest contribution to the reform movement by reforming itself. Every art and activity of play production underwent a change. The changes were so complete and so multiphasic that they constitute what can be called the theatrical renaissance of the twentieth century.

The conditions in the theatre that needed reform were many and varied. They have already been suggested; let us now make them explicit.

Playwriting. More American playwrights were practicing their art than ever before, yet the products of their pens were second-rate or worse. Of the hundred or hundred and fifty new plays that reached Broadway every year in the first decade of the twentieth century, there were an astonishing number of flimsy, stereotyped dramas; none had the stature to command world attention.

Acting. As the classic repertory in comedy and tragedy declined, so did the versatile tragedians and character comedians who were able to perform the great roles greatly. In their place appeared performers of the emotionalistic and personality schools and romantic heroes of the muscular school who adjusted their styles of acting to fit the popular second-rate plays of the period.

Stagecraft. The mounting of a play was generally as stereotyped as the play itself. On the one hand, the tradition of flat, two-dimensional painted scenery, so universal in the nineteenth century, lingered on, particularly in the playhouses outside New York City. Such settings as these alternated with the overly realistic settings of Belasco and his followers. Often these settings went to the extreme and filled the stage with so many real objects that the audience saw little else. The lighting of these scenes sometimes showed imagination, but more often it was the flat, uniform illumination that comes from footlights in front and rows of border lights overhead.

Playhouses. There were thousands of them throughout the United States, and promoters were continuing to build them at a rapid rate. But the playhouses followed a set pattern. They were slightly modified versions of the Restoration playhouse, which had been transplanted from England to America at the end of the eighteenth century. The proscenium doors and boxes had been eliminated, but all the other features were there: a pictureframe stage, with a few boxes and galleries rising above a lower floor. Sight lines were usually bad, leg room was inadequate, lobby space was cramped, dressing rooms and work areas were small and badly lighted. The fixed shape of the playhouse confined directors to one style of presentation.

Business management. The independent producer, who was often devoted to the art of the theatre, had practically disappeared. In his place were producers who turned out the popular plays demanded by the business tycoons of the Theatrical Syndicate. To do so, they applied to play production some of the mass techniques that were so successful in industry.

In summary, show business, like other businesses at the start of the twentieth century, was prosperous, lively, and colorful. But it was also complacent, commercialized, commonplace, and uninspired. The best of the ideals and traditions that had motivated the theatre of the nineteenth century were dead or dying. The inspiration was gone. In every art of the theatre there was a crying need for renewal and rebirth.

Like a miracle, the need was met. A marvelous outpouring of ideas and creativity swept through the theatres of Europe and America. Innovators and pioneers in every branch of theatrical art emerged to challenge old concepts and to supply fresh inspiration. These gifted men and women, both European and American, did not all appear at the same time or make their contributions during the same period. Many of them began their work in the late years of the nineteenth century; many introduced ideas that exerted little influence until several years later, at least in the United States. Nevertheless, by the first decade of the twentieth century, when the arts of the drama in the United States were ripe for change, the accumulated force and influence of these innovators was great enough to stir the American theatre into a creative ferment and to effect changes that we can call a theatrical renaissance.

It is appropriate to look first at the European innovators who appeared in various branches of dramatic art. Much of their work antedated that of the American innovators and, in many cases, influenced American contributions. To comprehend American contributions, we must understand the sources of their inspiration.

FOREIGN CONTRIBUTIONS
TO THE THEATRICAL RENAISSANCE

Four giants among foreign dramatists helped to free the world, including the United States, from the sterile traditions of nineteenth-century playwriting. The most influential of these was Henrik Ibsen (1828-1906), one of the great pioneers of the modern theatre. He began his career about 1850 by writing historical and poetic plays culminating in *Peer Gynt* (1867). Then he turned to realistic social-problem plays in prose, by means of which he opened up a new world of subject matter and of dramatic techniques. In play construction he rejected all the devious devices of melodrama: the contrived situations, the amazing discoveries, the startling climaxes, and so on. He began his plays just before the crisis of the action and, after skillfully exposing the past, he moved swiftly through the complications to the climax and conclusion. His plays are masterpieces of compact, uncontrived construction. He also rejected the stock characters of nineteenth-century melodrama; and by using his own sensitive understanding of human nature, he created contemporary people in contemporary situations and let them reveal their characters

Henrik Ibsen in Dresden, October 1873.

From *Life of Henrik Ibsen,* by Edmund Gosse. Charles Scribner's Sons, 1908. By permission of the publisher.

in speech and action. The speech he gave them was realistic prose, not the ornate rhetoric or pseudopoetry favored by so many nineteenth-century playwrights. But most important, perhaps, Ibsen chose to write his plays about serious social problems that had long been unmentionable. In *A Doll's House* (1878-79), he exposed the stultifying situation of nineteenth-century women; in *Ghosts* (1881), he dared to reveal the horror of hereditary syphilis and the hypocrisy that surrounded it; in *Pillars of Society* (1875-77), he showed the corruption and double-dealing of the leaders of society. Some of his themes seem trite and old-fashioned today, but they were new and startling in their time. In fact, when Ibsen's plays were first produced, they sent a shock wave throughout the Western world. But they opened up a new and exciting source of subject matter to the dramatists of Europe and America.

August Strindberg (1849-1912), a Swedish dramatist, was another pioneer in revitalizing dramatic composition. He was both amazingly prolific and startlingly innovative. In his more than fifty plays, he introduced subject matter and invented techniques that have influenced playwrights ever since. Strindberg began his career as a dramatist by writing historical plays such as *The Free-Thinker* (1870) and *Sir Bengt's Wife* (1882). Then he turned to realism with plays like *The Father* (1887) and *Miss Julie* (1888). In the final period of his life, he created a form that might be called a symbolic interpretation of actuality, or expressionism. The best known of these plays are *The Dance of Death* (1901), *A Dream Play* (1902), and *The Spook Sonata* (1907). Writing with far greater intensity than Ibsen, he went beyond Ibsen's exposure of social corruption to explore "the inarticulate impulses and processes of the human mind."

In Russia, Anton Chekhov (1860-1904) created another new kind of play. He abandoned plot in the old-fashioned sense and wrote dramas that seemed to start and end aimlessly. In his four masterpieces—*The Seagull* (1896), *Uncle Vanya* (1899), *The Three Sisters* (1901), and *The Cherry Orchard* (1904)—he showed the doomed, frustrated middle class of Russia playing out their troubled, meaningless lives. His plays reveal the sterility and hopelessness that characterize the lives of millions of people everywhere. The plays may seem formless and meaningless compared to the well-made plays of the melodramatists, but they have a subtle poetic form and a profundity of meaning that revealed new worlds for the dramatists of the twentieth century to explore.

The fourth of the innovative giants in playwriting is the Irish-Englishman George Bernard Shaw (1856-1950). Shaw began his career as a jack-of-all-writing, composing articles, advertisements, poems, and novels. He then turned to reviewing books, music, and drama. His essays on plays and players were brilliant, iconoclastic, and widely influential. In 1885, excited by the work of Ibsen, he started writing his first play, convinced that the stage offered him a lively forum for his ideas on social and political reform. *Widower's Houses,* his first drama, was produced in 1892. Shaw's playwriting continued for half a century and taught the world that the play of ideas, if constructed with wit and eloquence, could be as entertaining as contrived melodrama or sexual romance. In the course of his long career, Shaw exposed and ridiculed every sacred concept of the Victorian age and, like Ibsen before him, won the right to dramatize forbidden subjects such as prostitution, slum landlordism, religion, family relations, and a whole host of other topics. Among Shaw's most popular plays are *Candida* (1897), *Caesar and Cleopatra* (1899), *Man and Superman* (1903), *Major Barbara* (1905), *Pygmalion* (1912, better known to the younger generation as the musical play *My Fair Lady*), and *Saint Joan* (1923).

The four giants—Ibsen, Strindberg, Checkhov, and Shaw—were writing vigorous new realistic plays long before there were directors to accept them, theatres to house them, or sympathetic audiences to see them. All those things were essential if a new generation of playwrights was to be nurtured. In every country there was a response. Starting in Paris in 1887 with the Théatre Libre of André Antoine, the idea of *free theatres* to introduce new dramatists and to experiment with new methods of production spread from country to country. In Germany, Otto Brahm

George Bernard Shaw.
Hoblitzelle Theatre Arts Library, Humanities Research Center, University of Texas at Austin.

opened his Freie Bühne two years after the Théatre Libre was established. In England in 1891, J. T. Grein, a native of Holland, organized the Independent Theatre Society, which stimulated the creation of other experimental stages serving Great Britain. In 1898 the Moscow Art Theatre began its illustrious career under the aegis of two gifted artists, Constantin Stanislavsky and Vladimir Nemirovich-Danchenko. Finally, in 1899 the Irish Literary Theatre was founded by William Butler Yeats, Edward Martyn, and Lady Gregory. All of these groups featured new methods of production and new styles of acting. Also they sponsored the work of Ibsen and of other new, soon-to-be-distinguished playwrights.

Two other important necessities of play production also underwent reform and rejuvenation in the late nineteenth century. The first was the playhouse itself. Theatre architecture had long been dominated by the designs of Italian court theatres and English Restoration theatres. These, of course, included tiers of boxes and galleries arranged in a circular or a horseshoe pattern from one side of a picture-frame stage to the other. In 1876 Richard Wagner opened his festival playhouse in Bayreuth, and in 1907 the Munich Art Theatre, designed by Max Littman, was built. Both houses eliminated boxes, balconies, and galleries. All seats were placed on a single floor that sloped upward, arena style, from the stage. Every spectator had a full view of the stage. From these two houses spread the influence that revolutionized theatre design and eventually gave us the marvelously versatile, flexible playhouses found in many university and community centers today.

The revolution in stagecraft that came at the turn of the century was equally far-reaching and more immediately effective. The revolution was largely the work of two amazingly creative men: a Swiss, Adolphe Appia, and an Englishman, Edward Gordon Craig. Between 1895 and 1905, the writing and sketches of these two men demolished the old concepts of scenery and lighting and established the basis for modern stagecraft.

Appia's contributions began in the late nineteenth century with the publication of two books whose subject was the staging of grand opera. Appia declared that the aim of scenery and lighting is not to provide a colorful visual display, but solely to enhance and strengthen the action of the play. The scenery must also be simple and uncluttered to increase the focus on the actor. To relate and unify the actor and the three-dimensional scenery, "living light" should be used. By this Appia meant light that is constantly changing to enhance the changes in the action, tensions, and moods of the play. To illustrate his beliefs, Appia designed scenery and lighting for six productions between 1903 and 1924. His settings were always a simple but noble arrangement of platforms, ramps, and walls. Together with the living light, they provided a milieu that gave primary attention to the actor and the play.

Gordon Craig, the other pioneer in establishing the new stagecraft, was the son of the famous English actress Ellen Terry. He started his career as an actor but was soon puzzled and dismayed by the scenery and lighting he observed around him. He began to analyze what was wrong and presently reached many of the same conclusions as Appia. Like the older man, Craig decided that only simple, sugges-

Adolphe Appia's drawing (1896) for the setting of Act I, the sacred forest of Wagner's *Parsifal.* Ross Theatre Collection, University of California Library at Berkeley.

tive, three-dimensional scenery could possibly help the actor project the truth and beauty of a play. In 1900 he illustrated his ideas in a production of the opera *Dido and Aenas.* During the next few years he designed the settings for several plays, all of which had "simplicity and grandeur."

Craig turned his critical attention to many other problems of play production. In his books, starting with *On the Art of the Theatre* (1905), he challenged almost every established concept of the nineteenth-century theatre and introduced ideas that were shocking at the time—and enormously stimulating.

The ideas of Appia and Craig led to improvements in stage equipment, stage lighting, and many other areas. But the most important result of their pioneering was the emergence of a dazzling new corps of scene designers. Within a few years these artists replaced both the flat, painted scenery of the nineteenth century and the meticulous realism of Belasco with original, stunning settings that we now recognize as the *new stagecraft.*

The United States was first introduced to this stagecraft when Max Reinhardt brought his production of *Sumurun* to New York in 1912. The scenery and lighting of the production emphasized simplicity, suggestiveness, and poetic symbolism. Two years later, an American theatre man, Sam Hume, who had studied with Gordon Craig in Italy, staged the first exhibition of scenic designs inspired by the new stagecraft. Between 1916 and 1918, he used a simple arrangement of architectural forms in his productions at the Arts and Crafts Theatre in Detroit. In 1915 English producer Harley Granville-Barker excited the progressive playgoers of New York with a series of plays all featuring the simple, suggestive scenery and lighting of the new stagecraft. One of the most successful of these settings was for Anatole France's *The Man Who Married a Dumb Wife*. It turned out to be the creation of a young American artist, Robert Edmond Jones, who became one of the greatest American designers of the twentieth century. By 1917, when the Vieux Colombier company of French director Jacques Copeau exhibited their own version of the new stagecraft in New York, the ideals of the movement were well on their way to becoming an important influence in the American theatre.

AMERICAN CONTRIBUTION
TO THE THEATRICAL RENAISSANCE

The creative ferment of Europe influenced American stage design and almost every other theatrical activity as well. Many European innovations were eagerly espoused and elaborated; many original contributions were made.

The first American attempt to establish a modern repertory theatre similar to the Moscow Art Theatre was made in New York in 1909. There had been earlier attempts to organize an independent theatre, an art theatre, or an endowed theatre patterned after the free theatres of Europe. But not until 1909 did the growing dissatisfaction with commercial drama inspire a group of wealthy citizens to take decisive action. Financial and social leaders like John Jacob Astor, J. Pierpont Morgan, Cornelius Vanderbilt, and Otto Kahn banded together to build a grand new playhouse which they called, simply, the New Theatre. It seated three thousand and boasted a mammoth acting area with a revolving stage and all the latest technical equipment. A company was engaged with the understanding that it would be a permanent troupe and would be molded into an ensemble like the companies of the Moscow Art Theatre and the Comédie-Francaise. The man chosen to direct the troupe was a wealthy young American, Winthrop Ames, who had studied in Europe and was enthusiastic over the new ideals of theatrical art. The first production starred Julia Marlowe and E. H. Sothern in Shakespeare's *Antony and Cleopatra*. Subsequent productions also emphasized stars rather than plays or the ensemble. The noble experiment continued for two years, then, for a variety of reasons, it collapsed.

More successful in the growing battle against a debased commercial theatre was the founding of the Drama League of America in 1910. Its purpose was to organize audiences all over the nation and educate their tastes and their general appreciation of dramatic literature. Hundreds of study groups were formed throughout the country, and a national magazine, *The Drama*, was established. The study groups read and discussed new plays and listened to idealists speak on what good theatre should be. Communities everywhere became excited over developments

Robert Edmond Jones's drawing of a setting for a street scene in *Othello,* 1933.
Ross Theatre Collection, University of California Library at Berkeley.

in the theatre and over the value of drama as a unifying cultural force in society.
The league eventually dwindled and disappeared, but before it declined it enrolled
thousands of citizens in the movement against cheapness and vulgarity in drama and
made them a part of the theatrical renaissance of the new century.

The general ferment that produced the Drama League and that was intensified
by the league's activity resulted in two parallel movements of the greatest importance to the future of the American theatre. One was the introduction of theatre
arts into the curricula of colleges and universities; the other was the rise of the
little theatres, or community theatres, throughout the nation. In the beginning,
the movements developed separately, although they often shared the same sources
of inspiration. In the middle and late years of the century, the two movements
often became partners. Their origin, growth, and union are the most fruitful developments, perhaps, of the entire century.

The Dramatic Arts in the Colleges

Establishing the study of the dramatic arts as a legitimate discipline in the
colleges and universities of America was not quick or easy. Remember that American colleges, even in colonial times, had sponsored the study of classic drama and

the presentation of dramatic colloquies and dialogues. As early as 1736, students at the College of William and Mary performed Joseph Addison's *Cato*. From that time on, the staging of plays continued in many American colleges. But the activity was never a part of the curriculum. Plays were studied as literature in the English department. If those plays were staged, the activity was extracurricular and earned no college credit. Some professors deplored this conservatism and began to advocate that theatre arts be made a regular course of study. They were led by George Pierce Baker of Harvard, who in 1904 established a course in playwriting at Radcliffe College. A year later he was permitted to establish a similar course at Harvard, his famous English 47. When Baker struggled to establish a parallel course in which students could stage the plays they had written, his appeal was refused. As a result, he organized in 1913 an extracurricular 47 Workshop where students could learn about directing, acting, scene design, and lighting, but they received no course credit for the activity. Both the playwriting course and the workshop attracted brilliant students.* But Harvard University refused to encourage such activity. As a result, Baker moved to Yale in 1925, where he was given the direction of an exciting new graduate school of drama, complete with playhouse and a curriculum in theatre arts. Baker directed this ambitious program until his death in 1935.

Other university pioneers struggled like Baker to establish dramatic art in the curriculum and inspired generations of talented students. For example, Brander Matthews at Columbia University became the first professor of dramatic literature in America in 1900. At Carnegie Institute of Technology the first department of dramatic arts offering an academic degree was established in 1914; it was guided to outstanding success by Professor Thomas Wood Stevens. At the University of Pennsylvania, Arthur H. Quinn surveyed the entire history of American dramatic literature from its beginning to modern times and between 1923 and 1936 published a series of volumes that have never been duplicated. Other professors, like Thomas H. Dickenson of Wisconsin and Frederick H. Koch, first of North Dakota and then of North Carolina, not only taught the dramatic arts but also organized and directed highly successful college theatres. So did Alexander M. Drummond of Cornell, who was an unforgettable teacher, a brilliant director, and the promoter of widespread interest in writing folk drama. He was also the rare superartist envisioned by Gordon Craig, able to write a play; design the scenery, lights, and costumes; train the actors; and even discipline the reactions of the audience, if necessary. Men like Drummond and the other university pioneers firmly established dramatic art as a high-ranking academic discipline and as the source of renewed strength for the American theatre.

---

*Among the playwrights who studied with Baker were Edward Sheldon, S. M. Behrman, Philip Barry, Sidney Howard, Percy Mackaye, Edward Knoblock, George Abbot, and, the greatest of them all, Eugene O'Neill. Equally impressive is the list of directors, designers, actors, and critics who served an apprenticeship in the 47 Workshop. Some of the best-known of these are Alexander Dean, Sam Hume, Theresa Helburn, John Mason Brown, Robert Benchley, Kenneth Macgowan, Lee Simonson, Robert Edmond Jones, Mary Morris, and Osgood Perkins. Baker's courses evidently filled a pressing need and attracted talent of the highest order.

The Community Theatre Movement

Paralleling the surge of activity in American colleges and universities was the prodigious growth of community, or little, theatres all over the nation. Like the free theatres of Europe, these groups rejected the slick, superficial entertainment that the merchants of Broadway were turning out. They aspired instead to produce significant, thought-provoking plays and to involve the maximum number of participants from the communities they served. At the start they were more concerned with becoming "theatres for participation" than "theatres for audience." The movement resulted in the establishment of a variety of groups organized in many ways and carrying a variety of labels. Some were called little theatres, others community or civic theatres. In the 1920s, Edith J. R. Isaacs of *Theatre Arts Monthly* labeled them somewhat condescendingly "tributary theatres," explaining that "the center of American professional theatre life will probably always be New York," and therefore, "the Tributaries must feed the main stream; the states must feed New York."[1] Today there is no settled nomenclature, but the terms most often used to designate the three main divisions of the American theatre are *university* theatre, *community* theatre, and *commercial* theatre.

Typical of the community zeal for better drama were the hundreds of little theatres that blossomed in various shapes and forms all over the country. The first of these may have been the theatre built for the players of Hull House in Chicago in 1900. However, the nationwide craze came after 1910. In 1912, for example, three pioneer projects were started. One of these was the Toy Theatre of Boston, directed by Mrs. Lyman Gale, which lasted only two and a half years. A second was the ninety-one-seat Chicago Little Theatre, directed by Maurice Browne and Ellen Van Volkenburg, which lasted five years and delighted its audiences with poetic productions whose scenery and lighting were inspired by the ideas of Gordon Craig. The third of the 1912 pioneer projects was Winthrop Ames's Little Theatre in New York, built after the failure of the New Theatre, which he had directed. Ames's Little Theatre differed from the others because it was entirely professional and did not involve the customery participation by the clerks, bankers, and housewives of the community.

The little theatres were not confined to big cities like Chicago and New York. They flourished everywhere from Ypsilanti, Michigan, to Eureka, California. Some of the groups, despite their enthusiasm, survived only a few months. Others became modest but permanently successful community organizations like the Barker Playhouse of Providence, Rhode Island. Still others metamorphosed into strong and distinguished semiprofessional or professional centers of dramatic art like the Cleveland Playhouse and the Pasadena Playhouse.

In the early years of experimentation with community drama, developments in the large cities usually attracted the greatest attention and publicity. Often, too, they made the most enduring contributions. Three groups, each established in 1915,

---

[1] *Theatre Arts Monthly*, XII (September 1928), 620.

illustrate this: the Neighborhood Playhouse of New York, the Washington Square Players of New York, and the Provincetown Players of Provincetown and New York.

The Neighborhood Playhouse began as an activity of the Henry Street Settlement. Its theatre was built and endowed by Alice and Irene Lewisohn, and for twelve years it supplied the residents of the lower East Side with a colorful program of plays, revues, and concerts. During the first five years, the company was amateur. Later it became professional and presented a wide variety of dramas, some of them experimental. The producing group disbanded in 1927, but the name survived in the influential Neighborhood Playhouse School of the Theatre, directed for many years by Sanford Meisner.

The Washington Square Players began their brief lifetime of three years and three months in February 1915. The group, led by Edward Goodman, was composed of idealistic, talented nonprofessionals who wished to present plays of artistic worth. Involved in the experiment were designers like Robert Edmond Jones and Lee Simonson, playwrights like Philip Moeller and Zöe Akins, and gifted performers like Katharine Cornell and Roland Young. Although the group disbanded in the middle of 1918, the artistic success that had been achieved inspired several members of the group to unite their talents again in December 1918 to form an organization that became the most prestigious theatre group in America, the Theatre Guild.

The third of the three important dramatic groups organized in 1915 had a special claim to immortality. It was the Provincetown Players, and it introduced to the world stage the playwright who is generally considered to be America's greatest, Eugene O'Neill. The formation of the group was almost accidental. In the summer of 1915, a number of young artists and intellectuals, all interested in the theatre, met in the resort city of Provincetown, Massachusetts. With Susan Glaspell and her husband, George Cram Cook, as moving spirits, the group decided to band together into a theatrical company. The group presented four short plays during the summer of 1915, all of them written by members. At the end of the season the players disbanded and returned to their homes. The following summer the group reassembled in Provincetown to continue the experiments and activities of the previous year. Their number was augmented by a shy young man named Eugene O'Neill, who contributed two short plays to the new season: *Thirst* and *Bound East for Cardiff.* The interest generated by these and other plays produced during the second summer inspired the players to continue their activity during the ensuing winter. When they returned to New York, they opened their own playhouse on Macdougal Street in Greenwich Village. In this congenial and stimulating atmosphere, O'Neill's talent for playwriting developed rapidly. The group presented many of his one-act dramas and also staged his early full-length plays, including *The Emperor Jones* (1920),[2] *Diff'rent* (1920), and *The Hairy Ape* (1922). By the time the group disbanded in 1929, O'Neill was firmly established as a dramatist of world stature. In addition to this achievement, the Provincetown Players had presented the work of other writers like Paul Green and Edna St. Vincent Millay, and

[2]Date in parentheses is date of production at the Playwright's Theatre.

had given experience to a host of performers and designers like Walter Huston, Jasper Deeter, Cleon Throckmorton, and Donald Oenslager. Thus the Provincetown Players are remembered as one of the most productive groups to come from the ferment that created the community theatre movement.

Many other organizations and individuals too numerous to list contributed to the renaissance of theatrical activity in America. A brief account of two of them provides examples of the influence that individual talent was able to exert. The first example is that of Sam Hume, who began his interest in the theatre as a student at the University of California at Berkeley and continued it at Harvard. Then he went to Italy and studied with Gordon Craig, after which he returned to the United States to become director of the Arts and Crafts Society of Detroit from 1916 to 1918. Here he had an opportunity to practice the new stagecraft taught by Craig and to apply many of Craig's other ideas. Original, vigorous, and iconoclastic, Hume radiated stimulation and creativity wherever he went. After leaving Detroit, he returned to the University of California at Berkeley, to direct both the Greek Theatre and the Wheeler Hall productions. His influence was both healthful and widespread.

Another individual who exerted a great influence and was also a product of the University of California at Berkeley, was Sheldon Cheney. In 1916 he founded *Theatre Arts* as a quarterly publication. Under his able leadership it developed into a monthly magazine and became a source of inspiration and stimulation throughout the nation. Cheney was assisted in his editorship by distinguished colleagues like Stark Young and Kenneth Macgowan and was able to obtain articles and essays from the keenest thinkers and most successful doers in world theatre. Cheney and *Theatre Arts* became the unifying, galvanizing voice of the American stage throughout one of its most exciting periods.

MRS. FISKE AND THE NEW ACTING

Of all the voices and influences that helped rejuvenate the American theatre, none is more important than that of Minnie Maddern Fiske. Her role as a pioneer is often overlooked. Although she is rarely given credit for being an innovator, her career marks a clean break with the traditions of the nineteenth century and the emergence of the ideals that dominate the stage of our time. She was a champion of the works of Ibsen and encouraged plays that, like his, discussed modern problems in a truthful, realistic manner. She deprecated the star system and tried to develop a company of players in which the individual was subordinate to the ensemble and in which all elements of the production served the design of the dramatist. Most significant of all, she advocated a simple, natural style of acting based on psychological truthfulness and freedom from theatrical trickery—a style that eventually became dominant in American acting.

It is important to remember that Mrs. Fiske did not emerge at the end of one era and, by means of a brilliant new theory and practice, transform her contemporaries and inaugurate an entirely new era of acting. Mrs. Fiske's career extended from 1870 until 1931; she served her theatrical apprenticeship and reached stardom during a period when many other styles of acting were vigorous and flourishing. Her theory and practice in the theatre were not typical; not until her last years and the years that followed did her style and methods become generally accepted.

The school of acting that Mrs. Fiske pioneered can be termed the Modern School of Psychological Naturalism. A few characteristics sharply differentiate this school from those that preceded it and that were or are contemporary with it.

The Modern School may be identified by (1) emphasis on psychological truthfulness in the portrayal of a character; (2) concentration on inner feeling with simplified, repressed external action; (3) cultivation of a simple true-to-contemporary-life manner of moving and speaking; and (4) fidelity to the design of the play with all performers and effects subordinate to the overall purpose of the dramatist.

Many influences, both direct and indirect, have been responsible for the establishment of the Modern School in the United States. The most powerful foreign influence came from Russia, where the Moscow Art Theatre began applying the theories of Stanislavsky in the production of new kinds of plays by Anton Chekhov and other realistic dramatists. The Russian example, particularly Stanislavsky's system of training actors, became a major force in the classrooms and theatres of this country later in the century. However, before the theories of the Moscow Art Theatre gained currency in America, Minnie Maddern Fiske was teaching similar principles and applying them in her productions. She began her adult career as an actress in 1882, her ideals and methods reached maturity as early as 1897, and she organized her Manhattan Theatre Company in 1904 as a repertory company to demonstrate her theories of acting and play production. The Moscow Art Theatre was not founded until 1898, and the first Russian-trained player to

Holbrook Blinn and Minnie Maddern Fiske in *Salvation Nell.*

Hoblitzelle Theatre Arts Library, Humanities Research Center, University of Texas at Austin.

perform in the United States, Alla Nazimova, did not appear in America until 1905. So Mrs. Fiske can rightfully be called a pioneer in the establishment of the Modern School.

Minnie Maddern Fiske (she acquired the "Fiske" by marriage to Harrison Grey Fiske in 1890) was the daughter of theatrical parents who began her career as a babe in arms. Throughout her infancy and youth she was in steady demand as a child actress and thus had acquired extensive experience by the time she made her adult debut in 1882 at the Park Theatre, New York. Her active career continued until a few months before her death in 1932.

Mrs. Fiske was intellectual and analytical by nature. Her approach to any role was careful and studious. Before acting a character, she believed in understanding both the character's mind and heart and in knowing the reason or impulse which prompted the character's words and actions. When her character emerged, each detail counted; every gesture and tone had significance. She developed a gift for revealing her characters in deft, subtle strokes. Her mature style was quiet and repressed, yet at its best it was charged with vital intensity. The actress suggested rather than exhibited the emotions of her characters and thus gained powerful effects.

One trait of Mrs. Fiske's acting on which all observers agreed was its naturalness. In her very first roles, she was praised for being simple, charming, and *true to life*. During all her career she was admired for the "unstudied" realism of her performances. She acted the plays of Ibsen in a simple, repressed style that seemed far more natural than that of Clara Morris or any other actress of the time.

In preparing a role Mrs. Fiske worked slowly and carefully to identify herself imaginatively with the personality she had conceived. Concerning her method she once said, "For months before I attempt even to rehearse a part, and many weeks before I begin to study the words assigned for me to say, I am imagining myself to be the character to be assumed. Eating, reading, walking up and down the stairs even, I am Becky or Tess as the case may be."[3] On one occasion, preparing for the role of Hedda Gabler, she locked her cousin, Emily Stevens, out in the cold while she recreated a scene between Hedda and Lovborg; and later, when Emily expressed astonishment that the scene was not in the play—having been imaginatively conjured up by Mrs. Fiske—the older actress answered, "Ibsen shows us only the last hours. To portray them I must know everything that has gone before. . . I must know all that Hedda ever was. When I do, the role will play itself."[4]

Mrs. Fiske exerted a strong influence on the stage not only as an actress but also as a manager and a stage director. As a manager she encouraged other actors and managers to be independent and presented her plays in any theatre or makeshift auditorium she could find rather than surrender to the theatrical Syndicate. As a stage manager she adopted many of the practices of the modern régisseur. To

---

[3] From an interview reported in the *Brooklyn Eagle*, 31 August 1899.
[4] Archie Binns, *Mrs. Fiske and the American Theatre* (New York: Crown Publishers, 1955), p. 139.

In the foreground, Minnie Maddern Fiske in *Hedda Gabler,* with George Arliss.
Hoblitzelle Theatre Arts Library, Humanities Research Center, University of Texas at Austin.

realize her artistic ideal of expert ensemble playing, she and her husband organized the Manhattan Company into a permanent troupe. Playbills dating from September 1904 to February 1914 announce a varied list of plays in which "Mrs. Fiske and the Manhattan Company" are the stars. During this period at least three of Ibsen's plays—*Hedda Gabler, Rosmersholm,* and *Pillars of Society*—were performed both in New York and on tour.

Mrs. Fiske's artistic ideals and style of acting were necessary corollaries of the kinds of plays she preferred to produce. Her tastes and convictions led her to one kind of drama, and in turn, the successful staging of this genre inevitably influenced her methods and style. While Clara Morris, Fanny Davenport, and Mrs. Leslie Carter were titillating their audiences with the emotional dramas of such playwrights as Sardou, Dumas, Feuillet, Daly, and Belasco, Mrs. Fiske was introducing the United States to Ibsen's plays, was searching for new dramas like his, and was praising such plays not only for their substance and truth but also for their drawing power.

In the pursuit of her ideals, Mrs. Fiske's strongest ally and coworker was her husband, Harrison Grey Fiske (1861-1942), editor of the *New York Dramatic Mirror.* He was an essential part of every production in which his wife appeared. Sometimes he was advisor and critic; sometimes he wrote or adapted the script; sometimes he was the business manager and director; sometimes he was the producer. Always he was the idealistic man of the theatre who expended every effort to aid his wife in raising the standards of the American theatre.

Anyone who studies Mrs. Fiske's career must conclude that she was an accomplished actress with a strong personality who occasionally achieved moments of greatness; that she illustrated in both her acting and her directing many ideals and techniques which are still dominant; and that as a player, manager, and régisseur (in association with her husband) she was a pioneer who contributed significantly to the theatrical renaissance of the twentieth century.

The early years of the twentieth century constitute an era of phenomenal growth, expansion, ferment, and reform. The politics and the economy of the country were profoundly affected, and so was the stage. During these years, theatrical practices of the previous century, many of which had outlived their usefulness, were totally reshaped by the ideas and movements of European pioneers and American artists. As the theatrical renaissance accomplished more and more, the American playgoer felt justified in viewing the future with optimism and hope.

16

The New Playwriting

When the nineteenth century ended, realism in playwriting was beginning to up-stage melodrama; the play of ideas was beginning to attract audiences. During the first two decades of the twentieth century, these trends continued, with additional effectiveness derived from new ideas, new models, and renewed inspiration. The excitement of the theatrical renaissance stirred and exhilarated many of the old playwrights and almost all of the new. A half-dozen dramatists exerted key influence: such men as Augustus Thomas, William Vaughn Moody, Edward Sheldon, Langdon Mitchell, Percy Mackaye, and most important, Eugene O'Neill responded to the ferment at home and abroad with plays that had major significance in redirecting the course of American playwriting.

The plays written by other dramatists during the early years of the twentieth century show varying degrees and kinds of response to the influences of the theatrical renaissance. These plays and much of the work of the key dramatists fall roughly into four groups. The first and by far the largest are the plays written only to divert, amuse, and entertain. In this group are the hundreds of farces, melodramas, and comedies of all kinds that were the standard fare of the commercial theatre. A second group of plays combines amusement with ideas. These pieces are usually social comedies that discuss contemporary problems or human foibles and social incongruities within the framework of a more or less amusing play. A third category contains the romantic escapist plays, often melodramatic, that continue a tradition of long standing in American drama. The final group might be called romance with ideas. These plays make thoughtful comments on the human condition or advance a thesis within the framework of a poetic or fanciful setting.

PLAYS WRITTEN TO AMUSE

The plays of the first group, written solely to entertain, are of many varieties. Some of them, descendants of the Harrigan-Hoyt comics, create laughter by caricaturing well-known American types or characters. These characters, often given dialects or slangy colloquial speech, are moved with rollicking speed through a series of exaggerated predicaments and episodes. George Ade (1866-1944) wrote such plays in *The County Chairman* (1903) and *The College Widow* (1904). So did George M. Cohan (1878-1942) in *Broadway Jones* (1912) and *Get-Rich-Quick-Wallingford* (1910). Other dramatists of the same genre are Winchell Smith (1871-1933), whose play *Lightnin'* (1918) ran for 1,291 consecutive performances in New York; Frank Craven, whose greatest success, *The First Year* (1920), spoofs the difficulties of the first year of married life and ran for 740 performances; Alice Hegen Rice, who created an American folk character in *Mrs. Wiggs of the Cabbage Patch* (1903); and a final but fabulous example of this kind of comedy, Anne Nichols, whose *Abie's Irish Rose* (1922) ran for almost six years on Broadway and set a record of 2,327 performances. This play, the champion of its genre, presents the difficulties that arise when a Jewish boy secretly marries an Irish girl and each must overcome family prejudices. The play, like others of its kind, is good-natured and sentimental and demonstrates that true love between a girl and a boy plus the innate lovableness of all human beings will triumph in the end.

A special type of comic entertainment grew out of the humor inherent in the antics of boys and teenagers. Booth Tarkington wrote and inspired plays of this type. Edward Everett Rose's *Penrod* (1918) is adapted from the Tarkington stories. Tarkington himself, with the aid of collaborators, wrote *Seventeen* in 1917; two years later, without collaborators, he wrote *Clarence*. Both plays enjoyed tremendous popularity in their day. Other comedies featuring juvenile characters made their appeal not through humor but through sentiment or sentimentality. Austin Strong's romantic piece *The Toy Maker of Nuremburg* (1907-8) is an example. So is *The Little Princess*, which Frances Hodgson Burnett wrote in 1903 following the prolonged success of her earlier play, *Little Lord Fauntleroy* (1888). This play depicts an impossibly perfect boy who looks, talks, and acts as women once thought every boy should look, talk, and act. *The Little Princess*, which won less success as a play, presents Fauntleroy's counterpart, the impossibly lovable little girl who wins the hearts of all she encounters, both humans and animals.

A new type of melodrama also flourished and helped to satisfy what seemed to be an insatiable public demand. It continued the dominant tradition of the nineteenth century, reshaped for a more sophisticated audience. The contrivances of plot are not so far-fetched; the playwright introduces a degree of probability and motivation. The characters are less stereotyped; many of them now have individuality and their actions some plausibility. The dialogue has lost its artificiality; playwriters have taken pains to reproduce colloquial speech. The entire structure of the play is often livened with humor, sometimes gentle and sometimes wildly farcical. Melodramas without much humor but with the suggestion of a serious thesis were written by Elmer Rice (1892-1967) in *On Trial* (1914), by George Broadhurst (1866-1952) in *Bought and Paid For* (1911), by Charles Klein (1876-1915) in *The Lion and the Mouse* (1905) and *The Third Degree* (1909), and by Eugene Walter (1874-1941) in *Paid in Full* (1908) and *The Easiest Way* (1908).

Melodrama enlivened with farcical humor had many exponents and attracted large audiences. Such plays use any and every aspect of American life as a source of plot and laughter. Sometimes the American mania for making money and achieving business success is lampooned, for example, by Winchell Smith (1871-1933) in *Brewster's Millions* (1906) and *The Fortune Hunter* (1909), by James Montgomery (1882-1966) in *Ready Money* (1912) and *Nothing but the Truth* (1916), and by R. C. Megrue (1883-1927) and Walter Hackett (1876-1944) in *It Pays to Advertise* (1914). Sometimes college life and athletic success provide the material for the farce-melodrama, as in W. C. de Mille's *Strongheart* (1905) and Rida J. Young's

George M. Cohan in *Little Johnny Jones,* about 1904.

Hoblitzelle Theatre Arts Library, Humanities Research Center, University of Texas at Austin.

Brown of Harvard (1906). Still other plays of the genre grow out of domestic situations cleverly conceived and used for extended comic elaboration. Albert E. Thomas's *Her Husband's Wife* (1910) is an example. The action and humor of the play develop when a young wife, believing that she will soon die, starts planning her husband's second marriage. Another such comedy-melodrama is Margaret Mayo's *Baby Mine* (1910), which presents a series of comic mixups resulting from a wife's attempts to dupe her husband into believing that he is the father, first of twins and then of triplets.

The crook-detective play, made popular by William Gillette's *Sherlock Holmes*, grew in appeal during the early years of the century. The large following for this kind of play developed early and has remained steadfast throughout the years. Superior examples of this genre were written by Bayard Veiller in *Within the Law* (1912), *The Thirteenth Chair* (1916), and *The Trial of Mary Dugan* (1927); and by Harriet Ford and Harvey O'Higgins in several plays, the best of which is generally considered to be *The Argyle Case* (1912). Also belonging to this group is George M. Cohan's spoof on the crook-detective play, *Seven Keys to Baldpate* (1913), in which the melodramatic happenings that constitute the action of the play turn out to be only a piece of fiction written by Magee, the leading character, during the course of a night spent alone at the inn on Baldpate.

PLAYS OFFERING ENTERTAINMENT WITH IDEAS

Allied to the farce-melodramas for entertainment only was a second group of plays generally termed *social comedies*. They use sprightly dialogue and comic situations not as ends in themselves, but as the means of communicating ideas. Sometimes, following the tradition of *The Contrast* and *Fashion*, the ideas concern the foibles and pretensions of society. Sometimes they involve a specific social problem and represent the growing interest in thesis plays. The ideas that motivate these plays vary in seriousness and so does their treatment. Sometimes the treatment is wholly comic to the extent of being farcical; sometimes it is light and delicate; other times it is mostly serious with only an occasional touch of wit or humor.

The most successful play of this kind was written by Langdon Mitchell and first played by Mrs. Fiske in 1906. It is the comedy entitled *The New York Idea* and is a satire on the casual attitude toward marriage and divorce found in sophisticated social circles. The principal characters are John and Cynthia Karslake, both young, handsome, and dashing. They have recently been divorced and Cynthia is about to remarry, this time to the stuffy, wealthy, socially prominent Philip Phillimore. Philip's divorced wife, Vida, is trying to maneuver John Karslake into marrying her. The entire action of the play is a series of complications, intrigues, and misunderstandings which finally end when John and Cynthia discover that they are still in love with each other and actually are still married to each other. The four acts of complication and delay provide occasions for amusing repartee and the chance to ridicule not only casual marriage and divorce but a host of other things such as the manners, customs, and houses of stuffy New York society and the peculiarities of visiting Englishmen. As vehicles for ideas, the situations are cleverly conceived and the characters admirably drawn. The dialogue also serves the purposes of the play, although a modern reader finds it far less witty and sparkling than did the audiences who raved about it in the early years of its success.

Another social comedy analyzing the institution of marriage won the first Pulitzer Prize for drama in 1918. This is the play *Why Marry?* by Jesse Lynch Williams. The problem posed by it is one that the early twentieth century was debating vigorously: do love and marriage handicap a gifted man, in this case a scientist, in the pursuit of his career? Clustered around the central issue are numerous views and examples of other problems inherent in marriage and family life. The play has a good deal of wit, a fair amount of wisdom, and a liveliness that sometimes approaches farce. It would not win a Pulitzer Prize today, but fifty years ago it was considered the best of its genre, at least for the season of 1917-18.

Other exponents of the kind of play that combines comedy or melodrama with social comment were James Forbes (1871-1938), who used the ever-fascinating lives of theatre people as the material for his *The Chorus Lady* in 1906 and *The Show Girl* in 1914, but whose most important social comedy is a feminist play called *The Famous Mrs. Fair,* produced in 1919; Robert Housum (1886-?), whose drama *The Gypsy Trail* (1917) contrasts the ideals of a romantic young woman and a prosaic young man; Thompson Buchanan (1877-1937), whose play *A Woman's Way* (1909), dealing with a wife's attempt to keep her husband from falling for another woman, has been called "one of the most incisive social comedies that has been written in America"[1] and whose later drama, *Civilian Clothes* (1919), presents the perennial problem of a wife's reaction to the return of her soldier-husband to civilian life; and Clare Kummer (1874-1958), whose early plays such as *A Successful Calamity* (1917), *The Rescuing Angel* (1917), and *Rollo's Wild Oat* (1920) successfully combine social comment with lively dialogue and farcical situations. Other dramatists of social comedy, unlike Miss Kummer, sometimes emphasized the thesis of their plays more than the comedy. A representative example of this kind of play is *The Unchastened Woman* (1915) by Louis K. Anspacher (1878-1947), which exposes the hypocrisy of a predatory female who operates behind the facade of social and moral superiority. The early plays of Rachel Crothers might be mentioned here because several of her comedies with ideas appeared before 1920. However, her best plays were written and produced after this date.

A further development of the comedy with ideas were the realistic thesis plays of Edward Sheldon (1886-1946). Although his several romantic escapist plays such as *Romance* were more successful with the public, Sheldon's real claim to fame rests on four realistic social problem plays: *Salvation Nell* (1908), *The Nigger* (1909), *The Boss* (1911), and *The High Road* (1912).

Sheldon, born in Chicago and educated at Harvard, was a student in Professor Baker's English 47. A year after he graduated, *Salvation Nell* was produced by Mrs. Fiske. Its barroom and tenement settings were so realistic that they shocked

---

[1]Margaret G. Mayroga, *A Short History of the American Drama* (New York: Dodd, Mead & Co., 1934), p. 253.

audiences. Like Gorky's *Lower Depths* in Russia, *Salvation Nell* introduced in the United States an honest revelation of conditions, which the theatre sorely needed.

A year after *Salvation Nell,* the New Theatre of New York produced a thesis play by Sheldon entitled *The Nigger.* The only American play seen at the New Theatre during the season of 1909-10, it represents an early, courageous attempt to expose the evils of racism. Another of Sheldon's realistic plays appeared in 1911. Entitled *The Boss,* it is the strongest and most compelling of the dramas. The plot is tightly knit and moves swiftly from episode to episode, then to climax and conclusion. It stresses the plight of the little man who lives in the slums, exposes the cruel, unscrupulous methods of political bosses, and illustrates the need for protective unions of workers. Yet the ideas are incidental to the development of plot and character. They are not implicit in the action. *The High Road* is Sheldon's fourth play involving a social problem. It presents the struggle of a farmer's daughter to achieve a life of nobility and service to others.

A far better welding of plot, character, and theme is found in a play that appeared four years before *The Boss.* It is *The Witching Hour,* one of the best dramas of Augustus Thomas (1857-1934). In this play all of the events—and they are complicated—are developed to illustrate the power of thought transference and mental telepathy. The central action of the play begins when young Clay Whipple accidentally kills a man who has aroused Clay's psychopathic fear of the semiprecious gems called cat's-eyes. Clay is convicted of murder, but an appeal is made on the grounds that Clay's phobia, which caused his irrational behavior, was not given due consideration during his trial. Justice Prentice of the United States Supreme Court volunteers to testify in Clay's behalf because he was once in love with Clay's grandmother and has first-hand knowledge of the family fear of cat's-eyes. A second trial is ordered. When it is over and the jury is considering its verdict, Jack Brookfield, a gentleman gambler who has psychic powers, tries to reach and influence the jury through mental telepathy. More than this, he gives the newspapers a sensational exposé of the criminal behavior of the district attorney, Hardmuth, who prosecuted Clay Whipple. Brookfield believes that the hostile thoughts of thousands of newspaper readers will influence the jury against Hardmuth and in favor of Clay Whipple. He is right. The jury returns a verdict of "not guilty." Hardmuth then tries to kill Brookfield but drops the gun when both Brookfield and Justice Prentice use their psychic powers on him. In several concluding developments, Clay Whipple conquers his fear of cat's-eyes, Brookfield gives up gambling because he decides that his power to read minds gives him an unfair advantage, and finally, the reformed Brookfield wins the woman he has loved all his life.

An outline of the main events of the play gives a poor impression of its merits. Actually, there is skillful interweaving of character and action, there is persuasive dialogue, and what appears to be scientific nonsense is made dramatically acceptable and effective. Certainly the thesis of the play is not incidental. It is the element which fuses all the other elements.

Many critics believe that *The Witching Hour* is the best of Thomas's many plays. Other critics claim superiority for *The Copperhead* (1918), one of the best dramas about the Civil War. These are only two of fifty-one long plays that Thomas

George Nash (with pistol) and John Mason (holding light switch) in Thomas's *The Witching Hour.*

Hoblitzelle Theatre Arts Library, Humanities Research Center, University of Texas at Austin.

wrote in addition to twelve short ones. That output, which began in 1875 when Thomas was only eighteen and ended in 1926 when he was sixty-nine, makes Thomas one of the major dramatists of his time. The plays vary enormously in quality and subject matter. The best of them, like *The Witching Hour* and *The Copperhead,* show superior craftsmanship in construction, logical motivation of action, sharp and incisive dialogue, and plausible characterization. The poorest are blighted by melodrama and sentimentality.

ROMANTIC ESCAPIST PLAYS

A third major category of plays during the early years of the twentieth century is the romantic escapist drama. Such plays represent a hardy and enduring strain in American playwriting. The twentieth century, in fact, was ushered in by two hugely successful plays of this kind. One was *Ben Hur,* which began its spectacular career on November 29, 1899, just a month before the twentieth century began.

The other was *Madame Butterfly*, "a tragedy of Japan," by David Belasco and John Luther Long, which opened March 5, 1900, when the twentieth century was only two months old.

The love of the romantic is illustrated by many later dramas. Edward Knoblock (1874-1945) in 1911 provided Otis Skinner with an enduring vehicle entitled *Kismet,* a "romance of the Arabian Nights," in which Hajj, a beggar, accomplishes the remarkable feat of marrying his daughter to the caliph. Richard W. Tully (1877-1945) provided two outstanding examples of escapist romantic drama. One of these, *The Bird of Paradise* (1912), has a Hawaiian setting and reaches its climax when the beautiful native girl throws herself into a volcano as a sacrifice to the American she loves. The other is *Omar the Tent Maker* (1914), which tries to re-create the life and times of ancient Persia. A unique type of romantic drama written in 1912 by George C. Hazelton, Jr., and J. Harry Benimo was entitled *The Yellow Jacket.* It is an imitation Chinese drama complete with property man and chorus. The play succeeded in the commercial theatre and remained a favorite of the noncommercial theatre for many years.

A different type of romantic play using the fascination of the supernatural is found in such dramas as Belasco's *The Return of Peter Grimm* (1911) and in the works of Charles R. Kennedy. Belasco's play, already mentioned as an example of his penchant for sentiment, presents the nonrealistic, romantic situation of a stubborn old bachelor who returns after death to rectify the mistakes he has made in life. The ghost is a tangible character on the stage, visible to the audience but not to the other characters. Kennedy's use of the supernatural is different. Otherworldly elements are symbolized rather than represented. In the highly successful *Servant in the House* (1907), the character Manson symbolizes Christ. A later work, *The Chastening* (1923) is a play about Jesus as a youth, while *The Army with Banners* (1918) is an imaginative projection of occurrences in the millennium.

Many other dramatists, better known for a different type of drama, wrote romantic costume plays. Booth Tarkington, famous for his Penrod-type comedies, provided Richard Mansfield with a dashing, romantic role in *Monsieur Beaucaire* (1901). Edwin M. Royle (1862-1942), noted for his late-nineteenth-century melodramas, scored a great success with *The Squaw Man* (1905), which presents the romantic situation of a titled Englishman banished to the wild west territory of Wyoming, where he marries a beautiful Indian maiden who nobly kills herself for the sake of her husband's career. Philip Moeller (1880-1958), one of the original pioneers of the Washington Square Players and the Theatre Guild, used historical characters—with considerable liberty—to produce three costume plays: *Madame Sand* (1917), *Moliere* (1919), and *Sophie* (1919). All have a sheen of wit and sophistication that provides an antidote to their sentimentality.

ROMANTIC PLAYS WITH IDEAS

Far more important in the development of American playwriting were the romantic or poetic plays with a thesis, the fourth major group of plays. These dramas are not escapist; they use their romantic setting or their poetic treatment as a means of communicating ideas. Two significant playwrights head this group: Percy Mackaye and William Vaughn Moody. Mackaye was by far the more prolific, for he wrote twenty-six long plays and more than half a dozen short ones. Moody, in contrast, wrote only five plays, three of which were never staged. But the two plays that did receive professional production established him as a more influential dramatist than Mackaye.

Percy Mackaye (1875-1956), son of Steele Mackaye, was the principal promoter of civic drama through his persuasive books and his production of spectacular civic pageants. In addition, he wrote many plays for the commercial theatre. Few of them achieved real success, but many received high praise from the spectators and critics who enjoyed ideas poetically expressed. These observers noted that Mackaye's strength as a dramatist came from combining his gift for poetry and his love of literature. Thus his drama, *The Scarecrow,* is considered his most significant contribution to American playwriting.

The Scarecrow, first presented by the Harvard Dramatic Club in 1909 and produced professionally in 1911, is an absorbing fantasy inspired by Nathaniel Hawthorne's story *Feathertop.* The scene is colonial New England, the central character a scarecrow manufactured by Blacksmith Bess and Dickon, who is the devil in human guise. Bess and Dickon make their scarecrow an instrument of revenge. Years before, Gilead Merton had seduced Bess; the son who was born to her had died. Now Merton is a highly respected justice in the colony with a lovely marriageable niece, Rachel. He is aided by Dickon, the devil, disguised as a tutor. After complications with Rachel's human suitor, Richard, and after Justice Merton is terrorized by being told the truth and threatened with exposure, the two young people, Rachel and Lord Ravensbane, fall deeply in love. Lord Ravensbane, the scarecrow, starts to speak and move independently of Dickon. He tells Rachel that she has given him a soul and begins to wish he were a man. In a climactic scene the jealous human suitor, Richard, dares Lord Ravensbane to look into "the glass of truth," a magic mirror which Rachel has purchased from Blacksmith Bess. Lord Ravensbane does so and sees that he is only a scarecrow. Dickon now tries to complete the revenge plotted against Justice Merton. He almost convinces everyone that Lord Ravensbane is a living man. But Ravensbane, exercising his newfound free will, denounces Dickon, admits that he is only a scarecrow, and dies. As he is dying, he looks into the glass of truth and the reflection he sees is that of a man.

The play is an allegory presenting the author's conception of humanity and human destiny—namely, that human beings are scarecrows conceived in sin, made of worthless material, and shaped by evil—but love can give them souls, and free will coupled with sacrifice can make them human. In the play Mackaye provided an example of the more serious, elevated, and thoughtful kind of drama he recommended for the American theatre.

William Vaughn Moody (1869-1910), another playwright of significant influence, advocated the same kind of drama. He was an intellectual, a scholar, and a poet whose idealism effectively served the theatrical renaissance in America. Educated at Harvard and well-traveled in Europe, he taught English at the University of

Chicago for some years before retiring to devote full time to poetry and drama. Before he withdrew from active teaching in 1902, he had published a volume of lyric poems and a *History of English Literature,* the latter in collaboration with Robert M. Lovett. After his retirement he concentrated on completing an ambitious trilogy of poetic plays whose theme was "the unity of God and man." The first play of the trio, which had appeared in 1900, was entitled *The Masque of Judgment.* The second, *The Fire Bringer,* was published in 1904. The third, to bear the title *The Death of Eve,* was only partially completed. None of these poetic plays was staged, although their quality as closet drama was highly regarded by lovers of poetry.

While Moody was working on his poetic trilogy, his interest was diverted to the writing of two prose plays, both inspired by actual events reported in the newspapers. The results of this interest were *The Great Divide,* produced in 1906, and *The Faith Healer,* first presented in 1909. These two dramas are Moody's only contributions to the regular theatre. He died prematurely in 1910 at the age of forty-one, yet the two plays established him as a major contributor to American playwriting.

The Great Divide has been both condemned as a "hair-curling melodrama" and praised as "the first modern American drama." We cannot dispute that the initial situation of the play, although based on an actual occurrence, is the stuff of melodrama. Ruth Jordan, a genteel product of New England, is left alone in a cabin on an Arizona ranch that she and her brother are trying to develop. Three drunken ruffians break into the cabin and threaten rape. Ruth, in desperation, appeals to the youngest and most attractive, whispering, "Save me from these others, and from yourself, and I will pay you—with my life." The bargain is made. Stephen Ghent, the young man, buys off one of the ruffians and wins a shooting match with the other. The two losers ride away. As the first act ends, Ruth departs to marry Ghent and thus to fulfill her part of the bargain. The rest of the play relates the long, agonizing conflict between Ruth, who represents the refinement, culture, and inhibitions of Puritan society, and Ghent, who represents the freedom, strength, and power of the uninhibited man of the frontier. After a year and a half of suffering and torture, during which time Ghent's mine makes him rich, Ruth realizes that both of them have "cleansed" themselves through pain, as her Puritan principles have demanded, that her husband is a man reborn, and that she can now acknowledge her love for him and begin a free, joyful life unclouded by a sense of sin and guilt.

In the early years of the century, *The Great Divide* was a sensational success. The charge that it was a "sex play" (Ruth unwillingly sleeps with her husband and bears him a son) only increased its popular appeal. After more than a thousand performances in the United States, it was produced in London and later in Paris. It can still be seen in occasional revivals. What merits have enabled it to endure so long? They are precisely summarized in Richard Moody's introduction to the play, where he describes it as "a play of literary merit; truly realistic, with no mere superficial exploitation of lifelike details; filled with exciting action, yet not of the customary melodramatic action; and above all a serious psychological study of two aspects of American culture brought into collision against the picturesque background of the western landscape."[2] His conclusion is that it is correct to call the play the first modern American drama.

William Vaughn Moody's only other prose play, *The Faith Healer,* was not a commercial success. Yet in many respects it is a superior drama. Many critics believe that it has a more powerful theme that is more skillfully treated. Conceived by the playwright before *The Great Divide,* the second play did not achieve final form until 1908. It was produced a year later. Like *The Great Divide,* it was inspired by actual events. Moody became interested in a young man known as the "New Mexico Messiah," whose activities as a faith healer Moody found to be "intensely significant and eloquent." With this motivation, Moody devised a drama that presents the conflict between faith and love in plausible dramatic terms.

If Moody's *Great Divide* deserves to be called the first modern American play, his *Faith Healer* belongs in the same class. It shows a native dramatist who is free of the blight of melodrama, sentimentality, and contrived action and who is able to clothe a significant theme in convincing dramatic apparel.

Moody and Mackaye, Sheldon, Thomas, and Mitchell, together with a host of other dramatists, steadily moved American playwriting toward maturity and excellence. It remained for Eugene O'Neill to demonstrate this maturity to the world finally and indisputably. His emergence as a dramatist occurred between 1916 and 1920, so his early work must be considered here as another product of the theatrical renaissance of those fertile years.

EUGENE O'NEILL, 1888-1953

> The playwright of today must dig at the roots of the sickness of today as he feels it—the death of the old god and the failure of science and materialism to give any satisfactory new one for the surviving primitive religious instinct to find a meaning for life in, and to comfort its fears of death with. It seems to me that anyone trying to do big work nowadays must have this big subject behind all the little subjects of his plays or novels, or he is scribbling around the surface of things.[3]

These revealing words of Eugene O'Neill provide a key to our understanding of the playwright. They clarify his motivation and dedication; they explain his achievements and his failures. Throughout his entire career, O'Neill was obsessed with a search for the meaning of life and for a means whereby men can control their fear of death. In the search he never stooped to scribbling around the surface

[2] Richard Moody, *Dramas from the American Theatre 1762-1909* (New York: World Publishing Company, 1966), p. 727.

[3] Eugene O'Neill, quoted in Joseph Wood Krutch, *The American Drama since 1918* (New York: Random House, Inc., 1939), pp. 92-93.

of things. Whether his subject was big or little, he tried to do big work. Sometimes he succeeded, sometimes he failed. But he never ceased the search, and the more he wrote the larger grew his concepts and the more comprehensive his plays. His legacy to American playwriting is unmatched in the history of the American theatre.

O'Neill's unending search for fundamental meanings makes him unique among American dramatists, but his uniqueness does not end here. He was prolific. Not counting the plays he destroyed or left uncompleted, he gave the world at least thirteen major short plays and twenty-four major long plays in the twenty-nine years between 1914, when he wrote *Thirst,* and 1943, when he completed *A Moon for the Misbegotten.* This must be considered a large output when we remember that during the last eight years of his productive life he withdrew from active contact with the professional theatre and concentrated on writing a vast cycle of nine plays, most of which were destoyed before he died.

Another aspect of O'Neill's uniqueness was his single-minded devotion to playwriting once he had begun his career. His entire energy and talent were dedicated to his profession. Such dedication resulted in a considerable output and also in the steady development of his skill and power as a dramatist.

O'Neill was also unique in his search for effective methods of communicating meaning through the dramatic resources of the stage. He experimented with numerous techniques known to the theatre—symbolism, expressionism, masks, asides, verbalization of inner thoughts—and many techniques that he devised himself. HIs quest for a perfect way to communicate thought and emotion may be one of the reasons for the uneven quality of his plays. Some were triumphs when they were produced; others were failures; still others were rated somewhere in between. This unevenness of quality is apparent to a reader of O'Neill's plays as well as to a spectator.

O'Neill's literary reputation fluctuated. His gifts were recognized by the Provincetown Players in 1916. For the next four years his reputation increased. In 1920 he won his first Pulitzer Prize, and during the ensuing decade he was hailed as the great playwright of the United States. His fame reached its zenith in 1931 when his "masterpiece," *Mourning Becomes Electra,* was presented; his fame and greatness were confirmed five years later when he was awarded the Nobel Prize for literature. Thereafter, his reputation began to decline. As he isolated himself more and more to concentrate on his nine-play cycle, the public and the critics began to forget his earlier work or to discount its worth. But after his death, when *Long Day's Journey into Night* and *A Touch of the Poet* were produced, his reputation again skyrocketed. Today students, critics, and theatregoers are busy trying to evaluate the enduring worth of his plays. Whatever the final verdict may be—if there ever is one —no one can dispute that O'Neill is the first American dramatist of genuine world importance and that he thus represents the coming of age of American playwriting.

It is no wonder that O'Neill was obsessed with a search for the meaning of life and for a way to face death. His life was extraordinarily tormented and unhappy. The tragedies that beset a man with such a sensitive, introspective nature forced him to face and grapple with the most fundamental of all human problems: Why must good men suffer and die?

Eugene O'Neill was the son of the actor James O'Neill, who after a promising start as a versatile tragedian found himself trapped in the single role of the Count of Monte Cristo. The playwright was born, literally, on Broadway in 1888 and during the first years of his life had no home but theatrical dressing rooms and boarding-houses. From 1897 until 1906, he attended boarding schools, then spent a few months at Princeton University. In 1909 he accompanied a mining engineer to Honduras, where he contracted such a serious case of malaria that he had to be sent home. A year later, he began his experiences as a sailor, traveling to South America, South Africa, Europe, and finally back to New York. His experiences at sea had a profound effect on his outlook and provided him with the subject matter of his early plays.

During some of his summers, the young O'Neill lived with his family in New London, Connecticut, where his father maintained a summer home. It was as close to a settled home as Eugene ever knew. In 1912 it was discovered that he had tuber-culosis. The next several months, spent in a sanatorium, were another crucial period in his life because they gave him time to get well, to decide that playwriting was to be his life's work, and to struggle with his doubts and fears. Shortly after leaving the sanatorium he began writing one-act plays. In 1914-15 he attended Professor Baker's class in dramatic composition at Harvard and in the summer of 1916 joined the group that gained fame as the Provincetown Players. This launched his active career in the theatre.

During his childhood and young manhood, O'Neill was subjected to shatter-ing stress and distress. His father, always haunted by the fear of poverty, furnished his family only a cheap, second-rate living. His mother became a drug addict; his brother Jamie was a derelict and a drunkard. Eugene himself, during his years as a sailor, became a hard drinker. After one trip from Buenos Aires to New York, he tried to commit suicide by taking sleeping pills. Sometime later his roommate committed suicide by jumping from a window. The following year Eugene was hospitalized for tuberculosis.

Added to these troubles were his marital entanglements. In 1909 when he was twenty-one, he eloped with a girl named Kathleen Jenkins but left her soon after-ward. In 1910 a son, Eugene Jr., was born. The father visited the baby but not its mother, whom he divorced in 1912. O'Neill's next wife was Agnes Boulton, whom he met in 1917 and married in 1918. A son, Shane, was born and later a daughter, Oona. In the mid-1920s O'Neill, now established as the country's most promising playwright, met the actress Carlotta Monterey and fell in love with her. Meanwhile, his father, mother, and brother had died, his brother in a sanatorium. In 1929 the playwright divorced his second wife and married Carlotta. She was the great love of his life but their marriage was a tempestuous one, filled with bitter fights, separa-tions, and reconciliations. The years with Carlotta were also marked by periods of serious illness. In 1936, for example, the playwright was too sick to travel to Sweden to receive his Nobel Prize.

In 1942 O'Neill's daughter, Oona, began her romance with the great come-dian Charles Chaplin and finally married him. The marriage, bitterly opposed by the playwright, caused a break between father and daughter that was never mended. Oona's brother, Shane, became a drug addict and died in a sanatorium. Eugene Jr., the playwright's first son, began a promising career as a teacher and television performer, then became an alcoholic and finally committed suicide.

During O'Neill's last years he was crippled by a debilitating disease which caused his hands to tremble so that he could not use a pen. This ended the creative writing that had sustained him through so many horrors. When he finally died in Boston on November 27, 1953, his troubled life seemed to have been, truly, a long day's journey into night. No wonder he was obsessed with trying to understand the meaning of it all.

O'Neill's earliest plays are short; most of them are based on his experiences at sea and his relationship with men at sea. He began writing them in 1913 and continued until 1920. After that date his plays, with one or two exceptions, are full-length—and often more than full-length. A number of the early short plays have not survived. A few were lost; others were destroyed by the playwright himself, who felt they were unworthy to survive. In the summer of 1916, two of the short plays—*Thirst* and *Bound East for Cardiff*—were presented by the Provincetown Players, followed later in the year by a production of *Before Breakfast.* In the next four years ten more of the short plays were presented. Of these, the most impressive were *'Ile* and three plays which use the same memorable characters introduced in *Bound East for Cardiff.* These three plays are *The Long Voyage Home, The Moon of the Caribbees,* and *In the Zone.* Together with *Bound East for Cardiff,* they form a kind of tetralogy that can be produced as a unit. All these short plays present individuals groping for a meaning in life.

The central concern of O'Neill's plays—discovering a meaning or purpose of existence—was fully articulated for the first time in *Beyond the Horizon,* the dramatist's first long play. *Beyond the Horizon* also has the distinction of being the first of O'Neill's plays to be produced on Broadway and the first to win a Pulitzer Prize. It is an intensely human drama concerning the fate of the Mayo family. The characters are real enough to involve us in their suffering, and the circumstances which entrap them are understandable enough to frighten us into realizing that similar circumstances can entrap any of us. The play has no villain. Each character is well meaning but flawed and fallible in his own way. Thus, each contributes to the failure and defeat, and each suffers a full penalty for his mistakes.

Beyond the Horizon carries us far from the remote, romantic suffering of a Metamora or a Spartacus and even farther from the contrived anguish of an Uncle Tom or an Octoroon. It involves us in the lives of people like ourselves and our friends and reminds us that ordinary men and women can create misery and failure for themselves, not through wickedness or malice or rage, but simply through the flaws of their human nature and through unpredictable turns of fate. O'Neill makes us face the relentless question, What does it all mean?

The year in which *Beyond the Horizon* won the Pulitzer Prize (1920) also saw the production of three additional full-length plays by O'Neill. These were *Chris Christopherson, Diff'rent,* and *The Emperor Jones.* The first, *Chris Christopherson,* was tried out in Atlantic City and Philadelphia, then withdrawn. The following year, after considerable rewriting, it became the highly successful *Anna Christie.* *Diff'rent,* another 1920 production, was a bleak tragedy reminiscent of Strindberg, and failed quickly. The third play, *The Emperor Jones,* succeeded brilliantly and confirmed O'Neill's reputation as the best young American playwright.

The central character of *The Emperor Jones* is a Pullman car porter, Brutus Jones, who flees the United States to escape criminal prosecution and establishes himself on a West Indian island as the "Emperor Jones." Using fear, superstition, and unscrupulous methods learned from white society, Jones rules the black islanders cruelly and ruthlessly. When they revolt, he escapes into the jungle and tries to make his way to safety. Then follows a sequence of scenes in which the ghosts of his past rise to terrify him. All the scenes are accompanied by the steady beat of jungle drums that begin slowly and softly, and, as the scenes progress, gradually increase in tempo and volume. The drums reach their climax when Jones stumbles out of the jungle, not to safety, but to death at the hands of his fellow blacks. The gripping substance of the play, the unusual virtuoso monologues of Jones, the significant revelation of Negro character, the unique setting, and the exciting, compelling stage effects all made *The Emperor Jones* a celebrated production. In the opinion of many observers, it was an original, stunning contribution to American playwriting.

Thus, the first two decades of the twentieth century ended with high promise and great optimism. The theatrical renaissance, it appeared, had done its work. American playwriting, stagecraft, and acting had achieved a stature and quality equal to those of any other nation in the world. The sheer volume and variety of theatrical activity had set new records. Prospects for the future seemed bright indeed.

17

Enter the Motion Picture

During the first two decades of the twentieth century, while the living theatre was experiencing a ferment of change and rejuvenation, an entirely new form of theatre was being developed and perfected. Born of modern technology, it grew with incredible speed and attracted a vaster audience than any other form of theatre in history. It was destined to end, prematurely, the bright promise of the theatrical renaissance, and it was to inaugurate an entirely new era in public entertainment. This new form of dramatic art was, of course, the motion picture.

On April 14, 1894, in a phonograph parlor located at 1155 Broadway, New York City, the motion picture made its unheralded debut. On that date, Thomas A. Edison's "kinetoscope" was first offered to public view. It was a peephole box containing a spool of pictures photographed on George Eastman's new flexible film. When a spectator dropped a coin in a slot, turned a crank, and glued his eyes to the peephole, the spool of pictures revolved and created the illusion of motion.

ORIGINS

Edison's invention was the culmination of a series of discoveries that had begun milleniums before. The ancient Egyptians had noticed the phenomenon of the persistence of vision—that is, the phenomenon of the afterimage. They discovered that if a series of pictures is passed before the eye, the image of one picture lingers on the retina and seems to merge with the image of the succeeding picture. If the pictures represent a sequence of motion and if they change every sixteenth of a second, the illusion of continuous motion is created. Many centuries after this phenomenon was first noted, Leonardo da Vinci discovered the principle of photography with his *camera obscura,* and about 1645 Athanasius Kircher, a German Jesuit and professor of mathematics, demonstrated the principle of the magic lantern by projecting hand-drawn transparent pictures on a screen. Following these discoveries, curious men in several countries tinkered with machines that combined a series of photographs with a device for rotating them to create the illusion of motion.

Pioneers in many parts of the world contributed improvements to these devices. The final step in the creation of the motion picture is generally credited to Thomas A. Edison, who, in an effort to provide a visual accompaniment to his phonograph, experimented with pictures recorded in spirals on a cylinder. The first efforts were unsatisfactory, but when flexible photographic film was placed on the market by George Eastman, Edison found the material he needed and proceeded to build his first peephole moving-picture machine, the kinetoscope. In France the Lumière brothers, Louis and Auguste, manufacturers of photographic equipment, studied Edison's kinetoscope and decided to combine it with a projection device to free the moving picture from its peephole box. The resulting successful machine invaded the United States in 1896 and forced Edison to improve his kinetoscope. He combined it with a superior projector invented by Thomas Armat of Washington, D. C., and a new machine called the vitascope was born. It could project a series of photographs of moving pictures to whole groups of people. The vitascope began its commercial career on April 13, 1896, just two years after the debut of the kinetoscope, and it entranced an audience that had assembled to see a vaudeville show at Koster and Bial's Music Hall in New York City.

With the invention of the vitascope, the dazzling, incredible career of motion pictures was launched. Here was a new form of popular theatre with a magic destined to win the devotion of millions of people. During the nineteenth century the popular theatre had consisted of the sprightly, motley offerings of vaudeville, burlesque, minstrelsy, circus, and related entertainments. During the first two decades of the twentieth century, while the motion picture was developing, these forms of theatre continued to prosper in varying degrees; but the entertainment they offered reached at the most a modest 10 to 20 percent of the population. A less expensive, more available, and even more understandable form of theatre was needed for the remaining 80 percent. The motion picture came as a boon and a salvation to this gigantic group. It was destined to exert such a universal appeal that it destroyed the great circuits of vaudeville, burlesque, and circus—and almost wiped out these forms of theatre altogether.

EARLY DEVELOPMENTS

Once invented, vitascope booths featuring pictures that moved began to appear in penny arcades throughout the nation. The circuslike advertising used by their promoters helped the new form of theatre grow steadily. The early growth, however, was impeded by two handicaps. One was the fear of fire. Eastman's new flexible film was highly flammable, and disastrous fires were always a possibility and sometimes a fact. A second handicap was Edison's legal campaign to protect his inventions. He had not patented them abroad, nor was he fully protected at home. In 1897 he began a series of law suits to establish his rights. These lasted for several years and slowed the growth of the movies.

As the years went by, additional handicaps developed. Churches and saloons—an odd fellowship of institutions—became enemies of the new form of entertainment. People started to attend the movies instead of going to church or gathering at the local bar. So ministers and bartenders campaigned against the movies, declaring that they were a sinful influence on the community. The campaign, needless to say, met with little success. A more serious hindrance to development was an organization known as the Motion Picture Patents Company. This was a monopoly established when a group of businessmen, in cooperation with Edison himself, obtained exclusive authority to exploit the original Edison patents as well as other related patents. Thus armed, the Motion Picture Patents Company proceeded to dictate harsh terms to theatre owners and exhibitors. There was bitter fighting and often violence between independent producers and the Patents Company, yet the monopoly succeeded in dominating the industry until it was dissolved by court order in 1917.

Despite the handicaps, many influences speeded the development of the movies. The new form of entertainment had an enormous appeal to millions of people. The booths and parlors that housed the vitascopes were located in the most congested areas of the big cities and were open continuously from early morning until late at night. For the small sum of ten cents any immigrant or citizen could purchase admission and could lose himself in the marvel of pictures which moved, and which soon began to tell stories, report news events, and depict the exotic beauties of foreign lands. The pictures on the screen did not require a knowledge of the English language to be understood. They were silent and communicated their meaning through visual representation which everyone could grasp. An occasional subtitle in English did not detract from the visual enjoyment and might even be an advantage because it could be used as a simple aid to learning the language. The admission price of ten cents was not excessive, but to make the appeal of the movies even wider, the price was soon dropped to five cents.

The quality of the films offered in the vitascope parlors and the range of subject matter increased with surprising speed. Many inventive, enterprising pioneers were responsible. For example, in 1896 George Méliès, a professional French magician, started to film the tricks of his trade and discovered that he could create astonishing illusions by using dissolves, fadeouts, and double exposures, devices that became unique features of cinematic art. A year later, in 1897, R. G. Hollaman filmed a three-reel version of the passion play, which demonstrated the dramatic capability of the movies, and in the same year the Corbett-Fitzsimmons championship boxing match was filmed, which demonstrated the power of the movies to record actual events of history.

Of major importance to the growth of the movies were the developments of 1905. In that year John P. Harris and Harry Davis remodeled a storeroom in McKeesport, Pennsylvania, installed ninety-two seats and a piano, and announced their theatre as a "Nickelodeon," with an admission of five cents. Their first attraction was *The Great Train Robbery,* filmed in 1903 by an Edison cameraman. It was, as the title indicates, the story of how bandits invade a small railway station, bind and gag the station master, then rob the mail train and flee with their loot—only to be pursued and shot down by representatives of law and justice. The film, brief, crude, and melodramatic, is nevertheless credited with establishing the art of narration on the screen. So fascinating was a story picture like *The Great Train Robbery,* and so popular was the nickelodeon, that similar movie houses showing similar thrillers sprang up everywhere. Within four years there were at least eight thousand nickelodeons in the United States.

One influential factor in the shaping of film fare was the polyglot, poorly educated working-class audience. Another equally influential factor was the small businessman, the canny promoter who perceived the possibilities of the new medium and who devoted his life to establishing and building the motion-picture industry. In general, the stars, managers, and directors of the living stage were not interested. Leaders in the fields of art and entertainment, captains of finance, and the educated classes in general all ignored the new invention.

The men who perceived the potential of the movies and risked their careers to exploit it were a strange but remarkable group. One of them was a cowboy, Thomas Tally, whose imagination was so aroused when he saw his first motion picture that he sold his horse and invested the money in a vitascope booth. He pioneered in

The Great Train Robbery, 1903. Edwin S. Porter, director.

building public confidence and educating his audiences to the wonders of the motion picture. Even more influential were men like Carl Laemmle, Adolph Zukor, Marcus Loew, and William Fox, who forsook their positions in business to gamble on careers in the motion pictures. Carl Laemmle, for example, was a Bavarian immigrant who worked many years in a Wisconsin clothing store, scrimping and hoarding to amass enough money to start his own establishment. When he had made his stake, he traveled to Chicago in search of a suitable location. In the course of roaming the city, he ran across one of the new vitascope booths. Fascinated, he watched a steady queue of customers come and go in what seemed a never-ending stream. When he inquired into the finances of the operation, he discovered that a man could make as much money from the movies in one month as he had been able to save during twenty years of labor in the clothing business. He immediately abandoned his plans to open a store, and instead began a career that made him a leader in the motion-picture industry.

The movie industry from the very start grew and flourished without the leadership of people experienced in the ways of the legitimate theatre. A few of the early actors, directors, and producers had some stage experience, but in general, the founders of the movie industry were true pioneers. They were not hampered by a commitment to traditional ideas and practices, but they were often uncommited to artistic ideals as well.

MORE DEVELOPMENTS

Yet the artistic film appeared early in the history of the movies. European producers led the way. Unhampered by the patent difficulties and monopoly practices that plagued American film makers, they began making multireel films of high quality. One of these, a nine-reel feature entitled *Quo Vadis,* was imported to the United States in 1913 and shown all over the country at road-show prices. Another was a four-reel film entitled *Queen Elizabeth,* starring Sarah Bernhardt, which was so successful that it inspired Adolphe Zukor to organize a company called "Famous Players" with the avowed purpose of making superior films using the most famous players of the living stage. Such Broadway celebrities as Mrs. Fiske, Mrs. Leslie Carter, and Billie Burke were lured to Hollywood to appear in motion pictures. In 1914-15, D. W. Griffith produced his twelve-reel masterpiece, *The Birth of a Nation,* demonstrating how quickly American directors could equal and even surpass the pioneer work of European film makers. The Griffith masterpiece about the Civil War, even though it was highly controversial, swept the nation, playing to huge audiences that paid as much as two dollars per person for admission. Between 1915 and 1929 the picture earned eighteen million dollars.

The artistic film developed early, and so did comedy and melodrama. In 1912 Mack Sennett launched the madcap career of his Keystone Kops, a career that was long and successful. Two years later Pearl White began appearing in *The Perils of Pauline,* a serial of twenty installments recording the breathtaking adventures and sensational escapes of an intrepid heroine. It thrilled the audiences of its day, just as *The Great Train Robbery* had thrilled audiences of 1905. It symbolized the fact that the motion picture was an ideal medium for melodrama and henceforth would relieve the living stage of a major share of its obligation to supply this kind of entertainment.

To enhance the popularity of the movies even more, producers began to promote the star system. In the earliest popular films, the identity of the performer was carefully concealed. For example, the Biograph Company's leading lady was not advertised as Florence Lawrence but simply as "The Biograph Girl." Soon, however, this practice gave way to the exploitation of personality, and the first movie stars were born. Performers like Mary Pickford, John Bunny, William S. Hart, Charlie Chaplin, and Lillian and Dorothy Gish rose so rapidly in fame and fortune as to constitute a prodigy of history. By 1910 at least ten million moviegoers in America were worshipping their favorite players. By 1916 the number had swelled to twenty-five million fans, who were now able to view their celluloid heroes and heroines in movie houses that became increasingly lavish and comfortable.

Motion pictures were not only inexpensive, easily available, and easily understood, they also offered a unique style of acting whose appeal was entirely visual. The traditional means of communication used by living actors—voice and movement— were replaced by communication through pantomime and special photographic techniques. A pioneer group of talented performers began experimenting with and

The Birth of a Nation, 1914. D. W. Griffith, director.
Hoblitzelle Theatre Arts Library, Humanities Research Center, University of Texas at Austin.

perfecting the new techniques of acting. Some of them became so skillful and popular that they left an indelible stamp on the art of acting for the cinema.

TECHNIQUES OF EARLY FILMS AND FILM ACTING

In early silent films, two distinct kinds of presentation are evident. One represents the transplanting of stage techniques to the screen. Films of this kind are simply photographed stage plays. An early example is the classic film *Queen Elizabeth,* a four-reel tragedy starring Sarah Bernhardt that was made in France and first shown in the United States in 1912. Throughout this film the camera remains in one position, as though it were a spectator facing a proscenium arch, and all the performers move in and out of the frame. When a scene terminates, there is no fadeout, no dissolve, and no blending with the ensuing action; the scene simply ends, as though a curtain has been dropped. The camera angle never changes, and of course there are no closeups. Subtitles are freely used and there is much lip movement as the actor stands and recites his lines, unheard by the audience. This style of presentation disappeared when the pioneers of the motion picture began to discover how to use their cameras and how to direct their actors in performances that pleased the eye and stirred the heart of the spectator.

In the first movies that developed in the direction of true cinematic art, pantomime is the principal means of communication. It is crude, exaggerated, and obvious. If a character wishes to tell another character that he is about to leave a room, he points at himself, then at the door, then at himself again. Eventually he strides to the door, measures its outline, examines its knob, then swings it open with a flourish. No one in the audience, however dim his wit or however poor his command of the English language, can mistake the intention of such an action. But crude pantomime of this sort did not persist. Slowly but surely movie makers discovered the uses of pantomime for comic or emotional effects rather than for simple communication of ideas. As they learned their craft, they found that the intimacy of the camera allowed for pantomime that was more subtle even than stage pantomime. They also discovered the immense advantage of a camera that follows the action rather than remaining stationary. In so early a film as *The Great Train Robbery,* produced in 1903, we can see the beginnings of those techniques that are unique to the motion picture and have no connection with stage plays.

Motion pictures and the enthusiastic men who produced them progressed and developed with astonishing rapidity. Several of the young directors who began working with the new medium turned out to be men of talent and imagination. By the time that one of them, D. W. Griffith, produced *The Birth of a Nation* in 1914-15, cinematic art had already discovered its real potential and established its basic techniques. Griffith's film demonstrated magnificent use of such unique motion-picture devices as montage, the closeup, fadeouts and dissolves, angle shots, pan shots, the flashback, and many other techniques. These devices, with improvements and refinements, became the basis for the subsequent development of motion pictures.

The style of acting that evolved in motion pictures was shaped by the conditions of motion-picture production. These conditions, markedly different from those that surround stage performance, create significant differences between acting for the screen and acting for the stage. Style in motion picture acting can be understood only if these differences are perceived. Stage and screen performers do have much in common, however. The same endowments of body, mind, personality, and sensitivity are important to both, although they may be used in different ways. Many of the same techniques of assimilating character and projecting emotion are used by both. Yet some significant differences exist between acting for the stage and acting for the screen. Let us compare some of the conditions of stage acting with those of silent-film acting.

FILM ACTING AND STAGE ACTING

The stage actor performs in a theatre before a live audience; the screen actor performs in a studio or out-of-doors before a camera and a director. The consequences of this obvious and easily recognized difference are tremendous. A stage actor is confined in space and can be viewed from a limited range of angles only. He must project his voice, his facial expressions, and his movements to the entire audience. He must orient his acting in one direction, and he must enlarge it so that words, expressions, and movements will carry a considerable distance. If he is performing in a playhouse seating two or three thousand people, his effects must be exaggerated if they are to be effective. In contrast, the film actor is not confined to a single space but may roam the world at will, with the camera following him from any distance and at any angle. The film actor must not project his gestures or expressions; the camera will do it for him because it can catch and enlarge the smallest movement or the most subtle change of expression. The camera, with its omnipotent eye, can search out tiny details or minute objects and give them enormous significance. Thus the screen actor can perform with maximum realism; no action or reaction need be faked or simulated. Furthermore, he must perform with restraint and complete naturalness, for any exaggeration or artificiality will be enormously enlarged by the camera.

The presence of a live audience has great influence on the stage actor. It stimulates him to develop his personal magnetism and to find a way of projecting it to the spectators. The screen actor, on the other hand, faces only his director and the camera. He performs in isolation for one person and a machine. His personal magnetism can rarely be projected to an audience as a living influence. It may be captured, in part, on film, but more likely it is an effect created by the director through montage and skillful editing and enhanced by colorful publicity. The stage actor is a free agent who varies his performances to win the response of varying audiences. The film actor has no such freedom. He is almost a puppet in the hands of the director and must shape every movement and expression to suit the demands of his single spectator. This spectator, the director, establishes artistic dominance in many ways. A motion picture is not photographed as a continuous whole but is made in bits and pieces. Final scenes may be shot early and opening scenes may be photographed late, with the intervening scenes recorded in a jumbled sequence that only the director may understand. The actor may know the script as a whole but may be unaware of the position or purpose of individual scenes. He is thus completely dependent on the word of his director and must follow, often blindly, the suggestions given to him.

In the final editing, or piecing together, of the film, the director, again, is the controlling artist. He can create any effect he desires by joining scenes together in certain sequences. He can make an actor appear effective and powerful or awkward and dull. Many stars of the cinema have been created through ingenious directing and editing; many successful careers have been sustained by artful cutting. The style or effectiveness of any movie actor owes much to the director; it is often the creation of the director and not the performer.

The standard method of making films in bits and pieces has another effect on the technique of the performer. He must be able to summon a mood or an emotion instantly, sustain it a few moments for a particular scene, then shift to an unrelated emotion for a succeeding scene. The stage actor, following a coherent script, can develop his emotion logically and gradually as the play develops. However, he must repeat his performance *in toto* night after night for differing audiences and thus his performances will vary noticeably in style and effectiveness. As Lawrence Barrett remarked many years ago, the stage actor is forever carving "statues of snow."

The situation of the screen actor is completely different. Since he performs only for a director and a camera, he repeats a scene over and over again until the director is satisfied. When this performance is included in the finished picture, it is fixed and unchangeable—a statue in marble—that will remain exactly the same as long as the physical substance of the film endures.

The last and biggest difference between silent films and the stage is, of course, the silence. On the stage, voice and delivery are of paramount importance; they are major tools of the actor's art. In the silent film, however, the actor has no voice; delivery is of no consequence. The movie actor's appeal is purely visual. He must rely upon his facial expressions, his gestures, and his movements to communicate the narration as well as the thought and emotion that accompany it.

The absence of sound and the need for subtle but expressive pantomime created an admirable style of acting in the silent movies. It ranged from the hilarious slapstick of the Keystone comedies, through the graceful acrobatics of Douglas Fairbanks, to the expressive art of Charles Chaplin. The best way to study the acting of the silent films is to survey the style and achievements of a few outstanding performers. Four pioneers who deserve mention for their notable contributions to film acting are Mary Pickford, Douglas Fairbanks, William S. Hart, and Charles Chaplin.

MARY PICKFORD, 1893-1979

Mary Pickford, who earned the title of "America's Sweetheart," was identified with motion pictures for a large part of their history. Born Gladys Mary Smith in Toronto, Ontario, in 1893, she was attracted to the stage at an early age. When she was only five she made her debut with the Valentine Stock Company of Toronto and after four years of apprenticeship reached stardom—at age nine—in a play called *The Fatal Wedding*. She continued to play leading roles both in Canada and in the United States in such formidable favorites as *East Lynne* and *Uncle Tom's Cabin*. Then in 1907 David Belasco engaged her to create the part of Betty Warren in his production of *The Warrens of Virginia*. At the same time he persuaded her to drop the label of Gladys Smith and adopt a name that had more glamor and appeal.

Mary Pickford and Douglas Fairbanks in *Taming of the Shrew,* 1929.
Courtesy of Miss Mary Pickford.

Soon after *The Warrens of Virginia,* Miss Pickford made her first motion picture under the direction of D. W. Griffith at the Biograph Studio, and her career as America's Sweetheart was launched. She achieved a success that may never be duplicated in motion pictures. In three years her salary rose from forty dollars per week to two thousand dollars per week plus 50 percent of the profits of her films. In 1916, when the Mary Pickford Film Corporation was organized, her salary jumped again—to ten thousand dollars per week plus 50 percent of the net profits. At the time it was said that she "was receiving the largest salary ever paid to any woman in the world."[1]

During this period Miss Pickford made films in rapid succession, and each film increased her popularity. Such pictures as *Tess of the Storm Country, The Little Princess, The Poor Little Rich Girl, Rebecca of Sunnybrook Farm,* and *The Little American* won overwhelming acclaim for the actress and endeared her to millions of people throughout the world. In all these films she played essentially the same character and used the same appeals that had proven successful on the stage. She was always the wholesome child, alternately hoydenish and wistful, who won love and created happiness wherever she went. Like Maude Adams in her prime, Miss Pickford gave her audiences a clean, sweet sense of hope and enjoyment. She fulfilled their dreams of goodness and success.

To project her appeal, Miss Pickford adapted the style of performing that she had learned on the stage to the requirements of the camera, and quickly became a master of film acting. Her sensitive, expressive face and eyes perfectly mirrored the emotions of the moment. Her movements and gestures, shy and natural as a child's, communicated meaning without the need of subtitles.

In the early 1920s, after playing children's roles all her life, Miss Pickford decided to experiment with adult roles to see if her public would accept them. She produced a series of films that included *Rosita, Dorothy Vernon of Haddon Hall,* and *Little Lord Fauntleroy,* in the last of which she played both the mother and the son. These films fell far short of the popularity of her former pictures, so she returned to little girl roles—but only temporarily. Late in the 1920s, talking pictures made their debut and took the country by storm. Miss Pickford decided to cut off her curls, abandon children's roles for good, and make her talking debut in the adult role of *Coquette,* a play made famous on the stage by Helen Hayes. The picture won Miss Pickford an Oscar as the best motion picture actress of the year 1928-29, but it did not attract the popular following that Miss Pickford had come to expect. Following *Coquette* she made a few more films and then quietly retired from the screen to devote herself to civic and business enterprises and to the management of the large fortune she had accumulated. She died in 1979 at the age of eighty-six and will be long remembered as the sensitive child with the golden curls who mastered the techniques of film acting when the medium was new and who was able to project so appealing an image that she became America's Sweetheart.

[1] Elinor Hughes, *Famous Stars of Filmdom (Women)* (Boston: L. C. Page & Company, 1931), p. 270.

DOUGLAS FAIRBANKS, 1883-1939

Closely associated with Mary Pickford in the public mind is another pioneer film idol, Douglas Fairbanks. For fifteen years, from 1920 to 1935, he was Mary Pickford's husband. During these years the two celebrities represented the dream marriage of filmdom. They were the unofficial king and queen of Hollywood, and their mansion, Pickfair, was visited by notable men and women from all over the world. Like Mary Pickford, Douglas Fairbanks earned his distinction by creating a film personality and a style of acting that were unique and inimitable.

Fairbanks, born in Denver, Colorado, in 1883, won a reputation on the stage before he experimented with film acting. In the fall of 1900, at the age of seventeen, he made his debut with a road company in Richmond, Virginia, in the role of a lackey in a play entitled *The Duke's Jester*. A few minor parts followed, and then the restless young man left the stage for two years. He returned in 1902, joining Minnie Dupree's company in *The Rose of Plymouth Town*. He continued to act, with increasing popularity and success, and developed an exuberant, athletic manner of performance which Miss Dupree described, unflatteringly, as "a bad case of St. Vitus dance." But the public liked his happy athleticism, and by 1909 he was playing a starring part for William A. Brady in a play called *A Gentleman from Mississippi*. The play and its star were so successful that they enjoyed a run of two years.

In 1915 the producers of Hollywood persuaded more than sixty popular actors and actresses to leave their Broadway billets and join the rapidly growing movie colony in Hollywood. Few of them remained for long, but Douglas Fairbanks, lured with a salary of two thousand dollars per week, proved a smash hit. His high spirits and exuberant athleticism "brought to the camera an instinctive, natural grace that proved to be the best of silent movie acting," says Arthur Knight.[2]

During the first six years of his movie career, Fairbanks played the part of a healthy, optimistic young American who overcame obstacles with a leap and a grin, who exposed the evils of sham and pretense, and who preached the gospel of confidence and success at a time when America needed just such a tonic. Fairbanks's early films such as *The Americano* (1916) and his style of acting did more than entertain and inspire. They showed the visual rhythm and pictorial effectiveness that distinguished the motion picture from the legitimate stage. Louis Delluc, a French critic who stumbled on the early Fairbanks films long after they were withdrawn from general circulation, hailed them as "something not of the theatre, something which is simple, direct, sincere, with a vital rhythm . . . in fact a true moving picture."[3]

In 1920 Fairbanks produced his first costume picture, *The Mark of Zorro*. The exotic settings, romantic costumes, and deeds of daring found in this film were

[2] Arthur Knight, "Douglas Fairbanks," *Dictionary of American Biography* (New York: Charles Scribner's Sons, 1958), XXII:172.

[3] Alistair Cooke, *Douglas Fairbanks—The Making of a Screen Character* (New York: Museum of Modern Art, 1940), pp. 28-29.

perfectly suited to Fairbanks's temperament and style. Henceforth, with the exception of a film called *The Nut* (produced in 1921), he devoted himself exclusively to costume pictures and will be forever remembered as the dashing hero of such spectacular romances as *The Three Musketeers, Robin Hood, The Thief of Bagdad,* and *The Black Pirate.*

There has never been a style of acting quite like Fairbanks's. Heroes galore have graced the stage who could wield a sword, ride a horse, and rescue a woman with dash and style. But Fairbanks exceeded them all in grace, inventiveness, and dazzling dexterity. He was a superb athlete with a body so marvelously trained that it responded instantly and beautifully to any demand. His acrobatics had an effortless, instinctive grace that reminded many spectators of ballet rather than athletics. His physical feats delighted the viewer with their rhythm, fluidity, and ingenuity. The most unexpected and inventive exploits were continuously developing in a Fairbanks film. Everything from a simple entrance to a daring escape was performed in so clever and surprising a fashion that the spectator was forever gasping in astonishment and pleasure.

Fairbanks's spell remained potent and his popularity dazzling until the advent of talking pictures. Then, although he made a few successful talking films, his star began to decline. He continued to write, to direct, and occasionally to act, and he continued to live the same vigorous, athletic life he had always enjoyed. His death in 1939 was a shock to the world. It came without warning while he slept and removed him from the screen before decreptitude could destroy his image as the wholesome, unconquerable hero of a thousand wonderful adventures.

WILLIAM S. HART, 1872-1946

A third idol of the silent films was the original western hero of the movies, William S. Hart. He never achieved the world celebrity of Mary Pickford or Douglas Fairbanks, but he earned immense popularity and established a style of acting that influenced dozens of his fellow performers. Although his pre-cinema career has been forgotten, it is interesting to know that Hart was a successful stage actor for twenty-five years before he appeared on the screen; during much of that period he was a popular leading man in such plays as *The Squaw Man* and *The Virginian.*

Not until 1914 did he join the exodus to Hollywood, by which time he had already perfected the character of the strong, silent hero in western romances. He continued to play these roles in the movies. Although he had numerous competitors, he quickly outdistanced them to become the model of the firm-jawed, clear-eyed, square-dealing, hard-riding, straight-shooting western hero. The image he created has influenced western heroes ever since. Also, his style of underplaying roles set a new fashion in movie acting. When Hart began his film career, many actors continued to use broad gestures and exaggerated facial expressions before the camera. Hart perceived the camera's inherent power to enlarge and demanded the right to underplay his roles—that is, to suppress the overemphatic pantomime used by other players. His first film, made for the Triangle Corporation, was a great

William S. Hart in *Tumbleweeds,* 1926. King Baggott, director.

disappointment to the producers. They told Hart that his acting would be considered wooden, that he did not exaggerate enough, and that the public would feel that he was not acting at all. The Triangle people, fearful of losing money, sold Hart's first film to another releasing organization. The film proved a great success and Hart's style of acting was vindicated.

CHARLES CHAPLIN, 1889-1977

The actor of the silent screen who did most to establish cinema as an art and who perfected a comic character that won the hearts of the whole world was Charles Spencer Chaplin, the immortal "Charlie" of the toothbrush mustache, baggy pants, jaunty derby hat, and willowy cane. He became the foremost artist of the silent screen and firmly established his claim as one of the greatest comedians of all time.

Although generally considered an American actor because almost his entire film career was pursued in the United States, Chaplin was English by birth and never changed his citizenship. He was born in London in 1889 of theatrical parents and made his stage debut at age five when, on the spur of the moment, he substituted for his mother in a variety act because her voice had failed her. "That night," says Chaplin, "was my first appearance on the stage and my mother's last."[4]

At age twelve-and-a-half, Chaplin began regular stage appearances when he successfully acted the role of a newsboy in a play entitled *Jim, the Romance of a Cockney*. His first American appearance was with a traveling English company in a vareity sketch entitled *The Wow-wows*. Evidently, Chaplin's comic talents attracted notice because when he returned to the United States in the fall of 1912 on his second visit, the Keystone Film Company offered him one hundred fifty dollars per week. After completing his engagement in vaudeville, Chaplin accepted the offer and traveled to Hollywood to begin a film career that was to be meteoric. Within two years his salary jumped to ten thousand dollars a week plus a yearly bonus of one hundred fifty thousand dollars. The comedies he produced in a single year were sold by his studio to the British Empire for six hundred seventy thousand dollars, and the British distributors, in turn, made a handsome profit on the deal. This sensational rise to fame and fortune illustrates not only Chaplin's genius as a comedian but also the explosive popularity of the movies in the early years of the twentieth century.

Charlie Chaplin in *Modern Times,* 1936.
Courtesy of Charles Chaplin.

[4]Charles Chaplin, *My Autobiography* (New York: Simon & Schuster, Inc., 1964), p. 21.

The character of Charlie the tramp, which Chaplin was to immortalize, appeared in the second movie he made, a ten-minute film without plot or distinction except for the character Chaplin introduced. Chaplin had been standing by in Mack Sennett's studio watching the filming of a comedy when Sennett suddenly ordered him to put on comic makeup and introduce a few gags into the scene. On the spur of the moment, Chaplin donned baggy pants, a tight coat, a small hat, large shoes—and the little tramp was born.

Once created, the character of the tramp began to weave an irresistible spell. Audiences took an instant liking to the funny little man who, as one critic observed, "does all the absurd and wonderful things which people do when they think they are alone and not being watched."[5] At first the antics of the little clown—his ingenious battles with an exasperating world—were enjoyed as pure slapstick. Spectators both young and old roared with laughter at Charlie's inventive clowning and did not bother to analyze its unusual appeal. Much later, critics recognized in Charlie the tramp the epitome of the human condition in all its ridiculous poignancy and pathetic bravery. The little man in the baggy trousers wears a tragicomic mask that is somehow the mask of all of us.

During his first years in the movies Chaplin made many films. But as both Chaplin and the public developed a fuller appreciation of Charlie the tramp, more and more was expected of each film, so fewer and fewer pictures issued from the Chaplin studio. Instead of slapdash filming of almost impromptu scripts, each picture became an elaborate and carefully worked out production. Each one represented the creative genius of a single individual, Charles Chaplin. He wrote his own scenarios, composed the musical accompaniment, produced and directed the film, and of course performed the leading role.

The character of the little tramp who appears in these carefully wrought films is a fully and marvelously developed portrait—unforgettable in such pictures as *The Gold Rush, City Lights,* and *Modern Times.* The tramp appears, thinly disguised, as *The Great Dictator* in 1940, another unforgettable film. In *Monsieur Verdoux* (1947), the tramp wears a disguise so sophisticated as to make the character almost unrecognizable. This film disappointed the public and enraged many critics, yet it is considered by some to be a masterpiece. In Chaplin's last films, *Limelight* (1953) and *The King in New York* (1957), the classic character of the little tramp is almost entirely abandoned.

The introduction of talking motion pictures created a crisis in Hollywood and in Chaplin's career. Hollywood capitulated to the new Frankenstein of sound, but for many years Chaplin refused to do so. He felt that to adopt spoken dialogue was to destroy the uniqueness of motion pictures and to make them merely a mechanical imitation of the stage. He was willing to introduce synchronized music and special sound effects and demonstrated how such additions could enhance a silent picture without destroying its essential character. Not until the end of his picture-making career did Chaplin finally surrender to the overwhelming demand for spoken dialogue and introduce it into his last films.

[5] Robert Payne, *The Great Charlie* (London: A. Deutsch, 1952), p. 33.

The perfection of Chaplin's comic style is difficult to describe, but it can be studied by attending reruns of his films. He is a master of pantomime from the tiniest gesture to the wildest slapstick, from the most fleeting expression to the most violent pandemonium. Moreover, every one of his movements, gestures, and expressions has meaning and conveys with exquisite timing and clarity the precise emotion or idea Chaplin has in mind. Belly-laughs or tears, pathos or satire, Chaplin communicates them all without clumsiness or strain and with magnificent humor. The range of his inventiveness is limitless. His manipulation of people and things is endlessly surprising but always comically logical for the given situation. And all his superb clowning seems to result from the natural reactions of a dramatic character who has universal human appeal.

When the first two decades of the twentieth century ended, both the living stage and its newly developed rival, the motion picture, were living happily together. Each was strong and prosperous; each looked forward to new growth and development. The First World War, in which the United States participated for eighteen months, exerted no immediate adverse effect. To the contrary, it gave the United States a commanding lead in the making of motion pictures. Moreover, in the United States itself the war created a booming economy that increased the overall demand for plays and movies and added to the general prosperity of every kind of show business. The moral disillusionment and breakdown of traditional values in the aftermath of the war were to exert a profound influence on American playwriting but were not yet apparent. In 1920 the nation looked forward to continued prosperity and progress. People in all forms of theatre expected happy times to come in the new decade of the roaring twenties.

18

Triumph and Tragedy, Comedy and Failure

Developments, 1920-1940

The two decades from 1920 to 1940 constitute a strange, complex, and paradoxical period in American history. The 1920s began with roaring prosperity and ended with the collapse of the stock market; the 1930s began with the ordeal of the Great Depression and ended with the horror of the Second World War. The events of both decades had a profound effect on the American theatre.

When the 1920s began, the United States seemed, on the surface, to be stronger, surer, and richer than ever before. Below the surface, however, certain deadly viruses had taken hold that were soon to produce widespread malaise and unrest. One fatal virus was the loss of faith in religious and moral values. Ever since Charles Darwin had documented his theory of the origin of the species, the "sea of faith," as Matthew Arnold called it, had been receding. Almost every field of science—physics, chemistry, astronomy, physiology, psychology, and so on—had announced discoveries that contributed to the recession. The human race became diminished. Human beings were no longer considered children of God exercising free will on a planet that was the center of the cosmos. Instead, they appeared to be a biological accident entirely controlled by predetermined forces and maintaining an insecure place on an insignificant speck of cosmic matter.

Three special influences accelerated the collapse of belief in traditional values. One, of course, was the monstrous blood-letting of the First World War. After the debacle, which the United States had entered with gallant idealism, the principles that had drawn America into the war were discredited and repudiated. Within a few years Americans realized it had not been a war to end wars; the conflict had only sown the seeds of worse disasters. It had not been a war to make the world safe for democracy; the carnage had only created newer, more despicable dictatorships. In time the United States, bitter and disillusioned, withdrew into its traditional isolationism.

A second shattering influence that contributed to the unrest and questioning of values was the communist revolution in Russia. In that country the old order, which had been accepted for centuries, was suddenly swept away. After a bloody struggle against internal forces and against an international army, to which the United States contributed, the forces of Lenin triumphed. Capitalism was destroyed, God was abolished, and a strange and terrifying new social order was organized. One of its avowed aims was to invade and to conquer every other nation of the world.

The third special influence that helped to shatter humanity's conception of itself and its place in the scheme of things was Freudian psychology. The discoveries of a single Austrian neurologist, Sigmund Freud, exposed the dark inner workings of the human mind, revealed the nightmare of the id, and stripped away the pious pretensions that related human beings to the angels, showing instead that humans are savage, sexual animals. Freudian psychology destroyed the old image of humanity, just as the communist revolution shattered the old order of society.

All these influences affected the thinking of playwrights and other artists during the 1920s and '30s. Their work, as we shall see, reflected the crises in moral, social, and aesthetic values. The masses of the people, however, were only dimly aware of the underlying disillusionment and unrest. During the 1920s they were caught up and swept along by the spirit and activity of the era. There was new freedom for both men and women in personal behavior and social relationships. Women bobbed their hair, smoked cigarettes, and declared that the double standard of morals was obsolete. Men manufactured bathtub gin, wore racoonskin coats, and chased young women in fast automobiles. The thoughtless among both sexes believed that the booming prosperity that they enjoyed would last indefinitely.

BROADWAY AND THE COMMERCIAL THEATRE

During the roaring twenties, the commercial theatre, like most other businesses, enjoyed a period of great prosperity. In the season of 1920-21 a total of 157 new productions reached Broadway in New York. As the decade advanced, the number of new shows increased steadily. The peak came in the season of 1927-28, when Broadway saw a grand total of 280 new plays. This record has never been equaled.

When the prosperous decade ended and the depression era of the 1930s began, new productions on Broadway decreased alarmingly. They dropped from two hundred forty in 1929-30 to a mere eighty in 1939-40. International offerings, which had enriched America's theatrical life during the 1920s, also decreased but luckily did not disappear.

An interesting index of the spirit and prosperity of the '20s was the number of lavish revues among the new productions each season. The *revue* was a distinct type of musical show that since colonial times had been an important offering of the popular theatre. Originating in Paris and closely related to vaudeville, the revue eliminated a plot line on which to attach its musical numbers, dances, leg art, and dramatic sketches. Instead it presented a collection of heterogeneous, independent acts unified only by the presence of music and alluring girls. It was Florenz Ziegfeld who perfected the revue and who became the master producer of this kind of entertainment. Ziegfeld had started modestly in 1907 to "glorify the American girl" in a series of revue sketches. Each year he had steadily increased his reputation as a judge of beautiful women and as a Croesus who spared no expense to exhibit these women excitingly and spectacularly. By the 1920s his revues, called the Ziegfeld Follies, could only be described as colossal. They flourished until the end of the decade, when the Great Depression put them out of business.

Somewhat different in their appeal but still reflecting the prosperity of the decade were the all-Negro musical shows that developed during the 1920s and began to compete with the lavish revues of the period. The first of these, entitled *Shuffle Along,* reached New York in 1921 after a shaky beginning in Washington and Philadelphia. Within a few days the news of its lively, original appeal spread among theatregoers, business began to boom, and *Shuffle Along* settled down to a year's run in New York and a two-year run on the road. Its success was no accident. The show was created and performed by a group of Negro artists with astonishing talent. The composers and musical directors were Noble Sissle and Eubie Blake, who provided such hit tunes as "I'm Just Wild about Harry" and "Love Will Find a Way"; the chief comedians were the expert team of Miller and Lyles, who had already won a popular following in vaudeville; and the feminine star was the enchanting Florence Mills, appearing in her first important role. Of course, *Shuffle Along* was not the first all-Negro revue to be seen in New York. Six years earlier, *The Darktown Follies* and its successor *Darkydom* had been hits at the Lafayette Theatre in Harlem and had attracted crowds of white theatregoers from downtown. But *Shuffle Along* was something different: a big, colorful show presented on Broadway for a general audience. It was only the first of many such revues. It was followed by other Negro shows like *Runnin' Wild, The Plantation Revue, The Chocolate Dandies,* and *Blackbirds.* The 1928 version of *Blackbirds* is remembered because it introduced a vaudeville star named Bill "Bojangles" Robinson, who, it is said, danced the show to success.

Another memorable musical show of the boom period deserves special mention because it featured black and white performers in the same cast and because it represented an advance in dramatic excellence for musical drama. This was *Show Boat,* which opened in December 1927 and held the stage for two years before touring the United States and becoming a national institution. Four years after *Show Boat,* another enormously successful musical, *Of Thee I Sing* (1931), demonstrated the increasing versatility and scope of musical plays by showing that they could be used for hilarious political satire, again without sacrificing the old popular ingredients.

The success of the musical play *Show Boat* had an ironical aspect. While the production was captivating audiences all over the nation, the institution of the floating theatre that had inspired the musical play was steadily declining. It was an inevitable decline because the conditions that had created a demand for showboats had radically altered. Now the towns once isolated along the Middle Western rivers were connected by highways and railroads; now the audiences once starved for entertainment could attend movies, vaudeville, circuses, and every other kind of road show. Thus, the gaudy, colorful floating palaces of the drama lost their appeal. In 1910 there were at least twenty-six showboats doing business; by 1928, when the musical play *Show Boat* was at its peak of success, the number of floating theatres had dwindled to fourteen; in 1938 there were five; in 1943 only the famous *Goldenrod* was in service. Today the two or three showboats that still survive are permanently moored and used by local troupes as restaurants or novelty theatres.

Showboating declined during the 1920s, as did stock companies and road-show houses. During the early years of the decade, Broadway sent most of its successful productions on tour of the United States to play in the chain of theatres designated as road-show houses. It also shared many of its new productions of straight plays with a chain of stock companies that stretched from coast to coast and that were housed in theatres of their own. But as the century advanced and the motion picture gained in popularity, both stock-company houses and road-show houses declined. Between 1920 and 1930, their number dwindled from fifteen hundred to five hundred.

NONCOMMERCIAL AND SUMMER THEATRES

As if to compensate the playgoer for the decrease in road companies and stock companies, the noncommercial theatres in communities, colleges, and universities grew in strength and numbers during the 1920s. By the end of the decade, Kenneth Macgowan, who had traveled fourteen thousand miles visiting noncommercial theatres, was able to report that there were approximately one thousand of them functioning throughout the nation. During the following decade, some of them declined, some grew in strength, and others were converted into summer theatres located in vacation areas and geared to attracting the holiday crowds. The 1930s were the great era for the proliferation of summer theatres of all kinds. They spread from coast to coast, varying from earnest amateur groups performing in converted barns to professional companies presenting big-name players in well-equipped playhouses. They have become a permanent addition to American theatrical activity.

PROTECTION FOR PLAYWRIGHTS

Not directly related to the noncommercial theatre but of great importance to the American stage was the establishment in 1926 by the Dramatists' Guild of the now-famous "Minimum Basic Agreement," which guaranteed to a playwright the permanent ownership of his plays and a fair share of the profits derived from them. Despite the efforts of such men as Dion Boucicault and Bronson Howard, playwrights had lagged behind other theatrical workers in organizing themselves to protect their rights. Actors and backstage workers had already won protective contracts.[1] Now, in 1926, the playwrights finally gained comparable protection under the Minimum Basic Agreement. Thus ended the long exploitation of the American dramatist, an ugly feature of the theatrical scene for almost two hundred years.

THE THEATRE GUILD

Perhaps the happiest development of the 1920s was the success of the Theatre Guild of New York City. Its achievements reflected the prosperity of the period, but more important, they represented a culmination of the influences toward theatrical rejuvenation that had been at work for a quarter of a century.

The founding fathers of the Guild were veterans of the defunct Washington Square Players. In December 1918, a group of these veterans again banded together and organized a theatre dedicated to the production of fine plays which commercial managers were afraid to present. It was designed to be an art theatre and entirely professional. The first production was Benavente's *The Bonds of Interest.* The play, presented in April 1919, failed to attract an audience or to impress the critics. It lost money so rapidly that the life of the fledgling organization was threatened. To avert disaster, the Guild rushed its second offering into production. This was St. John Irvine's *John Ferguson.* It opened on May 12, 1919, at a time when the Guild's treasury had diminished to nineteen dollars and fifty cents. To the immense joy and relief of the Guild, *John Ferguson* was a success. It enjoyed a prosperous run and critical acclaim.

With this success the Guild launched a long, prosperous, and exciting career. For the next two decades its achievements were notable. During part of this time it maintained a permanent acting company using a kind of alternating system. According to Lawrence Langner, who developed it, the system consisted in "producing a play for a week, and then using the same actors in a second play for the second week, then back to the first play, and so on."[2] The original acting company that established this Alternating Repertory System included such distinguished players as Helen Westley, Alfred Lunt, Lynn Fontanne, Dudley Digges, Henry Travers, and Ernest Cossart. Later the group was enlarged to include other versatile performers. For several years this was the only company of its kind in the professional theatre.

---

[1] Those who are interested can find a detailed history of the Alliance of Theatrical Stage Employees from its beginning until 1933 in Robert O. Baker, *The International Alliance of Theatrical Stage Employees and Moving Picture Machine Operators of the United States and Canada* (Lawrence, Kan., 1933). A complete economic history of the theatre in 1932, including a history of Actors' Equity Association, can be found in Alfred L. Bernheim, *The Business of the Theatre* (New York: Actors' Equity Association, 1932).

[2] Lawrence Langner, *The Magic Curtain* (New York: E. P. Dutton & Co., Inc., 1951), p. 214.

In 1925, to house the company and to provide an adequate theatre for its productions, the Guild built its own million-dollar playhouse. Here were presented the best modern plays of both foreign and native playwrights. During the ten seasons from 1920-21 through 1929-30, the Guild offered sixty-seven different productions. Fifteen of them were the work of American playwrights and included Eugene O'Neill's *Strange Interlude, Marco Millions,* and *Dynamo;* Sidney Howard's *The Silver Cord* and *They Knew What They Wanted;* Elmer Rice's *The Adding Machine;* John Howard Lawson's *Processional;* S. N. Behrman's *The Second Man;* and Dorothy and DuBose Heyward's *Porgy.* Adding to this rich fare were plays from the theatres of Germany, Russia, Scandinavia, France, and several other foreign countries plus ten plays from the pen of George Bernard Shaw, who designated the Guild as his American agent in 1920.

During the 1930s, the Guild continued its distinguished activity, but at a somewhat slower pace because of the economic disasters of the period. The fifty-three dramas presented in the decade, despite the depression, included some of the Guild's proudest and most successful undertakings. One of these was Eugene O'Neill's *Mourning Becomes Electra* with Alla Nazimova and Alice Brady in leading roles. Lawrence Langner called the production "the greatest play the Guild ever did."[3]

Throughout these years the directors of the Guild maintained their ideals and their spirit of dedication, insisting on the highest standards of artistry and creativity in every Guild production. The artists whom they encouraged and helped to develop responded magnificently. A talented, vital, enthusiastic corps of playwrights, actors, directors, and designers set standards of excellence that inspired theatre groups all over the country. Among the scenic artists who did major work under Guild sponsorship were Robert Edmond Jones, Jo Mielziner, Stewart Chaney, Donald Oenslager, and Lee Simonson. Directors Philip Moeller and Rouben Mamoulian achieved their greatest successes as Guild directors.

The Guild was a stimulus and a pioneer in many areas other than play production. It rendered the American theatre a notable service in 1931 when it assisted in the founding of the Group Theatre. It built up subscription audiences in New York and in the other cities where the Guild regularly toured. In 1932 the interests of the Guild and the Shubert brothers were united by the formation of the American Theatre Society, Inc., which coordinated bookings for subscription audiences in twenty-three cities from New York to California.

The Guild, of course, was not without problems, disappointments, and failures even during its most flourishing years. Outstanding actors, directors, and scenic artists often left the Guild for more lucrative or glamorous positions elsewhere. These defections further complicated the troubles created by the depression of the 1930s. Everywhere in the United States audiences were dwindling, and money to support creative activity was diminishing. The Guild was forced to curtail its programs; it lost the playhouse that it had proudly opened in 1925; many of its

---

[3]See "A Long and Worthy Life, The Theatre Guild: 1919-1959," *Theatre Arts Magazine,* XLIII (September 1959), 21.

artists were forced to accept jobs with the Federal Theatre or with other groups. However, the Guild, as an organization and as an influence, continued to function largely through the leadership of Lawrence Langner and Theresa Helburn. Although its vitality was diminished and its program cut back and although it became essentially just another commercial producer, it was destined to continue making contributions to the American theatre during the 1940s and '50s.

During all of these years Lawrence Langner, one of the original directors, functioned as the leading figure in the management of the Guild's affairs. This amazingly versatile man, who was also a playwright and a successful patent attorney, supplied such a continuing stream of ideas and inspiration that when he died (in December 1962) he had earned the title of founder, lifelong director, and guiding spirit of the Guild. Following his death, the creative activities of the organization diminished until it became principally a backer of commercial plays and a booking agent for Broadway hits.

EVA LE GALLIENNE AND WALTER HAMPDEN

The dedication to great drama beautifully presented, which characterized the Theatre Guild throughout most of its career, was shared by two other producing groups that flourished in the 1920s. One was Eva Le Gallienne's Civic Repertory Theatre, which enjoyed a lifetime of six seasons from 1926 to 1932. Miss Le Gallienne wished to present significant plays in rotation, or repertory, at a low enough price to enable a large and varied audience to attend. She adhered to these ideals during the lifetime of her theatre. Opening with a production of Chekhov's *The Three Sisters,* Miss Le Gallienne presented a distinguished repertory of plays that included such classics as Ibsen's *The Master Builder* and *Hedda Gabler,* Chekhov's *The Sea Gull* and *The Cherry Orchard,* Tolstoy's *The Living Corpse,* and Shakespeare's *Romeo and Juliet.* When the Great Depression forced her to close, she could boast a total of thirty-four different productions representing the best dramaturgy of foreign playwrights.

The other producing group that joined the Theatre Guild and the Civic Repertory Theatre in presenting great plays was Walter Hampden's. This distinguished American-born actor, whose career had begun in England in 1901, had been producer with his own company since 1919. In 1925 he leased the Colonial Theatre in New York, which he renamed Hampden's; and here he trained his actors in the style he had learned during his long stay in England. For five years he presented a series of distinguished plays that included several of Shakespeare's tragedies, Ibsen's *An Enemy of the People,* Rostand's *Cyrano de Bergerac,* and a dramatization of Browning's *The Ring and the Book* entitled *Caponsacchi.* These productions, originating in New York, were regularly taken on extended tours throughout the nation. In 1930 Hampden relinquished his theatre but continued to tour the country in revivals of his popular successes during most of the succeeding decade.

NEW DESIGNERS

The general prosperity of the New York theatre during the 1920s and the inspiration of groups like the Theatre Guild and the Civic Repertory Theatre stimulated the development of a host of artists in every branch of theatre art. Especially notable was the group of designers who emerged. Disciples of the new stagecraft proposed by Appia and Craig, this group gave American productions a scenic style and artistry that they had never before possessed. The leaders of the new corps of designers were Robert Edmond Jones (1887-1954), Lee Simonson (1888-1967), and Norman Bel Geddes (1893-1958). Rivaling this early group was a younger group whose members quickly gained reputations for originality, artistry, and versatility. Among the most notable names were Cleon Throckmorton, Donald Oenslager, Stewart Chaney, and Jo Mielziner—the latter being, perhaps, the most prolific and versatile of the younger group.

NEW CRITICS

Equally important to the rejuvenated theatre was a brilliant new corps of dramatic critics. Their leader was James G. Huneker (1859-1921). Under his influence they brought to the theatre a completely transformed philosophy of aesthetics. The eminent reviewers of the nineteenth century, such as William Winter, represented the moral and aesthetic principles of the Victorian age; and when they were confronted with the plays of Ibsen, Chekhov, or O'Neill, their traditional standards of judgment proved wholly inadequate. The new critics, nurtured in a different climate, possessed a different standard of values, morals, and aesthetics and a deeper understanding of the aims of twentieth-century drama. Their work stimulated and educated theatregoers all over the nation. Some of the most active members of the new school of criticism were Brooks Atkinson (1894-   ), the veteran critic of the *New York Times;* Robert Benchley (1889-1945), who served both *Life Magazine* (the old version) and later *The New Yorker;* Heywood Broun (1888-1939), drama critic for the *New York World;* John Mason Brown (1900-1969), reviewer for the *Saturday Review of Literature* from 1944 to 1955; Sheldon Cheney (1886-1980), founder of *Theatre Arts Monthly* and its editor for five years; Barrett H. Clark (1890-1953), literary editor of Samuel French, Inc., and prolific writer on theatrical matters; and a host of other keen, perceptive men like Kenneth Macgowan, Burns Mantle, George Jean Nathan, and Stark Young. The level of criticism that these reviewers established was surprisingly high, despite occasional outbursts of disappointment from playwrights and producers. Brooks Atkinson and his fellow reviewers made a genuine contribution to greater understanding and appreciation of the art of the theatre.

THE TWENTIETH-CENTURY DIRECTOR

Closely associated with the renaissance of theatrical art were the stage directors who developed in the early years of the twentieth century. Régisseurs like Augustin Daly, who had emerged in the last years of the nineteenth century, were either dead or retired, with the exception of David Belasco. To replace them, a new corps of directors appeared. In the earliest years of the twentieth century, they included such gifted and idealistic men of the theatre as Winthrop Ames, Harrison Grey Fiske, and Arnold Daly. A group of manager-producers including Jed Harris, Gilbert Miller, John Golden, and William Brady combined idealism with a flair for commercial success and were a powerful force in the theatre for a time. Two directors of artistic integrity and theatrical talent who developed in the 1920s and '30s became outstanding representatives of the twentieth-century régisseur: Arthur Hopkins (1878-1950) and Guthrie McClintic (1893-1961). A brief review of their achievements and methods will illustrate the role of the master director in modern play production.

Arthur Hopkins began his career as a newspaperman, booking agent, and writer of vaudeville sketches. After moving to New York City from Cleveland, he produced his first play, *Poor Little Rich Girl*, in 1913. By 1920 he had produced seventeen plays, four of which had lasted more than one hundred performances and three of which had been plays by Ibsen starring the Russian actress Alla Nazimova. During the 1920s, Hopkins firmly established himself as a master director and as a man who could discern and develop the talent of young performers. He directed John Barrymore in *Richard III* and *Hamlet;* he directed Lionel Barrymore in *Macbeth;* and he presented Ethel Barrymore in a series of plays that included *Romeo and Juliet, The Laughing Lady,* and *The Second Mrs. Tanquery.* Hopkins also recognized the genius of Eugene O'Neill and in 1921 staged *Anna Christie.* In the same year he brought the Provincetown Players' production of *The Hairy Ape* to Broadway. Three years later he was the director of the famous Stallings-Anderson antiwar play, *What Price Glory?* He also introduced plays by Philip Barry, Sidney Howard, and Robert Sherwood. His successful career, which also included playwriting and the production of radio dramas, continued well into the 1940s.

In his method of directing a play, Hopkins differed from the earlier régisseurs like Daly and Belasco. They were absolute czars, dictating every intonation, gesture, and movement of their actors. In contrast, Hopkins followed a laissez-faire method, allowing his performers to develop their manner of performance slowly and individually. He was the coordinator of effects and the final authority in artistic decisions, yet his performers had the freedom to be original and creative. To get the best possible performances from them, Hopkins believed that a director must show both faith and confidence in their ability. A Hopkins production, when it reached the public, was characterized by a slow pace, the absence of theatrical tricks, a careful coordination of all effects, and a broad pictorial impact. Many critics felt that Hopkins, as a director, was like the little girl with the curl in the middle of her forehead. When he was good, he was superb; when he was bad, his productions were flat and sloppy. However, his successes justify his reputation as one of the best directors of the first half of the twentieth century.

Another eminent and representative director of this period was Guthrie Mc-Clintic, famous not only as a régisseur but as the husband and coworker with the notable actress Katharine Cornell. Although fifteen years younger than Hopkins, McClintic was active on Broadway during many of the same years.

McClintic, born in Seattle, Washington, was stagestruck early in life. After running away from home to join a road company, and refusing to attend high school, he was permitted by his parents to attend the American Academy of Dramatic Arts in New York. Following graduation at the age of nineteen, he joined a road company, then worked briefly in stock and vaudeville. In 1913 he wangled a job with the distinguished New York producer and director Winthrop Ames, and did so well in all his assignments that Ames offered to back him financially in the production of a play. Unable to find a satisfactory script, McClintic in 1920 joined Jessie Bonstelle's Detroit stock company for a season; here he met the new leading lady, Katharine Cornell. He had seen her perform with the Washington Square Players in 1917 and had noted that her talent was worth watching. Now he fell in love with her and the following year, 1921, he married her. In the same year— surely a memorable one for McClintic—he made his debut as a producer and director. The play, A. A. Milne's *The Dover Road,* ran for thirty-five weeks. This was the beginning of a career as a producer and director that lasted more than thirty years and that saw the presentation of ninety McClintic productions, many of which starred Katharine Cornell. The team of Cornell and McClintic became one of the most famous and creative of the twentieth century.

McClintic's method as a director was unique and individual. The preparation of every play began with an eight-day period during which the actors sat around a table and read their parts. They were not allowed to rehearse on their feet until they had established the tempo, rhythm, and timing of the play and had planned all the action and business. After eight days they took to the stage, which was often fully set, and started rehearsing the overall design worked out previously around the table. McClintic was a perfectionist, painstakingly suggesting, explaining, and experimenting. A McClintic production, when finally ready for public presentation, was noted for the smoothness of its detail and the overall shape and polish of its action. The critics usually praised these productions for being "fluid and interesting" and for demonstrating "vigor and pictorial effectiveness." They also admired McClintic's ability to blend his players, however individualistic, into an effective ensemble.

The careers of Arthur Hopkins and Guthrie McClintic illustrate how the function and methods of a play director have developed during the twentieth century and, perhaps of more significance, confirm how vitally important the position of director has become.

ACTING IN THE LIVING THEATRE
BETWEEN TWO WORLD WARS

During the years of the prosperous '20s and the depressed '30s, American players of the living stage continued to contribute notable performances. The old giants of the nineteenth century who had acted tragedy and comedy so notably were gone, but a few performers still practiced the methods of the classic school. The ladies of the emotionalistic school had faded, as had many of the representatives of the personality school. Mrs. Fiske was still active during the 1920s and many other practitioners of the modern school of psychological naturalism were making names for themselves.

The famous Barrymore family—Lionel, John, and Ethel, grandchildren of the celebrated actress-manager Mrs. John Drew—were leading exponents of the classical school during the 1920s, before Lionel and John succumbed to Hollywood and to the devitalizing influence of typecasting. Lionel (1878-1954), the eldest of the three, was originally a versatile character actor who identified so completely with his roles that he lived them off the stage as well as on. He demonstrated a remarkable power of transformation before he settled into the rut of a single line of roles in Hollywood, that of the crusty, shrewd old man with a heart of gold.

John Barrymore (1882-1942), the younger brother, was a devoted admirer of Lionel. In his early career on the stage, John was an actor who spared no effort or pains to prepare himself for a role. He worked tirelessly with his speech coach, Mrs. Margaret Carrington, to train his voice for Shakespearean parts. In rehearsals he was always on time, perfect in his lines, willing to repeat a scene to the point of exhaustion. He loved creating a part, and his first performances of a role were always his best. But he hated repeating a part, so during a long run his later performances became almost a parody of his earlier efforts. Probably his crowning achievement as an actor was his embodiment of Richard III in 1920. His director, Arthur Hopkins, says that in the part "John took his place in the classical gallery. He was unforgettable."[4] John's later embodiment of Hamlet was lavishingly praised, but according to Hopkins, who directed this production also, only the earliest performances were first-rate; the later ones were often "embarrassingly bombastic."[5]

Ethel Barrymore (1879-1959), the other member of this gifted trio, shared the family talent for acting and in addition added glamour and an unerring sense of theatrical effectiveness. She played a wide range of parts from Lady Teazle in *The School for Scandal* to Shakespeare's Juliet. Like her brothers, she was tireless in her study and preparation and so dedicated to the theatre that she often performed when she was physically ill or exhausted. She appeared in a few movie roles, but in general remained loyal to the living stage until the end of her career.

[4]Arthur Hopkins, *To a Lonely Boy* (Garden City, N. Y.: Doubleday & Company, Inc., 1937), p. 201.
[5]Ibid., p. 231.

John Barrymore as Richard III.

Hoblitzelle Theatre Arts Library, Humanities Research
Center, University of Texas at Austin.

Many other gifted players like the Barrymores carried on the traditions of the classic school. Some of the best of these were Margaret Anglin, Nance O'Neill, Alice Brady, Pauline Lord, Laurette Taylor, Jane Cowl, and Judith Anderson.

As widely known and universally admired as any performers of their time were four players of unusual grace and talent who achieved fame during the 1920s and 1930s: Lynn Fontanne (1882-   ), Alfred Lunt (1893-1977), Helen Hayes (1895-   ), and Katharine Cornell (1898-1974).

Lynn Fontanne, English by birth, first acted in the United States in 1916. Eight years later she joined the company of the Theatre Guild and demonstrated her exquisite skill as a comedienne in the Guild's production of Ferenc Molnar's play *The Guardsman.* In 1928 she excelled in the serious role of Nina Leeds in O'Neill's *Strange Interlude,* and in 1930 she gave one of her best performances as the Queen in Maxwell Anderson's *Queen Elizabeth.* Thereafter she devoted herself mostly to playing roles in high comedy, her leading man and costar being her husband, Alfred Lunt. Mr. Lunt, whose acting career began in 1912, made a great hit in 1919 in the leading role in Booth Tarkington's *Clarence.* In 1924 he appeared

Helen Hayes in *Victoria Regina.*

Hoblitzelle Theatre Arts Library, Humanities Research Center, University of Texas at Austin.

with Miss Fontanne in *The Guardsman* and since then has played a few serious roles but, like his wife, has preferred to perform in high comedy.

Like the Lunts, Helen Hayes had a varied career on the stage before she joined the Theatre Guild in 1925 and acted the role of Cleopatra in Shaw's *Caesar and Cleopatra.* Thereafter, her special charm, reminiscent of Maude Adams's appeal, illuminated such roles as *Coquette,* which she acted from 1927 to 1929, and *Mary of Scotland,* which she acted in 1933. Two years later she undertook the leading role in Housman's *Victoria Regina,* demonstrating her versatility by her convincing portrayal of Queen Victoria from the age of eighteen to the occasion, sixty years later, when the queen celebrated her diamond jubilee.

Katharine Cornell, another greatly admired actress of the period, studied dramatics as a girl and made her first New York appearance in 1916 with the Washington Square Players. She acted with this group for two years, then joined the Jessie Bonstelle stock company, where she had the useful experience of playing

Katharine Cornell as Joan of Arc in *Saint Joan,* by George Bernard Shaw.

a variety of roles in many popular plays. Her first portrayal to win national attention was her 1921 role of Sydney Fairfield in *A Bill of Divorcement.* Her performance was marked by the casual grace and refined intensity that became characteristic of all her acting. In the same year as *A Bill of Divorcement,* Miss Cornell married the soon to be distinguished director Guthrie McClintic, and from 1925 until his death all the plays in which she appeared were directed by him. Outstanding productions presented by this team of husband and wife included *The Barretts of Wimpole Street, Candida, Saint Joan,* and *Romeo and Juliet.* The leading lady illuminated all of them with a radiant personality, an intensity of emotion, and a command of stage technique that won her the accolade of "First Lady of the Theatre" from many critics.

Of special interest during the 1920s and '30s was the emergence of several Negro performers of great ability and appeal. The first of these and certainly the greatest Negro actor to get a hearing since the days of Ira Aldridge in the nineteenth century was Charles S. Gilpin (1878-1930). Born in Richmond, Virginia, Gilpin was forty-one years old when he was invited to play the role for which he is remembered, that of Brutus Jones in the original production of Eugene O'Neill's *The Emperor Jones.* By looks, temperament, and experience, Gilpin was the ideal actor for the play. He proved to be even better than anticipated. He had frightening intensity and wonderful flexibility; he understood and projected with absolute authenticity every emotion of the dramatic Brutus Jones, from swaggering cunning and evil to superstitious horror and guilt. Gilpin played the role almost continuously for four years. However, when the play was revived in 1925 he was not invited to resume the part.

The actor who replaced him was a young man destined to be greater and more versatile than Gilpin. His name was Paul Robeson (1898-1976). A graduate of Columbia Law School, handsome, popular, brilliant, and ablaze with talent, Robeson abandoned the law for a career on the stage. He had appeared in O'Neill's original production of *All God's Chillun Got Wings* in 1924; but the play, which concerned the marriage of a Negro man and a white woman, had not been popular. Now Robeson in 1925 performed the role made famous by Gilpin, but he did not yet have the experience or the technique to equal his predecessor. Yet Robeson's great talent was soon recognized in his concert singing; and later on, especially in his performances of Othello, his stature as a superb actor was confirmed.

Gilpin and Robeson were not the only black performers of the 1920s and '30s. It was a period when the old color prejudices were breaking down, at least on the stage, and many Negroes were winning admiration and applause. In 1926 Jules Bledsoe played the name part in *In Abraham's Bosom* and went on to star as Joe in *Show Boat,* singing "Old Man River" a total of 572 times on Broadway. In the season of 1927-28, *Porgy,* by DuBose and Dorothy Heyward, presented a brilliant cast of black players including Rose McClendon and Frank Wilson. Then early in 1930 came another smash hit with an all-Negro cast: Marc Connelly's *The Green Pastures.* In it Richard B. Harrison earned an international reputation for his beautiful portrayal of "de Lawd." The climax of what might be called the Negro breakthrough in theatre came in 1935 when the musical version of *Porgy,* now

Paul Robeson as *Othello.*

Theatre Collection, The New York Public Library at Lincoln
Center, Astor, Lenox and Tilden Foundations.

called *Porgy and Bess,* opened in New York and took the city—and later the nation
—by storm. The production, with music by George Gershwin, made stars out of
such performers as Todd Duncan, Anne Wiggins Brown, and John W. Bubbles.

Such players maintained the high standards of American acting between the
First and Second World Wars. However, the number of distinguished players who
attempted the great roles of classic drama was notably smaller in the 1920s and
'30s than in earlier periods. There were, of course, fewer playhouses devoted to the
living drama; the resident companies performing a wide repertory of plays were
practically extinct; the opportunities for actors to play the great roles were sharply
limited. It is little wonder, then, that although there were outstanding performances in this period, the number of such performances decreased.

MOTION PICTURES

The decade of the 1920s was a prosperous period for the living theatre; it was even
more so for the motion picture. In fact, the entire period between the two world
wars and including the years of World War II can be called the golden age of the

253

motion picture. During these years, the art of the cinema reached a remarkable maturity, and attending the movies became a national pastime. By 1930 the United States was producing 355 films per year, In 1940 this figure rose to 473, and in 1941 it reached an all-time high of 497. The number of fans who regularly attended the showing of these films reached astronomical figures.

To attract the customers, to impress them, and to give them a sense of comfort and opulence, grandiose cinema palaces were designed and built all over the nation. All these palaces offered the customer not only a feature film and selected short subjects but also, somewhat like the legitimate theatres of the nineteenth century, they added a potpourri of entertainment including singing, dancing, vaudeville acts, and big-name bands. The smaller movie houses, which could not afford such lavish attractions, lured the customer with double features and with such gimmicks as dish nights, bank nights, lotteries, and an ingenious variety of games and contests. By the 1940s movie attendance in the United States was ninety million per week and gross receipts were one and a half billion dollars per week.[6]

Several developments in the movies during the interwar years deserve to be mentioned. In May 1927, the Academy of Motion Picture Arts and Sciences was founded "to raise the standards of production educationally, culturally, and scientifically." The first Oscar awards were made in 1929, and they have been an annual event of national interest ever since.

In 1930 the first production code to regulate the moral standards of American films was voluntarily adopted and put into practice. The three general principles originally chosen to shape the code are the following:

1.   No picture shall be produced which will lower the moral standards of those who see it. Hence, the sympathy of the audience shall never be thrown to the side of crime, wrong-doing, evil or sin.
2.   Correct standards of life, subject only to the standards of drama and entertainment, shall be presented.
3.   Law, natural or human, shall not be ridiculed, nor shall sympathy be created for its violation.

The ambiguous language of the code, so clearly illustrated in the general principles, created continual controversy and equivocation. The code has been revised several times, always in the direction of greater permissiveness, and is still accepted as Hollywood's voluntary system of self-regulation.

A third and even more important development of the interwar years was the introduction first of sound and later of color. Both came largely as a response to the competition offered by the advent of radio.

[6]See Leo A. Handel, *Hollywood Looks at its Audience* (Urbana, Ill.: The University of Illinois Press, 1950), pp. 95-96.

RADIO AND TALKING PICTURES

There had been radio broadcasting as early as 1909 when a pioneer station in San Jose, California, station SJN, began to transmit regular programs of spoken announcements and phonograph music. However, not until 1920 and afterward did broadcasting begin to flourish on a grand scale. It grew fantastically and soon blanketed the nation with a network of stations transmitting an infinite variety of programs in a hectic, round-the-clock fashion. By 1939 there were an estimated forty-three million radio sets in operation.

In the mid-1920s the movies began to feel the competition. Film fans deserted the neighborhood cinema houses to listen to their favorite broadcasts. In alarm, the movies offered all manner of enticements. But the public remained at home, enchanted with the free entertainment offered in its living rooms. Then in 1927, Warner Brothers, one of the major film producers in Hollywood, introduced synchronized music and spoken dialogue in its film *The Jazz Singer,* starring Al Jolson. With the advent of sound, the film industry quickly recovered its audience. Talking pictures became so enormously popular that the weekly attendance at movie houses rose from sixty-five million in 1927 to ninety million by the end of 1929. The drawing power of talking pictures continued well into the years of the Great Depression. Eventually the movies felt the effect of the Depression, but not for long. Toward the end of the 1930s, war in Europe and the preparation for war by the United States created a new boom in Hollywood. Movie production was suspended in most foreign countries, so the demand for American films increased. With every citizen employed—in the armed forces or in war production—everyone had money; and everyone, servicemen and civilians alike, felt the need for entertainment. American movies prospered fantastically.

The appeal of these films was enhanced by the introduction of color. Through the efforts largely of the Technicolor Motion Pictures Corporation, a successful process for making color films was developed in the 1930s and notably displayed in such pioneer color films as *Becky Sharp* (1935) and *Snow White and the Seven Dwarfs* (1938). Once introduced, color became an indispensible addition to the art of the cinema. Today it is a rare film that does not use it.

Acting in Talking Pictures

The introduction of the talkies in 1927 caused a major revolution in the film industry. Production became vastly more complicated and expensive; acting now demanded voice as well as looks and pantomime. For awhile, the new dimension of sound arrested the development of cinema technique, and movies again resembled photographed stage plays, just as they had in their earliest infancy. Movie actors, anxious to maintain their jobs, flocked to teachers of elocution and often acquired an "elegant" delivery that was stilted and unconvincing. It took time for actors to realize that if they had reasonably pleasant and flexible voices they needed only to follow the usual patterns of conversation and to use the natural tones of normal speech to produce acceptable delivery. Projection of volume and exaggeration of articulation, so necessary for effectiveness in large legitimate theatres, were wholly unnecessary before a microphone that magnified every tone and syllable. Directors also needed time and experience to realize that the techniques they had learned in silent films were still valid, and that a good movie still depended on visual excitement. After much stress and strain and several false starts, Hollywood mastered the use of sound and learned that the basic differences between film acting and stage acting, which had long been accepted in silent pictures, were unchanged.

For a time, radio—another mechanical marvel of the twentieth century—developed a unique but limited technique of performance which was different from that of either legitimate stage or the motion picture. The silent film was visual entertainment and communicated thought and emotion through sight alone. Radio relies wholly on sound and requires a type of performance based exclusively on the power and expressiveness of the human voice. In a radio play, no movement, gesture, or physical expression can be seen. They exist only in the mind of the listeners, created imaginatively from the sounds the listeners hear. The radio gives them many clues and suggestions: doors are slammed, papers rattled, shots fired, and lips smacked—but the human voice is the principal medium of communication. In the early 1920s the marvelous and infinite flexibility of the human voice was recognized and cultivated once more. Actors discovered anew that emotion could be stirred and attitudes and states of mind could be revealed by nuances of tone and variation in vocal quality. Comedians returned to the verbal gags that had been a mainstay of vaudeville but had died with the movies. Performers who excelled in vocal expressiveness, either comic or serious, became stars of radio and commanded a popularity as great as the following of the film idols. To be sure, radio never duplicated the pageantry, spectacle, or visual excitement of the films, but it had an inherent advantage that the movies never offered. It was free and it was mobile. A broadcast could be listened to without charge in one's home or car, in public or private, on land or at sea. But the heyday of radio acting was brief. As soon as television invaded the living room, radio acting all but disappeared, except for re-broadcast of a few old programs in the late 1970s.

THE GROUP THEATRE AND THE FEDERAL THEATRE

During the depression years of the 1930s, two unique producing groups emerged, both of which were significant and influential. The first of these, the Group Theatre, reflected the unrest of the times and the aspiration for a theatre dedicated to higher social and artistic ideals. The formation of such a group was logical. During the 1930s, many plays of social protest were written. As commercial managers were not interested in them, new companies were needed to produce them. The groups that were formed to meet the need were mostly leftist and dedicated to political action. Their orientation is suggested by their names. Labor Stage, Theatre of Action, Theatre Union, Social Stage, Workers' Laboratory Theatre, Theatre Collective, and Group Theatre were a few of the troupes that appeared during the restless 1930s. Most of them enjoyed a brief flurry of activity, then vanished. The Group Theatre, whose aim was artistic instead of political, represents one of the most important developments of the depression years.

The idea of the Group Theatre was the inspiration of Harold Clurman, an apprentice actor and play reader for the Theatre Guild. He envisioned a company of young actors and directors who would dedicate themselves to helping each other achieve artistic maturity within a common set of ideals. He propounded his ideas to his fellow workers so persuasively that by the summer of 1931, with the assistance and blessing of the Theatre Guild, he had gathered a group of twenty-eight actors and three directors to form a summer colony at Brookfield, Connecticut. The colony drew its principal inspiration from the ideals of Stanislavsky and the Moscow Art Theatre, ideals that had been introduced to the United States by the writings of Stanislavsky, by the visit of the Moscow Art Theatre in 1923, and by two noted teachers of the Stanislavsky method, Richard Boleslavsky and Maria Ouspenskaya, who had taught at the American Laboratory Theatre in the 1920s. The influence that the Stanislavsky-inspired Group Theatre was later to exert on the American stage is indicated by the names found on its original roster. The directors included, besides Clurman himself, Lee Strasberg and Cheryl Crawford. The actors included Elia Kazan, Stella Adler, Clifford Odets, Franchot Tone, Morris Carnovsky, and J. Edward Bromberg. Most of them later became noted exponents or teachers of "Method" acting.

After a summer of study, self-analysis, and rehearsal at Brookfield Center, the Group opened its first production in New York City in September 1931. The play, Paul Green's *The House of Connelly,* achieved a run of ninety-one performances after receiving excellent reviews. Then followed three more productions, two of which were failures and one a moderate success. The financial position of the Group was precarious until it presented Sidney Kingsley's *Men in White,* which proved to be a smashing success. From then until the end of the decade the Group continued to produce plays and to achieve success in a variety of ways. It discovered that Clifford Odets, one of its apprentice actors, was a gifted playwright and helped him launch his career. It gave a hearing to other serious young playwrights like Paul Green, Irwin Shaw, and William Saroyan. It provided the training that made first-rate actors or directors of several of its people. And it spread the gospel of Stanislavsky's principles until his method became a major force in American acting. Although the Group ceased its operations in 1941, the fervency having diminished and many of the key members having been lured to other positions, its influence is still felt in the teaching and directing of such men as Kazan, Strasberg, Clurman, and others.

THE FEDERAL THEATRE

Of all the activities and developments of the 1930s, the most unusual by far was the Federal Theatre. Out of the disaster of the Great Depression was born a project unique in the history of American drama. The sire was an enlightened national administration: President Franklin D. Roosevelt and his lieutenant, Harry Hopkins; the midwife was a gifted, intrepid lady: Hallie Flannagan. The unique project they brought to life, the Federal Theatre, lived and flourished for only four short years before congressional ignorance, fear, and malice killed it, yet in that time it achieved unexpected success. It remains the only instance in two hundred years of American history when the government of the United States became a theatrical producer.

In the early years of the 1930s, the Depression took a grim toll of activity in the living theatre. Motion pictures and radio had already lured away thousands of playgoers. Now the growing unemployment and poverty closed hundreds of playhouses and threw thousands of theatre people out of work. There are no statistics for the nation as a whole, but in New York City alone Actors' Equity said there were five thousand unemployed performers plus fifteen to twenty-five thousand unemployed scene designers, directors, costumers, electricians, stagehands, and technicians of all kinds. The situation in the theatre was duplicated in almost every other profession, industry, and trade throughout the nation.

Immediately after his inauguration, following the national elections of 1932, President Franklin D. Roosevelt launched a vigorous program to create jobs for the unemployed. The Relief Act of March 1933 was followed by the Federal Emergency Relief Administration, then by the Civil Works Administration. In April 1935, the Works Progress Administration supplanted these agencies. Harry Hopkins, the president's trusted lieutenant, was the wise and farsighted administrator. He recognized the desperate condition of theatre workers and, as early as February 1934, invited Mrs. Hallie Flannagan, director of the Vassar Experimental Theatre, to devise a plan to help them. Mrs. Flannagan declined because of commitments abroad and because she felt herself unsuited to the job. But a year later, when the situation in the theatre was even worse, she was persuaded to accept the position of director of the Federal Theatre Project under the Works Progress Administration. With astonishing zeal and intelligence she went to work. After conferring with leaders all over the nation who represented both the commercial and noncommercial theatres, she announced that the Federal Theatre Project would function on the following premises:

1. That the reemployment of theatre people now on relief rolls is the primary aim.
2. That this reemployment shall be in theatre enterprises offering dramatic entertainment either free or at low cost.
3. That whenever possible regional theatres developing native plays and original methods of production shall be encouraged.
4. That the WPA will pay:
    a. *Labor costs* of unemployed people enrolled on the project at the wage stated by the local WPA administration.
    b. *Superintendence cost,* on an average of one person not on relief rolls to twenty who are, at a small wage.
    c. *A small percentage* (not to exceed 10 percent) of labor costs *for production costs,* depending on the nature of the project.

5. That if the sponsoring organization is a public enterprise, or a nonprofit-making cooperative, or can be incorporated as such, any funds made by admissions may accrue to the project.[7]

After the adoption of these policies, the nation was divided into five regions, eminent men were chosen to direct each of these, and a capital city was selected for each. Each capital city was organized to be a production center, a retraining center for actors, and a service, research, and playwriting center for its region. It was hoped that the centers would "lay the foundation for the development of a truly creative theatre in the United States with outstanding producing centers in each of those regions which have common interests . . ."[8]

During the first year, the project was expected to employ twelve thousand theatre workers at salaries ranging from $21 to $103.40 per month for a total pay-roll of $10,000,000 per year. Harry Hopkins announced bravely that the new Federal Theatre was going to be "kept free from censorship," a promise soon to be invalidated by Congress.

So new and so vast a project created enormous difficulties for its director, Mrs. Flanagan. She was always between Scylla and Charybdis. Scylla was the monstrous federal bureaucracy of endless red tape, delays, and quibbling with congressional suspicion always lurking in the background. Charybdis was the morass of artistic temperaments, jealousies, and conflicting ideals revealed by thousands of individual theatre workers when they were suddenly brought together in a vast network of producing units. Yet Mrs. Flanagan kept the project afloat and on course despite the bickering, resignations, suspicion, and red tape.

By the end of its first year of operation, the Federal Theatre was functioning in thirty-one states, using twelve thousand theatre workers, and presenting entertainment to hundreds of thousands of citizens. The offerings were varied and colorful. In New York City, which constituted a single region, there were five major producing units. One was the "living newspaper," a dramatization of current events designed to employ the maximum number of performers and using an exciting combination of speech, pantomime, motion pictures, acrobatics, and numerous other theatrical devices to relate, clarify, and comment on important events of the day. A second unit in New York presented original plays by new authors. A third experimented with new production techniques using original plays. A fourth was a Negro theatre, and the fifth was a tryout theatre, which allowed commercial managers to try out new and risky plays, with the Federal Theatre providing the actors and the commercial producers furnishing the other costs. In addition to the five major producing units, New York also had a Gilbert and Sullivan company, vaudeville, marionette shows, a minstrel show, and eventually a circus.

The variety of theatrical offerings in the other regions of the United States was equally great. Often they reflected the differing characteristics of the regions. In New Orleans, for example, Paul Green's *Roll Sweet Chariot* was successfully

[7] Hallie Flannagan, *Arena* (New York: Duell, Sloan and Pearce, 1940), p. 29.
[8] Ibid., p. 23.

The Supreme Court hearing arguments on the TVA appeal in a
"living newspaper" production entitled *Power,* in New York City, 1937.

Hoblitzelle Theatre Arts Library, Humanities Research Center, University of Texas at Austin.

staged by Negro actors and choruses. In Chicago a dance production, *Frankie and
Johnny,* attained a "robustness, lack of inhibition, and racy humor—the elements
which make Chicago what it is."[9] In Los Angeles there were units for producing
Yiddish plays, religious plays, experimental plays, classic plays, and children's
plays—as well as units for vaudeville and standard plays.

The Federal Theatre enjoyed many outstanding successes both as a producer
and as an agency to retrain and return workers to private industry. Among the
notable productions were *It Can't Happen Here,* a dramatization of Sinclair Lewis's
novel, which played simultaneously in twenty-one theatres in seventeen states; T. S.
Eliot's *Murder in the Cathedral;* a Negro production of Shakespeare's *Macbeth*
(reset in Haiti); Paul Green's *The Lost Colony;* Harry Minturn's *The Swing Mikado,*
adapted from Gilbert and Sullivan; a subsequent version, *The Hot Mikado,* produced by Michael Todd; Marlowe's *The Tragical History of Dr. Faustus,* produced
by John Houseman and Orson Welles; and E. P. Conkle's *Prologue to Glory,* a play
about the early years of Abraham Lincoln. Eight hundred thirty major titles were
produced by the nationwide Federal Theatre during its four years of activity. They

[9] Ibid., p. 142.

included nine plays by George Bernard Shaw and fourteen by Eugene O'Neill. Both these eminent dramatists were so impressed by the work of the Federal Theatre that they gave a blanket permission to use their plays on payment of only a token fee.

We must not infer, however, that the Federal Theatre was universally success-ful. For every triumph there was a failure; for every superior production there was a mediocre one; for every original idea of staging there were many trite ideas. Yet the overall quality of the productions was remarkably high, all things considered, and the overall success was impressive.

The Federal Theatre was eventually destroyed by the suspicion and censor-ship of Washington's bureaucrats. Endless red tape was always a problem. Then in 1937 the production of Marc Blitzstein's *The Cradle Will Rock* was forbidden be-cause the bureaucrats considered it subversive and dangerous. The producers of the play, John Houseman and Orson Welles, immediately resigned. The next phase in the attack on the Federal Theatre was the elimination of the *Federal Theatre Maga-zine,* a publication that recorded the nationwide activities of the project and unified and stimulated the producing units throughout the country. After the suppression of the magazine came criticism in Congress and then investigation by congressional committees, including the Dies Committee on Un-American Activities. The attackers claimed that the Federal Theatre was both immoral and communistic. The enemies of the project also alleged that it was a haven for the idle and the lazy. Sometimes the attackers provided memorable examples of ignorance. Mrs. Flanagan was sus-pect because she had visited play festivals in the USSR. One Congressman wanted to know if Christopher Marlowe was a communist; another asked if Shakespeare's *Coriolanus* was subversive.

As Congressional attacks on the Federal Theatre increased, the theatrical profession rallied to defend it. Actors, critics, and producers, notable men and women from every branch of the theatre, came forward to testify that the Federal Theatre was doing a superb job, that it was contributing richly to the cultural and intellectual life of the nation, and that it had rescued thousands of workers and artists from poverty and privation. But the campaign to save the project was too little and too late. The Federal Theatre was killed by act of Congress on June 30, 1939. After a unique and spectacular career that included 63,729 performances of twelve hundred productions, featuring everything from classic and religious plays to puppetry and the circus, and after playing to audiences that totaled 30,398,726, the Federal Theatre became a memory. The foundation it had laid for the building of strong regional theatres throughout the nation was dismantled and forgotten. The exciting dream of a nationally supported theatre, like those of the great civil-izations of Europe, dissolved and vanished. All we can say is that the dream and the promise were great while they lasted.

The years between the two World Wars were notable not only for develop-ments like the Federal Theatre but also for the great number and astonishing variety of the plays that were written. It is time to survey the developments in playwriting.

19

Playwriting between Two World Wars

The decade of the 1920s saw a record number of new plays produced on Broadway and then shared with stock companies and road-show companies throughout the nation. What kinds of plays were these? How many of them reflected the superficial activities of the period and how many recognized the underlying malaise and unrest? Unfortunately, the majority of the productions were slick, commercial shows—the same kinds of entertainment that had flourished from 1900 to 1920. There were hundreds of farce-melodramas, farce-comedies, comedies with ideas, detective melodramas, and the like. There were a fair number of romantic costume plays and a few poetic plays with ideas. Luckily for the serious American playgoer, there were in addition the dramas of Eugene O'Neill and of other new playwrights— dramas that portrayed the breakdown of traditional values and the search for meaning in a frightening new world. The average person and the average commercial producer of plays might not be aware of the crises—spiritual, moral, social, and religious—that were facing humanity, but the best dramatists certainly were. They turned their attention to these crises and produced significant plays about the dilemmas of modern life. Their immediate predecessors had liberated playwriting from the artificialities of melodrama and had introduced the realistic play of ideas. The newer playwrights and many of the old wrote penetrating plays of this kind and also began experimenting with new forms and techniques to communicate their interpretations of the crises around them.

ELMER RICE, GEORGE S. KAUFMAN, MARC CONNELLY

Elmer Rice (1892-1967), who had already made his debut as a successful play-wright with his courtroom drama *On Trial* (1914), wrote an effective expressionistic play in 1923 entitled *The Adding Machine,* which was given a forceful production

The Green Pastures, with Richard B. Harrison as "de Lawd"
in his private office with the Angel Gabriel (Wesley Hill).

by the Theatre Guild. Expressionism, as a method of communication, presents the inner life of man through dreams, symbols, and abstractions; thus, it is different from realism, which presents the external details of so-called objective reality. The description of a typical expressionistic play applies exactly to *The Adding Machine.* "The alienated hero is in quest of salvation. Searching for brotherhood and an end to spiritual isolation, he wants a new life. . . . But the mechanized, industrialized society in which he lives reduces men to robots enslaved by machines . . . in the cage of a dehumanized world."[1] Because of its theme and its style, *The Adding Machine* is a significant play in the history of American dramaturgy, probably the most significant of the many plays written by Rice. He tried his hand at many different types and kinds of drama: comedies, mysteries, and realistic tragedies like *The Subway* (1929) and *Street Scene* (1929). In the 1930s Rice turned to the writing of social protest and propaganda plays such as *We the People* and *Judgment Day,* whose reception by the critics stirred more anger in the playwright than they did in the audiences, which the plays were intended to arouse.

---

[1] Bernard F. Dukore and Daniel C. Gerould, "Explosions and Implosions: Avant-Garde Drama Between World Wars," *Educational Theatre Journal,* XXI (March 1969), 7-8.

The expressionist style used by Rice in *The Adding Machine* was also used by George S. Kaufman (1889-1961) and Marc Connelly (1890-   ) in their play of 1924 entitled *Beggar on Horseback*. Unlike *The Adding Machine,* the Kaufman-Connelly play is a comic satire, and the sequence of dreams in which the musician-hero, Neil McRae, foresees his future is full of delightful burlesque of machines, business efficiency, and the other creations that dehumanize contemporary man.

Kaufman, the coauthor of the play, is better known as the writer of the wittiest comedies of his time, and Marc Connelly is best remembered for his appealing fantasy *The Green Pastures,* the retelling of biblical stories within the context of Southern Negro experience. *The Green Pastures* won the Pulitzer Prize for the season of 1929-30.

Kaufman was the great collaborator of his era. Almost every play he wrote was done in association with another dramatist, with Kaufman supplying the zany situations and uproarious lines and his collaborator providing the structure and discipline. During the 1920s Kaufman wrote four comedies with Marc Connelly: *Dulcy* in 1921, *To the Ladies* and *Merton of the Movies* in 1922, and *The Deep Tangled Wildwood* in 1923—all in addition to *The Beggar on Horseback* of 1924. Later in the decade, Kaufman turned to other collaborators. He constructed two plays in association with the novelist Edna Ferber: *Minick* in 1924 and *The Royal Family* in 1928. He also wrote *The Good Fellow* with Herman J. Mankiewicz in 1926; *Animal Crackers,* a musical comedy, with Morrie Ryskind in 1928; *The Channel Road* with Alexander Woolcott in 1929; and *June Moon* with Ring Lardner in 1929. In 1925 he wrote *The Butter and Egg Man* without the help of a collaborator. Certainly the decade was a prolific one for Kaufman whether he worked with associates or without them.

Kaufman's fecundity continued in the following decade. With Morrie Ryskind he produced a memorably funny musical, *Of Thee I Sing,* in 1931, a spoof of politics featuring a vice-presidential candidate named Throttlebottom. It won the Pulitzer Prize as the best American play of 1931-32, the first musical drama to receive this honor. A sequel to it entitled *Let 'Em Eat Cake* appeared in 1933 but was a failure. In addition to these two musicals, Kaufman wrote *Dinner at Eight* with Edna Ferber (1932), *The Dark Tower* with Alexander Woolcott (1933), and *First Lady* with Katharine Dayton (1935). He also collaborated with Moss Hart to create several outstanding comedies, the most successful being *Once in a Lifetime* (1930), *You Can't Take It with You* (1936), and *The Man Who Came to Dinner* (1939). *You Can't Take It with You,* one of the zaniest, wittiest comedies of modern times, won a Pulitzer Prize and was successfully revived on Broadway in 1965.

Kaufman's comedies were written to make people laugh. He made devastating cracks at all kinds of people, situations, and events; his purpose was not to ridicule or to reform but simply to create laughter—and lots of it. For two decades he provided the funniest lines in the funniest plays of the period and counterbalanced the growing seriousness and anxiety of many other playwrights.

MAXWELL ANDERSON

Maxwell Anderson (1888-1959) is one of the serious playwrights who rose to pro-minence in the 1920s. A scholar, poet, and journalist, Anderson was reared in North Dakota and his first play, *The White Desert* (1923), was a somber tragedy set in that region. In 1924 he collaborated with Lawrence Stallings to write the most successful American play based on the First World War: *What Price Glory?* Even more serious and angry than the war play was a drama called *Gods of the Lightning* (1928), which Anderson wrote in collaboration with Harold Hickerson. It was a violent indictment of American justice as illustrated in the notorious Sacco-Vanzetti case. Although not a success in the United States, it provided the genesis of a later and better play by Anderson, the well-known *Winterset.*

Anderson, alone or with collaborators, wrote several other plays during the 1920s, but not until the following decade, when he began to write poetic tragedy, did he hit his stride and produce the serious dramas for which he is best remembered.

Maxwell Anderson, playwright.
Hoblitzelle Theatre Arts Library, Humanities Research Center, University of Texas at Austin.

The first of these was *Elizabeth the Queen* (1930), in which Lynn Fontanne portrayed the greatness and the agonies of the first Elizabeth of England. The second was *Mary of Scotland* (1934), in which Helen Hayes created a memorable portrait of the ill-fated rival of Elizabeth. The success of these romantic historical plays in verse, which links Anderson with the oldest tradition in American playwriting, inspired the playwright to try his hand at a verse tragedy using contemporary material. The result was *Winterset* (1935), which was admired extravagently in its time.

Winterset uses material from the famous Sacco-Vanzetti case, but it is much more adroit than the earlier play, *Gods of the Lightning*. Sacco and Vanzetti were two immigrants who were executed for the murder of a watchman, a crime which thousands of Americans believed they did not commit. They were poor men; they had no influence; they were unpopular because they had participated in political activity that was considered radical and subversive. The defense of such men had great appeal in the mid-1930s when the nation was in the grip of the depression and seething with social protest. In retrospect the play seems seriously flawed. Much of the verse is labored and banal. More important, the basic issues concerning truth and justice which the play raises are never resolved.

The success of *Winterset,* great in its time, marked the pinnacle of Anderson's career. For a time, when Eugene O'Neill's reputation was suffering a temporary eclipse, Anderson was considered America's best dramatist. He continued to write plays for many years. Some of them were historical tragedies, like his play about Joan of Arc entitled *Joan of Lorraine* (1946) and his play about Anne Boleyn called *Anne of the Thousand Days* (1948). Some of them were modern melodramas, like *Truckline Cafe* in 1946. None of Anderson's later plays achieved the success of *Elizabeth the Queen* and *Winterset.* Yet Anderson's long career, covering more than a quarter century, added considerably to both the realistic and poetic traditions of American playwriting.

PAUL GREEN, SIDNEY HOWARD

Another serious dramatist whose voice was first heard in the 1920s is Paul Green (1894-1981), who was inspired to become a playwright by Frederick H. Koch at the University of North Carolina. Green's early dramas are short and draw their inspiration from the folklore of the southern United States. His first long play, *In Abraham's Bosom,* was presented in New York in 1926 and won the Pulitzer Prize for that season. The play is a tragic story of the cruelty of racism. It presents with compassion and understanding the aspirations and struggles of a member of the persecuted black race. As a drama it is a vast improvement in structure, treatment, and characterization over Edward Sheldon's play of 1909, *The Nigger,* which used a similar theme. Green's play, when compared to Sheldon's, illustrates the greatly improved skill and maturity of American dramatists.

The year after *In Abraham's Bosom,* New York saw another long play by Paul Green entitled *The Field God* (1927), which revealed the playwright's sympathy for the poor whites of the South. The play, somber and depressing, was far less popular than *In Abraham's Bosom.* Both dramas presaged Green's primary concern, demonstrated in later years: an abiding interest in drama based on the life of the common man, both black and white. This interest is illustrated in Green's *The House of Connelly* (1931), which portrays the decadence and dissolution of Southern culture, and in his tragicomic *Johnny Johnson* (1936), with music by Kurt Weill, which traces the disillusionment of an American folk hero, his attempt to oppose war, and his end in an insane asylum.

The realistic modern problem drama of the United States was enriched during the 1920s and '30s by the work of California playwright Sidney Howard (1891-1939), who, after graduating from the University of California in 1915, took Professor Baker's playwriting course at Harvard. His first successful play, *They Knew What They Wanted,* won the Pulitzer Prize for 1924-25 and revealed Howard's "immense zest for life and his tolerant philosophy toward human beings seeking happiness within themselves."[2] It was later converted into a successful musical play with the appropriate title of *The Most Happy Fella.* Other successful plays among the twenty-four that Howard wrote, helped to write, or adapted during his short lifetime were *The Late Christopher Bean* (1932), an adaptation from a French play; *Dodsworth* (1934), a dramatization of Sinclair Lewis's novel; and *Yellow Jack* (1934), a drama about the medical conquest of yellow fever written in collaboration with Paul de Kruif. However, Howard's most notable play, which best illustrates his gift as a dramatist is *The Silver Cord,* produced in 1926. It is a gripping drama portraying an overpossessive mother who, like a black widow spider, has gobbled her husband and is now trying to suck the lifeblood of her sons. The playwright depicts every aspect of motherhood—devotion, sacrifice, loyalty, tenderness, affection, and so on and shows how each can be perverted and corrupted into something vicious and unhealthy.

The Silver Cord has great merit as a play. Its construction is compact and tight. The characters are sharply drawn and revealingly contrasted. The dialogue is precise and sure and moves the play along without tedium or fumbling. Throughout the drama the playwright has a sure grasp of his ideas and characters and has the skill to communicate them. If there are weaknesses in *The Silver Cord,* they are an unconvincing quality in the characterizations of the two sons, a transparency in the characterization of the overly possessive mother, and a certain distastefulness in the theme. Yet, overall, *The Silver Cord* is an excellent illustration of the maturity that had been achieved by American playwriting in the first quarter of the twentieth century.

ROBERT EMMETT SHERWOOD, LILLIAN HELLMAN

Two other dramatists whose chief interest became the writing of realistic problem plays enriched the dramatic offerings of the 1920s and '30s. They are Robert Emmett Sherwood (1896-1955) and Lillian Hellman (1905-   ).

[2]Barrett H. Clark, "Sidney Coe Howard," *Oxford Companion to the Theatre,* 3rd ed. (New York: Oxford University Press, Inc., 1967), p. 452.

Sherwood, the older of the two, began his career as a writer of sophisticated comedy. *The Road to Rome* (1927), *The Queen's Husband* (1928), and *Reunion in Vienna* (1931) were satirical, farcical, and witty; they accomplished their primary purpose of creating entertainment and laughter. In 1935 Sherwood enjoyed a great success with a different kind of play. It was *The Petrified Forest,* a serious drama that ends tragically when the young poet Alan Squire, representing the defeatism of the 1930s, confronts the gangster Duke Mantee, who has trapped several people in a roadside restaurant. Squire begs to be killed so that his insurance money can be used by his newfound sweetheart to pursue her art career. The gangster obliges and shoots the poet, who dies quoting lines from Francois Villon. The play is a kind of allegory representing "the failure of nerve in society and the suicidal impulse in civilization, which enable the barbarian to take over the world."[3] It captivated a nationwide audience in the late 1930s.

The seriousness of *The Petrified Forest* was continued and intensified in Sherwood's subsequent plays. In 1936 came *Idiot's Delight,* a Pulitzer Prize play that attacks munitions makers and other sinister figures who help create wars. In 1938 came *Abe Lincoln in Illinois,* a historical play that portrays the rise of the young Abraham Lincoln and ends with his election to the presidency and his departure from Springfield, Illinois, for Washington, D. C. In 1940 appeared another serious play, the last important one by Sherwood, which won another Pulitzer Prize for the playwright. The play, *There Shall Be No Night,* chronicled the Russian attack on Finland during the early years of the Second World War.

Following *There Shall Be No Night,* Sherwood took leave of the theatre to become active in national affairs. As a friend of President Franklin D. Roosevelt, he promoted the cause of American aid to the Allies before Pearl Harbor. After Pearl Harbor he served as a speechwriter for the president and as head of the Office of War Information. Following the war he wrote two more plays, one serious and one comic, but neither was successful.

Lillian Hellman, unlike Sherwood, never tried her hand at comedy. Her plays have been uniformly serious in theme and realistic in treatment. Beginning her career as a dramatist seven years after Sherwood's debut, Miss Hellman's first play, *The Children's Hour* (1934), aroused widespread interest and some shock. It relates the torment and tragedy caused by a vindictive, neurotic schoolgirl who accuses her teachers of being lesbians. Even more gripping and more revealing of the baseness of human nature was *The Little Foxes* (1939), which portrays the activities of a predatory Southern family who, in their greed for wealth, are willing to lie, cheat, steal, and even allow a man to die without handing him the medicine that might save his life. The action of the play illustrates the biblical reference to "the little foxes that spoil the vines." Tallulah Bankhead, in the leading role as Regina Hubbard, gave a cold, cruel, glittering performance which revealed the great talent she possessed but usually parodied.

---

[3] John Gassner, *Treasury of the Theatre, Ibsen to Ionesco,* 3rd ed. (New York: Simon & Schuster, Inc., 1960), p. 1272.

After her auspicious debut in the 1930s, Miss Hellman continued to write plays thoughtfully but sparingly. The later list includes *Watch on the Rhine* (1941), *The Searching Wind* (1944), *Another Part of the Forest* (1946), *The Autumn Garden* (1951), and *Toys in the Attic* (1959)—all of them deeply serious studies of evil and failure in various forms.

RACHEL CROTHERS, PHILIP BARRY, S. N. BEHRMAN, GEORGE KELLY

While serious dramatists were exploring serious themes in a variety of styles, many writers of comedy were discussing serious topics in a light and witty manner. Two of the best of these were Rachel Crothers (1878-1958) and Philip Barry (1896-1949). Miss Crothers's playwriting began in 1902; her last big hit, *Susan and God,* appeared in 1937. Philip Barry, the younger of the two dramatists, had a much shorter productive life. His first real success, *Paris Bound,* was produced in 1927 after several previous plays had failed to attract much notice; his last outstanding success, *The Philadelphia Story,* appeared in 1939 and was followed by three additional plays that were only moderately successful.

During Miss Crothers's long career as an active playwright, she treated a great variety of themes and topics. For example, her first long play, *The Three of Us* (1906), was set in a Nevada mining camp. More typical are her drawing-room comedies, which discuss contemporary problems—often marital problems—in a deft and thoroughly entertaining manner. Her talent for writing this kind of play was revealed early in her career. The comedy *He and She* (1912) is a good example. Its theme is perennially important: can a woman successfully combine her homemaking with a career? The discussion of the problem is pleasant but not profound. The play generates no violent emotion or unusual tension. The characters, action, and dialogue combine to produce an urbane, civilized discussion that entertains its audience but does not galvanize or shock it.

Similar comments might be made about Miss Crothers's other social comedies. Such outstanding hits as *Let Us Be Gay* (1929), *As Husbands Go* (1931), *When Ladies Meet* (1932), and *Susan and God* (1937) reveal her expert craftsmanship, her gift for light, amusing dialogue, and her keen grasp of the problems and psychology of the men and women of her time. She will be remembered as a worthy successor to Anna Cora Mowatt. Like Mrs. Mowatt, she wrote social comedy, but without the acid or the melodrama of a play like *Fashion.*

Philip Barry is also best known for his witty, appealing, drawing-room comedies, although he wrote other kinds of plays. *Hotel Universe* (1930), for example, is a philosophical and psychological study of the illusions men live by; *Here Come the Clowns* (1938) is an allegory depicting the conflict of good and evil in the world. In contrast to these, comedies like *Paris Bound* (1927), *Holiday* (1928), *The Animal Kingdom* (1932), and *Philadelphia Story* (1939) offer the best examples of Barry's skills. In them a whole gallery of American types—charming or boring, daring or conventional, intelligent or stupid—illustrate and illuminate many of the worries, frustrations, and problems that bothered the men and women of the 1920s and '30s. All the comic plays are written with wit, charm, and sophistication. *Holiday,* a great hit in 1928, is an example. Like the plays of Rachel Crothers, it is not profound, violent, or disturbing. It has enough charm, wit, and polish to amuse an audience, and it contains enough ideas about freedom versus conformity to give the pleasant illusion of being a thought-provoking play. However, it seems curiously dated in the world of the late twentieth century. Like many of the drawing-room plays of its time, it reflects a simpler world of more stable values, where some of the important problems are whether a prospective son-in-law has the right social credentials and whether an engagement party should be an intimate, informal affair or an elaborate, formal occasion. Many theatregoers remember comedies of this type with genuine nostalgia and mourn their passing and their replacement by the dark, tormented, or absurd comedies of a new, more complex era.

Several other adroit writers of social comedy enlivened the 1920s and '30s. One of them, S. N. Behrman (1893-1973), contributed several delightful plays written with a sparkle and sophistication closely related to Philip Barry's style. One of the first of these was *The Second Man,* produced by the Theatre Guild in 1927. Others were *Serena Blandish* (1929), *Biography* (1932), *End of Summer* (1936), and *No Time for Comedy* (1939).

The plays of George Kelly (1887-1974) are also social comedies, but not of the sophisticated drawing-room variety. Kelly's first full-length play, *The Torch-bearers* (1922), satirizes the little-theatre movement that was then sweeping the country. Two years later he wrote a hilarious exposé of a common and repellent American type, the phony, pompous braggart. This was *The Show-off.* Kelly followed this play with an exposé of a different type—a study of a scheming, possessive wife entitled *Craig's Wife* (1925), which won a Pulitzer Prize. Subsequent plays like *Behold the Bridegroom* (1927), *Philip Goes Forth* (1931), and *Reflected Glory* (1936) were received with decreasing enthusiasm by the public and by the critics and earned the playwright the reputation of writing "austerely moralistic" plays. Kelly retired from the theatre for a time. His return with two plays in the 1940s was not a great success.

OTHER PLAYWRIGHTS

Some other playwrights of lesser rank deserve mention for their contributions during the interwar period. The first is Susan Glaspell (1882-1948), a novelist remembered for two powerful one-act plays, *Suppressed Desires* and *Trifles,* written early in her career, and for her Pulitzer Prize play of 1930, *Alison's House.* The second is Zona Gale (1874-1938), another novelist who won the Pulitzer Prize in 1921 for dramatizing her novel *Miss Lulu Bett.* The third is Zoë Akins (1886-1958), whose successful plays range from *Déclassé* (1919) to *The Greeks Had a Word for It* (1930) and *The Old Maid* (1935). *The Old Maid,* a dramatization of Edith Wharton's novel, won a Pulitzer Prize for Miss Akins.

Another writer who had already established a reputation as a novelist made a greatly loved contribution to the stage at the very close of the 1930s. This was Thornton Wilder (1897-1975) whose play *Our Town* (1938) has become a kind of American folk classic. The simple, wholesome lives of two families living in the early twentieth century, the Gibbses and the Webbs, achieve universal appeal as representatives of the best qualities in the American character and way of life. Written with deep understanding and sympathy but without offensive sentimentality, and ingeniously staged without scenery and with a stage manager who acts as commentator and master of ceremonies, *Our Town* is loved and played by amateurs and professionals alike and has maintained its appeal for more than forty years as a "hauntingly beautiful play," as Brooks Atkinson called it. Wilder's subsequent plays, which also demonstrate his skill and originality as a creative artist, belong in the decades that followed the 1930s.

EUGENE O'NEILL

The decades from 1920 to 1940 produced many new and talented dramatists whose work gave variety, depth, and dimension to American playwriting. Overshadowing all of them, however, was one man: Eugene O'Neill. His major contributions to dramatic literature came in the 1920s and the early 1930s. He can truly be said to have dominated the theatre of these years.

In 1920 O'Neill produced his first long play, *Beyond the Horizon,* and later in the same year he brought out *Chris Christopherson, Diff'rent,* and *The Emperor Jones.* During the remainder of the decade, the following new O'Neill plays were produced:

Gold, 1921
Anna Christie, 1921
The First Man, 1922
The Hairy Ape, 1922
Welded, 1924
All God's Chillun Got Wings, 1924
Desire under the Elms, 1924
The Fountain, 1925
The Great God Brown, 1926
Marco Millions, 1928
Strange Interlude, 1928
Lazarus Laughed, 1928
Dynamo, 1929

After such a creative explosion—thirteen major plays in a single decade—it is no wonder that the 1930s brought a tapering off. Or did they? The following new O'Neill plays were produced:

Eugene O'Neill, playwright. Sculpture by Edmond T. Quinn.
Bust: Yale School of Drama Library.

Mourning Becomes Electra, 1931
Ah, Wilderness! 1933
Days Without End, 1934

After this, O'Neill withdrew from active participation in the Broadway theatre to concentrate on the composition of the heroic nine-play cycle that he had begun earlier in the decade. His withdrawal was necessary and prudent. By 1935 he was physically and emotionally exhausted and close to a complete breakdown from overwork. He needed quiet, rest, and recuperation.

In all the plays from 1921 to 1935, O'Neill continued searching and probing for answers to fundamental questions. What is humanity's place in the scheme of things? What is the meaning of death? Is there a power, idea, or place to which a human being really belongs? Do we shape our destinies or are we the puppets of inscrutable forces either external or internal? How can we create significant relationships with our fellow men? Is passion valid? Is faith attainable? Is suffering meaningful? Is fulfillment possible?

The plays which pose such questions cover an astonishing range of subject matter, structure, and style. *Anna Christie,* a rewriting of *Chris Christopherson,* is an earthy, realistic drama about a prostitute who returns to her father and his ship and finds the means of redemption in the love of Mat Burke, a stoker on the ship. *The Hairy Ape* is a combination of realism, symbolism, and expressionism in which Yank, a powerful, muscular stoker on a luxury liner, glories in his physical strength and his contribution to the power that propels the ship. But his world is shattered when an effete daughter of the rich, visiting the stoke hole, recoils in horror at Yank and calls him a "filthy beast." Yank begins a pathetic journey to find his place in a hostile, inhuman world; failing, he dies in the embrace of an ape whom he believes to be his friend.

Desire under the Elms has overtones of mysticism and symbolism, but it abandons the expressionism of *The Hairy Ape* and presents the realistic world of an isolated New England farm. The action of the play involves a moral struggle between three people: a patriarchal old father, Ephraim Cabot, who is as hard and lonesome as the God he worships; his son, Eben, who has both his dead mother's sensitivity and his father's strength; and Abbie, the young wife Ephraim marries in his old age to beget a son and heir who will dispossess Eben. In the tragedy that ensues, the characters reveal a terrible, elemental strength that raises them above their sordid behavior and gives them some of the stature of tragic heroes.

In his next significant play, *The Great God Brown,* the dramatist abandoned the realism of *Desire under the Elms* and experimented with "subjective" drama. Two complementary characters, representing the dual personality and divided soul of a single man, don masks to symbolize their inner and outer struggles. *Marco Millions,* which followed *The Great God Brown,* is a romantic satire on materialism; but in *Strange Interlude,* which came next, O'Neill returned to the challenge of presenting both the external action of his characters and their inner thoughts and torments. To do this, he invented the "interior monologue." Each character speaks both his public and private thoughts, a device that allows the play to develop on two levels. During nine acts lasting several hours, the leading character, Nina Leeds, and the people surrounding her reveal themselves and analyze each other. The play recounts Nina's life and her desperate search to find fulfillment and meaning after the death of the one man she truly loved. The length of the play, its epic intentions, and its experimental technique made it the most memorable production of its time.

The fame of *Strange Interlude* was soon to be exceeded by another epic drama of O'Neill, the trilogy in thirteen acts called *Mourning Becomes Electra.* Before the production was staged in New York, however, the Pasadena Community Theatre in California attracted national attention by producing one of O'Neill's heavily symbolical, philosophical plays, *Lazarus Laughed.* Laid in ancient Rome, the play uses masks, choruses, and spectacle to tell the story of the resurrection of Lazarus and his ultimate triumph over death.

While the world of the theatre was still talking about the Pasadena production of *Lazarus Laughed,* O'Neill presented his monumental *Mourning Becomes Electra.* It is based on the Oresteian trilogy of Aeschylus, three classic tragedies that recount the legendary story of the return of Agamemnon from the war with Troy; his murder by his wife, Clytemnestra; and the revenge that Orestes and Electra, the son and daughter, eventually take on their mother and her lover, Aegisthus. In O'Neill's trilogy the scene is not ancient Greece but New England at the close of the Civil War. Agamemnon becomes General Mannon; Clytemnestra is Christine; the children are Orin and Lavinia; and Aegisthus is Adam Brant. O'Neill's play follows the ancient story, with some alterations. Christine, in love with Brant, contrives her husband's death when he returns from the Civil War. Lavinia, fiercely loyal to her father, is convinced of her mother's guilt and aids her brother in murdering Brant. Then, implacably, she drives her mother and brother to suicide and shuts herself within the decaying family home to suffer the hell of living the remainder of her life with ghosts and her own guilt.

The alterations in plot that O'Neill adopts are not significant, but his altered concept of fate is of great importance. Instead of the Aeschylean concept of a god-given curse inherited by innocent members of a once-guilty family, O'Neill presents a Freudian explanation of the events in the Mannon family. He reveals the tangled complexes and psychoses of the characters and attributes their fate to these sources.

Mourning Becomes Electra was hailed as O'Neill's masterpiece when it was first presented in the 1930s—and O'Neill agreed with the judgment. In a letter to A. H. Quinn, February 10, 1932, he wrote,

> I am very satisfied with it—(taken all around it *is* my best, I think)—but at the same time, deeply dissatisfied. It needed great language to lift it beyond itself. I haven't got that. And, by way of self-consolation, I don't think, from the evidence of all that is being written today, that great language is possible for anyone living in the discordant, broken, faithless rhythm of our time. The best one can do is to be pathetically eloquent by one's moving, dramatic inarticulations.[4]

O'Neill was apparently conscious of one of his major limitations as a dramatist. That is, he was not a poet; he always struggled for language that would do justice to the greatness of his concepts. He struggled—and he often failed. However, the delivery of good actors can give O'Neill's lines a force and color that are not apparent upon reading the plays. However, after a lapse of fifty years, *Mourning Becomes Electra* reveals more serious deficiencies than the language alone. The drama seems overly long; much of it is sententious and repetitious; the Freudian psychology is overly simplified and obvious. Some modern critics now consider the play a hulking bore; others still judge it a great drama.

Following the epic achievement of *Mourning Becomes Electra,* O'Neill wrote the happiest and least characteristic play of his career, *Ah, Wilderness!* It is a nostalgic representation of the good life in a small town at the start of the twentieth

---

[4] Ibid., p. 258.

century. When the play was presented in 1933, it was assumed to be a record of O'Neill's own boyhood—the dramatist referred to it as a "comedy of recollection"— and the appealing teenage hero, Richard Miller, was believed to be O'Neill himself. We now know that the true record of O'Neill's early life is contained in the nightmare world of *Long Day's Journey into Night* and that *Ah, Wilderness!* portrays the kind of boyhood O'Neill would have *liked* to have had—but never did.

In 1936, after O'Neill's withdrawal from the Broadway scene, he was awarded the Nobel Prize in literature—the second American to win the literary prize and the

Alice Brady as Lavinia Mannon in Eugene O'Neill's
Mourning Becomes Electra, produced by the Theatre Guild.

Billy Rose Theatre Collection, The New York Public Library at Lincoln Center, Astor, Lenox and Tilden Foundations.

first American dramatist to do so. O'Neill was not heard from again until 1946, when *The Iceman Cometh* was presented. The major portion of his productive life was over.

DRAMA OF SOCIAL PROTEST

A summary of American playwriting from 1920 to 1940 cannot end with the works of Eugene O'Neill. It must include a special type of drama that gained general attention in the mid-1930s, the drama of social protest. Born of the Great Depression and nurtured by the miseries of the time, these angry plays are a unique addition to the literature of the period.

During the 1930s, with new productions on Broadway steadily decreasing and with the hardships of the depression steadily growing, it is no wonder that there was a sharp increase in the number of plays that denounced the social evils of the time and demanded change and reform. Much of the attack was against the capitalistic system, which was blamed for the breakdown of the economy, for war, and for social injustice—especially racial injustice—of all kinds. Many of the playwrights were leftists, some of them avowed communists. Often in their rage and bitterness they sacrificed dramatic values to propaganda values. This was the case with John Wexley's plays, which are considered superior representatives of the genre. In *The Last Mile* (1930), for example, the indictment against capital punishment rests on the appeal of a killer-hero who is so sentimentalized as to be incredible. In *They Shall Not Die* (1934), a play dramatizing the Scottsboro murder trial, the Negro victims of injustice lack appeal and conviction because they are not developed or individualized as people.

More successful both as drama and as propaganda is the play *Stevedore* by Paul Peters and George Sklar, presented by the Theatre Union in 1934. The subject is a race riot in Louisiana, and although all the sympathy is directed to the blacks and all the onus heaped on the whites, the play is skillfully constructed and succeeds as an exciting melodrama.

In 1935 two other propaganda plays gained a measure of success. One was *Black Pit,* the story of a miners' strike, by Albert Maltz; the other was *Let Freedom Ring,* by Albert Bein, which also presented the story of a strike but centered the interest in a worker-turned-boss who must decide whether to side with the mill owners or with the strikers.

Joining the angry dramatists of social protest were established writers like Elmer Rice and John Howard Lawson. Their plays, it turned out, were so angry that they failed as drama and, having done so, greatly increased the rage of the playwrights.

CLIFFORD ODETS, IRWIN SHAW

Two young dramatists who began as writers of propaganda plays and developed considerable skill as thoughtful advocates of social reform were Clifford Odets (1906-1963) and Irwin Shaw (1913-   ). Odets, who was born in Philadelphia but grew up in New York City, decided to become an actor after he graduated from high school. In this capacity he joined the Group Theatre in 1931 and remained an actor for several years. At the same time, he tried his hand at playwriting. In 1935 he attracted national attention with a long one-act play entitled *Waiting for Lefty,* which effectively dramatized the New York taxicab strike of 1934. The drama, set in a meeting room of the taxicab union, allows workers and their associates to argue their cases, to reveal their hardships, and finally to inflame their listeners into a thunderous vote to strike.

Odets's career, following this success, was meteoric. He blazed brightly in the dramatic sky for a while, then faded quickly. Three plays followed *Waiting for Lefty* in the same year, 1935. They were an anti-Nazi play in one long act called *Till the Day I Die,* a full-length drama dealing with the problems and passions of a Jewish family entitled *Awake and Sing,* which was highly successful, and a less successful play dealing with middle-class morality called *Paradise Lost.*

In 1937 Odets again impressed audiences and critics with *Golden Boy,* a success both on the stage and on film. Odets's subsequent plays had varying degrees of success or failure, but the tendency was toward failure. They included *Rocket to the Moon* (1938), *Night Music* (1940), *Clash by Night* (1941), *The Big Knife* (1949), an indictment of Hollywood following Odets's stint as a screen writer, *The Country Girl* (1950), and finally *The Flowering Peach* (1954). The latter plays confirm the suspicion held by several early critics that Odets never really became the major playwright he was first considered to be.

Irwin Shaw's plays have not stood the test of time any better than those of Odets. He first attracted attention in 1936 with a long one-act play entitled *Bury the Dead.* It was a stunning indictment of war based on the bizarre situation of six soldiers, dead on the battlefield, who refuse to lie down and be buried. Instead, they insist on telling their story of suffering and damnation to all who will listen. Shaw's second play, *Seige* (1937), was a failure; but when his third, *The Gentle People,* was produced by the Group Theatre in 1939 it achieved a long run and considerable critical acclaim. Through the story of two gentle people who are preyed upon by a racketeer, the play suggests that there are times when the meek of the earth must defend their rights. The play remains superior to Shaw's subsequent dramas such as *Quiet City* (1939) and *Retreat to Pleasure* (1940).

As the years of depression and social protest neared their close, Europe was overrun by Adolph Hitler's Nazi hordes and the Second World War began. The United States reorganized its industrial power and became the arsenal of the free world. The Great Depression was over, and America was preparing itself for the mighty role it was to play on the world stage during the new decade of the 1940s. The theatre also prepared to play a new role in the life of the nation.

20

Bright Lights, Then Curtain

Developments, 1940-1960

The decade of the 1940s was the era of global war. The First World War had been long and terrible; the second exceeded the first in every grim particular. It lasted longer and covered the whole globe; its toll of terror, treasure, and human life exceeded calculation. In this titanic debacle, the United States played a commanding part. Suddenly thrust into the active conflict by the attack on Pearl Harbor, American citizens united to form a fighting force and a production machine unmatched at any other time in history for size, capacity, and achievement. Almost every citizen served in the armed forces or in a job that was essential to the war effort. The conflict finally ended in 1945 after the explosion of two atomic bombs. The war ended—but the atomic age began and brought with it a new era of anxiety and terror.

The immediate postwar years were a time of readjustment and reconstruction. With miraculous smoothness, millions of men were demobilized and reintegrated into civilian life. The mighty American industrial machine was retooled to produce consumer goods and materials needed to rebuild the areas devastated by war. Through the Marshall Plan and other programs of foreign aid, the United States undertook to restore the cities and the economies of both its allies and its foes. Never before has a victor nation contributed so much in money, goods, and services for the benefit of its friends as well as its enemies. While this unprecedented task of rebuilding and restoration was in progress, the United States also was busy forging treaties and alliances for the security of the free world. Communism was still a menace; now it had the atom bomb at its disposal. The noncommunist world had to organize itself for security, with the United States as the leader.

The decade of the 1950s, which followed the era of global war and reconstruction, is remembered as an era of stability and quiet consolidation of previous gains. The father-figure of Dwight D. Eisenhower symbolized the era. As president from 1952 to 1960, he gave the country a sense of security and tranquillity. His administration was not innovative or crusading, but neither was it disruptive or demanding. Despite the cold war with the communists and the ever-present threat of annihilation by atomic bombs, the nation enjoyed remarkable prosperity and a welcome feeling of well-being. College and university students of the 1950s were representative of the general attitude: they earned the label of the "silent genera- tion" because they were content to study hard, to play vigorously, and to enjoy— for the first time in their short lives—a world without economic depression or general war.

WARTIME DEVELOPMENTS IN THE THEATRE

As always, the American theatre reacted to its social setting and made its charac- teristic contributions. One contribution during the 1940s was to supply entertain- ment and relaxation for soldiers and hard-working civilians. The motion-picture studios rose to the challenge and turned out more films than ever before. The commercial theatre of Broadway also increased its output. The number of new plays produced annually rose from seventy-two in 1940-41 to eighty-three in 1944-45. More of these plays were successful than in the prewar years. The number of musicals also multiplied. In periods of tension, it seems, the relaxation offered by a musical production has tremendous appeal to theatregoers. And a newer, better type of musical appeared during the war years and inspired the production of many similar superior products. The pacesetter, of course, was *Oklahoma!*, a musical adaptation of Lynn Riggs' play *Green Grow the Lilacs. Oklahoma!* opened in March 1943 and ran for 2,248 performances. It was superior and popular because it was based on a well-written play and adapted by the gifted team of Richard Rodgers and Oscar Hammerstein II. Its plot was reasonable, its characters convinc- ing, and its music and dancing—excellent in themselves—were fully integrated with the action, mood, and personalities of the play. The choreography received particu- lar praise. Devised by Agnes de Mille, daughter of the playwright and film director William C. de Mille, it included not only incidental dances that fit the music and the story but also a modern ballet that enhanced and vivified the whole production.

The combination of elements which made *Oklahoma!* so successful set a new standard for American musical shows. Productions that adopted these standards were notable for combining intelligent plots and characters with music and dancing that were an integral part of the development and mood of the production. Ever since *Oklahoma!* the Broadway theatre has loved the big musical show. Among the most memorable of these in the years from 1940 to 1960 were *Carousel* (1945), *South Pacific* (1949), *The King and I* (1951), *My Fair Lady* (1956), *West Side Story* (1957), and *The Sound of Music* (1959). The big musical continued to flourish in the 1960s. In the 1970s, the originality and novelty of *Chorus Line* made it the hit of the decade.

During the 1940s the American theatre supplied musical and dramatic enter- tainment not only to those on the home front but also to numberless troops garrisoned all over the world. This tradition, established during the Civil War and continued in the First World War, developed to a remarkable degree in the Second World War. During the years of the conflict, hundreds of motion pictures were supplied to servicemen everywhere, and more theatrical troupes traveled to more battle areas than ever before. Most of the live entertainment supplied to soldier audiences was vaudeville featuring singing, dancing, pretty girls, and comedy routines; a good example is the Bob Hope shows which, starting in World War II, continued for many years after the war was over.

Although vaudeville-type entertainment predominated during the Second World War, it was by no means the only kind. Eminent musicians like Jascha Heifetz toured the battlefronts to play for soldiers, and one of the First Ladies of the American theatre, Katharine Cornell, headed a superb company that performed *The Barretts of Wimpole Street* for soldiers all over Europe. Miss Cornell had been warned that soldier audiences would not enjoy or appreciate her production. She stubbornly maintained that they would enjoy it and declared that if she were going to tour the European battle areas she would appear in a good play or not at all. Her tour turned out as well as she had predicted. She presented *The Barretts of Wimpole Street* 140 times in Europe, and it was a remarkable success. One of the vivid memories of the author of this book is of the bitterly cold night in December 1944, when he rode with a truckload of GIs to an unheated playhouse in Dijon, France, to watch the Cornell company perform their play. The circumstances could hardly have been worse. The leading man, Brian Aherne, was so hoarse he could scarcely speak. The theatre was so cold that the breath of the actors froze. The crowded audience of soldiers was bundled to the eyebrows, like the actors, with scarves, overcoats, earmuffs, and woolen caps. Yet the men of that audience, most of whom had never seen a live stage play before, sat utterly entranced and spellbound. They reacted to the play with complete naturalness and lack of restraint—encouraging the heroine, Elizabeth Barrett, growling and hissing at her tyrannical father, and cheering her final decision to break away and elope with Robert Browning. The evening was a revealing illustration of the magic that good theatre can exert, contrary to the skepticism of those who habitually underrate both living drama and American audiences.

Theatrical activity of all kinds flourished during the war—except for the writing of significant war plays. To be sure, topical patriotic material is always included in wartime entertainment; but good drama, it seems, comes later, after an opportunity for reflection and introspection—or not at all. Before the Second World War was over, two moderately successful plays appeared: *A Bell for Adano* (1944), by Paul Osborn, based on the novel by John Hersey, and *Home of the Brave* (1945), by Arthur Laurents. Far more successful and popular were later plays such as Thomas Heggen and Joshua Logan's *Mister Roberts* (1947); *Stalag 17* (1951), by Donald Bevan and Edmund Trzcinski; John Patrick's play, adapted from a novel by Vern Sneider, *Teahouse of the August Moon* (1953); and Herman Wouk's *The Caine Mutiny Court Martial* (1954).

None of these plays is doctrinaire or propagandistic; neither do they have great scope or dimension. They dramatize incidents and events that were small parts of the great conflict. But they do not examine directly (with the possible exceptions of *Home of the Brave* and *Command Decision*) any of the major problems such as the causes and effects or the futility and horror of war itself. Of course, effective plays of such scope are rare and may never grow out of any particular war, however vast and terrible.

THE END OF WARTIME PROSPERITY

When the Second World War ended, an era of prosperity ended also, for both the commercial theatre and the motion picture. Commercial producers found themselves in worse shape than before the war. New York audiences dwindled, and road-show business disappeared except in a few cities like Chicago, San Francisco, and Los Angeles. The disappearance of audiences is painfully recorded in the diminished number of playhouses. In 1949 there were only 150 legitimate professional theatres serving the entire nation, or approximately one playhouse for every million inhabitants—a far cry from the palmy days of the 1870s when, for example, five legitimate playhouses and six vaudeville houses were needed to serve the thirty thousand inhabitants of Virginia City, Nevada—an exceptional case, to bc sure, but one worth noting.

Playhouses disappeared and audiences dwindled, but the price of tickets to Broadway shows climbed to new heights. So did unemployment among actors. Even during the war years only 10 percent of the performers registered with Equity were employed at any time. At the end of the war, even this meager figure decreased.

THE RISE OF TELEVISION

The golden age of the motion picture ended, too, for a very specific reason: television made its debut. Immediately motion pictures began to suffer the same fate they had dealt the living theatre earlier in the century. Experimentation with television, begun before the Second World War, was suspended during the conflict; but as early as 1945—with the war barely ended—television sets began to appear in the United States. By 1948 there were forty-eight TV stations in twenty-five cities sending programs to more than seven hundred thousand receiving sets. A year later there were seventy stations and two million sets in operation—and the numbers continued to increase by leaps. By 1958 the sending stations totaled five hundred twelve and the receiving sets fifty million. A year later the television industry claimed that 85 percent of the people of the United States were watching television.

The impact of this tremendous growth on the movies was cataclysmic. Spectators by the millions deserted the cinema and stayed home to watch "the big eye." Customers who for years had regularly attended the movies once or twice a week stopped abruptly. From an estimated weekly attendance of ninety million in 1947, the figure had dropped to twenty-eight million by 1957. In 1947 gross receipts had been $1,565,000,000; by 1956 they had shrunk to $1,185,100,000. In 1945 there had been 20,355 movie theatres in the United States. Ten years later 6,000 of them had closed. In panic, film producers tried to stem the tide. When radio had threatened them with a similar disaster, they had recaptured their audience by introducing talking pictures. Now they tried wide screens, three-dimensional effects, stereophonic sound systems, and epic spectacles. But the enticement of free motion pictures, however old or distorted on a TV screen, and the lure of occasional "live" programs, however cheap or heavily burdened with commercials, were far too great to be resisted. The shrinkage of movie audiences went on. As patronage decreased year by year, so did the number of films produced in Hollywood. In 1941 the number had reached an all-time high of 497, but in 1959 only 224 films were made.

Television had a different effect on radio. It altered the kind of programs produced and virtually destroyed the national networks and the presentation of radio drama. However, it did not eliminate the medium. Instead, the coming of national television gave a tremendous boost to local radio stations specializing in recorded music, local news and sports, and particularly local advertising. In 1962 home viewers were likely to watch the national network television program, but they listened to the local independent radio station. Since 1948, the first big year for television, the number of AM and FM radio stations has more than doubled. Now over three thousand of them broadcast programs to more than ninety million home receiving sets and forty million car sets.

Television Acting

With the demise of the national radio networks, radio acting died, too. Soap operas, comic serials, and adaptations of standard plays were transferred to television, and the hundreds of performers who had learned to act with voice alone while remaining stationary before a microphone had to adjust to the techniques of television—that is, to the techniques of the talking picture. The radio performers who remain today, employed by the hundreds of local radio stations, can hardly be called actors. They are disc jockeys, sportscasters, newscasters, and hucksters, and their style of performing is that of the public speaker or the circus barker.

Television itself had no significant effect on style or technique in acting because TV acting quickly became the same as motion-picture acting. In television's early period, many TV dramas were presented live. Soon, however, it became apparent that there were great advantages to filming a play in a studio and then presenting the perfected film to the public. Today, almost all the dramatic programs on television are filmed in a studio under exactly the same conditions as any other movie.

HOPEFUL DEVELOPMENTS

The years following the Second World War were not entirely disastrous for the living stage or for the cinema either. Although attendance at motion pictures dropped ruinously and although many cinema palaces were forced to close, there were a few compensatory developments. To replace some of the bankrupt indoor movies, outdoor drive-in movies appeared and drew a sizable audience among young people and among parents with small children, who could take their children along and save the price of a babysitter. To replace some of the grand movie palaces that had shut their doors, numerous art theatres appeared, specializing in foreign, experimental, and classic films of earlier days, and many of the large movie houses divided their auditoriums into two, three, or four smaller theatres showing different films but serviced economically by a single lobby and staff.

In the living theatre too there were a few happy developments in the post-World War II period. Although Broadway and the road suffered a serious decline, many kinds of noncommercial drama prospered. Children's theatres, for example, continued to grow slowly but steadily. Such theatres, specializing in plays written or adapted for youngsters and often using youngsters in the casts, have been an important part of the American theatrical scene since the 1920s. Two pioneer programs, both initiated in 1925, were the Children's Theatre of Evanston, Illinois, and the Children's Theatre program of the Goodman School of the Theatre in Chicago. The latter was directed for twenty-one years by one of the American leaders in the field, Charlotte Chorpenning. Theatres like these, unsubsidized and dependent on sponsoring organizations such as Junior Leagues, civic clubs, community theatres, and university departments of drama, have nevertheless managed to survive and grow—although not as vigorously as they would in a more ideal situation.

Far more prosperous and showing unusual capacity for growth have been the college and university theatres of the nation. George Pierce Baker began his 47 Workshop in 1913, and one year later the nation's first department of dramatic arts was established at the Carnegie Institute of Technology. Following these fairly recent beginnings, organized curricula in theatre arts have been established in hundreds of colleges and universities throughout the nation. The movement accelerated in the years following World War II; by 1960, 308 colleges and universities were offering a major in theatre arts, and an additional 293 institutions were offering a minor in the field. The importance of these developments is further emphasized by the building program that has accompanied them. Not a single major commercial playhouse has been built on Broadway since 1932, but in the 1950s alone dozens of opulent new playhouses were constructed by colleges and universities everywhere in the nation.

Paralleling the growth of college and university theatres is the development of community theatres. No longer called "little" or "tributary," these theatres, often housed in elaborate buildings, are a major contributor to the dramatic life of the nation. Their growth has been astonishing. A report in the third edition of the *Oxford Companion to the Theatre* gives the following figures for the early years of the 1960s:

> There were, at that time, 20,000 to 65,000 community theatres of all kinds in the United States.
>
> Three to six thousand of these theatres performed three or more plays a year in permanent buildings.
>
> Play agencies mailed their advertising to five, six, and seven thousand producing groups.
>
> There were 4,000 members of the American Educational Theatre to operate, support, and encourage the community theatres as well as the college and university theatres of the nation.[1]

The summer theatres, which grew so rapidly in number and variety during the depression of the 1930s, continued to increase during the following two decades. By 1950 there were at least two hundred of these groups operating in the vacation areas of the nation, chiefly on the East and West Coasts.

Besides the growth of several varieties of noncommercial theatre, the 1940s and '50s witnessed other developments which indicate that the living stage still has vitality and promise. Notable among these was the rejuvenation of the American National Theatre and Academy, better known as ANTA. This organization dates back to the era of the Federal Theatre. At that time, in 1935, Congress after considerable prodding enacted a bill to charter "the American National Theatre and Academy, a nonprofit corporation, without capital stock, to present theatrical productions of the highest type, advance public interest in the drama as an art belonging both to the theatre and to literature and thereby to be enjoyed both on the stage and in the study." Unfortunately for the goals described in the charter, no money was allocated to the project and nothing was done for eleven years. Then in 1946, after a new set of officers was installed and considerable enthusiasm had been regenerated, ANTA came to life. With money from a nationwide membership drive and from various benefit performances, an ambitious program was launched. The general aim of the program was no less than the betterment of all living theatre in the United States, both commercial and noncommercial. ANTA may not have realized this lofty aim, but it has made useful contributions to the well-being of the theatre, chiefly as a clearinghouse for ideas and information.

Another hopeful development of the 1940s and '50s was the growth of the off-Broadway theatre. Because the cost of presenting a play in a regular Broadway theatre was (and is) so extortionate, producers who wished to try out experimental or unorthodox plays or who had meager budgets started presenting their plays off Broadway in little theatres or makeshift theatres of various kinds where rents and production costs were relatively low. Some of them had remarkable success. For example, in 1952 the Circle in the Square Theatre, performing in a former night-

---

[1] *Oxford Companion to the Theatre,* 3rd ed. (New York: Oxford University Press, Inc., 1967).

club, made a resounding success of Tennessee Williams's *Summer and Smoke,* which had met with meager success on Broadway in 1948. The director, José Quintero, was both new and talented. He was to prove his ability in other off-Broadway productions like that of *The Iceman Cometh* in 1956; he was also to become a leading Broadway director through his successful staging of O'Neill's *Long Day's Journey into Night,* also in 1956. Of course, not all the Off-Broadway groups were as successful as this, but as a whole the Off-Broadway theatre was prosperous enough to encourage growth and expansion. In the season of 1956-57, for example, seventy-five Off-Broadway shows were produced, thus establishing the Off-Broadway activity as a worthy competitor and addition to the traditional Broadway activity.

During wartime prosperity and the postwar depression, the Broadway theatre as well as the theatres of other American cities continued to be enriched by companies, performers, and plays from abroad. From 1940 to 1960, for example, the Old Vic Company of London made four separate visits; and the D'Oyly Carte troupe, performing Gilbert and Sullivan operas, made three. In the 1950s the French theatre sent four companies, including one visit by the Comédie Francaise and two by the troupe headed by Jean-Louis Barrault. Marcel Marceau, pantomimist extraordinary, also paid three visits; and to further enrich the international flavor, there were appearances by troupes from Ireland, Spain, Italy, and Canada.

The 1940s and '50s also saw a few stirring productions of Shakespearean drama. Some of them were acted by the English companies that visited the United States, others by American performers. In the 1940s Judith Anderson and Maurice Evans produced a memorable *Macbeth,* while José Ferrer, Uta Hagen, and Paul Robeson produced an even more successful *Othello.* In the 1950s, in addition to the Shakespearean productions of the Old Vic Company, Louis Calhern performed *King Lear,* to the surprise of his movie fans, while Vivien Leigh and Laurence Olivier acted *Antony and Cleopatra,* to the delight of their American admirers. At the very end of the decade, John Gielgud headed a company that presented a colorful production of *Much Ado About Nothing.*

A final promising development in the postwar era was an increase in the use of theatre as an instrument to promote international understanding. Following the war, many agencies and individuals throughout the world voiced the belief that drama is truly international and can speak eloquently to people of every race and belief. To exploit its potential for peace and harmony, a variety of plans and projects were suggested. The most fruitful turned out to be the International Theatre Institute, sponsored by UNESCO, the educational, scientific, and cultural organization of the United Nations. After two years of collaborative work with theatrical leaders of many nations, UNESCO staged an international theatre conference in Prague in the summer of 1948. Here was born the International Theatre Institute, a world association of artists and craftsmen whose aim is "to promote international exchange of knowledge and practice of theatre arts." Almost at once, national centers were set up in fourteen countries including the United States and more were added later. Also, immediately following the conference, a bulletin entitled

World Premiers was established with the purpose of publishing essential information about each new play, opera, and ballet produced anywhere in the world.

Additional help in making the theatre an instrument for international understanding came from the governments of many nations. They set up cultural and educational exchange programs that have included the exchange of theatrical productions of all kinds. In the United States almost two dozen federal agencies, under the aegis of the State Department, contribute to educational and cultural exchange, with the result that many American theatrical companies, both professional and nonprofessional, have performed before foreign audiences.

PLAYWRITING

The decade of the 1940s witnessed the debuts of two new major American playwrights, Arthur Miller and Tennessee Williams. Miller's first play, *The Man Who Had All the Luck,* was produced in 1944. It was followed by *All My Sons* in 1947 and *Death of a Salesman* in 1949. Tennessee Williams's first Broadway play, *The Glass Menagerie* (1945), was followed by *You Touched Me* in 1946, *A Streetcar Named*

Arthur Miller, playwright.

Hoblitzelle Theatre Arts Library, Humanities Research Center, University of Texas at Austin.

Desire in 1947, and *Summer and Smoke* in 1948. The following decade brought further evidence of the talent of these two dramatists. Miller presented *The Crucible* in 1953, *A View from the Bridge* in 1955, *A Memory of Two Mondays* in 1955, and an adaptation of Ibsen's *An Enemy of the People* in 1958. Tennessee Williams was more prolific. During the 1950s he produced seven plays: *The Rose Tattoo,* 1950; *Camino Real,* 1955; *Cat on a Hot Tin Roof,* 1955; *Orpheus Descending,* 1957; *Garden District* (two short plays), 1958; and *Sweet Bird of Youth* and *Period of Adjustment,* 1959.

Arthur Miller, born in 1915, was educated at the University of Michigan, where he was active in journalism and playwriting and where his talent won him several prizes. Joining the Federal Theatre in 1938, he continued to write, and in 1944 Broadway produced his play *The Man Who Had All the Luck.* It ran only four performances. Miller's next play, *All My Sons,* was far more successful. It was a realistic thesis play illustrating the theme that a man must recognize "his ethical responsibility to the world outside his home as well as in his own home." Although the play received the Drama Critics Circle Award as the best American play of the season, it is below the standard of Miller's best writing. That was demonstrated in 1949 with the production of *Death of a Salesman.* Now widely known and admired, this play is perhaps the best example in modern literature of the tragedy of the little man betrayed by the false values of contemporary society. Willie Loman is the little man, the traveling salesman who dreams of material success through being well-liked and who corrupts everything he touches and fails in everything he attempts. In the end he commits suicide so that his life insurance money will go to the son who still loves him. People all over the world have identified themselves with the intensely human Willie Loman. Yet the play, compassionate and insightful as it is, does little to exalt the human spirit; rather, it leaves one feeling depressed.

The Crucible, Miller's next play, creates anger rather than pity or melancholy. A record of the Salem witch trials, it reveals the horror and tragedy that result from mass hysteria and injustice. *A View from the Bridge,* which followed *The Crucible,* again demonstrates Miller's intimate, compassionate knowledge of the common man. But Miller again presents a tragic hero who is self-deceived to the end. Thus, despite the play's merits, its hero cannot command the kind of admiration evoked by the heroes of great tragedy.

Tennessee Williams, the other major playwright to emerge in the 1940s, contrasts sharply with Miller in vision and style of writing. Born of pioneer Tennessee stock in Columbus, Mississippi, and christened Thomas Lanier Williams, he was reared in the household of his grandfather, an Episcopalian minister. The atmosphere was one of "Southern Puritanism," Williams says, but it was also genteel and gracious in the best tradition of the Old South. It gave Williams an affection for that tradition that he has never lost.

When Williams was thirteen years old, the family moved to St. Louis, Missouri, where Tennessee's father found a job in a shoe factory. The family found living quarters in a crowded little apartment where, to make his sister's closetlike room livable, Williams helped her paint the walls and the furniture white and also helped her install her collection of glass animals. He attended high school in St. Louis, then entered the University of Missouri. After two years he left college for work in the shoe factory where, he says, he was "a miracle of incompetence." He returned to college in 1936, first at Washington University in St. Louis and then at the University of Iowa, where he received a degree. During all this time his principal activity —and his passion—was writing. He continued to write, mostly plays, after he left college and during the subsequent years of vagabondage around the United States. His work gradually became known in theatrical circles. In 1939 the Group Theatre paid him one hundred dollars for a group of four one-act plays entitled *American Blues,* which depicted some of the miseries of the depression years. In 1940 the Theatre Guild bought his long play, *Battle of Angels,* and opened it in Boston, where it caused such a scandal that it was quickly withdrawn. Williams says that the experience showed him "you can't mix up sex and religion" as he did in *Battle of Angels.*

During the next three years, Williams won several grants and fellowships which enabled him to continue his writing. Then he tried his hand at producing movie scripts for Metro-Goldwyn-Mayer, but he so enraged his superiors that they allowed him to draw his salary so long as he stayed away from the studio. He spent his time profitably, writing *The Glass Menagerie,* his first great success.

The Glass Menagerie, a "memory play," is Williams's poetic, nostalgic tribute to his last years in St. Louis with his mother and sister. The plot is fragile: the mother's attempt to find a husband for her shy, slightly crippled daughter; the mood is fragile too, harmonizing the realm of dreams and recollection with a world of reality. The writing is rightly called "exquisite," and the appeal of the play is haunting. As performed by Laurette Taylor and Julie Haydon, who portrayed the mother and daughter in the original production, the play was an outstanding success.

Williams's next play, *You Touched Me* (1946), written in collaboration with Donald Windham, was disliked by both the critics and the public. His eleven one-act plays published in the same year under the title *Twenty-seven Wagons Full of Cotton* were harsh and sordid. Then in 1947 came one of Williams's best and most powerful dramas, *A Streetcar Named Desire.* Often described as "an unsavory tragedy of a woman's frustrations" dealing with "sordid matter of sexual depravity and madness in the New Orleans Latin Quarter," the play nevertheless has a compelling truth and a compassionate understanding that make it worthy of the acclaim it has received.

Williams's next play after *Streetcar,* entitled *Summer and Smoke,* ran only one hundred performances on Broadway. Its great success came in 1952 when the Circle in the Square Theatre produced it off Broadway. Like *A Streetcar Named Desire, Summer and Smoke* records the conflict between a man and a woman, only this time the woman is unsophisticated and sexually repressed. She rejects the advances of the virile young physician living next door and only when it is too late realizes her desperate need for physical love.

In the decade of the 1950s, Williams poured out a series of plays that varied greatly in quality and success. The one that achieved the greatest popularity and

Laurette Taylor and Eddie Dowling in a scene from Tennessee Williams's *The Glass Menagerie.*
Hoblitzelle Theatre Arts Library, Humanities Research Center, University of Texas at Austin.

acclaim bore the unpoetic title of *Cat on a Hot Tin Roof.* Produced in 1954, it won both the Pulitzer Prize and the Drama Critics Circle Award for that year. Yet its power and appeal are far inferior to those of *A Streetcar Named Desire.* Many scenes are theatrically effective, and Williams's characteristic compassion is recognizable in his portrayal of the leading characters, Maggie and Brick; yet the central situation of the play has limited appeal, and the characters exhibit little of the valor and endurance that ennoble the troubled people of Williams's better plays.

Another new voice in the American theatre after World War II was that of

Willian Inge (1913-1973). Born in Independence, Kansas, Inge was reared and educated in the Middle West and is an authentic spokesman for the people of that area. His plays present their problems and frustrations, pleasures and triumphs with insight and sympathy. The first of Inge's plays (not counting the unsuccessful *Farther Off from Heaven*, 1947) was *Come Back, Little Sheba*, produced in 1950 and notable not only because it introduced Inge to the American playgoer but also because Shirley Booth and Sidney Blackmer brought unusual distinction to the leading roles. Inge's next play, *Picnic* (1953), records the shattering effect caused by a handsome young drifter when he invades a small, sexually repressed community in the Middle West. It was rated highly enough to win a Pulitzer Prize. *Picnic* was followed by *Bus Stop* (1955); *The Dark at the Top of the Stairs* (1957), another drama of dislocation in a small-town family; and *A Loss of Roses* (1959), Inge's first failure on Broadway.

The debuts of Miller, Williams, and Inge were the most promising developments in American playwriting during the first fifteen years after the Second World War. They were not the only developments, however. Many of the established playwrights made valuable contributions. Plays were written by Maxwell Anderson, Clifford Odets, Lillian Hellman, and Robert E. Sherwood during the 1940s and '50s. In addition, the distinguished poet Archibald MacLeish, who had written some of the most powerful radio dramas of the 1930s, made from the Old Testament story of Job a fascinating, challenging modern play. Entitled *J. B.,* the drama ran for two hundred performances on Broadway. Finally, Thornton Wilder, who made such a deep impression with *Our Town* in 1938, startled the theatrical world in 1942 with another completely original play, *The Skin of Our Teeth*. It telescopes all the crises that have threatened mankind since prehistoric days and shows how the human race, represented by a typical American family, has managed to survive the crises by the skin of its teeth. Twelve years after *The Skin of Our Teeth,* Wilder resurrected his 1938 comedy, *The Merchant of Yonkers,* the plot of which had been borrowed from Austrian and English sources. After revising it and retitling it *The Matchmaker,* Wilder allowed it to be produced at the Edinburgh Festival. The happy, bustling comedy, which related how the widow Dolly Levi, a marriage broker, entraps a prosperous merchant into marrying her, was successful in Edinburgh and during subsequent runs in London and New York. In 1964 *The Matchmaker* became the popular musical comedy *Hello, Dolly!*

Four years after the production of Wilder's play, the old master, Eugene O'Neill, broke a silence that had lasted since 1934. In 1946 he gave the Theatre Guild a play he had written as a diversion during his long struggle with his epic cycle. It was a lengthy, difficult drama entitled *The Iceman Cometh,* and the Guild's production of it was not a success. But ten years later, the Off-Broadway Circle in the Square Theatre revived the play. As directed by José Quintero in the three-sided arena theatre, and as acted by Jason Robards, Jr., in the leading role, it was a triumph. The theme of the play is the illusions men live by. The scene is the back room and bar of Harry Hope's shabby roominghouse, which shelters a collection of derelicts, each of whom maintains a slender hold on existence by nurturing his life-giving dream. The action of the play portrays what happens to each of the derelicts when his illusion is shattered.

Five months after the triumphant staging of *The Iceman Cometh,* the co-directors of the Circle in the Square, José Quintero and Theodore Mann, were given the privilege of producing O'Neill's *Long Day's Journey into Night* on Broadway. The master American playwright had died in 1953, leaving instructions that his intensely autobiographical play not be published until twenty-five years after his death. Fortunately his widow, who possessed legal rights to her husband's literary estate, chose to disregard the ban. She authorized publication of the play early in 1956 and a few months later permitted its production on Broadway. The play was so successful, despite its length and pessimism, that it restored O'Neill's reputation, which had badly slipped; it won him a posthumous Pulitzer Prize and numerous productions by groups all over the country.

Long Day's Journey into Night records the events of one fateful day in the life of Eugene O'Neill and his family (called the Tyrones in the play). During the course of the day, the pretenses and illusions of each member of the family are destroyed; by the time night has come, the ugly truths about each one are revealed: the father is a money-conscious egotist; the mother is a dope addict; the older brother is an alcoholic; and the younger brother, who represents the playwright, is a victim of tuberculosis, condemned to spend the next several months in a second-rate sanitorium chosen by his pinch-penny father. In addition to revealing the tragedy of each life, the play raises the searching questions that occupied O'Neill in all his major works: What is the meaning of misery and suffering? Who or what is responsible for the tragedy?

Two other O'Neill dramas were produced before the end of the 1950s. *A Moon for the Misbegotten* was partially autobiographical, a sequel to *Long Day's Journey into Night,* but unlike *Long Day's Journey,* it did not achieve much success. The other play was *A Touch of the Poet.* This play received a great deal of attention because it represents the massive play cycle that O'Neill worked on from the early years of the 1930s until illness forced him to end his writing. The cycle, *A Tale of Possessors, Self-Dispossessed,* was to be a long series of plays portraying the growth of the American nation from its beginning until the 1930s, as revealed in the history of one American family. O'Neill was not concerned with political or economic history but with the spiritual and psychological development of the family, which he hoped to make symbolic of the possessiveness and materialism that have characterized and corrupted American history. O'Neill completed drafts of several plays of the cycle before his death but, unable to finish and perfect them, he destroyed most of them. All he saved was the long, uncompleted manuscript of the projected sixth play, *More Stately Mansions,* and the completed fifth play, *A Touch of the Poet.* Produced in New York in 1958, *A Touch of the Poet* portrays the aristocratic pretensions and self-deception of an Irish-American family living in New England during the early years of the nineteenth century. The play was successful on Broadway and proved even more popular in community and university theatres. Its impact, together with the admiration earned by *Long Day's*

Journey into Night and by the 1956 production of *The Iceman Cometh,* reestablished the reputation of Eugene O'Neill as America's master playwright.

THE RISE OF NEGRO PLAYWRITING

The years from 1940 to 1960 are remembered not only because they saw the debuts of several major playwrights and the renewal of belief in Eugene O'Neill's greatness; they also witnessed the beginning of significant activity by black American playwrights.[2] This was a development of genuine importance and promise.

The first Negro drama produced in the United States was *The Drama of King Shotaway,* written by Mr. Brown, the Liverpool steward turned impresario, performed at his African Theatre in 1823. The earliest extant play by a black American was William Wells Brown's *The Escape, or the Leap for Freedom,* written in 1858 but never produced. In the years that followed, blacks made numerous contributions to the music, skits, and jokes that comprised the material of the minstrel show, and later they contributed extensively to the vaudeville stage. Also, when the musical revue came along, they were original and productive. During these years, however, their output of regular plays was sparse and sporadic. As we have seen, a number of plays were written *about* blacks but almost all of them were written by white dramatists. Not until the early 1920s did the first black-authored plays appear on Broadway. These were Willis Richardson's *The Chipwoman's Fortune* in 1923 and Garland Anderson's *Appearances* in 1925. During the next thirty-four years only eighteen plays by fifteen black playwrights were produced professionally on the New York stage. Among the best of these were Hall Johnson's beautiful production, *Run, Little Children* (1933), which used words, music, dance, spectacle, and sensitive acting to relate the conflict between a pagan cult and a Baptist church; Langston Hughes's *Mulatto* (1934), which exposed the bitterness and suffering that can result from illicit relationships between the races and which gave Rose McClendon an opportunity to demonstrate her impressive talent; and *Native Son* (1941), Richard Wright's novel dramatized by Mr. Wright with the help of Paul Green, which starred Canada Lee as the young black who becomes a murderer through the relentless force of social injustice.

However, the greatest stimulus to black playwriting came in the 1950s as a result of the civil rights movement. Several new dramatists were galvanized into action. Alice Childress, already well established as an actress, began her career as a playwright with *Florence* and *Just a Little Simple.* William Branch produced an effective play called *A Medal for Willie* and later a stirring historical drama about John Brown entitled *In Splendid Error.* Ossie Davis, another actor turned playwright, presented *Alice in Wonder.* Louis Peterson wrote *Take a Giant Step,* which was first produced on Broadway with some success and later off-Broadway with

---

[2]"Negro" was the term used almost universally until the civil rights movement of the 1950s when "black" became popular. Today both terms are used. Hence, in the following pages, the term black will appear.

much greater success. Loften Mitchell dramatized the famous civil rights case involving the blacks of Clarendon County, South Carolina, and called his play *A Land Beyond the River.* It ran for a year at the Greenwich Mews Theatre. Finally, in the last year of the 1950s, Lorraine Hansberry's poignant drama about black family life, *A Raisin in the Sun,* won the New York Drama Critic's Award for the best American play of the year.

Although their output was still modest in the 1950s, black playwrights were serving notice that even greater productivity could be expected from them in the future.

Claudia McNeil and Sidney Poitier in *A Raisin in the Sun.*
Photo-Joseph Abeles Studio.

ACTING

American acting did not fare too well in the years after World War II. When the commercial theatre declines and presents fewer and fewer plays and television supplants the movie houses as the source of popular entertainment, it is inevitable that fewer actors will be employed to attempt challenging roles and that there will be fewer notable performances to record.

The dwindling corps of actors seen during the postwar years continued to represent many of the styles that had flourished in the past history of the American theatre. The heroic school of Edwin Forrest appeared in the acting of the muscular heroes of western drama and in costume epics seen on stage and screen. The personality school had many successful exponents, particularly among actresses. Such eminent and greatly admired performers as Lynn Fontanne, Katharine Hepburn, and Tallulah Bankhead belong to this group because, with rare exceptions, they substituted their unique personalities for the dramatic character they were playing, or they portrayed characters which exactly suited their personalities. In the cinema and television, practically all roles are cast strictly to fit the personality of the individual player.

Three actresses who continued their careers in the 1940s and '50s could claim kinship with the classic school: Judith Anderson, Helen Hayes, and Katharine Cornell. Miss Anderson continued as a powerful actress of the heroines of Greek tragedy. Helen Hayes, after her earlier appearances in such parts as Mary of Scotland and Queen Victoria, played roles like Viola in *Twelfth Night* and Harriet Beecher Stowe in *Harriet,* along with many comic roles. Katharine Cornell portrayed Shaw's St. Joan and Shakespeare's Juliet. Although no actress of the period demonstrated the range or the power of Charlotte Cushman or Helena Modjeska, Anderson, Hayes, and Cornell nevertheless gave to their acting an integrity, a devotion, and a quality which resemble the ideals of the classic school.

It is difficult to find male performers in the post-World War II period who fulfilled the ideals of the classic school. The only versatile tragedians who performed in the American theatre during these years were English by birth, training, and generally by citizenship. Sir Lawrence Olivier, Sir John Gielgud, Sir Ralph Richardson, Maurice Evans, Michael Redgrave, and Richard Burton all belong to the British tradition. They are versatile, gifted players, worthy of the standards established by Edwin Booth and E. L. Davenport, but alas, they are not American. Three native actors—Alfred Lunt, Orson Welles, and Frederic March—who might be considered exponents of the classic style rarely or never attempted the great roles of classic tragedy. Orson Welles acted a few Shakespearean parts including Macbeth and Othello successfully, but he was largely identified with so-called character roles in which, more often than not, he played Orson Welles.

Alfred Lunt specialized in comedy during much of his career, including the role of Shakespeare's Petruchio. Even when he could name his parts, his serious roles were not Hamlet, Lear, or Macbeth but the less challenging parts in modern plays like Sherwood's *There Shall Be No Night* and Duerrenmatt's *The Visit.* Never-

Lunt and Fontanne in *Amphitryon 38.*

theless, in these plays he revealed a capacity for intensity, conviction, and dramatic power that was not apparent in his high comic roles.

Frederic March (1897-1977) was a versatile actor who portrayed a wide variety of characters with skill and conviction. Although many theatregoers identify him only with motion pictures, he was primarily devoted to the living stage. He began his acting career in 1920 and remained on the stage for eight years before undertaking his first movie role. After ten years in Hollywood, he returned to New York and resumed his stage career, often teamed with his actress-wife, Florence Eldridge. He made a great impression as Mr. Antrobus in Thornton Wilder's *The Skin of Our Teeth* (1942), depicting the common man who survives the catastrophes of history as an irresistable optimist with resilience, a sense of humor, and a dogged faith in a brighter future. In Lillian Hellman's *The Autumn Garden*, he was the engaging but faithless modern man who reflects the shallowness and instability of the times. His greatest success during the 1950s was the part of James Tyrone in O'Neill's *Long Day's Journey into Night.* James Tyrone represents O'Neill's father, the actor James O'Neill. Without sentimentality or exaggeration, March showed the best and the worst of the character and made him an intensely understandable and pitiable human being. His achievement was recognized by the New

York drama critics, who named him the best actor in a straight play for the season 1956-57.

Other gifted American performers, like Morris Carnovsky and Jason Robards, Jr., have devoted themselves to roles in contemporary plays, although with the establishment of the Shakespearean festivals in Stratford, Connecticut, and Stratford, Ontario, they have met the challenge of a limited number of Shakespearean characters.

During the 1940s, several black performers reached maturity in their art and contributed notable performances to the American stage. Paul Robeson, already famous as an actor and a singer, portrayed Othello in 1943 with such power, passion, and richness of voice and presence that many critics declared him to be the greatest Othello of the twentieth century. At about the same time, Ethel Waters emerged as a powerful dramatic performer. Already famous, like Robeson, for her singing, she won acclaim in several straight plays.

Other black performers who earned recognition and admiration during this period were Canada Lee for his performance in *Native Son* (1941), the dramatization of Richard Wright's novel; Hilda Simms and Frederick O'Neal for their acting in *Anna Lucasta* (1944); Gordon Heath for his appealing portrayal in *Deep Are the Roots* (1945); and Dooley Wilson, Rex Ingram, Todd Duncan, and Katherine Dunham for their remarkable work in *Cabin in the Sky* (1940). These achievements and the appearance of productions like *Beggar's Holiday* (1946) and *Finian's Rainbow* (1947), which featured integrated casts of black and white performers, were clear evidence that the old color barrier in the theatre was slowly but surely disappearing. Ira Aldridge would have been pleased.

The style of acting most frequently seen and acclaimed on the American stage in the 1940s and '50s was the school of psychological naturalism, or the Stanislavsky method of acting. The two are identical in aim and similar in the means of achieving the aim. Both the method and the school of psychological naturalism, whose chief exponent and teacher in America was Minnie Maddern Fiske, emphasize psychological truthfulness in the portrayal of a role, concentration on inner feeling with repressed overt responses, cultivation of a simple true-to-contemporary-life manner of moving and speaking (which often leads to careless delivery), and fidelity to the overall design of the play.

The Actor's Studio of New York, under the artistic direction of Lee Strasberg, and the Neighborhood Playhouse School of the Theatre, directed for many years by Sanford Meisner, were two of the nation's leading centers for the teaching of Method acting in the post-World War II period. The Actors' Studio stirred the most interest because of Lee Strasberg's awesome reputation as a teacher of the Method. In addition, ideals similar to those of Stanislavsky and Mrs. Fiske are taught by the American Academy of Dramatic Art, the oldest professional school of acting in the United States. The late Aristide D'Angelo, for many years the authority on acting at the Academy, said that the ideal of the school "has always been to work from within: to build the idea, the concept, the truth of the character and scene—and let the form of expression follow naturally." Mr. D'Angelo also stated that the "Academy ideal and Stanislavsky's ideal are much the same, but Stanislavsky formalized the method of responding while the Academy has not."[3]

D'Angelo's statement names the principal difference between the Stanislavsky school of acting and the Fiske school or the Academy's style. Stanislavsky organized his principles and evolved a detailed method of teaching them. Stanislavsky's clarification and formalization of the means of liberating an actor's creativity have made his method sought-after and have caused many contemporary actors and theatregoers to forget that similar ideals were held by many great performers in the past and are particularly close both to the aim and to the method of Mrs. Fiske's school of psychological naturalism.

Most of the notable young actors in the United States today have been trained in the Stanislavsky method, in the style of psychological naturalism, or in some related school, and they all represent similar aims and ideals. Their achievements in many cases have been outstanding. In the post-World War II period, several young actresses achieved stardom through their vivid, authentic portraits of the troubled heroines of contemporary drama. They include Kim Stanley, Julie Harris, Uta Hagen, Maureen Stapleton, Geraldine Page, and Shirley Booth. These talented performers have not only embodied modern heroines; they also have been successful in certain Shakespearean roles, in the modern classics of Ibsen and Shaw, and in a variety of parts seen on movie and television screens.

Two male actors who deserve mention are Eli Wallach and Marlon Brando. Wallach, born in Brooklyn and educated for the stage at the Neighborhood Playhouse School of the Theatre in New York, had the beneficial experience early in his career of performing in such classics as Shakespeare's *Henry VIII* and *Antony and Cleopatra* and in Shaw's *Androcles and the Lion.* He made his first real hit playing opposite Maureen Stapleton in the role of the persistent suitor, Mangiacavallo, in Williams's *The Rose Tattoo* (1951). His other favorite role is the character Kilroy in another Williams drama, *Camino Real,* which Wallach acted in 1953.

Marlon Brando also made his first memorable impression in a Tennessee Williams play. That was *A Streetcar Named Desire* (1947) in which he created the role of Stanley Kowalski. He had earned recognition previously for his acting in *I Remember Mama* (1944), in *Candida* (1946) with Katharine Cornell, and in Maxwell Anderson's *Truckline Cafe* (1946). A year later, Brando's compelling embodiment of the strong, primitive, physically attractive Kowalski made him a star. He moved to Hollywood and continued to star in a series of successful movies.

DIRECTORS AND DESIGNERS

The importance of the director in the theatre, established at the end of the nineteenth century and emphatically confirmed during the first forty years of the twentieth, was demonstrated every time a successful play was produced between

[3]Statements from a private conversation with Mr. D'Angelo at the Academy in New York, September 1939.

1940 and 1960. By this time the original American régisseurs were dead and many of their immediate successors either dead or inactive. To replace them, a new group of teacher-directors had developed who were regarded as master artists, men able to perceive all the potentials of a drama and able also to embody them vividly and excitingly in a production. This group was so varied and numerous as to be almost bewildering.

A few of the old masters were still active. Arthur Hopkins was represented by a few productions in the 1940s; Guthrie McClintic continued to stage his wife's productions as well as others during the 1940s and '50s. Many playwrights, like Lillian Hellman, Sidney Kingsley, and Clifford Odets, undertook to stage their new dramas; and that expert writer of comedy, George S. Kaufman, often filled the role of director.

The continuing popularity of big musical shows produced a special breed of régisseurs who were expert at staging funny, fast-moving, spectacular productions. Among the most successful of these were George Abbott, Joshua Logan, Rouben Mamoulian, Hassard Short, and John C. Wilson. Their skills were soon challenged by younger talents like Jerome Robbins and Morton de Costa. Most of these men were as expert in shaping comedy and farce as they were in directing big musicals. Still others who established themselves as master directors were Bretaigne Windust, José Ferrer, David Ross, and José Quintero. Ross and Quintero were leaders in the development of the Off-Broadway theatre.

Of all the gifted directors who enriched the years from 1940 to 1960, none was more influential than three alumni of the Group Theatre: Harold Clurman, Lee Strasberg, and Elia Kazan. Their early theatrical experience falls in the decade of the 1930s, but because their best work was done after that they can rightly be considered as representative of the top directorial talent of the '40s and '50s.

Harold Clurman, after helping to organize the Group Theatre in 1931, became not only the guiding, galvanizing spirit of the enterprise but also a régisseur who staged many plays during the Group's ten years of activity, including its final production, Irwin Shaw's *Retreat to Pleasure* (1940). By the time the Group officially disbanded in 1941, Clurman was firmly established as one of the two or three most sought-after directors on Broadway. By 1959 he had more than fifty productions to his credit, including such popular and admired successes as *The Member of the Wedding* (1950), *Bus Stop* (1955), *The Waltz of the Toreadors* (1957), and *A Touch of the Poet* (1958). Clurman's dedication to the living theatre and his belief in its greatness are revealed in his intense emotional involvement when he directs a play. During rehearsals, his actors report that he is heated and volatile. He shouts and screams; he gesticulates and tears his hair; he begs, pleads, and cajoles. All of it is done to make the actors feel that they are engaged in a high and holy profession and must give their best during every moment of a performance.

One of the other cofounders of the Group Theatre and a long-time colleague of Clurman's is Lee Strasberg, famous as the artistic director of the Actors' Studio. Strasberg's renown as a superb teacher and as America's best interpreter of the Stanislavsky Method had somewhat obscured his reputation as a director, but that reputation is high indeed. His professional career began in 1924 when he became, like Clurman, an assistant stage manager for the Theatre Guild. During the next seven years he acted, stage-managed, rehearsed experimental plays, and dreamed about revitalizing the American theatre with a new kind of acting and a new concept of production. After cofounding the Group Theatre, he helped direct the Group's first production, *The House of Connelly*. He also directed its great popular and financial success, *Men in White*. The production won the Pulitzer Prize for drama in 1934.

In 1937 Strasberg resigned from the Group Theatre but continued his activity as a director of plays. After the Actors' Studio was founded in 1947, he was invited to join the enterprise, and in 1948 he became its artistic director. His inspired leadership made it America's most famous and sought-after training school for established actors. Although Strasberg continued to direct plays, his principal activity became that of master teacher. His students, including many stars of the contemporary stage, declared that he had an almost superhuman ability to diagnose an actor's shortcomings and to stimulate talent and increase creativity.

The third representative régisseur of this period, Elia Kazan, became a sought-after director of the Broadway theatre. He joined the Group Theatre in 1933 as an apprentice actor, but after one month he was told to leave because he had demonstrated no talent. He refused to depart, and instead stayed on as a handyman about the stage. His friendship with the newly discovered playwright Clifford Odets led to a resumption of his acting career. He appeared in several of Odets's plays and proved himself a capable actor despite his early failure. However, his greater talent lay in directing, as he shortly discovered. Beginning uncertainly, he steadily increased his strength and reputation as a director until in 1942 he won the assignment of staging Wilder's *The Skin of Our Teeth* on Broadway. The skill and imagination he demonstrated in this production won him the New York Drama Critics Circle Award for the best directing job of the year. His subsequent career produced a long succession of triumphs.

In all his productions, Kazan was admired for the power and simplicity of his staging. He is primarily interested in the major elements of the play—the structure, the plot, and the characters. After careful study, he decides where the emphasis should be and then spends several days discussing his concepts with his cast. He does not neglect details, but he never allows them to obscure the principal thrust of the play. Actors revere his judgment and trust his sense of the theatrical, which, they know, is always circumscribed by good taste. He continues to be one of the most impressive and influential talents in the American theatre.

Closely associated with the directors who enriched the period from 1940 to 1960 were their fellow artists, the scene designers. The success of many productions was due in no small measure to the creative artistry of these designers. Their names make an impressive list. Several of the old masters were still active during the period; Robert Edmond Jones, Norman Bel Geddes (who turned his attention chiefly to industrial designing), and Lee Simonson all designed a production or two. Their younger successors were even more active. Mordecai Gorelik and Aline Bern-

Scene from *Fall River Legend,* presented on "Omnibus," CBS TV.
Choreography by Agnes de Mille, design by Henry May.

Courtesy of Henry May.

stein did much good work. Donald Oenslager continued to design most of the productions of Guthrie McClintic. Stewart Chaney was busy with a variety of shows from *Blithe Spirit* and *The Voice of the Turtle* in the early 1940s to *The Moon Is Blue* and *Much Ado About Nothing* in the 1950s. Busiest of them all and unsurpassed in productivity was Jo Mielziner. However, he could not supply all the needs of the American theatre or of the Broadway stage during the 1940s and

'50s. Fortunately, he did not have to. A group of other gifted designers rose to prominence during these years, whose work enriched many productions and often invited comparison with Mielziner's best. The group was large and varied. Busiest and most successful were such men as Howard Bay, Boris Aronson, Raymond Sovey, Frederick Fox, Oliver Smith, and Peter Larkin. All of them created settings of great beauty and effectiveness, designed many kinds of shows, and were representative of the enormous talent available to the American theatre in the middle of the twentieth century.

21

The Phoenix in Flames

Developments, 1960-1980

The twenty years from 1960 to 1980 are immensely difficult to understand. The events of the period are too close for us to observe them with a sense of perspective; we are too involved in them to be objective. Certain developments in the theatre, such as the rise of regional professional companies and the increased interest in the performing arts, are easy to accept and to understand. They are welcome culminations of long-cherished ideals. Certain other new developments, such as the popularity of absurdity, cruelty, and nudity, are harder to grasp. As always, the social milieu may furnish the basis for understanding these developments.

The young people who reached maturity in the 1950s and who supported the theatre of that decade were called the "silent generation." They grew up in the years of world depression and world war; and when those traumatic experiences were over, they were, on the whole, content to enjoy without protest the security and prosperity their parents had won for them.

In contrast, the young people who set the tone of the 1960s and early 1970s were the restless, rebellious, outspoken generation. To them, the Great Depression and the Second World War were only events of history—but the evils they saw around them were real and horrifying. They rejected or despised the moral, religious, and social values of the past. They watched their elders pay lip service to high ideals and then all too frequently, repudiate them in practice. They were deeply troubled by the ugly war in Southeast Asia and the invasion of Cambodia; they were enraged by the injustices inflicted on minority groups, by the paradox of poverty amid plenty, by the despoliation of the land, by the shocking assassinations of national leaders, and by the increasing impersonalization of a society that diminished them and robbed them of their humanity.

The decade of the 1960s began with hope and promise. The president of the United States who took office at its beginning epitomized the qualities of youth, grace, accomplishment, and vigor. He lifted the spirits of the entire nation. After his brutal assassination, the mood of the country changed, the evils seemed to multiply, and restlessness increased. There was a momentary lifting of spirits at the end of the decade when American astronauts accomplished their magnificent voyages to the moon. Otherwise, the decade was a period of dissatisfaction and protest. This mood continued into the early 1970s and was intensified by other events: the dishonesty and corruption in Washington that forced a president to resign; the perils that were revealed in the production of nuclear energy; the gasoline shortage and the rampant inflation that went with it. As the decade neared its end, protest continued but at a diminished rate and intensity. The pendulum began to swing toward a mood of conservatism mixed with apathy and disillusionment. The latter attitude was intensified at the very end of the decade, when the United States Embassy in Iran was seized and its officials taken prisoner; mighty America apparently was helpless to defend its property or to rescue its citizens.

There have always been evils and problems in the world and young people have always protested them. Why did protest become so universal and so violent in the 1960s and the 1970s? The answer can surely be found in the background of these young people. Reared in comparative affluence, security, and freedom, they had a greater opportunity to examine the world around them and to think about its evils. Freed from the incessant labor that occupied their forefathers, and recipients of an accelerated, progressive education, they came face to face with the funamental problem of the meaning of evil and suffering in the world far earlier than any preceding generation. Subject to the constant barrage of televised news that dramatized and sensationalized every evil, they could never escape or forget the problems that surrounded them. It is no wonder that they were restless, demanding, and rebellious—and no wonder that the new trends in the theatre that they supported, the theatre of the absurd, the theatre of cruelty and revolution, the theatre of "happenings," and the theatre of sex and nudity, should reflect their restlessness and rebellion. Before we discuss these trends, let us examine the traditional activities of the theatre during this period.

RADIO, TELEVISION, AND MOVIES

During the 1960s and 1970s, radio, television, and motion pictures continued to prosper in the new interrelationships that had evolved during the '50s. Radio was active and prolific on the local level. Television was controlled by the great national networks, which also broadcast a continuous series of programs that can be accurately described, in the vernacular of the decade, as a "mixed bag." It continued to demonstrate its awesome power to influence manners, morals, and fashions—and its frightening power to make or break the candidates for public office. Motion-picture studios adjusted their facilities to the production of films for television and at the same time produced feature films that varied from artistic epics to run-of-the-mill cinema. Many fervent young directors experimented with new kinds of films that often featured innovative techniques and forbidden subject matter. In ever-increasing numbers, these films were shown in a large variety of small houses that were usually converted shops, markets, or commercial offices of various sorts. The neighborhood movie house began to reappear in new urban shopping centers. The new houses, smaller than the traditional movie palaces, were so mechanized that only two staff members were needed to carry on the whole operation.

The story of the theatre in New York City can also be briefly told. In the decade of the 1960s, productions on Broadway averaged in number around seventy-five per season; this figure includes straight plays, musicals, revues, imports from abroad (mostly from London), specialties, and revivals of old plays. The following decade saw a steady decline in the total number of productions to an average of fifty-seven per year. However, to balance this decline, both the Off-Broadway and the Off-off-Broadway theatres burgeoned and prospered. For example, the Off-Broadway theatre recorded 111 productions in the season of 1978-79, compared to 54 on Broadway. Once fugitive, experimental, and sporadic, Off-Broadway theatres are now almost indistinguishable from the Broadway scene. They have professional Equity casts, they are subject to union rules and high costs from which they were originally exempt, they offer themselves for review by the regular critics, and they play a regular eight-a-week schedule of public performances. They also win places on the yearly list of the ten "best plays" and compete for some of the prizes once reserved for on-Broadway productions.

The original impulses that created Off-Broadway—the desire to experiment and to save money—were reawakened in the early 1960s and resulted in a new wave of pioneering and experimentation. The phenomenon has been given the name "Off-off-Broadway." The editor of *The Best Plays of 1965-1966* wrote that the phenomenon "is almost impossible to define or to grasp statistically . . . it is relaxed, proud of it and suspicious of any attempt at regimentation or even definition."[1]

The credit for starting the Off-off-Broadway movement is generally given to Joe Cino, owner of the Caffe Cino. In 1958 he invited the first playwright to work in his coffeehouse, and thereafter his establishment became a tiny but vigorous and exciting theatre. Here, until Cino's suicide in 1967, a host of new playwrights had an opportunity to experiment with all kinds of scripts and with unorthodox methods of acting and staging.

Cino's activities earned him the title of father of the Off-off-Broadway movement. The mother of the phenomenon, "La Mama," was certainly Ellen Stewart, a gifted black clothes designer who in 1962 began staging plays in a basement coffeehouse on East Ninth Street. Now famous as the La Mama Experimental Theatre Club, it is credited with nurturing an impressive number of new plays and playwrights. In the first five years of its activity, Miss Stewart and her La Mama troupe presented 130 to 175 new plays, usually at the rate of one new play a week! In addition, La Mama has built up a corps of actors, designers, and directors (Tom O'Horgan, for example) and has taken several of its productions on highly successful tours of Europe.

---

[1] Otis L. Guernsey, Jr., *The Best Plays of 1965-1966* (New York: Dodd, Mead & Co., 1966), p. 34.

The fantastic growth and success of the Off-off-Broadway theatre have astonished everyone. In the middle of the 1970s, it was reported that there were 78 major Off-off-Broadway groups staging at least 650 programs each year plus 140 miscellaneous groups responsible for more than 200 other programs!

Certain other facts are important in understanding the theatre situation in New York City. One is the steadily rising cost of tickets. In the 1965-66 season, the top price of a ticket broke the "old sawbuck barrier" and reached eleven dollars and ninety cents. Since then it has continued to climb. The season of 1978-79 saw the price of popular musicals reach twenty to twenty-five dollars, with straight plays touching a twenty-dollar top. Such prices, of course, are the result of constantly soaring production costs, which in turn are dictated by the Frankenstein of inflation.

A significant consequence of runaway production costs is the invasion of Broadway by stage successes from London. Of course, there is nothing surprising in the presence on Broadway of British actors and productions. From colonial times to the present they have been an important part of the American theatre. What is surprising, however—and disturbing to many observers—is that while the number of successful American offerings has declined, the percentage of successful British offerings has risen. The reason is clear. When costs of producing new American plays reach staggering amounts, and when the chances for making a profit—or even for breaking even—constantly dwindle, producers naturally turn more and more to established successes from the London stage. The cost of importing them is relatively moderate, and their chances for success are relatively high.

The theatre in New York is not dead, not even the traditional on-Broadway theatre. It may be only a shadow of its former self, but it still functions despite the problems. Developments since 1945 have been such that now it shares the activities which it once monopolized with dozens of producing groups throughout the New York area. Nationally the same decentralization has occurred. Whereas the Broadway theatre was once practically the only source of new plays, the Mecca for all American playwrights and the staging ground for hundreds of road companies that traveled the length and breadth of the land, now these functions are shared with dozens of regional centers located in dozens of cities throughout the nation. Some devotees of the old monopolistic Broadway may mourn its passing, but most friends of the American theatre believe that decentralization is a healthy, long-needed development. They believe that Broadway will continue to function as one of the important theatre centers of the United States, but they also believe that the impressive size and rich diversity of the nation require many centers to serve a population that exceeds two hundred million potential playgoers.

REGIONAL PROFESSIONAL THEATRES AND UNIVERSITY THEATRES

The American dream of many centers of dramatic inspiration and activity was realized during the 1960s and 1970s. The period was outstanding for the spectacular development of professional regional theatres and of university theatres. New producing groups, centers for the performing arts, and university theatre complexes sprang up everywhere.

The remarkable growth of professional regional theatres is reflected by the reports contained in the annual volume of *Best Plays* (the Burns Mantle Yearbook), published each year as a record of professional theatrical activity in America. The 1960-61 volume described only the theatrical seasons in New York and Chicago. The following year activities in Washington, D. C., Boston, Dallas, and San Francisco were included, and these reports mentioned five professional regional companies in operation. By the end of the 1970s, sixty professional regional theatres were presenting 642 productions of 490 plays in 115 playhouses in fifty-eight cities (fifty-one of the cities in the U. S. A., seven in Canada). As the movement gained momentum, *Time Magazine* declared, "Broadway shows are having difficulty finding understudies . . . almost every serious young actor who can walk or crawl has gone off to a repertory company."[2]

The development of professional regional companies was generously supported by the private philanthropic foundations of the nation. Even more significant was the establishment of the National Foundation for the Arts and for the Humanities in the mid-1960s. After almost two hundred years, the federal government recognized its obligation to aid and encourage cultural activities which, unlike the sciences, had never received federal support. In 1965 the commitment was finally made and the foundation was established. It includes two groups, the National Endowment for the Arts and the National Endowment for the Humanities. Each endowment has a chairman and a council, and each is responsible for allocating the funds voted by Congress. In its first year of existence, the National Endowment for the Arts received a budget of five million dollars. Ten years later the sum had grown to two hundred million dollars. This amount is miniscule compared to the staggering federal expenditures for science, engineering, and war. The money nevertheless represents a revolutionary change of attitude and a long-sought development which, it is hoped, will nourish and enrich the cultural life of the nation.

The professional regional theatres are fascinating in their differences. No two are exactly alike in organization, management, or financial resources. A closer look at two of these theatres, one located on the East Coast and one on the West Coast, will illustrate the variety.

The McCarter Theatre of Princeton University is a university theatre—and yet it is not. Princeton has no department of drama. Students interested in theatre arts must get their knowledge and inspiration from association with the McCarter Theatre company, which is entirely professional and is directed by Michael Kahn. Its yearly selection of plays is supervised by a committee of Princeton University faculty members, but its operations are directed by its own professional staff. Although the university supplies some financial support, three-fourths of the operating budget must come from ticket sales and other nonuniversity sources. Part of this revenue is derived from a program of concerts, ballets, and other entertainment

[2] *Time Magazine*, LXXXIII, 7 (14 February 1964), 61.

presented in the playhouse when the repertory company is not using it. During the season about 230 performances of all kinds are presented in the 1,077-seat theatre.

About 35 percent of the spectators who support the McCarter Theatre come from the university and from the town of Princeton. All the rest are drawn from other communities both near and far. The McCarter Theatre is a true regional theatre serving a sizable area of both New Jersey and New York.

On the opposite side of the nation, serving the northern half of California, is the American Conservatory Theatre, whose major activities are centered in San Francisco. It differs from the McCarter Theatre and is more representative of another large group of regional professional theatres. The American Conservatory Theatre (or ACT, as it is better known) is not attached to any college or university, although as the "Conservatory" in its name suggests, it offers a continuous program of instruction and training in theatre arts. It was organized by a group of actors headed by William Ball, a graduate of the Carnegie Institute of Technology. In 1965 this company presented a season of plays at the Pittsburgh Playhouse. The following year the group traveled to California. Their first public appearance on the West Coast was at the University of California in Berkeley. Later they performed with spectacular success at the Stanford University Summer Festival. The enthusiasm aroused by the company led to the establishment of ACT as San Francisco's resident repertory theatre, succeeding the Actors' Workshop, which had left the city about the time ACT arrived. The new company, opening its first regular season in San Francisco in January 1967, presented 283 performances of sixteen plays.

ACT is sponsored by and partially supported by the City of San Francisco. Its budget comes from ticket sales, tours, grants from foundations, and funds raised by the California Theatre Foundation, a continuing support group organized by the city. Like most of the regional theatres, it is always in search of additional means of support for its extensive and varied activities.

ACT's ambitions are impressive and so is its record of activity. During the season of 1978-79, the company presented a repertory of eleven plays in 245 performances at the Geary Theatre. In addition, there were guest performances at both the Geary and the Marines Memorial Theatre plus five programs of "plays in progress." As if this were not sufficient activity, three Young Conservatory productions went on tour to celebrate the Year of the Child; and two of ACT's major productions visited five cities spaced from Claremont, California, to Westport, Connecticut. For both the quantity and quality of its activities, ACT was given a special Tony Award as the outstanding regional theatre of 1979-80.

Another gratifying development of the 1960s and 1970s was the continuing prosperity and growth of college and university theatres. A few professional regional companies were resident at universities—for example, at Princeton and Yale. More often, however, university theatres were not associated, except incidentally, with the regional companies. Instead, they were part of the drama departments of their institutions. Performers were students; directors, designers, and chief technicians were faculty members; productions were subsidized by university funds. The drama that resulted was supported not only by students and faculty members but, just as important, by the communities around the college or university—so much so that a special study of the performing arts by the National Association of State Universities and Land Grant Colleges concluded by declaring that ". . . the community at large has benefited as much if not more than the university" from the varied programs of drama and music offered by the universities and that "the vitality of our society may ultimately be said to rest on the strength and vitality of its universities."[3]

SHAKESPEARE FESTIVALS

Other evidence of the vitality of the American theatre in the period from 1960 to 1980 was provided by the continuing success of summer theatres and of summer Shakespearean festivals. Several of the Shakespearean festivals became firmly established institutions with enviable records for the quality and quantity of their productions. The four most successful are the American Shakespeare Festival at Stratford, Connecticut, which presents more than one hundred performances each summer; the New York Shakespeare Festival, founded by Joseph Papp, which

Shakespeare's *Measure for Measure,* directed by Jean-Bernard Bucky at the Zellerbach Playhouse, University of California at Berkeley, January 1970. Design by Henry May.

Courtesy of Henry May and the Department of Dramatic Art, University of California, Berkeley.

[3]Katherine Skogstad and Joyce Todd, "The Performing Arts: Another Dimension of University Service" (Lexington, Ky.: Office of Institutional Research, National Association of State Universities and Land Grant Colleges and the University of Kentucky Alumni Association, 1969), p. 28.

averages about seventy performances each year in Central Park; the National Shakespeare Festival at the Old Globe Theatre in San Diego, California, which presents more than one hundred performances per season; and the Oregon Shakespeare Festival at Ashland, which averages about fifty performances per summer. In addition to these four long-established festivals, new groups have appeared year by year. Some of them have grown to national recognition while others have achieved a good measure of regional fame.

PLAYWRITING

Playwriting was one art during the period from 1960 to 1980 that showed much activity and some accomplishment but not, perhaps, the abundant achievement that might be expected considering the size of the nation, the increased theatrical fervor everywhere, and the incentives offered to encourage good playwriting. The established dramatists continued to write, but their success was sporadic. Lillian Hellman, after her success in 1960 with *Toys in the Attic,* confined her playwriting to one adaptation, *My Mother, My Father, and Me* (1963), a satire based on a novel by Burt Blechman. William Inge began the 1960s decade with an Academy Award-winning film script and with the publication of a volume of short plays. Then he produced two unsuccessful long plays, *Natural Affection* (1963) and *Where's Daddy?* (1966). He died in 1973. Tennessee Williams authored two hits at the beginning of the 1960s, thus continuing his amazing creative output of the 1950s. But after the two successes, he seemed to have exhausted his fecundity, producing several failures in quick succession. The two hits were *Period of Adjustment* (1960), a comedy of dubious worth, and *The Night of the Iguana,* a play which, like Williams's earlier successes, featured sex, valor, and endurance.

Arthur Miller wrote fewer plays than Williams and was more consistently successful. He remained silent for eight years following *A View from the Bridge* and *A Memory of Two Mondays* in 1955. Then in 1964 the repertory company of Lincoln Center in New York made a great success of his *After the Fall,* a play that appeared to be an analysis of the guilt and failure involved in Miller's unhappy marriage to Marilyn Monroe. The following season (1965) Miller had another success with *Incident at Vichy,* a play about the Nazi persecution of the Jews that exposes the many kinds and degrees of guilt involved in that persecution.

Miller's third success came early in 1968 when *The Price* opened on Broadway. The play is a vivid portrayal of the confrontation between two brothers, one a rich, successful physician, the other a policeman who values his personal honor more than wealth or position. Out of the conflict comes an indictment of the materialism that corrupts the lives of modern men whether they are successful or unsuccessful.

Miller was again silent until the season of 1972-73, when he presented *The Creation of the World and Other Business.* The play received some favorable critical comment but was rejected by playgoers. It ran for only twenty performances and thus was one of Miller's few failures. However, his three plays of the 1960s, although they seemed old-fashioned to some critics, increased his reputation as a major playwright.

More exciting than the contributions of the established playwrights were the new voices that were heard during the 1960s and 1970s. Leading the chorus in the 1960s were two white authors, Neil Simon and Edward Albee, and a vigorous group of black dramatists. Simon astonished Broadway by his amazing gift for turning out one comedy hit after another in rapid succession; Albee startled the world of the theatre with the disturbing power and originality of his plays; the black playwrights shocked the public with their passion and explosive creativeness.

Neil Simon, born in the Bronx in 1927, began his apprenticeship as a dramatist by writing gags for such TV celebrities as Jackie Gleason, Sid Caesar, and Phil Silvers. Continuing his service to television, Simon helped to write situation comedies and to adapt old musicals. Later he worked on the Sergeant Bilko television show, starring Phil Silvers, and helped to write thirty shows in thirty-nine weeks. This strenuous apprenticeship behind him, he turned to the creation of comedies for the stage. His fabulous record is as follows:

Come Blow Your Horn (1961)
Little Me (a musical, book by Simon, 1962)
Barefoot in the Park (1963)
The Odd Couple (1965)
Sweet Charity (a musical, book by Simon, 1962)
The Star Spangled Girl (1966)
Plaza Suite (a program of three one-act plays, 1968)
Promises, Promises (a musical, book by Simon, 1968)
The Last of the Red Hot Lovers (1969)
The Gingerbread Lady (1970)
The Prisoner of Second Avenue (1971)
The Sunshine Boys (1972)
The Good Doctor (1973)
God's Favorite (1974)
California Suite (1976)
Chapter Two (1977)
They're Playing Our Song (a musical, book by Simon, 1978)
The Curse of Kulyenchikov (due in 1981)

The list does not include several screen plays. Simon's total output is astonishing. It is even more astonishing that *all* of the plays and *all* of the musicals were successful. Most of them, in fact, were smash hits. During the season of 1966-67, Simon had four hit shows running on Broadway at the same time, equaling the record set by Clyde Fitch in 1901.

Simon's plays have great appeal for audiences because their comedy grows out of believable characters and situations. *Barefoot in the Park* derives its humor from the tribulations of a newly married couple who, having been reared in luxury, try to make their marriage work while living on a modest income in a top-floor, walk-up flat. *The Odd Couple* depicts the friction and absurdity that result when two divorced men of opposite temperaments try to share the same flat. One is a fussy, meticulous housekeeper; the other is maddeningly careless and sloppy. Conflict is inevitable, and in Simon's deft playwriting, so is laughter. Both characters and situations are funny, and the dialogue that follows is naturally funny, too. So far Simon's instincts have been unerring. He is currently the most successful and popular writer of comedy in the nation—perhaps in the world.

Edward Albee has not equaled Simon's overall popular and financial success, but his plays have stirred greater excitement. They had a powerful relevance for the playgoer of the restless decade of the 1960s. Albee, born in Washington, D. C., in 1928, is the adopted child of Reed A. Albee, the son of E. F. Albee, who, with B. F. Keith, is remembered for organizing a chain of vaudeville theatres throughout the United States. Young Albee's interests in creative writing and in the theatre manifested themselves early in his life. He started attending plays when he was five and by the age of twelve had written a three-act sex farce. When he was seventeen and a student at Choate School, the school's literary magazine published his play called *Schism*. After graduating from Choate, Albee attended Trinity College for a brief time, and then, restless and dissatisfied, quit college and worked at a number of routine jobs. He continued to write, mostly poems and novels, but without much success. In 1953 Thornton Wilder suggested that he return to his first love, playwriting. Accepting the advice, Albee wrote four short plays: *Zoo Story* in 1958; *The Death of Bessie Smith* and *The Sandbox* in 1959, and *The American Dream* in 1960. The first two of these plays premiered in Germany, and only after being favorably received there did they and the other two plays earn production in the United States. Now all the short plays are immensely popular with community and university theatres. *The Sandbox* and *The American Dream* have been called contributions to the theatre of the absurd, but Albee denies that they are such. He does not deny, however, that his first long play, *Who's Afraid of Virginia Woolf?*, won him international fame and the claim to be considered a major playwright.

Who's Afraid of Virginia Woolf? was the smash hit of the 1962-63 season. The play, now well known even to the general public because of the successful movie version, is the record of an all-night drinking party during which two couples ruthlessly and sadistically rip each other to shreds. By dawn all illusions have been shattered, truth has been reduced to a weapon of torture, human relationships have been exposed as a sadomasochistic conflict, and existence itself is revealed as an ugly Walpurgisnacht. We may well ask how a play of this sort could achieve great public success. The answer lies in the skill of the dramatist. He can create vivid, lifelike—often repellent—people, juxtapose them so that tension and conflict instantly develop, and put such incisive, deadly dialogue into their mouths that an audience winces and laughs at the same time.

Albee's next long play, *Tiny Alice* (1964-65), was marred by false leads and murky symbols, so many of them that spectators were often completely baffled and found no meaning in the play at all. In fact, the original New York production

Paul Shenar as Brother Julian in Edward Albee's *Tiny Alice,* as presented by
the American Conservatory Theatre in San Francisco, directed by William Ball.

Courtesy of Hank Kranzler.

was not a great success. Since then, however, productions by repertory companies
and university theatres have steadily increased the reputation of the play until
today it is regarded as one of Albee's best. It deserves to be esteemed. In the
gorgeously theatrical production of it in 1967 by the American Conservatory
Theatre in San Francisco, the play became exciting, sensuous drama and its basic
meaning emerged clearly and strongly.

Following *Tiny Alice,* Albee adapted and dramatized two novels for the stage.
The first was Carson McCuller's *The Ballad of the Sad Cafe* (1963); the second was
James Purdy's *Malcolm* (1966). Although there were praiseworthy qualities in both
adaptations, neither one succeeded on the stage. Nine months after *Malcolm* closed,
an original play by Albee entitled *A Delicate Balance* appeared on Broadway. The
play presents a disturbing analysis of human relationships in an age of anxiety and
despair; and although it enjoyed only a moderate run on Broadway, it was chosen
as a best play for the season of 1966-67 and also won the Pulitzer Prize. Albee won
another Pulitzer Prize in the season of 1974-75 with his play entitled *Seascape.*
Although admired by the critics, it had a run of only two months. His 1980 play,
The Lady from Dubuque, aroused sharp controversy among the critics and closed
after twelve performances.

Black Dramatists

Even more significant to the development of American playwriting was a
creative explosion among black dramatists. During the 1960s the whole nation became acutely conscious of the need for racial justice and equality. Blacks every-

312

where demanded it, sometimes peacefully, sometimes violently. Black writers, especially playwrights, were aroused to express themselves with vehemence and passion, not only on the subject of racial justice but on the more enduring subject of the black's unique history, culture, and way of life. The result was the emergence of at least a dozen vigorous and talented new black dramatists.

The leader of the group in the 1960s was LeRoi Jones (1934-   ). Talented and articulate, angry and aggressive, Jones wrote poems, essays, and a novel in addition to his plays. But his plays had the greatest impact. In 1964 his short drama about the corruption of white society entitled *Dutchman* won an Off-Broadway award for the best American play of the year. In 1965 another one-act play, *The Toilet,* also produced off-Broadway, won a place on the list of best plays of the season. It is a bitter but moving play about hate and love set in the dirty toilet room of a ghetto school. Its subsequent production in various parts of the country created a good deal of shock and controversy. So did such plays by Jones as *The Baptism* and *Eighth Ditch,* which were closed by the police. In 1966 a short play by Jones, *The Slave,* won second prize at the International Art Festival in Dakar, Senegal. One of Jones's later plays, *Slave Ship,* produced off-Broadway in November 1969, is yet another bitter indictment of white society and counsels black revolution.

Another especially articulate black playwright who emerged in the 1960s and blossomed in the 1970s is Ed Bullins, a friend and disciple of Jones. Born in Philadelphia but a resident of California for most of his adult life, Bullins's career as a writer began when he tried his hand at novels, poetry, short stories, and newspaper articles. Then in 1965, under the influence of Jones and the civil rights movement, he turned away from what he calls his "middle-class orientation" and began writing angry plays about the life and problems of the black American. The range of Bullins's interest and talent is illustrated by his three short plays produced in 1968 under the title of *The Electronic Nigger and Others,* a title that was later changed to *Three Plays by Ed Bullins.* The three plays were *A Son, Come Home; The Electronic Nigger;* and *Clara's Ole Man.* All of them show Bullins's fierce pride in black identity and his outrage at the treatment of his race. In 1969 Bullins produced several other short plays, among them *The Gentleman Caller, How Do You Do, It Has No Choice,* and *The Corner.* He also wrote longer plays, two of which have been greatly admired. The first, which was produced off-Broadway in 1970, is entitled *The Pig Pen.* A sequel to it, *The Taking of Miss Janie,* was presented in 1975 to great acclaim. It won the best play award of the New York Drama Critics Circle and was included in the Burns Mantle Yearbook as a Best Play of 1974-75.

When Bullins's *The Gentleman Caller* was produced by the Chelsea Theatre Center in 1969, it was one of four short plays by four black dramatists all presented under the title of *A Black Quartet.* LeRoi Jones was represented by a play called *Great Goodness of Life (A Coon Show).* The other two playwrights were, like Bullins, new voices. One was Ben Caldwell, whose play was entitled *Prayer Meeting, or the First Militant Minister;* the other was Ronald Milner, whose play was *The Warning—A Theme for Linda.* Both dramatists continued to write, as evidenced by Milner's long play, *What the Winesellers Buy,* which was one of the admired plays of the 1973-74 season.

Still another new black dramatist (also an actor) who made an impressive debut in the 1960s was Lonne Elder III. His play, *Ceremonies in Dark Old Men,* was a notable production of the Negro Ensemble Company; it was seen not only in New York but also on an extensive tour of the United States. The star actor in *Ceremonies in Dark Old Men,* Douglas Turner Ward, is also a dramatist. In 1965-66 his two short plays, *Happy Ending* and *Day of Absence,* won an Off-Broadway, or Obie, Award for their excellence.

Joseph A. Walker is a favorite playwright and actor of the Negro Ensemble Company—the highly successful production group whose artistic director is Douglas Turner Ward. Walker's drama, *Harangues,* opened the company's 1969 season, his *Ododo* opened the 1970 season, and his prize-winning play, *The River Niger,* inaugurated the 1972 season.

Not all the black dramatists were men. Black women also showed their involvement and their talent. Adrienne Kennedy made significant contributions in plays like *The Funny House of a Negro* (1964) and *Cities in Bezique* (1969). Alice Childress, who had established herself in the 1950s with such plays as *Just a Little Simple, Gold Through the Trees,* and *Trouble in Mind,* continued to write, her most talked-of work in the 1970s being *Wedding Band.* Lorraine Hansberry, whose moving drama *Raisin in the Sun* was chosen by the New York drama critics as the best American play of 1958-59, lived to see the Broadway production of another play of hers, *The Sign in Sidney Brustein's Window.* The day after the play achieved its one hundred first performance, the playwright died of cancer at the age of thirty-four.

The decade of the 1960s ended with a play about a black that won all the prizes—the Pulitzer, the Drama Critics, and the Antoinette Perry—for being the best play of 1968-69. The drama, entitled *The Great White Hope,* was the first Broadway production of its author, Harold Sackler. It told the story of a black heavyweight boxer who wins a world championship only to be destroyed by the forces of American racial prejudice. This remarkable play had been produced very successfully during the previous season by the Arena Stage of Washington, D. C. When it reached Broadway, both the play and its star, James Earl Jones, were even more successful.

Black theatre groups and the black playwrights mentioned above are only a representative sampling of black creativity that has enriched the American theatre in the 1960s and the 1970s. The enormous talent which suddenly found expression and the passionate dedication of the leaders of the black arts movement indicate that tremendous development can be expected in the decades to come. The future of black drama, according to one of its leaders, Loften Mitchell, is based on the hope "that in the world's most powerful country a minority that has made undying contributions can make its greatest contribution and redeem the majority. This minority stands at a moment in time, poised, with new, vital allies, demanding to be reckoned with."[4]

[4] Loften Mitchell, *Black Drama* (New York: Hawthorn Books, Inc., 1967), p. 236.

OTHER NEW PLAYWRIGHTS

While Albee, Simon, and the new black playwrights were making headlines in the 1960s, other new dramatists emerged who were perfecting their craft and who were destined to make significant contributions to American playwriting in the 1970s.

One of the most prolific of these is Lanford Wilson (1937-   ), whose talent was nurtured by the Off-off-Broadway groups of New York. In 1963-64, the Caffe Cino presented three of his one-act plays, and in 1965 the Cafe La Mama produced his first long play, *Balm in Gilead.* Wilson continued to write, and his plays were produced with increasing frequency. By 1973 he had to his credit at least sixteen produced plays, long and short, plus a libretto and a film script. Many of these won prizes. In January, 1973, his play *Hot el Baltimore* was premiered Off-off-Broadway, then it moved to a commercial Off-Broadway theatre, where it set a new Off-Broadway long run record for an American play of 1,166 performances. It also harvested three major awards. Wilson's success continued with his *The Mound Builders* in 1975, his *Serenading Louie* in the same year, his *The 5th of July* in 1978, and finally, his *Talley's Folly,* which won the Pulitzer Prize in 1980. The last two plays were widely popular and widely honored for the elements that Wilson uses so effectively to appeal to modern audiences. His plots may be fragile but his people are real. They exhibit the same stresses and confusions and the same groping for meaning that are epidemic in late twentieth-century America. Playgoers can identify with these people and, in consequence, are touched, amused, enlightened, and comforted.

Sam Shepard (1942-   ) is an equally creative and successful playwright whose early dramas, like those of Wilson, were encouraged and performed by Off-off-Broadway groups. He began to hit his stride in 1973 with *The Tooth of Crime,* continued with *Geography of a Horse Dreamer* in 1975, and then made a striking impression in 1978 with *The Curse of the Starving Class.* The latter achieved a considerable run at Joseph Papp's Public Theatre in New York. The "starving" in the title of the play refers as much to spiritual and emotional hunger as to physical hunger. The play metaphorically examines the human condition and the gloomy choices open to humanity. Shepard quickly followed this success with an even greater one when *Buried Child* was presented in the season of 1978-79. It won the Pulitzer Prize and was produced by regional theatres all over the United States. Like *The Curse of the Starving Class,* it is an example of the "New Realism" in playwriting. Using realistic setting and dialogue and representative American characters, the play examines the relationships within a disintegrating family and symbolically suggests what is happening to families everywhere. It is a play which intrigues spectators and challenges them to study and understand the symbols and meanings that are buried, like the child, within the play.

Shepard's next play opened in July 1980, at the Magic Theatre in San Francisco (which had also premiered *Buried Child* and other plays by Shepard) to critical acclaim and sold-out houses. Its title is *True West.* It records the conflict between two brothers, the younger one a sensitive, aspiring screenwriter, the older one a derelict, a bully, and a petty thief. The play begins in a mood of Pinteresque menace, moves to hilarious, slapstick farce, and ends in murderous confrontation between the brothers. Like *Buried Child,* it is sharply realistic in action, setting, and dialogue and again suggests the contemporary disintegration of relationships within families—including the family of the human race.

The New Realism of Shepard—and it can also be applied to the plays of Lanford Wilson—has influenced other productive young American playwrights. There are a whole host of these—far more than playgoers suspect. When the San Francisco Bay Area Playwrights Festival issued a call for new scripts to compete for production in the Festival, more than eight hundred entries were received! Only four could be chosen. Obviously the greatly expanded theatrical activity throughout the nation in the 1960s and 1970s has inspired hundreds of new dramatists.

Several of the new writers, in addition to Wilson and Shepard, have already achieved considerable success. David Rabe (1940-   ) attracted attention with his first two plays, which grew out of his war experiences in Vietnam. They were titled *The Basic Training of Pavlo Hummel* and *Sticks and Bones* and both were presented in 1971. Other successes followed, one of which was *Streamers* of 1976, which won the New York Drama Critics Circle Award for the best American play of the year. Mark Medoff, born in the same year as Rabe, earned major acclaim for his third play, *When You Comin' Back Red Ryder?* It received three awards for distinguished playwriting and was followed by other successes, including *Children of a Lesser God,* which won the Tony Award for best play of the 1979-80 season. David Mamet (1947-   ), who is seven years younger than Rabe and Medoff, received the 1975-76 Obie award for the best new playwright of that season for his *American Buffalo* and his *Sexual Perversity in Chicago.* Arthur Kopit (1937-   ), who began his career in the early 1960s with his *Oh Dad, Poor Dad, Mama's Hung You in the Closet and I'm Feelin's So Sad,* continued to write plays both long and short and had the satisfaction of seeing his *Indians* given its world premiere by the Royal Shakespeare Company in London in 1968. His latest success is *Wings,* which started as a production of the Yale School of Drama and reached Broadway in 1979 for a run of one hundred thirteen performances. Terrence McNally (1939-   ), like Kopit, began playwriting in the 1960s and has had two of his plays appear in the Burns Mantle Yearbook as Best Plays. They were a one-acter, *Next,* of the 1968-69 season, and a long play, *Where Has Tommy Flowers Gone?* of the 1971-72 season. Michael Cristofer (1946-   ) and Preston Jones (1936-   ) each scored hits in their professional New York debuts in the season of 1976-77. Cristofer won both the Pulitzer Prize and the Tony Award for his play *The Shadow Box;* Jones was lauded for the satiric insight and the realism of his three Texas plays: *The Last Meeting of the Knights of the White Magnolia, Lu Ann Hampton Laverty Oberlander,* and *The Oldest Living Graduate.* The first and third were chosen as Best Plays of 1976-77.

There are many other dramatists, young and youngish, who are enriching the life of the American theatre in the last years of the twentieth century. Although the list is too long to set down, at least these additional names should be recognized: Megan Terry, Albert Innaurato, Maria Irene Fornes, Thomas Babe, Thomas Meehan, Jean-Claude Van Itallie, Rochelle Owens, Paul Foster, and Michael McClure.

NEW DIRECTORS

The rise to prominence of Edward Albee as a playwright is related to the development of one of America's new breed of directors. Alan Schneider. During the 1960s and 1970s, the older, established directors continued their contributions, and several new ones—particularly in the flourishing regional theatres—met with success. But just as Albee created the most excitement among the new dramatists in the 1960s, so Alan Schneider won the most attention among the new Broadway directors. During the decade he staged all but two of Albee's plays, introduced several works of Harold Pinter and Samuel Beckett to the United States, and enhanced the reputation of Bertolt Brecht. He well deserves his reputation as the foremost interpreter of certain types of avant-garde drama in America. Equally unusual is his knowledge of the theatre on all levels. He represents a new breed of director because he is equally at home in the university theatre, in the regional community theatre, and in the commercial Broadway and Off-Broadway theatres. Thus, he symbolizes an ideal of closer relationship between the several major areas of theatrical activity, a relationship that has long been considered important and desirable.

In his directing Schneider followed no single theory or method but adapted his style to fit the needs of each production. Thus, he is representative of that group of directors whose talents and methods are described by the critic Howard Taubman in these words:

> [They are] strong personalities with clear minds and firm viewpoints, but they have no desire, expressed or inarticulate, to remake every play in their own images. They have a grasp of the literature of the drama, they have imagination, they think of theatre in larger terms than its commercial possibilities. They look upon their labors with a play as an effort and a duty to let the play speak for itself.[5]

Another young director who became widely influential and popular in the closing years of the 1960s is Tom O'Horgan, famous for staging *Futz!* and *Tom Paine* for the Cafe La Mama and for making *Hair* an international hit. As director he bombards his audiences with a frenetic combination of music, dancing, pantomime, and acrobatics, and his audiences, especially the younger playgoers, love it.

[5] Howard Taubman, *The Making of the American Theatre* (New York: Coward-McCann & Geoghegan, Inc., 1967), p. 365.

O'Horgan's fame as a director began when he joined the La Mama group. Before this his career had been colorful but uncertain. Then in 1964 Ellen Stewart asked him to direct Jean Genet's *The Maids.* The success of this production led to more and more assignments and resulted in a series of exciting productions. By 1968 O'Horgan had directed some fifty plays, films, and happenings with the La Mama troupe and had led the troupe through three successful tours of Europe. Among O'Horgan's most notable productions were *Futz!* in 1967 and 1968, for which he received an Obie award from *The Village Voice,* and *Tom Paine,* produced at the Edinburgh Festival in 1967 and in New York in 1968. For his direction of this play, O'Horgan received another prize, the Drama Desk-Vernon Rice Off-Broadway theatre award. Incidentally, O'Horgan composed the music for both *Futz!* and *Tom Paine.*

O'Horgan's international reputation increased enormously when he restaged *Hair* in 1968. The famous "American tribal love rock musical" was originally presented in 1967 as an attraction of Joseph Papp's New York Shakespeare Festival. It ran eight weeks. Then a wealthy Chicagoan, Michael Butler, bought the rights to the show and hired O'Horgan to restage it. The La Mama director made the show a dazzling, vibrating, joyous, fast-moving melange of music, dancing, acrobatics, sexuality, and antiwar, antiestablishment propaganda. It was a smash hit in New York, Chicago, San Francisco, Paris, Belgrade, Sydney, and every other city where it was done with the O'Horgan staging.

Almost equally successful and popular was O'Horgan's production of *Jesus Christ Superstar*—called "*Hair* in Galilean dress." It opened in 1971 and used the same elements that made *Hair* a smash hit. It has held the stage in some city somewhere ever since.

The elements that made *Hair* and *Jesus Christ Superstar* so popular illustrate O'Horgan's ideas of directing and stage effects. He believes that actors should be so versatile and so many-talented that they can sing, dance, play instruments, perform acrobatics, and speak lines simultaneously or, at least, two or three at a time. He asks his actors for total physical commitment, and he tries to involve his spectators emotionally, physically, and viscerally. The success of his theories and his practice has made him one of the most sought-after directors of the contemporary theatre.

Schneider and O'Horgan are only two examples of the new breed of gifted, innovative directors. There are many more. One could cite glowingly such names as Mike Nichols, Harold Prince, Bob Fosse, Gower Champion—but the list would be much too long. It may be sufficient to observe that in the hundreds of theatrical groups throughout the country, there are now a greater number of experienced, creative directors than at any time in the history of the American theatre.

RESULTS OF THE SPIRIT OF REVOLT

Critics of the American theatre writing fifty years from now will have a tremendous advantage. The perspective of time will permit them to evaluate developments in the years from 1960 to 1980 and to determine which ones had lasting significance.

It is likely that they will give high rating to the liberation of the theatre from the stranglehold of Broadway commercialism and the explosive growth of professional regional theatres, college and university theatres, and producing groups of every kind. They will also know whether the remarkable increase in playwriting resulted in dramas of more than temporary interest. But of all the developments of the period, they will probably be more intrigued and titillated by the spirit of revolt of the late 1960s and early 1970s that influenced the writing and staging of plays in many ways.

One result of the revolt was the appearance of the theatre of the absurd, when certain playwrights tried to illustrate the bitter hopelessness and ridiculousness of existence by banishing logic and meaning from their plots, characters, and dialogue. Another result was the theatre of cruelty and violence, one of whose forerunners was the French actor-producer Antonin Artaud (1896-1948). Theatre of this sort seeks to strip away the veneer of civilization and to shock the spectator into visceral reactions and orgiastic participation with the performers. The productions of the Living Theatre of Julian and Judith Beck and the Open Theatre of Joseph Chaikin were examples of this kind of theatre.

Along with absurdity and violence, there was also guerrilla theatre and the theatre of "happenings." The former is, of course, dramatized propaganda, often performed in the streets, to advocate causes and to foment revolt. The theatre of happenings aims at stirring the physical senses of the audience by the use of every means and medium available: sound, light, color, film, projections, and so on.

Far more shocking than any consequences of the spirit of revolt was the appearance on public stages and screens of nudity, sex, and dirty words. This development aroused a furor of rage and controversy far more intense, perhaps, than it deserved. A critic fifty years from now may smile at the thought of such a furor in the same way as a playgoer of 1980 smiles at Victorian prudery.

There has been nudity in Western theatre from the time the medieval mystery plays presented Adam and Eve in the garden of Eden to the modern era of the Folies Bergère; sexual activity has been portrayed on the stage from the satyr plays of ancient Greece to the stag movies of modern times. Yet the free use of sex, nudity, and dirty words in plays and films designed for general public consumption is a recent development. It was made possible by judicial decisions that invalidated long-standing censorship laws, and it was encouraged by the rebellion of the younger generation against established mores and morals. Of course, it has been exploited and degraded by flesh peddlers eager to make a fast buck; yet the appearance of sex, nudity, and forbidden words in serious plays and movies represents something more than the exploitation of prurience. It signifies a revolt against the last restrictions of censorship and the demand for complete freedom to use whatever subject matter and materials playwrights or directors believe are important to their productions. It may also represent, at least in its early uses, an act of affirmation on the part of the young performers who participate in the nudity and sex displays. In the age of the diminished man, when individuality is submerged in numbers and identity is lost in computerized living, the young performer who takes off his clothes and flaunts his nakedness before an audience may be saying, Now you must look at me! Now you must pay attention to me as a person!

The displays of nudity and sex take many forms. They may be dull and smutty, as in several of the skits of *Oh! Calcutta!* They may be joyous and incidental, as in the youthful musical *Hair*. They may be boring and repetitious, as in the Swedish film *I Am Curious (Yellow)*. They may be appropriate and effective, as in Gus Weill's two short plays, *Geese* and *Parents and Children*. In other words, sex and nudity, like any other material, can be well or poorly used. When they are well used, when they serve a valid dramatic purpose, they are defensible; when they are poorly used, dragged in for the sake of shock or presented dully and tastelessly, they are repellent and unnecessary. But the same can be said for any other element or material a dramatist chooses to use. Certainly the problems of sexual love are as crucial as the problem of hereditary syphilis, for example. Certainly the playwright who can illuminate and contribute to the solution of sexual "hangups" has as much right to do so as Ibsen had when he illuminated the ugly problem of hereditary syphilis in *Ghosts*. In this connection, it is interesting to note the appearance of plays dealing with love between members of the same sex—a strictly taboo subject until recently. Playwrights have finally claimed the right to dramatize the problems and agonies of homosexuals—and they have had considerable success. Mart Crowley's play *The Boys in the Band* opened off-Broadway in 1968 and ran for one thousand performances. Martin Sherman's *Bent,* which records the love of two male prisoners in a Nazi concentration camp, was mentioned as a candidate for the Pulitzer Prize in 1980. Probably the use of sex, nudity, and homosexuality on

The original cast of *Oh! Calcutta!*
Friedman-Abeles from the original production.

the stage will be with us for a long time, and probably after the shock, the rage, and the cheap exploitation have ended, the use of such material will be judged on the same basis as the use of any other material: Does it serve a valid dramatic purpose and is it effectively handled?

ATTENDING THE THEATRE OF TODAY

Attending the theatre in the 1980s can offer American playgoers an unusual range of experiences. If they choose to see a traditional play presented in a traditional playhouse, their experiences will be very much the same as if they had attended the opening of David Belasco's theatre in 1902. The air conditioning will be better and the traffic will be worse, but the physical features of the playhouse and many aspects of the production will be little changed. However, if playgoers attend an experimental play or a happening, they will undergo very different experiences. They will find themselves in an untraditional playhouse, perhaps a comfortable cafe with a stage at one end or a bare basement with no stage at all. Within such a place-for-performance, anything bizarre or unconventional might happen. The performance, whatever it might be or however it might develop, may shock them, delight them, repel them, or stir them deeply.

Probably the most representative choice modern playgoers can make is that of a play presented in one of the new centers for the performing arts and acted by a professional regional company. Playgoers who choose such an experience will buy tickets at a neighborhood outlet of one of the new computerized ticket services that instantly tells playgoers what seats are available and instantly prints a ticket for the desired location. When the evening of the performance arrives, playgoers will drive to the playhouse with the assurance that parking for their cars is available, that the playhouse will be perfectly ventilated and air conditioned, and that it will be adjacent to bars and restaurants as well as to gardens and galleries where they can find refreshment and relaxation. Inside the playhouse, they are not likely to find the traditional proscenium-framed stage or the traditional arrangement of galleries, balconies, boxes, and orchestra seats. Rather, they will find marvelously flexible facilities that can be adjusted to produce a thrust stage with the audience on three sides, an arena stage with the audience on four sides, or a traditional picture-frame stage with the audience on one side only. During the course of a single performance all of these arrangements may be used in succession, and playgoers will find their seats reoriented mechanically to conform to the changing arrangement of the stage. In this new protean playhouse, the stage machinery, the lighting, and the sound effects are also marvelously flexible and ingenious, all operated electronically. The drama that playgoers are likely to see in such surroundings will be new experimental offerings or established plays from a repertory that includes dramas of every nation and every period of time. The actors are likely to be sincere, direct, and skillful, and they will adjust their style of performance to fit the kind of play being presented. Many members of the company may be familiar to playgoers because the company makes the community its permanent home and has developed friendly associations with the citizens. When the performance ends, playgoers are likely to return home full of enthusiasm for the theatrical experience they have enjoyed, and full of pride because the living theatre is once again flourishing in their community.

AFTERWORD

Yes, the American theatre *is* a fabulous phoenix, forever declining and forever rising again in new shapes and varieties. It has a tenacity and a vitality that are phenomenal. Its diversity and complexity are astonishing. Its golden age is always in the past, yet always in the future. The palmy days of one period give way to equally palmy days of a different kind in another period. Today the forms of theatre that have survived since colonial times continue to delight audiences, while fabulous new forms like cinema and television bring the magic of the theatre to millions of people who have never before experienced it. In these powerful new media, in the growth of regional and university theatres, in the increased support being given to the performing arts, and in the restless, unorthodox experimentation seen on modern stages and screens, it is possible that the phoenix is once more undergoing rebirth and may emerge more glorious, more powerful, more persuasive, and more significant than in any period in the past. That is the hope of those who love the American theatre; it is the faith of all who know its long history and who take pride in its record of creativity and achievement.

Selected Bibliography

The following books and magazine articles are examples of source material for studies in the history of the American theatre. For greater usefulness they are grouped under general headings. For additional titles see the footnotes in each chapter.

GENERAL HISTORIES OF THE THEATRE

BLUM, DANIEL. *A Pictorial History of the American Theatre, 100 Years—1860-1960.* New York: Crown Publishers, Inc., 1960.

BOGARD, TRAVIS; MOODY, RICHARD, and MESERVE, WALTER, J. *The Revels of the Drama in English, Volume VIII: American Drama.* London: Methuen & Co., Ltd., 1977.

COAD, ORAL SUMNER, and MIMS, EDWIN, JR. *The American Stage.* New Haven, Conn.: Yale University Press, 1929.

CRAWFORD, MARY CAROLINE. *Romance of the American Theatre.* New York: Halcyon House, 1940.

DUNLAP, WILLIAM. *History of the American Theatre.* 2 vols. New York: J. & J. Harper, 1832; Burt Franklin, 1963. The 1963 reprint also contains John Hodgkinson's "A Narrative of His Connections with the Old American Company 1792-1797."

HEWITT, BERNARD. *Theatre U. S. A., 1668 to 1957.* New York: McGraw-Hill Book Company, 1959.

HORNBLOW, ARTHUR. *A History of the Theatre in America from its Beginnings to the Present Time.* 2 vols. Philadelphia: J. B. Lippincott Co., 1919.

HUGHES, GLENN. *A History of the American Theatre 1700-1950.* New York: Samuel French, Inc., 1951.

MESERVE, WALTER J. *An Emerging Entertainment: The Drama of the American People to 1828.* Bloomington: Indiana University Press, 1977.

MOODY, RICHARD. *America Takes the Stage.* Bloomington: Indiana University Press, 1955.

MORRIS, LLOYD. *Curtain Time: The Story of the American Theatre.* New York: Random House, Inc., 1953.

SEILHAMER, GEORGE O. *A History of the American Theatre.* 3 vols. Philadelphia: Globe Printing House, 1888-1891.

LOCAL AND REGIONAL HISTORIES

BAGLEY, RUSSELL E. "Theatrical Entertainment in Pensacola, Florida: 1882-1892." *Southern Speech Journal,* XVI (1950), 62-84.

BERNARD, JOHN. *Retrospections of America, 1797-1811.* New York: Harper & Row, Publishers, 1887.

BLAKE, CHARLES. *An Historical Account of the Providence Stage.* Providence, R. I.: G. H. Whitney, 1868.

BROWN, T. ALLSTON. *A History of the New York Stage from 1732 to 1901.* 3 vols. New York: Dodd, Mead & Co., 1903.

CHURCH, V. "Colonial Theatres." *Theatre,* XI (June 1910), 181-82, 184.

CLAPP, WILLIAM. *Record of the Boston Stage.* Boston: James Monroe and Company, 1853.

CLURMAN, HAROLD. *The Fervent Years* (Group Theatre). New York: Alfred A. Knopf, Inc., 1945.

DURANG, CHARLES. "The Philadelphia Stage from the Year 1749 to the Year 1855." *Philadelphia Sunday Dispatch* (7 May 1854, 29 June 1856, 8 July 1860).

EATON, WALTER PRICHARD. *The Theatre Guild: The First Ten Years.* New York: Brentano's, 1929.

EMERY, G. M. "Passing of the Walnut Street Theatre." *Theatre,* XXXI (June 1920), 506-8, 572.

FLANAGAN, HALLIE. *Arena.* New York: Duell, Sloan and Pearce, 1940.

FREE, JOSEPH M. "The Ante-Bellum Theatre of the Old Natchez Region." *Journal of Mississippi History,* V (January 1943), 14-27.

GAGEY, EDMOND M. *The San Francisco Stage.* New York: Columbia University Press, 1950.

GAISFORD, JOHN. *The Drama in New Orleans.* New Orleans: J. B. Steel, 1849.

IRELAND, JOSEPH N. *Records of the New York Stage from 1750 to 1860.* 2 vols. New York: T. H. Morrell, 1866-67.

KENDALL, JOHN. *The Golden Age of the New Orleans Theatre.* Baton Rouge, La.: Louisiana State University Press, 1952.

LARSON, CARL F. W. *American Regional Theatre History to 1900: A Bibliography.* Metuchen, N. J.: The Scarecrow Press, 1979.

LOVELL, JOHN, JR. "The Beginnings of the American Theatre." *Theatre Annual,* X (1952), 7-19.

McGLINCHEE, CLAIRE. *The First Decade of the Boston Museum.* Boston: Bruce Humphries, 1940.

ODELL, GEORGE C. D. *Annals of the New York Stage.* 15 vols. New York: Columbia University Press, 1927-1949.

RANKIN, HUGH F. *The Theater in Colonial America.* Chapel Hill: University of North Carolina Press, 1965.

San Francisco Theatre Research: W. P. A. in Northern California. 20 vols. San Francisco: W. P. A., 1938-1942.

SHAW, MARY. "The Boston Museum and Daly's Theatre." *Saturday Evening Post,* CLXXXIII, 4 (20 May 1911), 14-15, 34-35.

STAPLES, F. "History of the Theatre in San Francisco." *Overland Monthly,* LXXX (January 1927), 22-23, 25.

TOMPKINS, EUGENE, and KILBY, QUINCY. *The History of the Boston Theatre, 1854-1901.* Boston: Houghton Mifflin Company, 1908.

WEMYSS, FRANCIS COURTNEY. *Chronology of the American Stage from 1752 to 1852.* New York: W. Taylor & Co., 1852.

WILSON, ARTHUR H. *History of the Philadelphia Theatre, 1835-1855.* Philadelphia: University of Pennsylvania Press, 1935.

WOODRUFF, JACK. "America's Oldest Living Theatre—The Howard Athanaeum." *Theatre Annual,* VIII (1950), 71-81.

THE POPULAR THEATRE: VAUDEVILLE, MINSTRELSY, MUSICALS, AND THE LIKE

BARAL, ROBERT. *Revue: A Nostalgic Reprise of the Great Broadway Period.* New York: Fleet Press Corporation, 1962.

BARNUM, P. T. *Life of P. T. Barnum.* Buffalo, N. Y.: The Courier Company Printer, 1888.

CAFFIN, CAROLINE. *Vaudeville.* New York: Mitchell Kennerley, 1914.

CSIDA, JOSEPH and JANE B. *American Entertainment: A Unique History of Popular Show Business.* New York: Watson-Guptill Publications, 1978.

DULLES, FOSTER RHEA. *America Learns to Play.* New York: Appleton-Century-Crofts, 1940.

EWEN, DAVID. *Complete Book of the American Musical Theatre.* New York: Holt, Rinehart & Winston, Inc., 1965.

GILBERT, DOUGLAS. *American Vaudeville: Its Life and Times.* New York: McGraw-Hill Book Company, 1940.

GRAHAM, PHILIP. *Showboats.* Austin: University of Texas Press, 1951.

GREEN, STANLEY. *The World of Musical Comedy.* New York: Ziff-Davis Publishing Co., 1960.

GREENWOOD, ISAAC J. *The Circus: Its Origin and Growth Prior to 1835.* New York: The Dunlap Society, 1898.

HUTTON, LAURENCE. *Curiosities of the American Stage.* New York: Harper & Row, Publishers, 1891.

KAHN, E. J., JR. *The Merry Partners: The Age and Stage of Harrigan & Hart.* New York: Random House, Inc., 1955.

LAWRENCE, W. J. "The Rise of Spectacle in America." *Theatre Magazine,* XXV (1917).

LEWIS, PHILIP C. *Trouping.* New York: Harper & Row, Publishers, 1973.

MATES, JULIAN. *The American Musical Stage Before 1800.* New Brunswick, N. J.: Rutgers University Press, 1962.

MOODY, RICHARD. *Ned Harrigan. From Carlear's Hook to Herald Square,* Chicago, Nelson-Hall, 1980.

PASKMAN, DAILEY, and SPAETH, SIGMUND. *Gentlemen, Be Seated!* Garden City, N. Y.: Doubleday & Company, Inc., 1928.

SMITH, CECIL M. *Musical Comedy in America.* New York: Theatre Arts Books, 1950.

SOBEL, BERNARD. *Burleycue: An Underground History of Burlesque Days.* New York: Farrar & Rinehart, 1931.

————. *A Pictorial History of Burlesque.* New York: G. P. Putnam's Sons, 1956.

TAUBMAN, HOWARD. *The Making of the American Theatre.* New York: Coward-McCann & Geoghegan, Inc., 1965.

WILMETH, DON B. *American and English Popular Entertainment: A Guide to Information Sources.* Detroit: Gale Research Co., 1980.

WITTKE, CARL. *Tambo and Bones: A History of the American Minstrel Stage.* Durham, N. C.: Duke University Press, 1930.

HISTORIES OF THE DRAMA

MAYORGA, MARGARET G. *A Short History of the American Drama.* New York: Dodd, Mead & Co., 1934.

MOSES, MONTROSE J. "The Drama, 1860-1918." *The Cambridge History of American Literature,* III, 266-98. New York: G. P. Putnam's Sons, 1921.

QUINN, ARTHUR HOBSON. *A History of the American Drama from the Beginning to the Civil War.* New York: Appleton-Century-Crofts, 1923 and 1943.

————. *A History of the American Drama from the Civil War to the Present Day.* 2 vols. New York: Appleton-Century-Crofts, 1927, 1937, and 1943.

ACTORS, PLAYWRIGHTS, MANAGERS, AND PLAYHOUSES

ALGER, WILLIAM ROUNSEVILLE. *Life of Edwin Forrest, the American Tragedian.* 2 vols. Philadelphia: J. B. Lippincott Co., 1877.

BARRETT, LAWRENCE. *Charlotte Cushman.* New York: The Dunlap Society, 1889.

BINNS, ARCHIE. *Mrs. Fiske and the American Theatre.* New York: Crown Publishers, Inc., 1955.

BOST, JAMES S. *Monarchs of the Mimic World.* Orono: University of Maine at Orono Press, 1977.

BROWN, T. ALLSTON. *History of the American Stage.* New York: Dick & Fitzgerald, Publishers, 1870.

CLAPP, HENRY AUSTIN. *Reminiscences of a Dramatic Critic.* Boston: Houghton Mifflin Company, 1902.

CLAPP, J. B., and EDGETT, E. F. *Players of the Present.* Series 2. Vols. IX, XI, XII. New York: The Dunlap Society, 1899-1901.

————. *Plays of the Present.* New York: The Dunlap Society, 1902.

CREAHAN, JOHN. *The Life of Laura Keene.* Philadelphia: The Rodgers Publishing Company, 1897.

DOTY, GRESDNA ANN. *The Career of Mrs. Anne Brunton Merry in the American Theatre.* Baton Rouge: Louisiana State University Press, 1971.

FORD, GEORGE D. *These Were Actors—The Story of the Chapmans and the Drakes.* New York: Library Publishers, 1955.

GOODALE, KATHERINE. *Behind the Scenes with Edwin Booth.* Boston: Houghton Mifflin Company, 1931.

GROSSMAN, EDWINA BOOTH. *Edwin Booth: Recollections by His Daughter.* New York: The Century Company, 1902.

HENDERSON, MARY C. *The City & the Theatre: New York Playhouses from Bowling Green to Times Square.* Clifton, N. J.: James T. White & Company, 1973.

IRELAND, JOSEPH N. *Fifty Years of a Playgoer's Journal, 1798-1848.* New York: Samual French, Inc., 1860.

————. *Mrs. Duff.* Boston: James R. Osgood and Company, 1882.

JEFFERSON, JOSEPH. *Autobiography.* New York: The Century Company, 1889.

KIMMEL, STANLEY. *The Mad Booths of Maryland.* Indianapolis: The Bobbs-Merrill Co., Inc., 1940.

LEACH, JOSEPH. *Bright Particular Star: The Life & Times of Charlotte Cushman.* New Haven and London: Yale University Press, 1970.

LEAVITT, MICHAEL. *Fifty Years in Theatrical Management.* New York: Broadway Publishing Co., 1912.

LEMAN, WALTER M. *Memories of an Old Actor.* San Francisco: A. Roman Co., 1886.

MACKAYE, PERCY. *Epoch—Life of Steele Mackaye.* 2 vols. New York: Boni & Liveright, 1927.

MAMMEN, EDWARD W. *The Old Stock Company School of Acting.* Boston: Trustees of the Public Library, 1945.

MOODY, RICHARD. *Edwin Forrest: First Star of the American Stage.* New York: Alfred A. Knopf, Inc., 1960.

MORRIS, CLARA. *Life on the Stage.* New York: McClure, Phillips & Co., 1901.

MURDOCH, JAMES E. *The Stage, or Recollections of Actors and Acting from an Experience of Fifty Years.* Philadelphia: J. M. Stoddart & Co., 1880.

PERRY, JOHN. *James A. Herne—The American Ibsen.* Chicago: Nelson Hall, 1978.

REIGNOLDS-WINSLOW, CATHERINE MARY. *Yesterdays with Actors.* Boston: Cupples and Hurd, 1887.

SKINNER, OTIS, and SKINNER, MAUD. *One Man in his Times.* Philadelphia: University of Pennsylvania Press, 1938.

STRANG, LEWIS C. *Famous Actors of Today in America.* Boston: L. C. Page and Company, 1900.

————. *Players and Plays of the Last Quarter Century.* Boston: L. C. Page and Company, 1903.

TOWSE, JOHN RANKEN. *Sixty Years of the Theatre: An Old Critic's Memories.* New York: Funk & Wagnalls, Inc., 1916.

WEMYSS, FRANCIS C. *Twenty-Six Years of the Life of an Actor and Manager.* New York: Burgess, Stringer and Company, 1847.

WILSON, GARFF B. *A History of American Acting.* Bloomington: Indiana University Press, 1966.

WINTER, WILLIAM. *Shadows of the Stage.* New York: The Macmillan Company, 1892.

————. *Life and Art of Edwin Booth*. New York: The Macmillan Company, 1893.

————. *Life and Art of Joseph Jefferson*. New York: The Macmillan Company, 1894.

————. *Other Days: Being Chronicles and Memories of the Stage*. New York: Moffat, Yard and Company, 1908.

————. *Life and Art of Richard Mansfield*. 2 vols. New York: Moffat, Yard and Company, 1913.

————. *The Wallet of Time*. 2 vols. New York: Moffat, Yard and Company, 1913.

————. *Life of David Belasco*. 2 vols. New York: Moffat, Yard and Company, 1918.

WOOD, WILLIAM B. *Personal Recollections of the Stage*. Philadelphia: Henry Carey Baird, 1855.

YOUNG, WILLIAM C. *Documents of American Theater History: Volume 1, Famous American Playhouses, 1716-1899; Volume 2, Famous American Playhouses, 1900-1971*. Chicago: American Library Association, 1973.

ANTHOLOGIES OF AMERICAN PLAYS

CLARK, BARRET H., ed. *America's Lost Plays*. 20 vols. Princeton, N. J.: Princeton University Press, 1941; Bloomington: Indiana University Press, 1963-65.

————. *Favorite American Plays of the Nineteenth Century*. Princeton, N. J.: Princeton University Press, 1943.

DOWNER, ALAN. *Fifty Years of American Drama, 1900-1950*. Chicago: Henry Regnery Co., 1951.

GASSNER, JOHN, ed. *Best Plays of the Modern American Theatre*. New York: Crown Publishers, Inc., 1939, 1947, 1952.

HALLINE, ALLAN GATES, ed. *American Plays*. New York: American Book Company, 1935.

MOODY, RICHARD, ed. *Dramas from the American Theatre 1762-1909*. New York: World Publishing Company, 1966.

MOSES, MONTROSE J., ed. *Representative Plays by American Dramatists*. 3 vols. New York: E. P. Dutton & Co., Inc., 1921.

————. *Representative American Dramas, National and Local*. Boston: Little, Brown and Company, 1939.

QUINN, ARTHUR HOBSON, ed. *Representative American Plays*. New York: Appleton-Century-Crofts, 1953.

FRONTIER THEATRE

CARSON, WILLIAM G. B. *The Theatre on the Frontier*. Chicago: The University of Chicago Press, 1932.

————. *Managers in Distress*. St. Louis: St. Louis Historical Documents Foundation, 1949.

JENNINGS, JOHN J. *Theatrical and Circus Life: or, Secrets of the Stage, Greenroom and Sawdust Arena*. St. Louis: Herbert & Cole Publishing Co., 1886.

LUDLOW, NOAH. *Dramatic Life as I Found It.* St. Louis: G. I. Jones and Company, 1880.

MacMINN, G. R. *Theatre of the Golden Era in California.* Caldwell, Idaho: The Caxton Printers, Ltd., 1941.

ROURKE, CONSTANCE. *Troupers of the Gold Coast.* New York: Harcourt Brace Jovanovich, Inc., 1928.

SMITH, SOL. *Theatrical Management in the South and West.* New York: Harper & Row, Publishers, 1868.

WATSON, MARGARET G. *Silver Theatre: Amusements of Nevada's Mining Frontier, 1850 to 1864.* Glendale, Calif.: The Arthur H. Clark Company, 1964.

BLACK THEATRE IN AMERICA

ABRAMSON, DORIS E. *Negro Playwrights in the American Theatre 1925-1959.* New York: Columbia University Press, 1969.

BOND, FREDERICK W. *The Negro and the Drama.* Washington, D. C.: The Associated Publishers, Inc., 1940.

BULLINS, ED, ed. *New Plays from the Black Theatre.* New York: Bantam Books, Inc., 1969.

DOWD, JEROME. *The Negro in American Life.* New York: The Century Co., 1926.

HATCH, JAMES V. *Black Image on the American Stage: A Bibliography of Plays and Musicals, 1770-1970.* New York: DBS Publications, Inc., 1970.

ISAACS, EDITH J. R. *The Negro in the American Theatre.* New York: Theatre Arts, 1947.

MARSHALL, HERBERT, and STOCK, MILDRED. *Ira Aldridge, the Negro Tragedian.* Carbondale: Southern Illinois University Press, 1968.

MITCHELL, LOFTEN. *Black Drama.* New York: Hawthorn Books, Inc., 1967.

THE MOTION PICTURE

ADLER, MORTIMER J. *Art and Prudence.* New York: Longmans, Green and Co., 1937.

ARNHEIM, RUDOLF. *Film.* London: Faber and Faber, 1933.

BETTS, ERNEST. *Heraclitus on the Future of Films.* New York: E. P. Dutton & Co., Inc., 1928.

CHAPLIN, CHARLES. *My Autobiography.* New York: Simon & Schuster, Inc., 1964.

CHAPLIN, CHARLES, JR. *My Father, Charlie Chaplin.* London: Longmans, Green and Co., 1960.

COLLIER, JOHN W. *A Film in the Making.* London: World Film Publications, 1947.

COOKE, ALISTAIR. *Douglas Fairbanks—The Making of a Screen Character.* New York: The Museum of Modern Art, 1940.

COWIE, PETER. *Seventy Years of Cinema.* South Brunswick, N. J.: A. S. Barnes, 1969.

DE MILLE, WILLIAM C. *Hollywood Saga.* New York: E. P. Dutton & Co., Inc., 1939.

EDITORS OF TIME-LIFE BOOKS. *Life Goes to the Movies.* New York: Time-Life Books, 1975.

HART, WILLIAM S. *My Life East and West.* New York and London: Benjamin Blom; Reissued 1968.

HOUSTON, PENELOPE. *The Contemporary Cinema.* Baltimore: Penguin Books, Inc., 1963.

JACOBS, LEWIS. *The Rise of the American Film.* New York: Harcourt Brace Jovanovich, Inc., 1939.

KAEL, PAULINE. *I Lost It at the Movies.* Boston: Little, Brown and Company, 1965.

————. *Deeper into Movies.* Boston: Little, Brown and Company, 1973.

————. *When Lights Go Down.* New York: Holt, Rinehart and Winston, Inc., 1980.

KUHNS, WILLIAM, and STANLEY, ROBERT. *Exploring the Film.* Dayton, Ohio: G. A. Pflaum, 1968.

LAHUE, KALTON C. *World of Laughter: The Motion Picture Comedy Short, 1910-1930.* Norman: University of Oklahoma Press, 1966.

MACGOWAN, KENNETH: *Behind the Screen: The History and Techniques of the Motion Picture.* New York: The Delacorte Press, 1965.

PAYNE, ROBERT. *The Great Charlie.* London: A Deutsch, 1952.

SELDES, GILBERT. *The Movies Came from America.* New York: Charles Scribner's Sons, 1937.

THRASHER, FREDERIC, ed. *Okay for Sound . . . How the Screen Found its Voice.* New York: Duell, Sloan and Pearce, 1946.

Index